'In recent years, many moral philosophers have returned to the idea of virtue in the hope of filling gaps left by traditional consequentialist and deontological ethics. This suggestive and wide-ranging book takes that approach in the direction of environmental ethics, providing answers to questions left unresolved by economic cost–benefit analysis.'

Roger Crisp, University of Oxford, UK

'Mark Charlesworth argues powerfully that virtue ethics, as well as better science, is key to better climate policy. Specifically, he argues that moderation of production and consumption is essential for sustainability. The book is truly transdisciplinary, and Charlesworth demonstrates a deep understanding of natural science, philosophy and social science in arriving at his conclusions.'

Andy Dobson, Keele University, UK

'It's hard to find a book with as much breadth and ambition than Charlesworth's *Transdisciplinary Solutions for Sustainable Development*. He resolutely insists we go "back to basics" concerning the hubristic presumption of the possibility of predicting our socio-environmental futures, and thus of modelling and managing the planet for sustainability, and the need thus to embed approaches to sustainability firmly in reconstructed ethics, epistemology and expanded participation in socio-environmental decision making. He never uses the word but this is an invaluable contribution to thinking about the politics of the anthropocene.'

Matthew Paterson, University of Ottowa, Canada

'This book is part of a new generation of transdisciplinary and interdisciplinary sustainability research. Just as it has long been part of the thinking of green/sustainability advocates that we need a new worldview, values and culture to help make the transition from unsustainability, Charlesworth's book convincingly makes the argument for new paradigms in research and thinking about that transition. Integrating, inter alia, climate and ecological science, environmental management, political theory, earth system science, ethics and philosophy, *Transdisciplinary Solutions* is a real *tour de force*. *Transdisciplinary Solutions* not only challenges us to rethink how we think about unsustainability, but suggests solutions to unsustainability, and how we might begin to move towards global sustainable development. This opens up the possibility that many of the solutions to unsustainability may be found not in transforming or managing the earth (as often suggested by "anthropocene dreams" such as "geo-engineering"), but managing our relationship to and (always incomplete) understanding of our planetary home.'

John Barry, Queen's University Belfast, Northern Ireland

Transdisciplinary Solutions for Sustainable Development

Global environmental issues such as climate change and species loss are intensifying despite our best efforts to combat them. The key reason for this is that the drivers of these problems are closely linked to the industrialism and consumerism that are promoted by governments and other organisations the world over.

This innovative book identifies the key issues that block progress in sustainable development and proposes transdisciplinary solutions. Presenting a review of the epistemology and ethics of this policy field including current policy responses, it examines the ethical and policy implications from a multidisciplinary perspective. The book explains the current limitations of scientific prediction for global environmental issues and develops innovative approaches to respond to these difficulties, drawing out lessons that will make sustainable development policy more democratic, plural and open.

This book will be of great interest to students and researchers in environmental policy, development studies, politics, economics and sustainable development.

Mark Charlesworth is Honorary Research Fellow at the School of Social Sciences, Keele University, UK.

Routledge Studies in Sustainable Development

This series uniquely brings together original and cutting-edge research on sustainable development. The books in this series tackle difficult and important issues in sustainable development including: values and ethics; sustainability in higher education; climate compatible development; resilience; capitalism and de-growth; sustainable urban development; gender and participation; and well-being.

Drawing on a wide range of disciplines, the series promotes interdisciplinary research for an international readership. The series was recommended in *The Guardian*'s suggested reads on development and the environment.

Urban Waste and Sanitation Services for Sustainable Development
Harnessing social and technical diversity in East Africa
Bas van Vliet, Joost van Buuren and Shaaban Mgana

Sustainable Capitalism and the Pursuit of Well-Being
Neil E. Harrison

Implementing Sustainability in Higher Education
Matthias Barth

Emerging Economies and Challenges to Sustainability
Theories, strategies, local realities
Edited by Arve Hansen and Ulrikke Wethal

Environmental Politics in Latin America
Elite dynamics, the left tide and sustainable development
Edited by Benedicte Bull and Mariel Aguilar-Støen

Transformative Sustainable Development
Participation, reflection and change
Kei Otsuki

Theories of Sustainable Development
Edited by Judith C. Enders and Moritz Remig

Transdisciplinary Solutions for Sustainable Development
From planetary management to stewardship
Mark Charlesworth

Transdisciplinary Solutions for Sustainable Development

From planetary management to stewardship

Mark Charlesworth

First published 2015
by Routledge

2 Park Square, Milton Park, Abingdon, Oxon OX14 4RN
711 Third Avenue, New York, NY 10017, USA

Routledge is an imprint of the Taylor & Francis Group, an informa business

First issued in paperback 2017

British Library Cataloguing-in-Publication Data
A catalogue record for this book is available from the British Library

Library of Congress Cataloging-in-Publication Data
A catalog record has been requested for this book

ISBN: 978-1-138-90116-2 (hbk)
ISBN: 978-1-138-74364-9 (pbk)

Typeset in Goudy
by GreenGate Publishing Services, Tonbridge, Kent

Contents

Acknowledgements

Profound thanks are owed to readers of earlier versions of this work: Andrew Stirling, John Horton, Matthew Paterson, John Barry, John Proops and Andrew Dobson for their wisdom, patience and for posing many of the most important questions that prompted this research to have the shape it has. Obviously, I take full responsibility for any faults that remain.

Thanks are also due to many inSPIREations and other colleagues at Keele and elsewhere for discussions on questions of environmental policy theory, Earth System science as well as the smaller things that make life so much more pleasant. Particular thanks are due to Carme Melo-Escrihuela, Chukwumerije Okereke and Hannes Stephan for invaluable help and encouragement.

Deep thanks are owed to Edwin and Ann Charlesworth (my parents) for all the love, support and forbearance that they have given me. The forbearance also applies to my friends who have put up with me being 'busy' for so long. Equally, colleagues at Stroma – in particular Mark Rollins – are owed thanks for taking on 'real' work that they might have expected me to do, when instead I was finishing this book.

Sincere thanks are owed to Khanam Virjee, Helen Bell and Bethany Wright at Routledge plus Karen Wallace at GreenGate Publishing Services for their encouragement and expertise.

Abbreviations

CBD	Convention on Biological Diversity
CSD	Commission on Sustainable Development
EMAS	Eco-Management and Audit Scheme
EMS	environmental management system
EU	European Union
CFC	chlorofluorocarbon
GDP	Gross Domestic Product
GHG	greenhouse gas
GNP	Gross National Product
ICIDI	Independent Commission on International Development Issues
ILO	International Labour Organization
IMF	International Monetary Fund
IPCC	Intergovernmental Panel on Climate Change
IPPC	Integrated Pollution Prevention and Control
ISO	International Standards Organization
IUCN	International Union for Conservation of Nature
NAFTA	North American Free Trade Agreement
NGO	non-governmental organisation
OECD	Organisation for Economic Co-operation and Development
STS	science and technology studies
TC	Technical Committee
UN	United Nations
UNCED	United Nations Conference on Environment and Development
UNFCCC	United Nations Framework Convention on Climate Change
UNWTO	United Nations World Tourism Organization
WCED	World Commission on Environment and Development
WHO	World Health Organization
WSSD	World Summit on Sustainable Development
WTO	World Trade Organization

1   Introduction

This book proposes transdisciplinary solutions to unsustainable development. It does this by looking across policy and academic disciplines to identify key issues that have blocked progress in sustainable development since the 1987 Brundtland Report (World Commission on Environment and Development – WCED) and proposes ways forward with those issues. Thus, the principal aim of this book is to discuss how sustainable development might be better addressed in the context of an unpredictable Earth System. As the highest per capita stress to the Earth System comes directly or indirectly from high income unsustainable households – principally in 'developed' nations – the emphasis of this book is on sustainable development as it applies to these high income countries. That many of the newly industrialised nations contain increasing numbers of higher income households is not irrelevant but these households are typically broadly imitating 'Western' unsustainable lifestyles – hence a focus on the 'developed world'. A key feature of this research is a survey of 'official' sustainable development literature, selected from documentation produced in relation to key moments in international discourse building around the project of sustainable development. From this documentation I isolate the key assumptions and recommendations in three areas: epistemology, ethics and the nature of citizen participation in policy-making, as key issues for sustainable development. Against a background of unpredictability, the book attempts to suggest possible ways forward in respect of these issues in the sustainable development context. The ways in which the terms 'epistemology' (theories of knowledge) and 'ethics' (e.g. consequential, deontological, virtue) are to be used in this book are discussed in some detail in the next chapter. Also discussed is the 'open society' notion of Popper – which, it is claimed here, can perhaps act as a catalyst for appropriate ways of thinking about participation, in the context of an objective such as sustainable development.

A principal reason for attempting this study[1] is that it appears there is little discussion of whether humans can predict and control the Earth System. There is less direct discussion of how policy with regard to global sustainable development might be made if prediction and control is not possible. Of course, the precautionary principle, which states that action should be taken under uncertainty and can apply at the level of the Earth System, deals with these issues. However, as we shall see in Chapter 6, the precautionary principle still leaves vital questions open, particularly with regard to what actions might follow from the principle.

We have become used to the fact that there are numerous definitions of sustainable development available to us, and none of them is definitive. This suggests the appropriateness of a plural approach to sustainable development, and to its constituent aspects – including its epistemological, ethical and participatory dimensions. What emerges from the survey of governmental sustainable development literature, though, is a rather narrow picture of the content of these dimensions. One reason for a lack of progress towards sustainable development is in part due to the mismatch between sustainable development's contested nature, and the way in which 'official' approaches to it have coalesced around a rather narrow set of claims and assumptions.

At a basic level the book is transdisciplinary in the sense that it discusses the science of sustainable development, in a way that is unusual for social science treatments of sustainable development. An assumption of the need to move beyond discipline boundaries is typical for environmental questions and other questions implicit in sustainable development. This is demonstrated by the WCED report, which could readily be described as transdisciplinary. To illustrate, the WCED (1987) takes a holistic perspective, covering questions from potable water supply to space debris in an admirably integrated way; more specifically it addresses these issues using insights from a variety of science disciplines as well as economics and politics, to name some prominent examples. This book adds to the range of consideration of the WCED a more detailed and explicit consideration of epistemology, ethics and participation.

The 'solutions' proposed in the book are not of the 'do this and the consequences you desire will result' form, rather they indicate reasons why certain approaches or attitudes might be considered good or 'virtuous' in the context of the questions raised by the concept of sustainable development. In other words, it is hoped that this book can hasten the time when we stop going in the wrong direction and start going in the right direction – that would be real progress (cf. Foster, 2014).

The broad approach of the book is to compare official sustainable development policy documents and academic sustainable development literature, in order to identify and suggest possible alternatives or even improved epistemology, ethics and policy-making processes. Much of the content of the book – particularly Chapters 2, 3, 4 and 6 – is discourse analysis inspired by the ideas of John Dryzek (e.g. 1997).

The broad philosophical assumption for policy-making in this book follows Dewey in broadly these terms: (1) identify the problem; (2) describe the problem; (3) suggest solutions to the problem as described; (4) choose solutions; (5) implement chosen solutions; (6) monitor effectiveness; and (7) go through the stages iteratively from (1) as experience suggests is necessary. As will become clear, if it is not already, only stages (1) to (4) can be attempted in this book. Much of the first half of this book is taken up with describing the problem and noting the limits of current and possible descriptions. Levin *et al.* (2010) is one recent relevant example that attempts something of this process for a key issue for sustainable development – climate change. This has some helpful suggestions; however, their description of the problem focuses on the nature of their perception of the climate change policy problem – broadly their starting point is society. What they do not do is go back the stage further to describe and wrestle with the limitations of natural science in predicting the Earth System. As we shall see in the next chapter, the Earth System cannot be predicted robustly enough for those predictions to be plugged in to cost–benefit analysis without gross unwarranted assumptions. That is, dominant policy approaches, for climate change and sustainable development, are based on what policymakers wish natural science could tell them, rather than what natural science can actually tell policymakers. Similar focus on the complexity of climate policy processes, not the complexity of the Earth System, results in similarly limited analysis by Hoffmann (2011). Perhaps worse is that although he acknowledges the dangers of the unintended, uncontrolled experiment humans are conducting on the Earth System (Hoffmann, 2011, 26), he does not examine the limitations of advocating social experimentation as a response to the initial experiment. That is not to say that some of the experiments that he discusses will not have a part to play in addressing climate change and unsustainable development. The question raised is whether the out-of-control Baconianism of our global experiment on the planet can best be addressed principally by more Bacon inspired experiments.

To orient the reader, let me summarise the argument of the book here. (1) Suggestions for sustainable development need to take into account that both the earth's systems and the human social systems are complex to the point that they cannot be robustly predicted for policy purposes – broadly Chapters 2 and 5. (2) As evidenced in Chapters 3, 4 and 6, dominant models of sustainable development both in theory and as embedded in governance practices, do not operate this way (cf. Grubb, 2014). In particular formal and informal cost–benefit analyses are the dominant and imposed models of sustainable development policy. This is at the heart of their various failures, in particular because costs cannot be robustly predicted and the ethics of economics promotes unsustainable behaviour. Conventional economics is irrational. (3) Chapters 7 and 8 outline three suggestions as being better able to cope with these difficulties in prediction. These are (i) virtue epistemology (prudence/wisdom/precaution); (ii) virtue ethics; and (iii) more participative governance arrangements to implement prudence collectively. Global virtue tradition can readily incorporate the knowledge of natural science and holds the predominant allegiance of more people in the world than the ethics of conventional economics. That is, economics is an undemocratic and irrational response to unsustainable development.

Given the transdisciplinary nature of this book and perhaps the radical nature of the conclusions, decisions have been made in the writing that may be worth making explicit to aid people from different disciplinary backgrounds. There is a good deal of evidence for the assumptions of existing sustainable development policy presented in the book, as results of discourse analysis. Those readers who are immersed in sustainable development policy might skim these chapters as long as they agree with the analysis of the book that conventional economics cannot be used to achieve sustainable development – Chapters 2, 5, 7 and 8 will remain important. If a reader does not agree or is unfamiliar with this policy field, all the chapters will bear close reading. If a reader agrees with the prior analysis but believes that technology will be largely sufficient to achieve sustainable development, then Chapter 5 will be vital. If a reader does not have faith in either economics or technology to achieve sustainable development, then Chapter 5 might be skimmed but Section 5.7 should still be closely read as it illustrates the profundity of the limits of technological approaches. Chapter 2 is the vital description of unpredictable unsustainable development and Chapter 7 describes the centre of the best 'solution' to that unpredictable unsustainable development. A more detailed outline chapter by chapter will now be helpful.

The next chapter outlines some key ideas that will frame the discussion in the rest of the book. First there is discourse analysis of the physical science underpinning sustainable development, highlighting the limitations of this science. Considering those limitations in more depth, epistemological issues relating to understanding the Earth System are discussed, with particular consideration being given to the idea of 'managing' the Earth System. Varieties of ethical framework for policy are considered in the light of current and anticipated capacities for Earth System management. The ideas of Francis Bacon and Karl Popper are examined as possible loci of the widespread adoption of managerial attitudes to nature and a possible way of moving towards sustainable development, respectively. Chapter 2 encapsulates the overall argument of the book.

Chapter 3 draws out and analyses the epistemology, ethics and notions of citizen participation discourses in early sustainable development literature, in particular *Our Common Future*, the report of the WCED, otherwise known as the Brundtland Report. Chapter 4 examines epistemology, ethics and participation for key later sustainable development policy literature from the United Nations (UN), European Union (EU) and the Organisation for Economic Co-operation and Development (OECD). By this point in the book we should have a sedimented sense of the centre of gravity of the 'official' approach to sustainable development, and how it developed. This might be summarised as:

- an implicit desire to 'manage' the Earth System, which is ...
- ... based on a desire for Baconian prediction and control of 'nature' as epistemological and ethical assumptions, which in turn appears to entail ...
- ... the ethical assumption that extracting the maximum possible material wealth out of the Earth System will bring maximum 'utility', and that this should dominate other ethical frameworks for policy such as deontological and virtue approaches.
- This appears to be combined with an implicit (neo-Platonic) assumption that experts can and should tell us how to manage the Earth System to maximise material utility.

These instrumental and utilitarian ethical assumptions, plus the arrogant predictive epistemological assumptions, are embedded in current (sustainable development) policy practice, which, as we shall see, can barely distinguish between economic development and sustainable development. Perhaps the paradigm case of this undemocratic, unethical and irrational practice is the use of economic cost–benefit analysis, to propose business as usual policies, where the costs used in the analysis are derived using opaque methods based on uncritical use of climate models, which are acknowledged to be far from perfect.

It should be noted that difficulties in predictions were clear over twenty years ago and that little has changed significantly. If the reader accepts the above characterisation of the tone of intergovernmental sustainable development literature, then the details of the analysis of documents in Chapters 3 and 4 need not detain them too much. If the reader is unconvinced, or wishes to gain a more detailed and nuanced understanding of the key assumptions of sustainable development policy, then Chapters 3 and 4 will be thought provoking.

In the context of this set of managerial assumptions for policy, Chapter 5 analyses practical environmental management responses to sustainable development, to identify if these responses have transcended the epistemological limitations identified in earlier chapters. There is also mention in this chapter of the ethical and participatory aspects of practical environmental management. In other words, the chapter asks and attempts to answer the question: does 'management' work?

Chapter 6 mines some key academic sustainable development sources for possible ways forward, again particularly from a point of view of epistemology and ethics. Here, broader perspectives on knowledge limits (particularly those of Earth System science) and ethical contestations begin to take shape.

Chapter 7 proposes epistemological responses and considers ethical responses to difficulties in prediction of the Earth System, setting out an account of ecological virtue that it is argued is more rational than cost–benefit analysis.

Chapter 8 explores democratic theory to gain insights into how the participatory policy processes, called for in the sustainable development policy literature, might be implemented and improved, particularly in the light of limits to knowledge and the contested nature of ethics in the sustainable development context. Based on the previous analysis, criteria are suggested that might be used to evaluate participatory processes.

The book concludes that a transdisciplinary analysis of sustainable development leads to the case being put forward that the Earth System is not predictable with current theories of knowledge. This in turn implies the desirability of a greater plurality of ethical assumptions in the policy-making process, with these being mediated by decision-making processes that better promote participation of citizens. There are many options, concepts and methods to promote citizen participation in policy-making. Further development of existing practices, innovations and analyses of how to choose between different methods for different situations and different constituencies are recommended.

The conclusion briefly draws together suggestions about how humanity might respond to the threats it now faces. A first sense in which humanity is under threat is that closed totalising 'market fundamentalism' (to use a phrase of George Soros) and possible eco-dictatorships are potential responses to issues such as abrupt climate change; both of these threaten the humaneness of societies. Second, market fundamentalism and the near imposition of consumerism threaten what can be regarded as the best aspect of individual humans (their humanity) and the humaneness of societies. For example, consumerist societies' typically selfish responses to immigration pressures, to refugee crises and to the global injustices that are key drivers of these issues. Finally, unpredictable abrupt changes in the Earth System, brought about by industrial activity, threaten complex human societies and conceivably Homo sapiens. The ideas described in this book are intended to allow us to be sufficiently wise to save ourselves from irrational undemocratic blind industrialism, whether communist or capitalist.

Note

1 Beyond any hoped for increase in sustainability of development of human societies.

References

Dryzek, J. (1997) *The politics of the Earth: Environmental discourses*, Oxford: Oxford University Press

Foster, J. (2014) *After sustainability: Denial, hope, retrieval*, Abingdon: Routledge

Grubb, M. (2014) *Planetary economics: Energy, climate change and the three domains of sustainable development*, Abingdon: Routledge

Hoffmann, M. (2011) *Climate governance at the crossroads: Experimenting with a global response after Kyoto*, New York: Oxford University Press

Levin, K., Cashore, B., Bernstein, S. and Auld, G. (2010) *Playing it forward: Path dependency, progressive incrementalism, and the 'super wicked' problem of global climate change*, http://environment.research.yale.edu/documents/downloads/0-9/2010_super_wicked_levin_cashore_bernstein_auld.pdf. Accessed 30 December 2011

WCED (1987) *Our common future*, Oxford: Oxford University Press

2 Can humans manage the earth?

No! Implications[1]

2.1 Introduction

This chapter outlines the key concepts used in the analysis in the rest of the book. It also indicates the broad thrust of the overall argument of the book.

Section 2.2 of this chapter will outline the science of key environmental issues that are of concern to sustainable development, noting that critical thresholds or tipping points in the Earth System mean that science cannot predict consequences of policy robustly. Section 2.3 will describe and consider some key concepts of epistemology (theories of knowledge) relevant to this book. Section 2.4 will briefly outline some ethical theories as they apply to sustainable development, including the place of prediction in these theories. Section 2.5 will look at the ideas of Francis Bacon and indicate the importance of these in 'modernity' as a key locus of a managerial assumption, which may be a key part of the causes of current unsustainable development. Section 2.6 considers the ideas of Karl Popper, and particularly his ideas regarding the 'open society', as a key treatment of alternative assumptions that may open the way to allowing human societies to develop more sustainably. The chapter will conclude that currently dominant epistemological and ethical assumptions of policy may need to be re-examined, in a situation of unimagined tipping points and hundreds of years of inertia in the Earth System.

Before that, it is worth noting that sustainable development is taken here to be a contested concept (e.g. Jacobs, 1999; Pezzey, 1992, Appendix 1; Reid, 1995, xiii–xx). A key starting point is the WCED (1987) report. The 'definition' of sustainable development typically highlighted from that report is: 'Sustainable development is development that meets the needs of the present without compromising the ability of future generations to meet their own needs' (WCED, 1987, 43).

To indicate some of the ways in which this 'definition' might be contested, let us at this point raise the following questions. Is 'development' synonymous with economic growth and economistic utilitarian ethical[2] assumptions or should development include other ideas such as 'democracy'? Are 'needs' purely those of subsistence or can deeper needs count? If so, how can we distinguish what are needs and what are wants? How can we know what the needs and wants of future generations will be?

The WCED (1987) will be discussed in more detail in Chapter 3. It is sufficient to suggest at the moment that sustainable development is the key policy idea for environment and development questions that will affect whether tipping points in the Earth System are crossed. To that end an alternative 'definition' from Earth System science literature will be helpful:

> At the international level, a broad consensus can be discerned that sustainable development should be development that, over the next two generations, promotes progress 'to meet the needs of a much larger but stabilizing human population, to sustain the life-support systems of the planet, and to substantially reduce hunger and poverty'.
>
> (Schellnhuber *et al.*, 2004, 16–17)

This 'definition' raises further questions; however, it is useful context to the literature from which it is taken. This literature is discussed in the next section.

2.2 Science of sustainable development

There is obviously a great deal of science that touches on questions relevant to sustainable development and it is not my intention to deal with it all here. This section will indicate some key scientific findings of studies of global environmental questions, in particular those that are important for theories of knowledge and ethics.[3]

Much of the discussion around sustainable development is about more local issues, for which uncertainty is perhaps less. However, these local issues are connected to global issues at least via emissions implicated in climate change and so cannot be completely separated from global issues. Nonetheless, for these more local issues uncertainties and difficulties in prediction may be less of a problem for policy-making and action. Detailed discussion of these local sustainability questions is beyond the scope of this book, which will focus on the global environment. At the global level, difficulties around prediction are perhaps at their greatest, yet difficulties in prediction in relation to policies for sustainable development appear under-discussed. In addition, these global issues appear to be some of the most important. In this connection, two areas will be discussed in detail: climate science, as this is an area where questions of the limitations of predictions are routinely discussed in 'authoritative' and mainstream natural science literature; and Earth System science for similar reasons and also because the Earth System appears to be the correct level of analysis for many global environmental issues. Thus, these examples are paradigmatic of the issues being wrestled with in this book. Literature that indicates similar policy relevant difficulties in prediction, with regard to biodiversity loss, toxic chemicals and genetic modification, are also mentioned.

This book assumes that the 'Western' physical sciences are the most robust and reliable forms of knowledge of the physical world. Indeed, they may produce ever-closer approximations of 'true' understanding of material reality, including ecosystems. However, this book will suggest that in the terms of science itself and for the sake of policy-making, there are significant limitations of current science, in particular for understanding large, complex systems such as the Earth System.

As an indication of this, let us take climate science as an example. The following quotation is a reasonable summary of the state of knowledge in this context: 'With a rapidly changing external forcing, the non-linear climate system may experience as yet *unenvisionable, unexpected,* rapid change' (IPCCWG1, 2001, 96, emphasis added). It should be noted that in Intergovernmental Panel on Climate Change (IPCC) terminology, 'external forcing' includes industrial activity. The IPCC admit deep epistemological difficulties with climate science:

> The evaluation of uncertainty and the necessary precaution is plagued with complex pitfalls. These include the global scale, long time lags between forcing and response, the impossibility to test experimentally before the facts arise, and the low frequency variability with the periods involved being longer than the length of most records.
>
> (IPCCWG3, 2001, 656)

The inertia implied in 'long time lags' may be hundreds of years (IPCCWG1, 2001, 558) for some components of the Earth System and conceivably thousands of years (IPCCSR, 2001, 16–21). This suggests that predictive efforts will need to be robust for these lengths of time for predict and control management of the climate and earth systems to be effective.[4] Nevertheless, the overall policy assumption seems to be that prediction of levels of stress[5] to the earth is possible and that such prediction will ensure the avoidance of catastrophic change to the Earth System. For the sake of brevity, this assumption is typically termed 'predict and control' in this book. However, what if this assumption is flawed? The IPCC's own evaluation of current limitation in human theories of knowledge is as follows:

> Some of these uncertainty aspects may be *irreducible in principle,* and hence decision makers will have to continue to take action under significant uncertainty, so the problem of climate change evolves as a subject of risk management in which strategies are formulated as new knowledge arises.
>
> (IPCCWG3, 2001, 656, emphasis added)

In *The Concise Oxford English Dictionary* (Thompson, 1995) the most relevant definitions of manage are 'organize; regulate; be in charge of ... gain influence with or maintain control over ... take or have charge or control of (an animal or animals)'. With regard to climate science, 'risk management' and the use of the term management more generally by the IPCC, management appears to indicate an assumption that quantified thresholds of greenhouse gas (GHG) concentrations can be identified and avoided before 'dangerous anthropogenic interference with the climate system' (UNFCCC, 1992, Article 2) is inevitable. This section questions whether such thresholds can be identified before they are crossed. It can be suggested that, in assuming management as the correct response to uncertainty, the IPCC perhaps make a normative assumption in favour of utilitarian ethics (cf. Jamieson, 1992; Padilla, 2004; Smith, 2003, 29–51);[6] specifically, the utilitarianism of conventional economics that is typical of IPCC ethical assumptions (e.g. IPCCWG2, 2001, 120–6, particularly 124). The potential consequences of climate change are illustrated as follows:

> Finally, a series of potential large-scale geophysical transformations ... have been identified and examined more closely in recent years. These imply thresholds that humanity might decide not to cross because the potential impacts or even the associated risks are considered to be unacceptably high. *Little is know [sic] about these thresholds today.*
>
> (IPCCWG3, 2001, 673, emphasis added)

The last quotation is almost the IPCCWG3's concluding remark and is perhaps their clearest indication of the stakes that may be involved in climate change. It is democratically significant that the IPCC has not made it clear to the *general public* what these 'large-scale geophysical transformations' might be *and* that '[l]ittle is known about these thresholds today' so that 'humanity might decide [to try] not to cross' them. Indeed, IPCCWG3 (ibid.) is not explicit about what these transformations are. IPCCWG3 (ibid., 677) appears to suggest the possibility of events such as the shutdown of the North Atlantic Thermohaline Conveyor or the collapse of the West Antarctic Ice Sheet, which would almost certainly have a very detrimental effect on human societies.

IPCCWG2 (2001, 129) appears to assume that the assessment of the 'low probability [of] ... the occurrence of extreme climate outcomes such as a "runaway greenhouse effect"' is known in an objective sense from 'subjective probabilities' from 'experts'. This may be the best process humans have for making this type of assessment, but it is hardly 'objective science'[7] and appears to make no assessment of factors that may affect these experts' views, such as:

- Commitment to particular ontological assumptions, scientific paradigms, scientific methods, ethical frameworks, economic and political arrangements.
- Supra-rational beliefs about the robustness or otherwise of the Earth System, and the basis of those beliefs.
- Level of expertise in the philosophy of science, in particular understanding of any current limitations of science.

Shackley and Wynne (1995) suggest that a conclusion of low probability of extreme events might be as much conditioned by the answers policymakers want as what science on its own can justify. Policymakers might find it hard to react effectively to unpredictable events because their standard tools are designed to cope with 'smaller ranges' of unpredictability. This book attempts to offer rational responses to unpredictability under conditions where the premises for standard policy tools do not operate.

Sarewitz *et al.* (2000, 385–6) tackle something of these questions; they provide a valuable indication of the emphasis policymakers put on prediction, as well as the issues that there are around assuming the need for prediction in policy. Their conclusions are:

> Given the uneven performance and our lack of understanding of the prediction enterprise, a good argument can be made for the following: First, our dependence on scientific prediction has become uncritical, and at times excessive and counterproductive. Second, we need to be more careful about how and when to make prediction a central activity in addressing environmental questions. Third, as soon as new environmental problems begin to command public attention, we need to resist the urge to immediately prescribe a predictive approach and should consider a range of possible actions. And finally, we should worry less about making good predictions and more about making good decisions.
>
> (Ibid., 386)

Similarly, Webster *et al.* (2003) is a valuable source that directly addresses questions of uncertainty and difficulties in prediction of climate change as they relate to policy. Early on they state (ibid., 295): 'While continued basic research on the climate system to reduce uncertainties is essential, policymakers also need a way to assess the possible consequences of different decisions, including taking no action, within the context of known uncertainties.'

The need to consider 'possible consequences' is quite reasonable; however, they then arguably proceed to implicitly assume policy needs to be based on (quantitative?) predictions of those consequences (ibid., 295–317). However, they eloquently illustrate the difficulties of this (ibid., 295): 'A significant part of our uncertainty about future climate change may be unavoidable – details ... are likely to remain unpredictable to some degree, and uncertainty in projecting future levels of human activities and technological change is inevitable.'

In their conclusion they also illustrate a 'significant' limitation in current climate policies based on prediction of consequences, 'therefore abrupt-changes or "surprises" not currently evident from model studies, including our uncertainty studies ... may occur' (ibid., 317).

When the analyses of Sarewitz *et al.* (2000) and Webster *et al.* (2003) are added to the Shackley and Wynne (1995) view, which problematises the very framing of scientific questions, a further level of difficulty in relation to the assumption that climate science can be used as a predictive basis for policy emerges. Thus, we can then see that a policy process that takes prediction as a sine qua non for effective decision-making is fraught with complications.

The possibility of 'rapid' or 'abrupt' climate change was discussed at least as long ago as 1992 (Mintzer, 1992, 55–64). However, significant discussion of the policy implications of this appears to be quite recent. Let us consider this literature, particularly noting any epistemological and ethical assumptions.

Hulme (2003) indicates a broadly predictive approach to 'slow' and rapid climate change. He admits there are currently limits to the effectiveness of predictive approaches but asserts that 'it is premature to argue therefore that abrupt climate change ... constitutes a dangerous change in climate that should therefore be avoided at all reasonable cost' (Hulme, 2003, 2001). Apparently this is on the basis that few studies of the possibility have been done. This appears to assume that the climate system will not change abruptly until humans have done some (robustly predictive) studies[8] before it rapidly changes or inertia commits it to rapidly changing.

The Committee on Abrupt Climate Change (2003) is a study of the science and potential impacts of abrupt climate change. It starts with this claim:

> Recent scientific evidence shows that major and widespread climate changes have occurred with startling speed. For example, roughly half the north Atlantic warming since the last ice age was achieved in only a decade, and it was accompanied by significant climatic changes across most of the globe. Similar events, including local warmings as large as 16°C, occurred repeatedly during the slide into and climb out of the last ice age. Human civilizations arose after those extreme, global ice-age climate jumps. Severe droughts and other regional climate events during the current warm period have shown similar tendencies of abrupt onset and great persistence, often with adverse effects on societies.
>
> (Ibid., 1)

The report of the committee, though, gives little insight into how to make policy in the context of the possibility of rapid climate change, other than a call for better science and a discussion of potential impacts of abrupt climate change if it did happen. This is perhaps because of an assumption that prediction of abrupt climate change (e.g. ibid., 4–5), or even prediction of the financial costs of abrupt climate change (e.g. ibid., 152, 157–9), is needed before policy can be made. An update in 2013 by the now Committee on Understanding and Monitoring Abrupt Climate Change and its Impacts (2013) still places faith in human abilities to anticipate abrupt climate change, which this book calls into question.

A useful discussion of 'decision-making under uncertainty' with regard to the Earth System is provided by Schneider *et al.* (2002, 53–87). This makes broadly economistic utilitarian ethical assumptions but illustrates the difficulties of these types of approach. Despite this, the authors state that 'unwarranted complacency may result from the inability to foresee nonlinear events' (ibid., 65). In the conclusion to the chapter they write:

> In view of the wide range of plausible climatic change scenarios available in the literature – including a growing number of rapid non-linear change projections – it is important for costing analyses to consider many

such scenarios, including the implications of rapid changes in emissions triggering nonlinear climatic changes with potentially significant implica- tions for costing.

(Ibid., 79)

It might be suggested that 'potentially significant implications for costing' is quite a euphemistic phrase. Schneider (2003) is a report for the OECD about abrupt climate change. In this he argues that research 'which neglects surprises ... of the Earth System ... is indeed questionable, and should carry a clear warning to users of the fundamental assumptions implicit in it' (ibid., 16). Once again, how is policy-making, and related areas such as political theory, economics and political philosophy, to take 'surprise' into account?

POST (2005) is a UK Parliament report that addresses rapid climate change, making clear that in spite of significant uncertainties it is a question that policy- making needs to consider. However, the most concrete policy responses are to 'instigate coordinated research; install monitoring systems; implement win–win strategies to reduce vulnerabilities; and ultimately stabilise atmospheric GHG concentrations at a level that would lower the risk of rapid changes in the future' (ibid., 4).

These appear largely based on the assumptions that humans can predict the level of stress to the Earth System, before significant harm to human socie- ties is inevitable. But given the uncertainties surrounding climate science, and our knowledge of the Earth System in general, there may be considerable risk attached to policy processes that simply assume uncertainties can be removed. Indeed, this perhaps has normative consequences in allowing an economistic utilitarian ethical assumption, based on the further assumption that science can predict the level of stress that the Earth System will withstand from industrial activity, before thresholds are reached.

An interesting discussion of climate change policy from the Congressional Budget Office (2005) explicitly considers abrupt climate change. However, this report only seriously considers economic responses or a cap on GHG emissions, both of which need (implicitly or explicitly) an agreed threshold to be predicted before significant policy action can be taken. This again illustrates the difficulties of economistic utilitarian approaches or other predict and control approaches to policy, where levels of stress to the Earth System before tipping points are reached cannot be robustly identified. Given the discussions of abrupt climate change in the document, an alternative would be a virtue approach that includes moderation. Since at least Aristotle, virtue ethics has considered questions of consumption, for example consuming enough but not too much food. In the light of evidence for the possibility of abrupt climate change, moderation could be extended to involve the reduction of climate change gas emissions immediately, without needing to wait for predictive evidence. Linden (2006) suggests that unpredictable abrupt climate changes have been, at least partly, responsible for the fall of numerous civilisations in the past.

Lowe (2006) reflects on whether communication of catastrophic climate scenarios is effective in producing action by citizens to reduce the GHG emissions associated with their lifestyle. This is a complex document whose assumptions are not made clear. However, it appears reasonable to characterise it as arguing that scare stories, on their own, are not effective in producing the 'desired effect'. The following appear key assumptions: 'We cannot predict with any great accuracy how, when or to what extent rapid, catastrophic, or runaway climate change will occur' (ibid., 2) and 'What is clear, however, is that the problem must be made tangible and manageable if the warnings are to have a real impact' (ibid., 4).

Thus, prediction and management appear key assumptions here. Lowe does not exclude the possibility of climate catastrophe, instead he emphasises that predictions of such are incomplete. This appears to mean that Lowe wants to manipulate citizens by feeding them just sufficient fear to make them take the action that he feels is best. If this is so, it is questionable morally and strategically. Strategically, it is questionable as the 'scare stories' are already in the public domain, including documents such as the 2001 IPCC reports as illustrated earlier. Morally, it is questionable in a number of ways. First, it is condescending and in some sense undemocratic. Second, it assumes that scary information can only be released as is, without taking measures to reduce the 'fatalism and apathy ... rejection and anger' (ibid., 1), this might result in. This book argues that virtue ethics schemes that include both hope and moderation are one basis of action to reduce the stress to the climate system from consumerism, without the need for prediction or management of the Earth System. Hulme (2006) and (2007) appear to be based on Lowe's (2006) analysis and can be questioned in a similar way.

The Stern Discussion Document (2006) contains only minor discussion of rapid or abrupt climate change, which perhaps indicates the difficulties that policymakers have in approaching questions of rapid climate change through economics. The completed Stern Review (2006) mentions abrupt, rapid or non-linear climate change frequently; however, this discussion illustrates the difficulties economics has with responding to the levels of uncertainty that there are in climate science. For example:

> The science is becoming stronger ... higher temperatures will bring a growing risk of abrupt and large-scale changes in the climate system, such as melting of the Greenland Ice Sheet or sudden shift in the pattern of monsoon rains. Such changes are still hard to predict, but their consequences could be potentially catastrophic.
>
> (Ibid., 84)

> With 5–6°C warming, models that include the risk of abrupt and large-scale climate change estimate a 5–10% loss in global GDP, with poor countries suffering costs in excess of 10%. The risks, however, cover a very broad range and involve the possibility of much higher losses.
>
> (Ibid., 143)

The most worrying possible impacts are also among the most uncertain, given that so little is known about the risks of very high temperatures and potential dynamic instability ... they would imply very large estimates of potential losses from climate change.

(Ibid., 164–5)

What is the current science of (rapid) climate change? Stainforth *et al.* (2005) address the question of climate prediction directly and suggest a wider range of temperature change than that accepted by the 2001 IPCC reports. However, their efforts so far appear not to transcend the difficulties with epistemology discussed in this chapter. Given the existing melting of the Arctic ice cap (NASA, 2006; NSIDC, 2005) and the permafrost in Siberia (Walter *et al.*, 2006), it could reasonably be argued that the climate and climate related systems are already rapidly changing (cf. Conkling *et al.*, 2011). Schellnhuber *et al.* (2006) do not robustly dispel this possibility. GHGs are being emitted more rapidly from permafrost than scientists predicted (Walter *et al.*, 2006, 71), although it is not yet clear that there is runaway climate change.

All this gives an indication of the nature of current climate science and our current lack of robust predictive abilities. Authors who appear wedded primarily to considering consequences in the rest of their article, still suggest the following policy implications: 'Hence, it appears that one should not rely on prediction as the primary policy approach to assess the potential impact of future regional and global climate change' (Rial *et al.*, 2004, 31).

Beyond the specific instance of climate change, Groombridge (1992), Haywood (1995), Power *et al.* (1996) and Tickner (2003, 175–89) suggest that similar limits of human knowledge currently affect questions around biodiversity. Cox and Tait (1991), Adams (1995), RCEP (2003), Weinberg (1986) and Porritt (2000, 47–62, 93–4) suggest that these types of limits also currently affect knowledge of harm from the use of chemicals. The Committee on Genetically Modified Pest-Protected Plants, National Research Council (2000), Medical Research Council (2000), The Royal Society of Canada (2001), Committee on Environmental Impacts Associated with Commercialization of Transgenic Plants, National Research Council (2002), Department of the Environment (1995, particularly 144), Tickner (2003, 157–70), European Communities (2005), Ho (1999), Porritt (2000, 41–2) and Rifkin (1999) suggest that genetic modification may be affected by the limits of human capacity to robustly know the consequences of human actions. Porritt (2000, 116) even suggests that humanity may have 'lost control of the biosciences'. These issues appear not to be convincingly addressed by ACRE (2002, 2006), European Federation of Biotechnology – Task Group on Public Perceptions of Biotechnology (2001), Sambrook and Russell (2001), European Federation of Biotechnology – Task Group on Public Perceptions of Biotechnology and The Green Alliance (1997) and Brown (1995). To give an indication of the limits of our understanding of molecular genetics, we are now beginning to understand that the 'non-coding' 98 per cent of the human genome that was labelled 'junk' by scientists in the past may have a variety of functions (e.g. Callaway, 2010). Stirling (Berkhout et al., 2003, particularly 47) might be interpreted as giving reason to suggest a lack of effective predictive ability for the effects of climate change, persistent chemicals and genetically modified organisms.

Boehmer-Christiansen (1992, particularly 144–5) insightfully addresses questions of the relationship between science and policy stating that

> politicians seem to need predictions. An engineer may shorten the policy process and argue: fund me instead and I will reduce these discharges as much as technologically will permit. Discovering the future first, i.e. to understand pollutions in the environment sufficiently so that it may be costed, is not essential for preventative policy.
>
> (Ibid., 144)

The second and third sentences of the quotation offer a useful indication of what might be done where prediction is difficult. It might be asked if the activity that causes the pollution is necessary, or at least is the activity moral in one or more sense? Boehmer-Christiansen (ibid., 152–3) specifically recommends 'open political systems' as an essential response to contested science, interests and ethics.

Ecological science suggests that it is heuristically effective to view life on earth as being connected through large and global systems. Examples include food chains, the hydrological cycle, the nitrogen cycle and the carbon cycle. These each involve any number of biological organisms as well as non-biological systems such as the atmosphere, which all coexist within the ecosphere.[9] Moreover, each system is connected to some extent to those around it. For example, plants absorb carbon dioxide from the air; use the carbon and release oxygen, which is then breathed in by animals, which in turn breathe out carbon dioxide. This dependence is normally organised in self-regulating systems.

To give an uncomfortable example of the connection of ecological systems, a recent El Niño/La Niña event was of such increased strength and duration that it might have been caused by global warming (McPhaden and Soreide, 2004). This in turn might have caused 'Hurricane Mitch, [to be] the strongest October hurricane ever recorded, [which] was marked by its duration, strength and persistent, destructive rains over Central America' (WMO, 1999). These effects were probably made worse by deforestation (FAO, 1999). Burkett et al. (2005) illustrate the linear and non-linear links between climate change and ecosystems and the difficulties this raises for policy-making, even if they appear to assume science will enable predictive policy in the future without making clear how (ibid., 386).

Schellnhuber (1998, 1999, 2001), Steffen and Tyson (2001), Schellnhuber and Held (2002), Steffen et al. (2004), Schellnhuber et al. (2004), Lenton et al. (2008) and Modvar and Gallopín (2005) suggest similarly significant connections exist within the Earth System. Modvar and Gallopín (ibid., 11) write that at least for the 'socio-ecological system … our knowledge on the inter-linkage is still insufficient'.

Current industrial and other activities induce stress on the Earth System. Reid (1995, 108–9) illustrates the possible implications of stress to this system when he writes:

> Some of the impacts of human activity on biophysical systems may have passed a threshold, which may mean unpredictable and possibly catastrophic change before the global system finds a new balance ... Even if such a threshold has not been passed we do not know how long we have before we reach it ... Unless action is taken soon, there is a real prospect that the sustainable system eventually achieved will represent a much ... impoverished lifestyle ... The breakdown ... of ecosystems to the point where they no longer provide essential services is not necessarily an even, gradual, plainly visible ... process, but may possibly be triggered by some slight modification in conditions, or by the loss of some inconspicuous species.

Ehrlich (1989, 13) suggests something of the difficulties of predicting the consequences of stress to the Earth System and something of the significance of this: 'Industrial civilisation ... [may] ... grind to a halt ... before the middle of this century. Steffen and Tyson (2001) is perhaps the clearest brief treatment of Earth System science, the potential risks of current human behaviour and implicit policy implications. For example,

> changes taking place are, in fact, changes in the human-nature relationship. They are recent, they are profound, and many are accelerating. They are cascading through the Earth's environment in ways that are difficult to understand and often impossible to predict. Surprises abound ... these human-driven changes to the global environment ... may drive the Earth itself into a different state that may be much less hospitable to humans and other forms of life.
>
> (Ibid., Foreword)

The authors go on to indicate more specifics:

> The human enterprise drives multiple, interacting effects that cascade through the Earth System in complex ways ... The Earth's dynamics are characterised by critical thresholds and abrupt changes. Human activities could inadvertently trigger changes with catastrophic consequences for the Earth System ... the Earth System has recently moved well outside the range of the natural variability exhibited over at least the last half million years. The *nature* of changes now occurring *simultaneously* in the Earth System, their *magnitudes* and *rates of change* are unprecedented.
>
> (Ibid., emphasis in original)

They later give concrete examples including 'the palaeo-record shows that ... recorded changes were often rapid and of high amplitude; in some cases temperature over large regions changed by up to 10°C in a decade or less' (ibid., 10).

Other important indications of the stakes of human decisions and actions include Schellnhuber *et al.* (2004, 5–6). Less stress to the Earth System from human activity is fundamentally what Schellnhuber and Wenzel (1998), Reid (1995, particularly 109–25), Costanza (1989, 4–5), Steffen and Tyson (2001), Schellnhuber and Held (2002), Steffen *et al.* (2004) and Schellnhuber *et al.* (2004) recommend. The question asked in this book is whether policy-making based on the possibility of prediction, leading to approximation to thresholds, is likely to be a robust way of reducing such environmental stress. The book will try to draw out some other assumptions that can be brought to bear as part of reasoned decision-making processes, which will make more likely the reduction of stress to the Earth System.

Rayner indicates something of the political significance of the limitations of prediction of the Earth System by science when he writes:

> Rather than resolving political debate, science often becomes ammunition in partisan squabbling, mobilised selectively by contending sides to bolster their positions. Because science is highly valued as a source of reliable information, disputants look to science to help legitimate their interests. In such cases, the scientific experts on each side of the controversy effectively cancel each other out, and the more powerful political or economic interests prevail, just as they would have without the science.
>
> (2006, 5)

2.3 Epistemology and sustainable development

This section will explore whether there are ideas that indicate that humans will be able to predict and control (manage) the Earth System (Newton, 1999; Schellnhuber *et al.*, 2004; Schellnhuber and Held, 2002; Steffen *et al.*, 2004; cf. Biermann, 2007). There are a variety of opinions about the possibility of managing the Earth System in this literature, and perhaps the most clearly argued is Steffen *et al.* (2004, 286, see also 295, 297–8):

> Systems theory suggests that complex systems can never be managed; they can only be perturbed and the outcomes observed. Furthermore many of these outcomes will be likely unpredictable ... This property of complex systems is manifest in the Earth System ... Humans ... cannot be in a position to manage the Earth System.

Epistemology is a term often used to describe theories of knowledge; for example, the processes humans use to understand physical and social systems (Klein, 1998). Important scientific forms of knowledge for understanding the Earth System include natural science, ecological science, systems science and Earth System science.

The philosophy and sociology of science both reflect on these domains of scientific activity and endeavour. A brief review of developments in these fields will help us to see whether there are ways that have been suggested in which the Earth System might become predictable. Important schools of philosophy of science, philosophers and sociologists of science such as logical positivism (Popper, 1972; Kuhn, 1970; Lakatos, 1970; Feyerabend, 1970, 1975) have not suggested ways in which complex systems such as the Earth System can be predicted. Let us consider what these authors do say about science in a little more detail.

Popper (1972) suggests that anything worthy of the name of science should be predictive in order to allow those predictions to be tested and to allow theories to be falsified. However, Kuhn (1970) argues that science develops by paradigm shifts rather than by falsification. Climate and Earth System science do tend to try to be predictive and do use falsification tests. However, as we have seen, climate science is not yet robustly predictive and it is not clear that Popper or anyone else has suggested ways in which it might become predictive. Lakatos (1970) attempts 'a "synthesis" of the accounts of science given by Popper and Kuhn' (Worrall, 1998, Vol. 5, 342). Lakatos' view has not been found widely convincing as a complete description of the process of science. Feyerabend (1970) suggests that reasoned debate about theories, observations and experimental results is the closest thing that science has to method. Indeed, he

> denied that there is such a thing as 'scientific method': there are no universally valid methodological precepts by which scientific practice either is or should be governed. If we must insist that there must be some such precept, the only defensible candidate is 'anything goes'.
>
> (Williams, 1998, Vol. 3, 640)

The tensions between Popper, Kuhn, Lakatos and Feyerabend broadly appear to illustrate the current state of the art in descriptions of science. Literature such as *Science and the Retreat from Reason* (Gillott and Kumar, 1995) suggests that this make some advocates of science uncomfortable; however, Gillott and Kumar do not suggest how science can be predictive of complex systems – particularly the Earth System.[10] There is, though, one way in which Gillott and Kumar are critical of trends in contemporary science that is important and relevant to this book. They suggest that emphasising an assumption of difficulties in prediction may become a new universalising orthodoxy, replacing a mechanistic ontology on the basis of inadequate evidence (ibid., 217–19). Gillott and Kumar also argue that epistemological assumptions that tend to be pessimistic about human predictive abilities have the normative social consequence of making society more cautious, particularly about attempting to control nature. There may be some truth in this suggestion, and it is indeed part of the argument of this book that this could be a step in the right direction.

A further pertinent discipline is science and technology studies (STS). Relevant authors in this field such as Wynne and Shackley have already been mentioned and others such as Jasanoff will be mentioned when applicable. However, given that this is a large, pertinent and growing field in academia, a brief general comment may help some readers. Some specific insights of STS are clearly helpful; however, moving forward now with sustainable development, Latour (2004) may well be right in wondering if some forms of STS are not an irrelevance at best and at worst dangerous, with regard to environmental issues such as climate change.

Authors such as von Bertalanffy (1971), Laszlo (1972) and Jantsch (1980) discuss systems theory and systems science; with Jantsch (1980) giving a key reason to suggest that prediction of the Earth System is not currently possible. Specifically, Jantsch discusses systems that change state at a specific or 'critical' level of disturbance, noting everyday occurrences of this phenomenon, such as flow of water from taps moving from smooth to turbulent as the tap is opened more. Jantsch does not describe how to find critical thresholds where switches in state will take place, except with laboratory systems where repeatable experiments can be done. This difficulty in finding 'tipping points' still appears true for Earth System science (Lenton et al., 2008; Rial et al., 2004; Schellnhuber, 1998, 1999; Schellnhuber et al., 2004; Schellnhuber and Held, 2002; Steffen et al., 2004), and there is at least one journal devoted to 'Nonlinear Processes in Geophysics'. Despite Rockström et al. (2009), all this appears to indicate that, at present, there is no robust way of finding all critical thresholds in global and more local ecological systems that appear essential to life, other than at the risk of blowing up the 'laboratory' along with the experimenters.

An example of critical thresholds in relatively simple systems is metal fatigue, where a crack propagates for months or years from a small imperfection, until the material is sufficiently weakened for it to break in fractions of a second (Mann, 1967, 11). This can 'take place even though the peak stress is well below the ultimate tensile stress' (Cox and Tait, 1991, 42). Given that metal fatigue was only widely recognised after numerous fatal 'real world experiments' and is still an issue that leads to fatalities in industries such as aviation, this suggests that the assumption that humans can spot all thresholds in the Earth System in time to stop them being crossed is highly questionable. It is also important to note that many materials, once stressed to a certain level, cannot return to their original state and will break even if the stress on them is reduced (Boyer, 1987; White, 1999, 288).

Rahmstorf (1994, 1995, 2003) argues that critical thresholds might exist in complex ecological systems, suggesting in particular that the North Atlantic Thermohaline Conveyor may shut down because of climate change. This example, and others, leads Schellnhuber (1998) to write: 'One of the most burning questions of modern environmental research is therefore whether there is a possibility that *critical thresholds* ... exist in the ... complex Earth System for certain global conditions' (ibid., 21, emphasis in original). He appears to assume that these can, for practical purposes, be established, but gives no explicit indication of how, and certainly none that indicates how they can all be robustly found.

Indeed, he goes on to write: 'The future of the Earth System cannot be predicted – due to *irreducible* cognitive and voluntative uncertainties' (ibid., 181, emphasis in original).

Schellnhuber (2001, 50–1) returns to these types of question, suggesting that control and management of the Earth System is both possible and desirable via repeated small 'steering adjustments' (cf. Jamieson, 1992, 142–6). However, this leap of faith by Schellnhuber appears to ignore questions such as the hundreds of years of inertia in the Earth System which probably means humans cannot see much past the end of the 'car' let alone far enough to effectively 'brake or steer'. In addition, it seems in tension with other analyses by Schellnhuber (e.g. 2001, 48–9) and Schellnhuber *et al.* (2004, 7–8). There are similar tensions within the Earth System science documents already referred to in this book. This assumption in favour of management by Schellnhuber may be because of an ethical assumption in favour of economistic utilitarianism (e.g. Schellnhuber, 1998, 67–74, 122, cf. 75–127; 2001, 42–8; Schellnhuber *et al.*, 2004, 20–1[11]) (cf. Jamieson, 1992, 142–6; Padilla, 2004; Smith, 2003, 29–51) or at least working in an intellectual context where utilitarian assumptions are dominant and unquestioned. This is perhaps inconsistent, given that Schellnhuber (e.g. 2001, 23–4, 43) notes severe problems with past managerial projects. Schellnhuber and Held (2002, 5) recall Steffen and Tyson (2001), which suggests predict and control management of the Earth System will be difficult or impossible (cf. Jamieson, 1992, 142–6). However, the rest of Schellnhuber and Held (2002), as well as Steffen *et al.* (2004, 38), seems to make managerial assumptions similar to those discussed in the other Earth System science literature; this is all apparently heavily influenced by Schellnhuber (1998, 48–127). To tease some of this out, 'management' tends to seek control, and utilitarian ethics tend to seek control over nature (at least), in order to maximise utility. By way of contrast, in many virtue ethic traditions, self-control by humans for the sake of self and the 'other' is a strong element.

Allan and Curtis (2005) indicate that there are significant difficulties at the local level with the adaptive management or steering, advocated by Schellnhuber above, let alone at the global level. Keilis-Borok *et al.* (2002) do offer some intriguing possibilities for future research from earthquake prediction. However, these processes are in their infancy. If they had been operating faultlessly for at least fifty years, then entrusting such techniques to predict and control the stress the Earth System will withstand from human activity might be reasonable. Even then, there would still remain questions around inertia, the possibility of unknown mechanisms in the Earth System and the worry that these 'management' tools have not yet been operating faultlessly even on smaller systems.

Schellnhuber (1998, 48–127) is a detailed discussion of possible sustainable development paradigms from the perspective of Earth System science, and these appear to have been influential on later Earth System science. These paradigms are summarised in Steffen *et al.* (2004, 38):

Standardisation. The management objective is to maintain the evolution of the Earth System within a safe range of environmental qualities or aggregated functions defined as sustainability indicators.

Optimisation. In an ideal world the most attractive of all of the management approaches would aim to maximise generalised utility over a prescribed time period, where utility is defined in a broad, normative way through millions of acts and interactions by individuals around the world.

Pessimisation. The primary emphasis in this approach is placed on the precautionary principle of preventing the worst from happening, for example, abrupt changes with potentially catastrophic effects.

Equity. Management approaches focussing on equity aim to achieve a relative balance amongst the various participants who have a stake in global management (i.e. virtually the entire human population), but taking into account the nature of Earth System dynamics.

Status quo. The goal of this paradigm is to define and maintain a stable equilibrium in the global environment.

The standardisation and optimisation paradigms, at least, appear to assume predictability of a sort that this book puts into question. The situation is less clear for the other three paradigms. In recent Earth System science literature, there appears to have been little discussion of possible relationships between the paradigms. Schellnhuber (1998, 121–7) does discuss this question though he does not make definitive suggestions; however, he does propose a possible hierarchy:

1   Pessimisation.
2   Status quo.
3   Equity.
4   Optimisation.

(Ibid., 126)

The relationship between the 'standardisation' paradigm and the above hierarchy is not clear; though it is perhaps implicit that standardisation is an essential prerequisite for the other four paradigms. It appears quite reasonable that we should prioritise planning for worst-case scenarios over maintaining the status quo, equality and maximising generalised utility. The relative priority of the others is more questionable. Maintaining the economic global status quo might be politically acceptable in globally powerful countries, but its acceptability elsewhere, and its morality, is questionable. Thus, levels 2 and 3 may need to be addressed simultaneously in order for either to be achieved. However, it is suggested here that the currently dominant global political and policy assumption of those who have power is to put maximisation of generalised utility above increased equality between humans (without even considering non-humans). This book (with the above reservations) tends to agree with the broad spirit of the hierarchy by

Schellnhuber. However, it can be argued that the difficulty in achieving the other levels will tend to exclude the utilitarianism implied in the fourth level. That is, implementing the other levels will be so difficult that optimisation will never need to be considered.[12]

The above Earth System science discusses chaos theory (Gleick, 1987) in a number of places, suggesting that it applies to large and global ecological systems. If chaos theory applies to the Earth System, this makes problems of prediction clearer and more problematic.

Human actions, manifest in widespread use of technology, are simultaneously disturbing many of the earth's systems. This may mean that multiple tipping points are crossed in quick succession. Given the interconnection of systems in the Earth System, one tipping point in one subsystem of the Earth System may cause other tipping points to be crossed. Lenton *et al.* (2008) discuss a number of these tipping points and tipping elements and include:

- melting of permafrost (Pearce, 2005; Schaefer *et al.*, 2011; Walter *et al.*, 2006);
- shut down of the North Atlantic Thermohaline Circulation (Rahmstorf, 1994, 1995, 2003; Rahmstorf *et al.*, 2005);[13]
- potential loss of much of the Brazilian rainforest (Betts *et al.*, 2004; Cox *et al.*, 2000; Lewis *et al.*, 2011);
- melting of the Arctic ice cap (NASA, 2006, 2010, 2011; NSIDC, 2005);
- collapse of Antarctic ice shelves (Ferrigno *et al.*, 2009; NSIDC, 2011a).

Chains of events or domino effects of tipping points appear to be a possibility that Earth System scientists have generally not considered in detail (Kemp, 2005; Lenton *et al.*, 2008; Modvar and Gallopín, 2005; Schellnhuber *et al.*, 2004, 19; Steffen *et al.*, 2004, 232–3, 244, 260–2; Steffen and Tyson, 2001, 22), though the evidence they present supports the possibility. Indeed, given current theories of science (particularly Popperian falsification as the best standard of 'proof'), it is not clear how science could disprove such a possibility. Given the difficulties of understanding the Earth System indicated previously, it is not clear how an opinion on the likelihood of this type of scenario, beyond an educated guess, can be formed for the foreseeable future (cf. Rockstrom *et al.*, 2009). If we add in other stresses to the Earth System, beyond stress from climate change, then a policy assumption that humans can predict and control the Earth System is even more questionable. Indeed, if the references above about tipping points or elements are interrogated through the lens of epistemological difficulties highlighted in this book, then they are clearly overconfident in how soon they state that tipping point will be crossed. This overconfidence relates first to the overconfidence in predictive abilities because of a lack of examination of current predictive abilities; and second, overconfidence leads to estimates of crossing of tipping points that are further in the future than can be supported by the science alone. To illustrate, it can be argued that the 2001 IPCC predictions of 'a substantial decrease of Arctic sea-ice cover ...

roughly 20% reduction in annual mean Arctic sea-ice extent by the year 2050'
(IPCCWG1, 2001, 446) are already in sight with the 2010 average relative
to 1979–2000 being reduced by 11.5 per cent (NSIDC, 2011b). Open ocean
reflects less light back than ice so less sea ice on its own will further increase
warming in the Arctic. This is a clear indication science cannot be relied upon
to predict in a way that can be depended on to make policy.

The problem of induction appears to make predictive knowledge of the Earth
System even more problematic, where induction is used as the philosophical
basis for policy shaping predictions. In many situations 'scientific theories' and
induction aid effective prediction; however, induction can be logically questioned and experience shows it is not always effective (e.g. Crutzen, 1996; cf.
Berkhout *et al.*, 2003, 22–3).[14] The problem of induction is an issue that has
been recognised in philosophy (particularly the philosophy of science) for a
long time (Hume, 1748/1975; Popper, 1972, 27–30) yet does not appear to
have been overcome so far (Caws, 1965, 256–65; Worrall, 1989), notwithstanding Bostrom (1996). Howson (2000) does present a 'solution', but this
clarifies the limits of inductive approaches rather than removes them. It is just
these limits that this book argues need to be respected by policy processes (cf.
ibid., 4). Until recently, the practical implications of the problem of induction
were perhaps not important, or at least not recognised as such. Norgaard (1989,
44) argues that 'the re-emergence of the problem of induction – after decades
of faith in unpractised falsification' is important in questioning the usefulness
for policy of 'modern' notions of science (cf. Lemons 1996, 18–19). For policy
relevant questions about issues such as climate change, persistent toxic chemicals, genetic engineering, etc., we might argue that the problem of induction
should not now be ignored, particularly with regard to risk assessment. Earlier
in history, the problem of induction was not as significant a practical issue, as
the issues humans had direct control over were local. However, in an era of
Earth System science and industrial societies, it is extremely significant, as we
have only one Earth System and it is not clear how big a mistake we can make
with it before the 'experimental apparatus' is wrecked.

To illustrate the possible importance of this type of question to unsustainable development, let us consider ozone depletion. It is not clear how the
stratospheric ozone depleting effects of chlorofluorocarbons (CFCs) could have
been anticipated when these chemicals were first developed. Indeed, it is suggested by Crutzen (1996) that if bromine had been used rather than chlorine,
ozone depletion would have been much worse. This is another example of the
difficulties involved in assuming that the side effects of new technology can be
anticipated and 'managed'. Schellnhuber *et al.* (2004, 8–10, 17) suggest that this
type of incompleteness in analysis currently affects Earth System science, and
they give us no reason to believe that it will not always affect Earth System science. However, they also claim (ibid., 10) that a 'comprehensive list' of critical
thresholds in the Earth System will 'support, in the not-too-distant future, global
stewardship'. Our question might be: how wise is it to organise policy around
thresholds when our knowledge of the processes surrounding them is so imprecise

and insecure? Whether the reasons for this assertion of the possibility of a comprehensive list are based in a Baconian predict and control assumption or a more robust epistemological scheme is not clear. Schellnhuber *et al.* (2004, 10–14) assert that critical facets of society are less well understood than critical thresholds in the Earth System, before illustrating profound epistemological difficulties in understanding the social components of the Earth System and the interaction between the social and ecological spheres.[15] Indeed, they specifically argue in the context of limits of prediction in climate science:

> So long as opponents of management have been able to declare – as did U.S. President George W. Bush in opposing the Kyoto Protocol – that 'no one knows what that (dangerous) level is' (press conference, June 11, 2001), science-based management remains a ready excuse for inaction.
>
> (Ibid., 18)

This quotation is an interesting reflection on the relationship between policy and prediction, especially in relation to the use of the term 'management' by Schellnhuber *et al.* When seen in context, the first use of the term management in the quotation is perhaps with regard to managing human behaviour (implicitly reducing stress to the Earth System), whereas the second is management of the Earth System including human societies, probably on the basis of predictive management. The next sentence of Schellnhuber *et al.* (2004, 18) is: 'The S&T [Science and Technology] community could therefore significantly improve "the prospects for humanity consciously managing a transition toward sustainability" by developing an understanding of the vulnerability and resilience of the Earth's life-support systems to "dangerous" disruption.'

Another alternative would be to question (or even challenge) the assumption of prediction being needed for policy. Particularly if there is reason to believe that a robust 'understanding of the vulnerability and resilience of the Earth's life-support systems to "dangerous" disruption' may never be developed, or at least may always be reasonably questioned by sceptics. To make the situation more difficult still, Schellnhuber *et al.* (2004, 20) argue that

> natural scientists have not contributed effectively to specifying goals and indicators for 'protecting life-support systems' ... only with respect to the global atmosphere was a reasonably integrated system of specific goals, targets, indicators, and monitoring in place. For the dimensions of 'life-support systems' relating to ocean productivity, freshwater availability, land-use change, biodiversity, and toxic releases, no such system exists.

If we consider the difficulties there are around 'managing' the climate with current policy processes, this is a further indication that successful, predictive approaches to Earth System policy are a long way off, and may not be possible at all.

A philosophical analysis of knowledge by Faber *et al.* (1998, 205–29) suggests further epistemological limitations: imperfect communication, inability to check all assumptions, the emergence of novel 'natural systems' and technology. These all suggest that robust predictive knowledge of the Earth System is even more problematic.

It should be clear from the preceding that prediction of the development of the 'natural' component of the Earth System is surrounded by difficulty. Similar problems affect the human social component of the Earth System; for example, that societies may react to predictions about themselves, either to try to reinforce predictions they like or avoid those they do not like. Sayer (1992, e.g. 134), Bernstein *et al.* (2000) and Gerring (2001, 118–27) among others argue that prediction is problematic for social science; Ruben (1998) among others also argues that controlled experiment is problematic. Popper (1966, 1989, 336–46) argues that assumptions of predictability of the development of societies can lead to the kind of historicist totalitarianism implicated in some of the most unpleasant regimes of the twentieth century.

In sum, the current science and epistemology of the Earth System suggest that the Earth System is not predictable, and is not likely to become so in the foreseeable future (cf. Adger, 2006, 276).

2.4 Ethics and unpredictable sustainable development

We have examined what humans can know of the Earth System; let us now consider in broad terms how we might react to that lack of knowledge.

A full analysis of how different types of political ideology will react to the inability to predict and control the Earth System for the sake of making policy is beyond the scope of this book. However, it is worth suggesting that modern political ideologies are perhaps just that, 'modern' in the sense that they assume something of the attitude to 'nature' in *New Atlantis* by Francis Bacon, discussed later in this chapter (Engel and Engel, 1990, 34, 78, 104–6, 238; Hay, 2002, 30–1, 75–6, 122–3, 140–1; Merchant, 1983).

An arguably smaller and perhaps more valuable task is to consider how different types of ethics respond to the inability to predict and control the Earth System. Ethics is a term often used (Crisp, 1998a) to describe theories of how humans (individually or collectively) decide what behaviour is right and wrong in a particular situation. Crisp (1998b), Baron *et al.* (1997) and Brown (2001) (cf. Hinman, 1999) argue that philosophy suggests that one way to consider ethics is to broadly divide it into the following three categories:

- Consequentialist or utilitarian ethics.
- Virtue ethics.
- Deontological or rights-based ethics.

This is not uncontroversial (cf. German Advisory Council on Global Change, 1999), but will suffice for the purposes of this book. To illustrate, economic thought is typically broadly utilitarian, which means that more money is assumed to broadly mean more 'happiness' or 'utility' and thus decisions are made on the basis of maximising money or economic growth. This contrasts with laws that often express broadly deontological ideas or rights (e.g. human rights, property rights). A second contrast can be drawn with virtue ethics: if someone is described as immoral they are typically being accused of not being virtuous rather than not utilitarian enough or insisting on rights. There appears to be no agreement about what relationships between these different types of ethics there are or should be, though there is research trying to see how they might fit together (Brown, 2001) including in a plural way (e.g. Hinman, 1999). Pettit and Slote (Baron *et al.*, 1997, e.g. 256–60, 267–74) each appear to support initiatives to see how consequentialism, rights and virtue ethics might fit together; as does Baron (ibid., 5–64) if to a lesser extent. A little more detail about each of these three ethical schemes will be worthwhile.

There are numerous types of consequentialism (ibid., 92–169). As we shall see in the next two chapters, the currently dominant type in policy-making, even in the area of sustainable development, is 'economistic utilitarianism'. This seeks to maximise economic growth as indicated by concepts such as Gross Domestic Product (GDP) or Gross National Product (GNP) within the bounds of broadly deontological rights and law. Consequentialism judges moral quality on the basis of the consequences of actions (ibid.; McNaughton, 1998). Utilitarianism is typically seen as a subset of consequentialism that seeks to maximise some notion of utility or welfare. The term economistic is intended to indicate a focus on monetary economies as an indicator of a measure of the welfare to be maximised (cf. Ludwig, 2001, 760–1). Thus, 'economistic utilitarianism' is intended to convey an ethical assumption that the primary aim of governments, other organisations and individuals is to maximise the financial wealth of nations, organisations and individuals (typically focusing on their own nation, organisation or themselves), based on the assumption that this will maximise happiness. Pettit (ibid.) makes clear that there are many other types of consequentialism. He indicates that most consequentialist philosophers are probably uncomfortable with economic growth as a single or dominant metric for the morality of a system of government.[16] Pettit (Baron *et al.*, 1997, 92–169) also indicates that many of these consequentialist notions have a poor understanding of at least some important virtue ethics schemes. It can be suggested that at least utilitarian notions of consequentialism need to predict consequences in order to attempt to maximise utility. In a situation where consequences are significantly difficult to predict, this calls into question policy-making processes that rely on predicting consequences (cf. Adger, 2006).

Virtue ethics schemes often (e.g. Aristotle) also seek to promote happiness. The distinction between virtue ethics and consequentialism/utilitarianism can appear unclear, but there are two important distinctions between the two for our purposes. First, consequentialism judges right and wrong by the consequences of actions, whereas, oversimplifying, virtue ethics tends to focus on questions of character. Second, utilitarianism tends to see happiness as coming through maximising welfare[17] and in practice often sees welfare as having a single metric such as material wealth, whereas virtue ethics typically aims to 'maximise' a set of virtues to 'maximise' happiness.[18] The logic for important virtue ethics schemes is reversed in comparison to consequentialism (including utilitarianism). Virtue ethics typically sees happiness as coming through having a stable disposition to be virtuous.

To illustrate, if a parent was purely consequential and selfish they might have and care for children for reasons of children conferring social status and in the expectation that the children will care for the parents when they get older. However, parents who have a virtue of love will care for their children because it is the right thing to do irrespective of the consequences, e.g. whether society approves of it or whether the children care for the parents in old age.[19] Virtuous parents might also receive satisfaction simply from caring for the children, but this would be secondary.

Deontological or rule-based ethics can be based on a range of assumptions. One example is a notion of the nature of humans, to give examples; autonomy (e.g. Baron *et al.*, 1997, 14), particular notions of equality (e.g. Baron *et al.*, 1997, 76) or freewill. Alternatively, rule-based ethics can be constructed to promote either virtue[20] (e.g. ibid., 13–16) or utility (e.g. property rights)). The particular distinguishing feature of deontological or rule-based ethics is that they generate laws, duties or rights often intended to be 'universally' applicable. It is not clear, to the author at least,[21] how these types of notion can help us make decisions about the Earth System if we cannot predict the consequences of policies or actions.

To illustrate the limitations of deontological approaches, let us consider the Kantian approach of Westra (Sandler and Cafaro, 2005, 79–91). She asserts rights to 'unpolluted air, unpolluted water, adequate food, adequate clothing, adequate shelter' (Shue, 1996, 23 quoted in ibid., 84); however, she does not make clear how these will be guaranteed even in principle. Although powerfully argued, sincere and well intentioned, difficulties in knowing who is responsible for causing particular levels of pollution and resource deprivation, and the effect this will have, are perhaps the key reason why 'punishment' (ibid.) of those who breach such rights is difficult. Thus, van Wensveen (ibid., 27, emphasis in original) can say 'virtue language ... may ... [have] a *good* chance at achieving moral breakthroughs ... [with] ... problems ... that are already getting stale (such as the question whether trees or rivers have rights)'. We have now reviewed something of how major types of ethical schemes might respond to our inability to predict the Earth System. Mention of these schemes will be made throughout the book, but some broad points of reference can be made at this stage, in regard to the issue of sustainability. First, any scheme driven by the idea of 'maximisation' (e.g. economic growth, material wealth and throughput) is likely to be problematic in the context of 'thresholds' and 'unpredictability', given everything that has been said earlier about the status of Earth System science. This suggests that 'economistic utilitarianism' is a problematic ethical scheme, in our context. Second, any system that has no 'eye' for consequences will perhaps be a problem in an Earth System showing signs of stress as a result of allowing processes to take their course (e.g. North Sea fishing), with no consideration of the scale of activity in relation

to its context. This suggests that deontological ethics may not be the most promising framework for determining 'right action' in our sustainability context. This
leaves virtue ethics, which is perhaps analytically most help in making decisions
where consequences cannot be predicted (Jamieson, 1992, 150–1) but still typically makes some non-predictive consideration of consequences. However, virtue
ethics is not sufficiently clearly better than other forms of ethics that it could
claim to exclude these others.

One possible way forward is to increase efforts to see how different forms of
ethics can and should relate to each other; and add in the lack of prediction as
a key assumption. Probably the most important conclusion is that economistic
utilitarian ethics should not be privileged by sustainable development policy-
making processes in the way that we shall see it typically is (cf. Jamieson, 1992;
Padilla, 2004; Smith, 2003, 29–51). Let us expand on this last point.

Jamieson (1992, 139–46; cf. Berkhout *et al.*, 2003, 223) argues that because of
limitations of human abilities to predict the climate, management approaches to
climate change 'must fail', particularly management in the form of economics:

> When our ignorance is so extreme, it is a leap of faith to say that some analy-
> sis is better than none. A bad analysis can be so wrong that it can lead us to
> do bad things, outrageous things – things that are much worse than what we
> would have done had we not tried to assess the costs and benefits at all.
>
> (Jamieson, 1992, 146)

Jamieson (ibid., 146–51) goes on to suggest that virtue ethics responses are analytically more robust in situations where consequences cannot be assumed to be
known. Reasons given for this, beyond the above, include that it is difficult to
assign individual responsibility for harm, making duty-based approaches difficult
(ibid., 148–50). Jamieson (ibid., 150) then argues that:

> One of the most important benefits of viewing global environmental prob-
> lems as moral problems is that this brings them into the domain of dialogue,
> discussion and participation. Rather than being management problems that
> governments or experts can solve for us, when seen as ethical problems they
> become problems for all of us to address both as political actors and as every-
> day moral agents.

Thus, sustainable development can be said to be, in part, about the habits that
produce our everyday actions and how these are connected to economic and
political processes. If these became stable dispositions to be ecologically virtuous, this should allow development to be more sustainable. Jamieson (ibid.,
150–1) also criticises managerial utilitarian approaches as tending to systematically reduce the virtuousness of societies in which they operate (cf. Berglund and
Matti, 2006; Le Grand, 2003).

Ethics will be discussed in more detail in Chapter 7; however, it is worth indicating at this point what a 'sustainable' virtue ethic might look like. Based on a

survey of ecological literature, van Wensveen (Sandler and Cafaro, 2005, 186–8)[22] argues that cardinal (pivotal) environmental virtues might be quite similar to cardinal virtues of existing virtue traditions: namely prudence, justice, moderation and courage. Cafaro (ibid., 135–58) and Wenz (ibid., 197, 205–6) both argue that the traditional seven deadly sins are ecological vices and are typically treated as virtue and encouraged by consumerist industrial societies. Connelly (2006, 70–2) broadly concurs and even adds that 'faith, hope and love seem appropriate to any list of virtues' (Connelly, 2006, 70).

There is one further ethical concept that needs to be introduced before we proceed – 'global virtue tradition'. This can be illustrated if we consider the use of virtue ethics as a concrete response to unsustainable development in Palmer and Finlay (2003) (cf. Sponsel, 2007), which is an interesting and important book for a number of reasons. Perhaps most interesting is that it was published by the World Bank with a foreword by the then president of the Bank but, in a context of 'conservation', it is significantly critical of economistic utilitarianism and tends to favour a range of virtue ethics schemes as the appropriate response to sustainable development questions. Indeed, in key ways the virtue schemes are broadly similar. Before discussing the specifics of this agreement between these virtue schemes, it is worth considering the reasons why Palmer and Finlay (2003) might or might not be used to promote dialogue about choices of ethics for sustainable development. First, most of the discussion is around conservation, that is, broadly questions about the interactions of humans and nature at a local level. However, there are no obvious reasons why these responses would not scale to the global level. In addition, the responses comfortably integrate development and environment questions. One possible reason for this comfortable integration is that Palmer and Finlay present the views of eleven world religions and their on-going dialogue on environment and development questions since 1986. For many of these religions, their responses are based on traditions of adapting to ecosystems for hundreds or thousands of years. These points are well illustrated in the first half of the book, which describes practical conservation initiatives that these traditions have been involved in, in recent years.[23] Before going any further, it might be worth suggesting that to dismiss these positions simply because they are religious might, to say the least, be characterised as undemocratic and 'closed' (cf. Popper, 1966). Indeed, in discussing environmental virtue ethics Taliaferro (Sandler and Cafaro, 2005, 159–61) gives five reasons to consider religious ethics, with the most important of these perhaps being that

> the majority of the world population is … affected by religious traditions. So long as you wish to carry out environmental ethics in a way that engages vast proportions of the world population, some acquaintance with religious ethics is pivotal. An intelligent encounter with religious traditions may be especially important … when, for example, secular and religious values clash. An environmental ethic that ignores religious values is in danger of failing to engage and respond to the world population as it is today, substituting in its place an engagement with a limited academic community.
>
> (Ibid., 160)

To continue, the second half of Palmer and Finlay (2003) presents statements of principle from each world religion about how humans should interact with ecosystems. The level of authority that might be accorded the statements is significant; to illustrate the Christian statement was jointly 'compiled and endorsed by the Ecumenical Patriarchate of Constantinople, the World Council of Churches, and the Vatican Franciscan Center of Environmental Studies' (Palmer and Finlay, 2003, 83).

Thus, this virtue response to ecological questions perhaps 'represents' a quarter of the global human population. With regard to the whole book, in the foreword the then president of the World Bank states the '11 faiths ... represent two-thirds of the world's population' (ibid., xi). It can be contested how much the broadly virtue ethical views presented in Palmer and Finlay (2003) actually represent the views of those the world religions might claim to represent; more particularly in the context of larger global sustainable development questions and also when moving from ethical principles to practical political economy questions. However, what is more significant is that the book was published by the World Bank and suggests that economistic utilitarian assumptions can at least be put under significant scrutiny, with virtue schemes being the implied alternative.

Now it is appropriate to illustrate what the agreement is about. Palmer and Finlay indicate that the traditions represented are often at least implicitly critical of economistic utilitarian assumptions (Palmer and Finlay, 2003, 74, 80–2, 85, 88–90, 91–3, 98, 106, 108, 111–12, 114–16, 129, 131, 135; Palmer, 1990) even if the Christian (Palmer and Finlay, 2003, 86) and Jewish (ibid., 111, 114, 118, 122) responses do perhaps give some support to economistic utilitarian assumptions.[24] That this book was published by the World Bank perhaps suggests that, even in key global advocates of economistic utilitarianism, doubts are surfacing about the appropriateness of trying to value everything with money.

Many of the traditions are implicitly or explicitly critical of exploiting humans and nature (ibid., e.g. 20, 83–5, 89–90, 96–7, 108, 117, 131–2, 136–8) to fuel human greed (ibid., e.g. 81–2, 85, 91, 93, 108, 135). Something akin to temperance or moderation is found in the responses of the following world faiths to environmental and development issues: Baha'i, Buddhism, Christianity, Daoism, Hinduism, Islam, Jainism, Judaism and Sikhism (ibid., 72, 76, 79–81, 85–6, 88–90, 91–2, 104–6, 108, 118–19, 135). There is discussion of 'rights' in Palmer and Finlay (2003); however, it is as common for this to be critical of people assuming they have the right to use and abuse nature as they are about asserting rights of humans. There is little clear discussion of rights for nature. Connelly (2006), Sandler and Cafaro (2005) (particularly chapters by van Wensveen, Cafaro and Wenz) along with Palmer and Finlay (2003) indicate a democratically significant 'global virtue tradition' that stretches back at least as far as ancient Greek philosophy, including Aristotle, much religious thought and also encompasses much recent environmental literature. For the sake of brevity, the term 'global virtue tradition' will be used in this way in the rest of this book. In the light of earlier discussions of difficulties around predicting the stress that the Earth System will withstand before thresholds are crossed, it is significant to note that none of these virtue schemes need to predict such limits before moderating consumerism. Indeed, significantly in the light of discussion in this book of catastrophe, the following indicates that care for nature could be virtuous even if immediate 'change in civilisation' appeared inevitable.

> Imagine you are busy planting a tree, and someone rushes up to say that the Messiah has come and the end of the world is nigh. What do you do? The advice given by the rabbis in a traditional Jewish story is that you first finish planting the tree, and only then do you go and see whether the news is true. The Islamic tradition has a similar story, which reminds followers that if they happen to be carrying a palm cutting in their hand when the Day of Judgment takes place, they should not forget to plant the cutting.
>
> (Palmer and Finlay, 2003, xiii)

A cynical interpretation can be put on the above quotation, that care for nature might be motivated by a desire to be a little more righteous for the sake of salvation if the end comes; however, it can be argued that the analytical point still remains that virtue tradition can advise dignity, care and justice to nature even if 'the end is nigh'. The agreement between Jewish and Islamic tradition is not insignificant.

Given the normative significance of the above, a few further comments are relevant. The following appears to be typically accurate for social scientists and policy professionals: 'It is a striking fact of modern intellectual life that we often seek to evade the value dimension of fundamental social questions' (Jamieson, 1992, 147). By evading values in such a fashion, social scientists and policy professionals perhaps make an implicit assumption in favour of the economistic utilitarian status quo. Perhaps particularly relevant to the 'global virtue tradition', Jamieson (ibid., 147) goes on to argue that 'values are more objective than mere preferences ... A value has a force for a range of people' and that our differences

> tend to occur around the edges of our values system. The vast areas of agreement often seem invisible because they are presupposed or assumed without argument. I believe that our dominant value system is inadequate for guiding our thinking about global environmental problems.
>
> (Ibid., 148)

Jamieson then goes on to attribute the dominant materialist utilitarian value system to a number of authors, including and perhaps primarily Francis Bacon, and something of this will be discussed in the next section. Jamieson then particularly criticises assumptions that individual responsibility can be taken for collective actions[25] such as carbon dioxide emissions, before recommending virtue ethics over economics as a response to unpredictable, human caused, Earth System change.

2.5 Prediction, instrumentalism and Bacon: key locus of the 'problem'?

Having now established that the Earth System is not predictable for the foreseeable future, suggested that policy processes typically assume this prediction and further suggested that the ethics of conventional economics underpin this instrumental approach to 'nature', some analysis of the origin of these ethical and epistemological assumptions will be insightful.

Complementing the analysis by Jamieson above, Attfield (1994, 13–86) provides a broad introduction to 'traditional attitudes to nature', highlighting the significance of these for environmental questions and to a lesser extent for broader sustainable development issues. Marangudakis (2001) provides an important (and entertaining) alternative relevant perspective, which outlines suggestions of the theological, philosophical and sociological underpinnings of 'pre-modern', 'Western' technological progress. This section is intended to provide a more specific orientation to readers unfamiliar with the development of 'modern' attitudes to 'nature'. To this end, it will draw out something of the origin and significance of the 'modern' epistemological assumption of 'prediction and control' and an ethical assumption that nature only has value for the use that can be made of it by humans. Emphasis here is on *New Atlantis* by Francis Bacon as key in promoting utilitarian or instrumental attitudes, that nature can and should be predicted and controlled purely for the benefit of humans.

As mentioned earlier, and discussed in more detail later, particularly in Chapters 3 and 4, it appears that prediction and control of the physical world is a key, though questioned, assumption for contemporary policy-making (e.g. Jamieson, 1992; Moore in Engel and Engel, 1990, 104–6), including sustainable development policy. This is normally implicit, or at least not reflected upon, perhaps because it appears deeply embedded in policy-making attitudes of 'modernity'. A key 'modern' articulation of prediction and control assumptions comes from Francis Bacon and can be captured in the phrase 'knowledge is power' (Bacon: *Meditationes Sacrae*).[26] This knowledge and power comes from systematic observation and systematic repeatable experiment organised by underlying reasonable theory (Milton, 1998, Vol. 1, 627–8). Milton goes on to write of Bacon: 'It was the ability of a theory to endow its holders with power over nature that provided the best, and indeed the only genuinely satisfactory, evidence for its truth' (ibid., 628). Or in Bacon's own words:

> Human knowledge and human power meet in one, for where the cause is not known the effect cannot be produced. Nature to be commanded must be obeyed; and that which in contemplation is as the cause is in operation as the rule.
>
> (*Novum Organum*, 1620, i 3, quoted in ibid.)

This epistemological and ethical assumption has profound implications for ecological questions and could be said to be based on an instrumental (some would say arrogant) anthropocentric ethical assumption (cf. Attfield, 2003, 31–6). Bacon applied his perspective on 'science' to politics primarily in a 'utopian' literary work[27] *New Atlantis* (Bruce, 1999, xxviii). It might be argued that much of the epistemology and ethics of *New Atlantis* are still foundational assumptions in much contemporary policy-making. To tease out and illustrate what is meant in later discussion of the application of Baconian assumptions (epistemological and ethical) in this book, let us also consider this text and something of its influence. Bruce argues that Bacon saw 'the reform of the natural sciences as the great project of his life; and that *New Atlantis* is intended to further this aim' (ibid., xxix–xxx). Bruce (ibid., 149–85) presents a standard edition of *New Atlantis* (ibid., xliv), which will be the version discussed in this book. The vision of science that Bacon paints in *New Atlantis* (ibid., 177–85) is much more of technology or at least applied physical sciences including physics, chemistry and biology, than pure science. This vision appears founded on prediction and control assumptions (ibid., e.g. 179; cf. Bacon: *Novum Organum*).

Given the possibility that *New Atlantis* is assumed implicitly to be an inspirational utopia in 'modernity', let us examine the utopian credentials that *New Atlantis* can claim. There is much relevant analysis by Bruce (ibid., xiv, xxx–vi). Specifically, Bruce (ibid., xxxii–v) argues that there is little evidence in *New Atlantis* that it is an ideal society for average citizens, indeed for anything except the notion of science as Bacon conceived it.[28] It is noted that the society of *New Atlantis* is well served by medical science (ibid., xxx, xxxii, 152–7) and the account of *New Atlantis* by Bacon does imply that average citizens are at least materially well provided for. In a less positive light, Bruce (ibid., xxxii–v) notes that the society of *New Atlantis* is authoritarian, secretive for the sake of control and power,[29] hierarchical, repressive, 'imperialist' and possibly xenophobic. Given the technological prowess of the people of *New Atlantis* if they had sought empire over other lands, this should have been easy to accomplish; however, in the account this was discouraged by an early monarch of the society. This attitude to empire was probably quite different from that of Europe at the time *New Atlantis* was written. The 'empire' (ibid., 177) for which science and technology are used appears to be the understanding (prediction) and control of nature, without any consideration of ecological issues.[30] This is also the type of empire that Bacon considers in his *Novum Organum*. To illustrate from *New Atlantis*, these are the words used by Bacon to describe the purpose of the Atlantean equivalent of the Royal Society: 'The end of our foundation is the knowledge of causes, and secret motions of things; and the enlarging of the bounds of human empire, to the effecting of all things possible' (ibid., 177).

It is this notion of empire that has deep implications for ecological questions, sustainable development and as an epistemological and ethical assumption that this book will call into question. In a more positive light, the text does suggest that the society of *New Atlantis* possesses the following, which might be described as virtues:

- It is implicitly critical of corruption (ibid., 155).[31]
- It is hospitable and generous (ibid., 153–8, 185).
- It prizes self-respect as a 'bridle of all vices' (ibid., 174), particularly lust. The society is suggested as generally more virtuous than the Europe of the travellers visiting it (ibid., 174).

Bruce (ibid., xxx) suggests that Bacon believed that science itself should be 'managed'. Overall, whether contemporary societies would consider a secretive, self-regulating technocracy, as outlined in *New Atlantis*, utopian is an interesting question. The intimate connection of empirical knowledge, power and 'empire' (prediction and control of nature) is suggested (ibid., xxxv–vi) as the key idea that Bacon intended to convey. Bruce leaves open the question of any moral implications of this.

Let us consider something of the explicit 'analytical' discussions of ethics by Bacon. In the essay on 'goodness' by Bacon, he gives precedence to the Christian virtue of love or charity and echoes something of the virtues of Aquinas; however, perhaps inspired by Machiavelli[32] whom he mentions in the essay, there are hints at a materialist instrumental or even utilitarian ethic. The latter is the tone of the ethical assumptions of *New Atlantis*. Thus, in both *New Atlantis* and *Of Goodness & Goodness of Nature*, both a virtue ethic and materialist utilitarian ethic coexist without any relationship being clear. Hence, even if Bacon was not the direct cause of any dominance of materialist utilitarian ethics, if Bacon is influential generally it will not be surprising for the materialist utilitarian ethics in the writing of Bacon to leave their imprint on society.

It is argued (ibid., xxix; Milton, 1998, Vol. 1, 630–1) that contemporary opinion of Bacon as a scientist is not as high as it was, Bacon being more influential as a philosopher of science (ibid., 631). For example, Milton (ibid., 626) argues that *New Atlantis* had a 'profound influence … on the founders and early practice of the Royal Society'. As is illustrated by this book, it appears that the epistemological and ethical assumptions that modern society inherits from Bacon, particularly through the institutions of science, go significantly beyond the early days of the Royal Society.

Overall, it is reasonable to question whether the epistemology and ethics of *New Atlantis* would be chosen by contemporary societies if they made an explicit thorough reflection on this 'utopia'. It can be argued that those assumptions of *New Atlantis* implicit in contemporary societies should be made explicit and interrogated, particularly if they are closely implicated in stress to the Earth System from industrialism, as appears the case.

It is not clear just how the above Baconian types of idea affect 'modernity'; however, commentators such as Jung (1993), Norgaard (1989, 38, 53), Davidson (2000) and Simpson (2005) suggest they are important, and Norgaard (1989, 42–3) suggests that they are still key to attitudes to policy-making. Williams (1992, 132) highlights the significance of Bacon and also connects this significance to questions of policy advice and the limitations of science for this purpose. *On the Intellectual Origins of the Ecological Crisis* is an analysis of Kochetkova

(2005). She usefully distinguishes between epistemology and attitudes to 'nature' post-Renaissance, suggesting that it is attitudes or ethics that are a more important intellectual origin of the ecological crisis and implying that it is the types of attitude or anthropocentric ethical assumptions that *New Atlantis* articulates that are the key cause. Other ecological discussions of Bacon such as Rodman (1975), Merchant (1983, particularly 80–6, 164–89) and Hay (2002, 75–6, 123) echo this and these make only minor reference to the epistemological assumptions of Bacon. That is, they tend to be critical of an ethical assumption in favour of exploiting 'nature' rather than questioning human ability to sustain its societies on the basis of controlling nature. More bluntly, they ask whether we should control nature rather than whether we can ultimately control nature or know the limits of our control. It is important that we are clear about the epistemological legacy Bacon has bequeathed us, as well as the better known and much discussed ethical legacy.

Attfield (1994, 17, 29–31, 48) is also critical of ethical attitudes to nature by Bacon (and Descartes and their followers) more than his epistemological assumptions. The analysis by Attfield (1994) goes deeper than the preceding literature by indicating other important factors than *New Atlantis* in the development of economistic utilitarian attitudes;[33] however, it still appears reasonable to characterise Bacon's fable as a key locus of unsustainable development.

As later chapters will show, Baconian attitudes and epistemological assumptions are recurring and perhaps dominant themes in governmental sustainable development literature, including the WCED report (1987). In contrast, this book suggests that 'we' do not have the power of predictive understanding of the challenges of sustainable development in this Baconian sense, at least where this equals an ability to control the Earth System for the material benefit of humanity or to predict the limits of the stress we can cause to the Earth System. Whether the correct attitude to nature is one of using it for human benefit or a less instrumental attitude is an ongoing debate that shows no sign of being resolved. However, Palmer and Finlay (2003) indicate that the 'global virtue tradition' would join environmentalists in contesting the dominant exploitative attitude of contemporary policy-making.

Connecting this analysis of *New Atlantis* with the earlier review of Earth System science, this book suggests that it is currently a significant leap of faith to assume that humans can successfully control, manage or know the 'tensile strength' of the Earth System (Newton, 1999; Schellnhuber, 2001; Schellnhuber *et al.*, 2004; Schellnhuber and Held, 2002; Steffen *et al.*, 2004; Steffen and Tyson, 2001). Much Earth System science does talk about management of the Earth System (Schellnhuber *et al.*, 2004, e.g. 7, 9, 14, 18–19, 25–6; Schellnhuber and Held, 2002, 16, 27–9; Steffen *et al.*, 2004, e.g. 188, 255, 265, 285–98; Steffen and Tyson, 2001, 3, 27–9); however, they also talk about stewardship (Schellnhuber *et al.*, 2004, e.g. 10, 23; Steffen *et al.*, 2004, 255, 285–6, 298; Steffen and Tyson, 2001, 3) or probably imply it (Schellnhuber and Held, 2002, 27–9).

What exactly is meant by either of these terms in this literature is not clear; however, where the literature considers limits to human abilities to predict, the emphasis is on reducing stress to the Earth System (broadly stewardship) from humans rather than predicting and controlling the Earth System (broadly management). Stewardship is explicitly recommended as the ecological virtue by Barry (1999); however, his justifications for this are not particularly clear. Nonetheless, the logic that Barry (ibid., 72) indicates of stewardship, as a balance between overconfidence in human abilities to control nature and paralysis in the face of difficulties in knowing the consequence of human actions, broadly accords with the global virtue tradition. Attfield (1994, particularly 41–62) is a useful discussion of the notion of stewardship that suggests 'stewardship' is less instrumental than 'management' and perhaps makes less strong assumptions about abilities to predict. Further, this indicates (ibid., particularly 13–62) how the historical notion of stewardship did not assume anthropocentric human interests as always paramount and could underpin a notion of sustainable development. A reasonable broad definition of stewardship would be care on behalf of others. More specifically the notion of stewardship could be to minimise interference (stress) at the global level, but encourage intelligent husbandry at the local level.[34] To give concrete indications, at the global level minimising stress could occur with something akin to 'The Natural Step' (Natural Step, 2011), whereas at the local or micro level, global principles such as The Natural Step could be worked towards with models such as Permaculture (Mollison, 1988). That is, humans can perhaps manage their local productive environment to minimise stress to the Earth System.

There is a tendency for economistic utilitarian assumptions to be made in Earth System science literature, without clear reasons being given. If detailed consideration is given to these discussions of management, it is reasonable to suggest that where they consider limitations of human knowledge, management is much closer to stewardship than it is to global prediction of limits and control. That is they recognise the limits of Baconian predict and control, instead adopting a more humble 'pre-Baconian' attitude of stewardship. Where more Baconian predict and control assumptions are made, the bases of these assumptions are not clear. For example, the best that Steffen and Tyson (2001, 25) can suggest is:

> There are now methods developed in biophysics that try to anticipate when critical systems thresholds will be crossed by detecting warning signs of the imminent phase transition. The latter approach is particularly relevant to Earth System analysis that attempts to identify the switch and choke points in the planetary machinery that might be inadvertently activated by human activities. In fact, science can even benefit from the existence of strong nonlinearities in the Earth System by devising an inverse sustainability strategy that calculates the critical anthropogenic perturbations to be avoided at all costs.

However, they do not provide details or references to how calculations of levels of these critical perturbations may be achieved. Kleinen et al. (2003) do offer one possible method. This is tested by a 'simple two-box model of the hemispheric thermohaline circulation' (Kleinen *et al.*, 2003, 53), but at the current level of development this perhaps suggests that robust processes cannot be assumed as much as anything else. When Steffen and Tyson along with other authors return to these types of question (Steffen *et al.*, 2004), their suggestions appear to offer no firmer basis for robust Earth System Baconian predict and control assumptions.

It is beyond the scope of this book to analyse in detail exactly how Baconian predict and control epistemological assumptions affect contemporary policy assumptions. However, official discussion of rapid climate change (e.g. POST, 2005), the Bush Administration's attitude to climate change (Schellnhuber *et al.*, 2004, 18) and much of the regulation processes for genetically modified organisms (e.g. European Union, 2001, Annex II Section C) suggests that at least for these examples, something of this ethos is used for important policy questions.

2.6 Popper and the open society: key locus of the 'solution'?

So far we have shown that the assumption that humans (including experts) can predict and control the Earth System is highly questionable. It has been suggested, and the next two chapters demonstrate, that this type of assumption is broadly implicit in much sustainable development policy-making. This then begs the question of whether an alternative assumption or assumptions exist and could be adopted. There is much discussion in ecological literature in favour of an attitude of humility or caution (particularly the precautionary principle) in our approach to 'using' the Earth System. This book indicates that greater humility and caution would probably be wise. However, humility or caution as an absolute would lead to 'quietism' (Barry, 1999, 72) leading to the end of humanity more surely than current 'arrogance'. Barry (ibid., 72) suggests that what is needed is a balance between quietism and arrogant humanism as a form of virtue ethic similar to that of some of the virtue ethics of Aristotle.[35] This is quite reasonable, but there is still a need for an epistemological model, not least to decide where the balance between quietism and arrogant humanism lies.

A predict and control assumption is often connected with a belief that experts can know best what to do. This is distinct from a belief that experts best understand a problem.[36] Experts who take a reductive approach to understanding problems can mean that they are particularly prone to not seeing all the potential consequences of any solutions they might suggest (cf. Holden, 2002, 43–4, 49; Berkhout *et al.*, 2003, 12–13). In addition, there is no necessary reason why experts should have the best suggestions to solve a problem, as long as they communicate the nature of the problem effectively enough to society, for others in society to engage with the questions raised. From an 'open society' viewpoint, communicating difficult problems is likely to lead to better 'solutions'. Expert perspectives will be invaluable for the rational evaluation of potential solutions, but a process independent of the assumptions of the experts should give a more objective evaluation. Popper (1966, vi) offers a concise statement of this situation in the following quotation from Edmund Burke:

In my course I have known and, according to my measure, have co-operated with great men; and I have never yet seen any plan which has not been mended by observations of those who were much inferior in understanding to the person who took the lead in the business.

Popper (1966) offers probably the most prominent treatment[37] of these questions so will be worth exploring in detail. Indeed, Popper (1989, 363) is specifically critical of Bacon (and Plato) both in focusing on power over humans and the environment, but also individuals (experts) 'claiming power on the basis of one's superior intellectual gifts'. Popper (1966) offers the 'open society' as a model that aims 'at humaneness and reasonableness, at equality and freedom'[38] and to counter 'totalitarianism' (ibid., Vol. 1, 1) or 'might is right' (e.g. ibid., Vol. 2, 41, 208, 234). Popper makes clear that there is much precedent for the idea in historical philosophy and political action; however, the articulation by Popper is probably the most important recent treatment of these ideas. Popper's model is intrinsically participatory and democratic with regards to politics and policy-making (e.g. ibid., Vol. 1, vi, 1–5, 169–71, 185–91, 195–200; Vol. 2, 125–33, 151–2, 160–3, 224–40). To give one illustration,

> we not only owe our reasonableness to others, but we can never excel others in our reasonableness in a way that we establish a claim to authority ... Reason, like science, grows by way of mutual criticism; the only possible way of 'planning' its growth is to develop those institutions that safeguard the freedom of this criticism.
>
> (Ibid., Vol. 2, 226–7)

For Popper, the 'open society' supports decisions by reason rather than power (e.g. ibid., Vol. 1, 5; Vol. 2, 224–40) with Popper holding up his understanding of Socrates as a paradigm (ibid., Vol. 2, 227). Popper (ibid., Vol. 2, 225, emphasis in original) clarifies decisions by reason[39] when he specifies what he means by 'rationalism' which is

> an attitude of readiness to listen to critical arguments and to learn from experience. It is fundamentally an attitude of admitting that *I may be wrong and you may be right, and by an effort, we may get nearer to the truth.*

Popper is critical of the 'worship' of success, power, fame and Great Men (e.g. ibid., Vol. 2, 269–80), 'hysterical ... ethics of hero-worship, of the ethics of domination and submission' (ibid., Vol. 2, 276) at the expense of rational mundane individuals 'who are just as worthy, or worthier' (ibid., Vol. 2, 277) and the societies these individuals inhabit.

The 'open society' is offered as a response to difficulties in prediction in social science and based on an awareness of the limitations of scientific method (e.g. ibid., Vol. 1, 3; Vol. 2, 84–99, 212–58). Indeed, Popper argues that in 'politics' the appearance of certainty is dangerous (e.g. ibid., Vol. 2, 279) and this can be usefully compared with the 'certainty' with which cost–benefit analysis is often portrayed (cf. Smith, 2003, 29–51).

Key procedural aspects of the 'open society' in the account by Popper are summarised in the following quotation:

> Ironically enough, objectivity is closely bound up with the *social aspect of scientific method*, with the fact that science and scientific objectivity do not (and cannot) result from the attempts of an individual scientist to be 'objective', but from the *friendly-hostile co-operation of many scientists*. Scientific objectivity can be described as the inter-subjectivity of scientific method.
>
> (Popper, 1966, Vol. 2, 217, emphasis in original)

Thus, for Popper, it is criticism (hostile) within bounds (friendly) that leads to objectivity. This leaves unclear important questions such as the basis for deciding what counts as friendly and who is to be counted as a scientist to be admitted to the process of achieving objectivity. Popper (ibid., Vol. 2, 221) glosses over this question when he writes, 'anybody may criticize [what] constitutes scientific objectivity'. This is probably the irony Popper indicates at the beginning of the above quotation given how scathing he is earlier of Plato, Aristotle and Hegel for privileging the knowledge of particular groups of people over others. Popper goes on to clarify and gives a further criterion for the objectivity of natural science methods:

> Two aspects of the method of the natural sciences are of importance ... *free criticism* ... [and second] ... scientists try to avoid talking at cross-purposes ... express their theories in such a form that they can be tested, i.e. refuted (or else corroborated) by ... experience.
>
> (Ibid., Vol. 2, 217–18, emphasis in original)

The recommendations for social science by Popper (ibid., Vol. 2, 221–3) are vague beyond criticism of the closed 'oracular historicist' epistemological assumptions of Hegel and as well of the 'sociology of knowledge' that was popular in his day, in particular the Hegelian desire to make social scientists aware of and abandon their subconscious normative assumptions. Popper regards this last point as unhelpful and unnecessary. What Popper recommends is 'practical actions ... necessary for establishing the democratic institutions which alone can guarantee the freedom of critical thought, and the progress of science' (ibid., Vol. 2, 223).

In the 'open society', Popper does not make clear what these institutions will be like, at least with regard to social science. The final phrase of the above quotation perhaps indicates a preference by Popper for the physical sciences to solve social problems, particularly by production technology giving people more 'leisure' time (cf. ibid., Vol. 2, 241). Popper (1989, 345–54) offers some ideas that might promote open societies, but he does not make these explicit, nor are these ideas incontestable.

Popper (1966, Vol. 2, 232–40) also argues that there is a moral implication of epistemological choices. In particular, he argues that a choice of the critical rationalism of the 'open society' tends to promote

> the belief of the unity of mankind ... [however] ... Irrationalism ... may be combined with any kind of belief ... it lends itself easily to support of a romantic belief in the existence of an elect body, in the division of men into leaders and led.
>
> (Ibid., Vol. 2, 232)

He concludes that chapter by quite reasonably suggesting that 'brotherhood' of humankind is linked to 'faith in reason' (ibid., Vol. 2, 258).[40]

To summarise, with regard to epistemology, Popper advocates collective processes, even if he is unclear how these should be institutionalised, beyond holding up, as discussed earlier, natural science as a model of the 'open society'. With regard to ethics, Popper (e.g. ibid., Vol. 1, 173; Vol. 2, 55, 232–3, 237, 243, 271–3) tends to assume a consequentialist or even a materialist utilitarian ethic. However, he (e.g. ibid., Vol. 2, 274–9) suggests that he saw a central role for virtues and rights such as openness, justice, freedom, service, equality, humility, moderation, faith and hope operating through individual 'conscience' (ibid., Vol. 2, 279). He does not, though, give a systematic account of these ethical ideas and their relationship.

As can be seen from the preceding, Popper's analysis is not unproblematic. This can also be seen in responses to his critics, by Popper, in the 1966 edition and work such as Jarvie and Pralong (2003). However, it still appears to be analytically a more robust response to difficulties in prediction than relying purely on experts.

One further question needs to be raised about the discussion of the 'open society' by Popper in the context of this book. That is, Popper perhaps appears to see openness and participation as a good in itself; however, his defence is perhaps centred around greater effectiveness in a broadly utilitarian sense. This is not necessarily a criticism, as this probably means that it can promote impulses for participation for those who largely adopt a utilitarian ethical assumption. However, given the plurality of possible ethical positions, this 'instrumentality' by Popper is worth bearing in mind.

For the sake of clarity, it is worth at this point contrasting participatory policy with administrative policy-making and implementation (Torgerson, 1999) and making clear that policy-making and implementation is likely to involve an administrative element as well as participation by citizens. Thus, participatory policy-making is assumed to put a greater emphasis on participation of citizens rather than exclude administration and 'experts'. Detailed discussion of processes for making decisions about the relationships between expertise and participation is beyond the scope of this book, though Torgerson (1999) and Stirling (Berkhout et al., 2003) will be good starting points for such questions. I shall come back to these issues particularly in Chapter 8.

Explicit discussions of the 'open society' of Popper and sustainable development are scarce in the academic literature, though discussions of participation
perhaps assume this concept. One 'exception', Morris (1998), argues for an
incremental approach to policy, including preservation of existing institutions
in largely their existing form. Morris tends to advocate a largely free market
approach, implicitly on the basis that the existing evidence of harm from existing market structures may be falsified. However, if the logic of his arguments
were followed then no significant changes to any 'institutions' would ever be
warranted. The evidence offered in this book suggests that significant changes are
warranted to current industrial practices. Morris (ibid., 2–3) argues that directing
research funding to research that will reinforce received wisdom of the scientific
and policy establishment is an important limitation on the openness of academic
research. This appears a valid and important criticism of current funding structures. However, he appears to assume (for normative reasons?) that this should
direct funding towards research that will indicate less harm from environmental issues than typically assumed, rather than towards research that will indicate
more harm to societies from stress to the Earth System than is typically assumed,
as well. Barry (1999, 204) does allude to the 'open society' and Popper in broadly
the way used by this book.

As market approaches to policy are so prevalent and often associated with
Popper's notion of the 'open society', it is worth clarifying and expanding on the
question of markets and unpredictable unsustainable development. First, Local
Exchange and Trading Schemes (Barry and Proops, 2000) and similar may have
a part to play in increasing the sustainability of societies. Nonetheless, nothing in this book raises questions about the appropriateness of using money in
local free markets to distribute provisions. Beyond this, the picture is less clear
with the epistemological issues described in this book raising profound difficulties with market-based approaches to policy. To illustrate, global environmental
issues have intrinsic difficulties with private property. People making good use
of private property is a cornerstone of market approaches to policy and generally
works well when the property is personal and easily managed by individuals and
small groups. With scandals around illegal corporate malpractice and the many
publicly contentious corporate practices, the situation is less clear with corporations (cf. Korten, 1996). Beyond this, at the global level experts cannot grasp all
of unsustainable development in detail even if that is their sole focus. Thus, it
is fantasy to assume that individuals can manage the Earth System to maximise
corporate profit up to the absolute limits of stress that the planet will withstand.
Where this is implicitly assumed and imposed or explicitly promoted it is a clear
case of 'market fundamentalism' (Soros, 2000).[41] The innate connectedness of
the Earth System means that the planet cannot be reductively divided in order
to be parcelled out to subdivisions of corporations, to be managed piece by piece
as would be typical corporate practice for complex issues. To illustrate with one
issue that is connected to most others, how can humans know levels to set carbon
emission targets for trading purposes if it is not clear what levels the Earth System
will withstand? Indeed, as this book suggests and the 350.org movement assumes,

we may already have exceeded the limits of the Earth System. To add further difficulties for markets, legal systems that surround markets will be stretched to cope in policing economic activity, if the cause of harm is the global middle class and beyond, but all humans (and much 'nature') and particularly the poorest will be harmed most. It is worth noting that research in 'common pool resources' by authors such as Ostrom *et al.* (1994) have raised questions about the effectiveness of free market approaches to resource management. This work instead demonstrates in some circumstances the long-term sustainability of more politically mediated rather than market mediated resource management. Beyond all this, as Berglund and Matti (2006) have demonstrated, at least in some circumstances economistic approaches reduce ecological good behaviour – e.g. ecological virtue. Thus, to be plural, democratic and (ecologically) rational, advocates of market-based approaches to sustainable development will need to adequately address the above and all the questions raised by this book if their advocacy of markets is not to be based on quasi-religious faith in markets.

2.7 Conclusions

This chapter has outlined the key ideas for this book and indicated the overall argument that

1   the Earth System is unpredictable;
2   Baconian predict and control assumptions are a poor response to unpredictable, unsustainable development;
3   aspects of Popper's 'open society' constitute a more appropriate response; and
4   policy processes tend to assume economistic utilitarian ethics in a way that perhaps presupposes greater predictability of the Earth System than is justified. Imposing economistic utilitarianism may not directly contradict human rights; however, it might be globally undemocratic in the light of the 'global virtue tradition'.

Chapters 3 and 4 will conduct a discourse analysis of the ethical and epistemological assumptions and practical suggestions in key sustainable development policy literature. Chapter 5 will look at environmental management as a key practical response to this literature, to see how successful these broadly Baconian approaches have been in addressing the practical, epistemological and ethical concerns raised by sustainable development. It will also indicate where management approaches are appropriate and where epistemological limitations indicate that a more open, humble approach is appropriate. Chapter 6 will look at theoretical responses to sustainable development, to see what other insights are to be gained here for epistemological and ethical responses to difficulties in prediction surrounding sustainable development. Chapter 7 will consider ethical responses in more depth and perhaps provides the most significant specific advance that should enable policy to better respond to an unpredictable Earth System. Chapter 8 will discuss how participatory processes might be used to address the issues raised by this book. Chapter 9 will attempt to draw together lessons that can be learned from the analysis presented, but the reader should not expect simple answers to complex and difficult questions.

Notes

1 A version of this chapter, in particular the next two sections, appeared as Charlesworth and Okereke (2010) which will add some more technical depth for readers looking for this.

2 The notion of economistic utilitarianism is discussed in Section 2.4. To give an indication here it is a term to indicate that maximum utility is the key aim of policy and comes through maximising economic growth.

3 Modvar and Gallopín (2005) is also a reasonable summary of these questions, it also connects these to policy-making and theories of knowledge; however, it does not clearly draw out the connections of these to ethical assumptions.

4 The 2001 IPCC third assessment reports put more effort into discussing inertia in economic systems than they do into discussing inertia in the climate or Earth System. This perhaps implies a normative assumption in favour of economistic utilitarian ethics by the 2001 IPCC reports.

5 Stress is intended to indicate pressure put on or disturbance to the Earth System or its components. It is used in a similar sense to that used in engineering stress–strain curves. All human activity causes 'stress' to the Earth System; as will become clear numerical estimates of this stress will be impossible to establish. The purpose of the term is to aid thinking not specify solutions.

6 The link between management and utilitarian ethics may not be immediately apparent. Wilson and Bryant (1997, 71) and Premeaux and Mondy (1993) do indicate the link. To clarify, one might have a right or a duty to manage something and it is conceivable that management might bring about more virtue; however, typically management is conducted to increase some notion of utility.

7 For example, compare this approach with the motto of the Royal Society: 'On the words of no one' or 'take nobody's word for it' (http://royalsociety.org/about-us/history or Royal Society, 1988, 7).

8 Later, Hulme (2003) perhaps implies that probabilistic estimates of abrupt climate change are needed before significant decisions can be made. He does call for the assumptions of these estimates to be transparent. Whether he means purely scientific assumptions or epistemological, ethical, political, faith in the robustness of the Earth System, etc. assumptions is not clear.

9 The ecosphere includes the biosphere and also non-biological systems such as the atmosphere.

10 Despite focusing on complexity, Northrop and Connor (2013) largely ignore difficulties in prediction and similarly do not go beyond this paradigm.

11 Schellnhuber *et al.* (2004, 21) write: 'What sorts of inducements or feedback will best assure the provision of adequate constraint in individual human uses of nature's commons', which with the rest of that section perhaps points analytically to the need of a virtue of temperance or moderation, more than it does to economistic utilitarian assumptions implied by 'inducements'. Unfortunately, there is no significant coherent discussion of ethics in the Earth System literature identified by the author.

12 It is worth noting that Schellnhuber (1998, 56) suggests that the paradigms are related to a virtue structure, even if he is not explicit where the 'virtues' and 'vices' come from, or what their relationship to each other or the rest of the research is, or should be.

13 Thompson and Sieber (2011) suggest that current efforts to predict tipping points are making huge contestable assumptions about future applications and are years away from being successful even if the deeper difficulties in prediction discussed in this chapter are ignored. The blind faith in prediction displayed by the authors, despite the difficulties they do recognise, is worth noting in the light of the discussion of faith in Chapter 7. It would be foolish indeed for policy-making to be solely dependent on such research until it has been proven by many years of unquestionable success.

14 In the light of later discussions of Francis Bacon, it is interesting that adoption of inductive processes in science were 'popularised' by Bacon (Milton, 1998, Vol. 1, 629–30).

15 If social can be analytically separated from ecological.

16 Pettit (Baron *et al.*, 1997, 106) suggests that there is a 'folk moral theory that gives us our bearings in discussions of rightness' without investigating this. In the 'West' this 'folk' morality may be primarily Christianity.

17 Though Pettit suggests that consequentialists (of which utilitarians are usually assumed to form a subset) are not clear 'what is truly of value' (Baron *et al.*, 1997, 254).

18 Given the apparent current preference of 'scientific empirical' (Baconian) notions in policy-making, it is worth noting that it is easier for utilitarianism than alternatives to be turned into empirically derived numbers that allow mathematics to be applied, particularly in the form of economics. This may mean that if a 'mathematical scientific empirical' epistemology is chosen then utilitarianism may be the ethical scheme preferred, whatever the philosophical rightness or wrongness of utilitarian ethics in comparison to other ethical schemes.

19 At least according to some accounts of love as a virtue.

20 Indeed, in places the description of Kantian ethics by Baron (Baron *et al.*, 1997, e.g. 19–21) make those ethics appear very closely related to the ethics of Aquinas. It can be contrasted with discussion by Baron herself of ethics. For example, she writes: 'It is not as if the more virtuous you are the more humanity you have' (Baron *et al.*, 1997, 26–7); whereas Aquinas would argue that the more virtuous you are the more fully human you become. Baron *et al.* (1997, 28–9) also conceptualises love in a very unsophisticated way.

21 Cf. McDonald (2001).

22 Cf. van Wensveen (2000).

23 The first half also includes a section called 'The World Bank and Other Faiths' (Palmer and Finlay, 2003, 12).

24 For the Jewish response, at least, this may be down to the approach of the particular author. Evidence for this can be seen from Engel and Engel (1990, 56–8, 183–8).

25 As is perhaps typically assumed by liberal theorists e.g. those who focus on ethical consumption as a response to environmental issues.

26 See Attfield (1994, 17, 29–31). Cf. also 'For knowledge, too, is itself a power' (Bacon: *Treatise De Hoeresiis*) and 'Knowledge and human power are synonymous, since the ignorance of the cause frustrates the effect' (Bacon: *Aphorism III*). It is worth noting that Bacon may have put the above into the ethical context of 'The desire of power in excess caused the angels to fall; the desire of knowledge in excess caused man to fall; but in charity there is no excess, neither can angel or man come in danger by it' (Bacon: *Essay – On goodness*); as well as 'Knowledge bloweth up, but charity buildeth up' (Bacon, *Rendering of 1 Corinthians 8:1*, www.worldofquotes.com/author/Francis-Bacon/2/index.html).

27 Bruce (1999, xxxi) notes that in the preface (ibid., 151) to the first publication of *New Atlantis*, it was described as a fable.

28 Bruce (1999, xxii) argues that this is a case of Bacon not taking his own advice on literary form.

29 Indeed, the scientists and technologists of *New Atlantis* keep some things secret even from the 'state' (Bruce, 1999, 184).

30 Unsurprisingly given the epoch in which Bacon was writing.

31 This might have been inspired by hard lessons that Bacon had himself learnt (Bruce, 1999, xxvii; Milton, 1998, Vol. 1, 625).

32 Bruce (1999, xxviii) states that Bacon was 'an admirer of Machiavelli'.

33 Attfield (1994, 34–5, see also 49–54, 84–6) concludes that it is less Christian attitudes (cf. White, 1967) to nature that are responsible for unsustainable development, than 'secular' consumerist attitudes that grew out of (some of) them. However, he does not consider the importance of epistemological assumptions in detail. Jackson (2002) suggests a further related factor.

34 This would accord with the historical account by Attfield (1994) but also with how stewardship is often used in the Earth System science literature reviewed.

35 Cf. Foster (2002).

36 It is not always the case that experts understand every aspect of the nature of a problem best (Wynne, 1996).

37 Dryzek (1987, 1990, 2000) and Torgerson (1999) are important and useful treatments of these issues from a specifically ecological perspective and would bear further study. However, detailed discussion of these is beyond the scope of this book. Modvar and Gallopín (2005) concur that the general idea of openness is a good response to epistemological problems and sustainable development.

38 In the context of global virtue tradition, it is worth noting that Popper (1966, Vol. 1, 184, see also Vol. 2, 231–8, 242) asserts that 'faith in reason, freedom and the brotherhood of all men' is 'the only possible faith of the open society'. It is not in the spirit of Popper (ibid.) to suppress other 'faiths' that do not share these articles of faith but it does raise interesting questions about how open societies should react to those who may have 'power' to close them. Popper (ibid., Vol. 2, 246) makes this question more pointed when he probably suggests that the key question facing humanity is a choice between 'a faith in reason and in human individuals and a faith in the mystical faculties of man by which he is united into a collective'. Popper (ibid., Vol. 2, 258) clarifies: 'I feel no hostility towards religious mysticism.' It appears (quite reasonably) that he objects to elitist mystical arguments being used to dominate humans who are not of 'the chosen'. The faith in 'humanism' by Popper (ibid., Vol. 2, 258) to be always positive does not distinguish between totalitarian humanist regimes and more open alternatives. In a broadly similar vein, Popper (ibid., Vol. 2, 238–9) writes approvingly: 'Socratic reason … does not aspire to coerce … even into happiness', which begs the question of whether it is possible to coerce into happiness, openness or rationality.

39 Popper (1966, Vol. 2, 239, 243, 246) is critical of the use of language that is not attempting to be 'rational communication', which suggests that he is not particularly 'open' to poetic forms of communication, at least beyond between two individuals, even though he uses exactly this type of literary device (e.g. ibid., Vol. 2, 243).

40 This leaves unresolved the question of whether a person needs to be minimally rational to be morally considered as being worthy of human 'rights'.

41 In a rumbustious and entertaining manner, Ferrara (2007) expands on the cultish nature of the Mises Institute – one key church of free market fundamentalism. It is not irrelevant that he explicitly states that key theologians of market fundamentalism such as 'neo-Thomist' Murray Rothbard base their faith in greed, on partial and incomplete (i.e. heretical) immoral theology that wrenches ideas of Aquinas and other scholastic thinkers nonsensically from context, to present them as infallible truisms. The truth or otherwise of market fundamentalism is less important than the neo-religious normative nature of this faith/ideology, which makes it one religion among others, albeit with a less 'fully developed' theology. A longer and more widely discussed treatment of these questions is available in Ferrara (2010).

References

ACRE (2002) *ACRE open hearing on the criticisms of the risk assessment for T25 GM Maize*, London: Defra

ACRE (2006) *Advisory committee on releases to the environment – annual report – Number 12: 2005*, London: Defra

Adams, J. (1995) *Risk*, London: UCL Press

Adger, W.N. (2006) 'Vulnerability', *Global Environmental Change*, 16: 268–81

Allan, C. and Curtis, A. (2005) 'Nipped in the bud: Why regional scale adaptive management is not blooming', *Environmental Management*, 36: 414–25

Attfield, R. (1994) *Environmental philosophy: Principles and prospects*, Aldershot: Ashgate

Attfield, R. (2003) *Environmental ethics: An overview for the twenty-first century*, Cambridge: Polity Press

Baron, M., Pettit, P. and Slote, M. (1997) *Three methods of ethics*, Oxford: Blackwell

Barry, J. (1999) *Rethinking Green politics: Nature, virtue and progress*, London: Sage

Barry, J. and Proops, J. (2000) *Citizenship, sustainability and environmental research: Q methodology and local exchange and trading systems*, Cheltenham: Edward Elgar

Berglund, C. and Matti, S. (2006) 'Citizen and consumer: The dual role of individuals in environmental policy', *Environmental Politics*, 15: 550–71

Berkhout, F., Leach, M. and Scoones, I. (2003) (eds) *Negotiating environmental change: New perspectives from social science*, Cheltenham: Edward Elgar

Bernstein, S., Lebow, R.N., Stein, J.G. and Weber, S. (2000) 'God gave physics the easy problems: Adapting social science to an unpredictable world', *European Journal of International Relations*, 6(1): 43–76.

Betts, R., Cox, P., Collins, M., Harris, P., Huntingford, C. and Jones, C. (2004) 'The role of ecosystem-atmosphere interactions in simulated Amazonian precipitation decrease and forest dieback under global climate warming', *Theoretical & Applied Climatology*, 78: 157–75

Biermann, F. (2007) '"Earth system governance" as a crosscutting theme of global change research', *Global Environmental Change*, 17: 326–37

Boehmer-Christiansen, S. (1992) 'How much "science" does environmental performance really need?', in Lykke, E. (ed.) *Achieving environmental goals: The concept and practice of environmental performance review*, London: Belhaven

Bostrom, N. (1996) *What we should say to the skeptic*, www.nickbostrom.com/old/skepticism.html. Accessed 9 May 2011

Boyer, H. (1987) *Atlas of stress-strain curves*, Metals Park, OH: ASM International

Brown, C. (2001) *Ethical theories compared*, www.trinity.edu/cbrown/intro/ethical_theories.html. Accessed 9 May 2011

Brown, T. (1995) (3rd edn) *Gene cloning: An introduction*, London: Chapman and Hall

Bruce, S. (ed.) (1999) *Three early modern utopias*, Oxford: Oxford University Press

Burkett, V., Wilcox, D., Stottlemyer, R., Barrow, W., Fagre, D., Baron, J., Price, J., Nielsen, J., Allen, C., Peterson, D., Ruggerone, G. and Doyle, T. (2005) 'Nonlinear dynamics in ecosystem response to climatic change: Case studies and policy implications', *Ecological Complexity*, 2: 357–94

Callaway, E. (2010) '"Junk" DNA gets credit for making us who we are', *New Scientist*, 16: 11

Caws, P. (1965) *The philosophy of science: A systematic account*, London: Van Nostrand

Charlesworth, M. and Okereke, C. (2010) 'Policy responses to rapid climate change: An epistemological critique of dominant approaches', *Global Environmental Change*, 20: 121–29

Committee on Abrupt Climate Change (2003) *Abrupt climate change: Inevitable surprises*, Washington, DC: National Academy Press

Committee on Environmental Impacts Associated with Commercialization of Transgenic Plants, National Research Council (2002) *Environmental effects of transgenic plants: The scope and adequacy of regulation*, Washington, DC: National Academy Press

Committee on Genetically Modified Pest-Protected Plants, National Research Council (2000) *Genetically modified pest-protected plants: Science and regulation*, Washington, DC: National Academy Press

Committee on Understanding and Monitoring Abrupt Climate Change and its Impacts (2013) *Abrupt impacts of climate change: Anticipating surprises*, Washington, DC: National Academies Press

Congressional Budget Office (2005) *Uncertainty in analyzing climate change: Policy implications*, The Congress of the United States: Congressional Budget Office, www.cbo.gov/ftpdocs/60xx/doc6061/01-24-ClimateChange.pdf. Accessed 7 May 2011

Conkling, P., Alley, R., Broecker, W. and Denton, G. (2011) *The fate of Greenland: Lessons from abrupt climate change*, Cambridge, MA: MIT Press

Connelly, J. (2006) 'The virtue of environmental citizenship', in Dobson, A. and Bell, D. (eds) *Environmental citizenship*, Cambridge, MA: MIT Press

Costanza, R. (1989) 'What is ecological economics?', *Ecological Economics*: 1: 1–7

Cox, P., Betts, R., Jones, C., Spall, S. and Totterdell, I. (2000) 'Acceleration of global warming due to carbon cycle feedbacks in a 3D coupled model', *Nature*, 408: 184–7

Cox, S.J. and Tait, N.R.S. (1991) *Reliability, safety and risk assessment*, Oxford: Butterworth-Heinemann

Crisp, R. (1998a) 'Ethics', in Craig, E. (ed.) *Routledge encyclopedia of philosophy*, London: Routledge

Crisp, R. (1998b) 'Virtue ethics', in Craig, E. (ed.) *Routledge encyclopedia of philosophy*, London: Routledge

Crutzen, P. (1996) 'My life with O-3, NOx, and other YZO(x) compounds (Nobel Lecture)', *Angewandte Chemie-International Edition*, 35: 1758–77

Davidson, J. (2000) 'Sustainable development: Business as usual or a new way of living?', *Environmental Ethics*, 22: 25–42

Department of the Environment (1995) *An Evaluation of GENHAZ as a risk assessment system for proposals to release genetically modified organisms into the environment*, London: Department of the Environment

Dryzek, J. (1987) *Rational ecology environment and political economy*, Oxford: Blackwell

Dryzek, J. (1990) *Discursive democracy: Politics, policy, and political science*, Cambridge: Cambridge University Press

Dryzek, J. (2000) *Deliberative democracy and beyond: Liberals, critics, contestations*, Oxford: Oxford University Press

Ehrlich, P. (1989) 'The limits to substitution: Meta-resource depletion and a new economic–ecological paradigm', *Ecological Economics*, 1: 9–16

Engel, J.R. and Engel, J.G. (eds) (1990) *Ethics of environment and development: Global challenge, international response*, London: Belhaven

European Communities (2005) *European communities: Measures affecting the approval and marketing of biotech products (DS291, DS292, DS293)*, Geneva: European Communities

European Federation of Biotechnology–Task Group on Public Perceptions of Biotechnology (2001) *Report of a European workshop stakeholder dialogue on environmental risks and safety of GM plants*, http://files.efbpublic.org/downloads/GMPlant.pdf. Accessed 8 May 2011

European Federation of Biotechnology – Task Group on Public Perceptions of Biotechnology and The Green Alliance (1997) *How can biotechnology benefit the environment?*

European Union (2001) 'Directive 2001/18/EC of the European Parliament and of The Council of 12 March 2001 on the deliberate release into the environment of genetically modified organisms and repealing Council Directive 90/220/EEC', *Official Journal of the European Communities*, L 106/1–38

Faber, M., Manstetten, R. and Proops, J. (1998) *Ecological economics: Concepts and methods*, Cheltenham: Edward Elgar

FAO (1999) *Countries hit by Hurricane 'Mitch' on long road to recovery*, www.fao.org/english/newsroom/highlights/1999/990102-e.htm. Accessed 9 May 2011

Ferrara, C. (2007) *Opposing the Austrian heresy*, http://distributist.blogspot.com/2007/01/opposing-austrian-heresy.html. Accessed 26 May 2011

Ferrara, C. (2010) *The church and the libertarian: A defense of the catholic church's teaching on man, economy, and state*, Forest Lake, MN: Remnant

Ferrigno, J.G., Cook, A.J., Mathie, A.M., Williams Jr, R.S., Swithinbank, C., Foley, K.M., Fox, A.J., Thomson, J.W. and Sievers, J. (2009) *Coastal-change and glaciological map of the Palmer Land area, Antarctica: 1947–2009*, U.S. Geological Survey Geologic Investigations Series Map, http://pubs.usgs.gov/imap/i-2600-c. Accessed 9 May 2011

Feyerabend, P. (1970) 'Consolations for the specialist', in Lakatos, I. and Musgrave, A. (eds) *Criticism and the growth of knowledge*, London: Cambridge University Press

Feyerabend, P. (1975) *Against method: Outline of an Anarchistic theory of knowledge*, London: NLB

Foster, S. (2002) 'Aristotle and the environment', *Environmental Ethics*, 24: 409–28

German Advisory Council on Global Change (1999) *World in transition: Environment and ethics*, www.wbgu.de/fileadmin/templates/dateien/veroeffentlichungen/sondergutachten/sn1999/wbgu_sn1999_engl.pdf. Accessed 21 May 2011

Gerring, J. (2001) *Social science methodology: A criterial framework*, Cambridge: Cambridge University Press

Gillott, J. and Kumar, M. (1995) *Science and the retreat from reason*, London: Merlin Press

Gleick, J. (1987) *Chaos: Making a new science*, Harmondsworth: Penguin

Groombridge, B. (ed.) (1992) *Global biodiversity status of the earth's living resources: A report compiled by the World Conservation Monitoring Centre*, London: Chapman and Hall

Hay, P. (2002) *Main currents in Western environmental thought*, Bloomington: Indiana University Press

Haywood, V.H. (1995) (Executive Editor) *Global biodiversity assessment*, Cambridge: Cambridge University Press

Hinman, L. (1999) (2nd edn) *Contemporary moral issues*, Upper Saddle River, NJ: Prentice Hall

Ho, M-W. (1999) (2nd edn) *Genetic engineering – dream or nightmare? – turning the tide on the brave new world of bad science and big business*, Dublin: Gateway

Holden, B. (2002) *Democracy and global warming*, London: Continuum

Howson, C. (2000) *Hume's problem: Induction and the justification of belief*. Oxford: Oxford University Press

Hulme, M. (2003) 'Abrupt climate change: can society cope?', *Philosophy and Transactions of the Royal Society London (A)*, 361: 2001–21

Hulme, M. (2006) 'Chaotic world of climate truth', BBC News, 4 November, http://news. bbc.co.uk/1/hi/sci/tech/6115644.stm. Accessed 7 May 2011

Hulme, M. (2007) 'Newspaper scare headlines can be counter-productive', Nature, 445(7130): 818

Hume, D. (1748/1975) Enquiries concerning human understanding and concerning the principles of morals, Oxford: Clarendon Press

IPCCSR (2001) Climate change 2001: Synthesis report, Cambridge: Cambridge University Press

IPCCWG1 (2001) Climate change 2001: The scientific basis, Cambridge: Cambridge University Press

IPCCWG2 (2001) Climate change 2001: Impacts, adaptation, and vulnerability, Cambridge: Cambridge University Press

IPCCWG3 (2001) Climate change 2001: Mitigation, Cambridge: Cambridge University Press

Jackson, T. (2002) 'Consumer culture as a failure in theodicy', in Consumption, Christianity and creation: Proceedings from an academic seminar held on 5 July 2002, Sheffield: Centre for Sustainable Consumption

Jacobs, M. (1999) 'Sustainable development as a contested concept', in Dobson, A. (ed.) Fairness and futurity: Essays on environmental sustainability and social justice, Oxford: Oxford University Press

Jamieson, D. (1992) 'Ethics, public policy, and global warming', Science, Technology and Human Values, 17(2), 139–53 (also in Light, A. and Rolston III, H. (2003) Environmental ethics: An anthology, London: Blackwell)

Jantsch, E. (1980) The self-organizing universe: Scientific and human implications of the emerging paradigm of evolution, Oxford: Pergamon

Jarvie, I. and Pralong, S. (eds) (2003) Popper's open society after fifty years: The continuing relevance of Karl Popper, London: Routledge

Jung, H. (1993) 'Francis Bacon's philosophy of nature: A postmodern critique', Trumpeter, 10(3)

Keilis-Borok, V.I., Shebalin, P.N. and Zaliapin, I.V. (2002) 'Premonitory patterns of seismicity months before a large earthquake: Five case histories in Southern California', Proceedings of the National Academy of Sciences, 99: 16562–7

Kemp, M. (2005) 'Inventing an icon', Nature, 437: 1238

Klein, P. (1998) 'Epistemology', in Craig, E. (ed.) Routledge encyclopedia of philosophy, London: Routledge

Kleinen, T., Held, H. and Petschel-Held, G. (2003) 'The potential role of spectral properties in detecting thresholds in the Earth System: Application to the thermohaline circulation', Ocean Dynamics, 53: 53–63

Kochetkova, T. (2005) 'On the intellectual origins of the ecological crisis: Towards a gestalt solution', Ethics, Place and Environment, 8: 95–111

Korten, D. (1996) When corporations rule the world, West Hartford, CT: Kumarian Press

Kuhn, T.S. (1970) (2nd edn) 'The structure of scientific revolutions', in Neurath, O., Carnap, R. and Morris, C. (eds) Foundations of the unity of science, Vol. 2, Chicago, IL: University of Chicago Press

Lakatos, I. (1970) 'Falsification and the methodology of scientific research programmes', in Lakatos, I. and Musgrave, A. (eds) Criticism and the growth of knowledge, London: Cambridge University Press

Laszlo, E. (1972) Introduction to systems philosophy toward a new paradigm of contemporary thought, New York: Gordon and Breach

Latour, B. (2004) 'Why has critique run out of steam? From matters of fact to matters of concern', *Critical Enquiry*, 30(2): 225–48

Le Grand, J. (2003) *Motivation, agency, and public policy: Of knights and knaves, pawns and queens*, Oxford: Oxford University Press

Lemons, J. (ed.) (1996) *Scientific uncertainty and environmental problem solving*, Cambridge, MA: Blackwell

Lenton, T., Held, H., Kriegler, E., Hall, J., Lucht, W., Rahmstorf, S. and Schellnhuber, H-J. (2008) 'Tipping elements in the Earth's climate system', *Proceedings of the National Academy of Sciences*, 105(6): 1786–93

Lewis, S., Brando, P., Phillips, O., van der Heijden, G. and Nepstad, D. (2011) 'The 2010 amazon drought', *Science*, 331: 554

Linden, E. (2006) *Winds of change: Climate, weather, and the destruction of civilization*, New York: Simon & Schuster

Lowe, T. (2006) *Tyndall briefing note no. 16*, Norwich: Tyndall, www.tyndall.ac.uk/sites/default/files/bn16.pdf. Accessed 7 May 2011

Ludwig, D. (2001) 'The era of management is over', *Ecosystems*, 4: 758–64

Mann, J. (1967) *Fatigue of materials: An introductory text*, Victoria: Melboune University Press

Marangudakis, M. (2001) 'The medieval roots of our environmental crisis', *Environmental Ethics*, 23: 243–60

McDonald, H. (2001) 'Towards a deontological environmental ethics', *Environmental Ethics*, 23: 411–30

McNaughton, D. (1998) 'Consequentialism', in Craig, E. (ed.) *Routledge encyclopedia of philosophy*, London: Routledge

McPhaden, M. and Soreide, N. (2004) *Frequently asked questions about El Niño and La Niña*, National Oceanic and Atmospheric Administration, www.pmel.noaa.gov/toga-tao/el-nino/faq.html#warming. Accessed 23 March 2015

Medical Research Council (2000) *Report of a MRC expert group on genetically modified (GM) foods*, London: Medical Research Council

Merchant, C. (1983) *The death of nature: Women, ecology, and the scientific revolution*, San Francisco, CA: Harper & Row

Milton, J. (1998) 'Bacon, Francis', in Craig, E. (ed.), *Routledge encyclopedia of philosophy*, London: Routledge

Mintzer, I. M. (1992) *Confronting climate change: Risks, implications and responses*, Cambridge: Cambridge University Press

Modvar, C. and Gallopín, G. (2005) *Sustainable development: Epistemological challenges to science and technology*. Report of the workshop Sustainable development: Epistemological challenges to science and technology, Santiago, Chile, 13–15 October 2004, Santiago: UN Economic Commission for Latin America and the Caribbean, www.eclac.cl/publicaciones/MedioAmbiente/3/LCL2273P/lcl2273.pdf. Accessed 7 May 2011

Mollison, B. (1988) *Permaculture: A designers' manual*, Tyalgum, NSW: Tagari Publications

Morris, J. (1998) *Popper, Hayek and environmental regulation*, speech to the Adam Smith Society, Milan, 24 June 1998, www.fraserinstitute.org/WorkArea/DownloadAsset.aspx?id=3439. Accessed 7 February 2015

NASA (2006) *Arctic ice meltdown continues with significantly reduced winter ice cover*, www.nasa.gov/centers/goddard/news/topstory/2006/seaice_meltdown.html. Accessed 7 May 2011

NASA (2010) *Arctic sea ice minimum for 2010*, http://earthobservatory.nasa.gov/IOTD/view.php?id=46282. Accessed 7 May 2011

NASA (2011) *Record low arctic sea ice extent for January*, http://earthobservatory.nasa.gov/IOTD/view.php?id=49132. Accessed 7 May 2011

Natural Step (2011) *The four system conditions*, www.naturalstep.org/the-system-conditions. Accessed 11 May 2011

Newton, P. (1999) 'A manual for planetary management', *Nature*, 400: 399

Northrop, R.B. and Connor, A.N. (2013) *Ecological sustainability: Understanding complex issues*, Boca Raton, FL: CRC Press

Norgaard, R. (1989) 'The case for methodological pluralism', *Ecological Economics*, 1: 37–57

NSIDC (2005) *Sea ice decline intensifies*, http://nsidc.org/news/press/20050928_trendscontinue.html. Accessed 7 May 2011

NSIDC (2011a) *Ice shelves*, http://nsidc.org/sotc/iceshelves.html. Accessed 7 May 2011

NSIDC (2011b) *Sea ice*, http://nsidc.org/sotc/sea_ice.html. Accessed 7 May 2011

Ostrom, E., Gardner, R. and Walker, J. (1994) *Rules, games, and common-pool resources*, Ann Arbor: University of Michigan Press

Padilla, E. (2004) 'Climate change, economic analysis and sustainable development', *Environmental Values*, 13(4): 523–44

Palmer, M. (1990) 'The encounter of religion and conservation', in Engel, J.R. and Engel, J.G. (eds) *Ethics of environment and development: Global challenge, international response*, London: Belhaven

Palmer, M. and Finlay, V. (2003) *Faith in conservation: New approaches to religions and the environment*, Washington, DC: World Bank, http://go.worldbank.org/3L9IDQNFO0 or www.arcworld.org/books_resources.asp. Accessed 9 May 2011

Pearce, F. (2005) 'Climate warning as Siberia melts', *New Scientist*, 2512: 12

Pezzey, J. (1992) *Sustainable development concepts*, Washington, DC: World Bank

Popper, K. (1966) (5th edn) *The open society and its enemies*, London: Routledge and Kegan Paul

Popper, K. (1972) (3rd edn) *The logic of scientific discovery*, London: Hutchinson

Popper, K. (1989) (5th edn) *Conjectures and refutations: The growth of scientific knowledge*, London: Routledge

Porritt, J. (2000) *Playing safe: Science and the environment*, New York: Thames & Hudson

POST (2005) *Rapid climate change*, London: Parliamentary Office for Science and Technology, www.parliament.uk/briefing-papers/POST-PN-245.pdf. Accessed 6 February 2015

Power, M.E., Tilman, D., Estes, J.A., Menge, B.A., Bond, W.J., Mills, L.S., Daily, G., Castilia, J.C., Lubchenco, J. and Paine, R.T. (1996) 'Challenges in the quest for keystones', *Bioscience*, 46: 609–20

Premeaux, S. and Mondy, R. (1993) 'Linking management behavior to ethical philosophy', *Journal of Business Ethics*, 12(5): 349–57

Rahmstorf, S. (1994) 'Rapid climate transitions in a coupled ocean-atmosphere model', *Nature*, 372: 82–6

Rahmstorf, S. (1995) 'Bifurcation of the Atlantic thermohaline circulation in response to changes in the hydrological cycle', *Nature*, 378: 145–50

Rahmstorf, S. (2003) 'Thermohaline circulation: The current climate', *Nature*, 421: 699

Rahmstorf, S., Crucifix, M., Ganopolski, A., Goosse, H., Kamenkovich, I., Knutti, R., Lohmann, G., Marsh, R., Mysak, L., Wang, Z. and Weaver, A. (2005) 'Thermohaline circulation hysteresis: A model intercomparison', *Geophysical Research Letter*, 32: L23605

Rayner, S. (2006) 'What drives environmental policy?', *Global Environmental Change*, 16: 4–6

RCEP (2003) *Chemicals in products: Safeguarding the environment and human health, reducing the risks from chemicals*, Royal Commission on Environmental Pollution, London: TSO

Reid, D. (1995) *Sustainable development: An introductory guide*, London: Earthscan

Rial, J., Pielke Sr, R.A., Beniston, M., Claussen, M., Canadell, J., Cox, P., Held, H., de Noblet-Ducoudre, N., Prinn, R., Reynolds, J. and Salas, J.D. (2004) 'Nonlinearities, feedbacks and critical thresholds within the Earth's climate system', *Climatic Change*, 65: 11–38

Rifkin, J. (1999) *The biotech century: How genetic commerce will change the world*, London: Phoenix

Rockström, J., Steffen, S., Noone, K., Persson, Å., Chapin III, F.S., Lambin, E.F., Lenton, T., Scheffer, M., Folke, C., Schellnhuber, H-J., Nykvist, B., de Wit, C.A., Hughes, T., van der Leeuw, S., Rodhe, H., Sörlin, S., Snyder, P.K., Costanza, R., Svedin, U., Falkenmark, M., Karlberg, L., Corell, R.W., Fabry, V.J., Hansen, J., Walker, B., Liverman, D., Richardson, K., Crutzen, P. and Foley, J.A. (2009) 'Planetary boundaries: Exploring the safe operating space for humanity', *Ecology and Society*, 14(2): 32

Rodman, J. (1975) 'On the human question: Being the report of the Erewhonian High Commission to evaluate technological society', *Inquiry*, 18(2): 127–66

Royal Society (1988) *The yearbook of the Royal Society of London*, London: Royal Society

Royal Society of Canada, The (2001) *Expert panel on the future of food biotechnology*, Ottawa: The Royal Society of Canada

Ruben, D-H. (1998) 'Social science, philosophy of', in Craig, E. (ed.) *Routledge encyclopedia of philosophy*, London: Routledge

Sambrook, J. and Russell, D.W. (2001) (3rd edn) *Molecular cloning a laboratory manual*, Cold Spring Harbor, NY: Cold Spring Harbor Laboratory Press

Sandler, R. and Cafaro, P. (eds) (2005) *Environmental virtue ethics*, Lanham, MD: Rowman & Littlefield

Sarewitz, D., Pielke Jr, R. and Byerly Jr, R. (2000) *Prediction: Science decision making and the future of nature*, Washington, DC: Island Press

Sayer, A. (1992) *Method in social science: A realist approach*, London: Routledge

Schaefer, K., Zhang, T., Bruhwiler, L. and Barrett, A.P. (2011) 'Amount and timing of permafrost carbon release in response to climate warming', *Tellus B*, 63: 165–80

Schellnhuber, H-J. (1998) 'Earth System analysis: The concept', in Schellnhuber, H-J. and Wenzel, V. (eds) *Earth System analysis: Integrating science for sustainability*, Berlin: Springer Verlag

Schellnhuber, H-J. (1999) '"Earth System" analysis and the second Copernican revolution', *Nature*, Supplement, 402, 6761: C19–C23

Schellnhuber, H-J. (2001) 'Earth System analysis and management', in Ehlers, E. and Krafft, T. (eds) *Understanding the Earth System: Compartments, processes and interactions*, Berlin: Springer Verlag

Schellnhuber, H-J. and Held, H. (2002) 'How fragile is the Earth System?', in Briden, J. and Downing, T. (eds) *Managing the Earth: The Linacre lectures 2001*, Oxford: Oxford University Press

Schellnhuber, H-J. and Wenzel, V. (eds) (1998) *Earth System analysis: Integrating science for sustainability*, Berlin: Springer Verlag

Schellnhuber, H-J., Cramer, W., Nakicenovic, N., Wigley, T. and Yohe, G. (eds) (2006) *Avoiding dangerous climate change*, Cambridge: Cambridge University Press

Schellnhuber, H-J., Crutzen, P., Clark, W., Claussen, M. and Held, H. (eds) (2004) *Earth System analysis for sustainability*, Boston, MA: MIT Press

Schneider, S. (2003) *Abrupt non-linear climate change, irreversibility and surprise*, working party on global and structural policies – OECD workshop on the benefits of climate policy: Improving information for policy makers – ENV/EPOC/GSP(2003)13/FINAL, OECD, www.oecd.org/dataoecd/9/59/2482280.pdf. Accessed 7 May 2011

Schneider, S., Rosencranz, A. and Niles, J. (eds) (2002) *Climate change policy: A survey*, Washington, DC: Island Press

Shackley, S. and Wynne, B. (1995) 'Global climate change: The mutual construction of an emergent science-policy domain', *Science and Public Policy*, 22: 218–30

Simpson, D. (2005) 'Francis Bacon', *Internet encyclopaedia of philosophy*, www.iep.utm.edu/bacon. Accessed 11 May 2011

Smith, G. (2003) *Deliberative democracy and the environment*, London: Routledge

Soros, G. (2000) *Open society: Reforming global capitalism*, New York: Public Affairs

Sponsel, L.E. (2007) 'Religion, nature and environmentalism', in Cutler, J. (ed.) *Encyclopedia of Earth*. Cleveland, OH, Washington, DC: Environmental Information Coalition, National Council for Science and the Environment, www.eoearth.org/article/Religion,_nature_and_environmentalism. Accessed 9 May 2011

Stainforth, D., Aina, T., Christensen, C., Collins, M., Faull, N., Frame, D., Kettleborough, J., Knight, S., Martin, A., Murphy, J., Piani, C., Sexton, D., Smith, L., Spicer, R., Thorpe, A. and Allen, M. (2005) 'Uncertainty in predictions of the climate response to rising levels of greenhouse gases', *Nature*, 433: 403–6

Steffen, W. and Tyson, P. (eds) (2001) *Global change and the Earth System: A planet under pressure*, Stockholm: International Geosphere-Biosphere Programme, www.igbp.net/download/18.1b8ae20512db692f2a680007648/1376383135421/science-4.pdf. Accessed 7 November 2014

Steffen, W., Sanderson, A., Tyson, P., Jäger, J., Matson, P., Moore III, B., Oldfield, F., Richardson, K., Schellnhuber, H-J., Turner, B.L. and Wasson, R. (2004) *Global change and the Earth System: A planet under pressure*, Berlin: Springer-Verlag, Executive Summary, www.igbp.net/documents/IGBP_ExecSummary.pdf. Accessed 9 May 2011

Stern Discussion Document (2006) *What is the economics of climate change? Discussion paper – 31 January 2006*, www.fanrpan.org/documents/d00109/Stern_review_Climate_change_Jan2006.pdf. Accessed 6 February 2015

Stern Review (2006) *Stern Review on the economics of climate change*, http://webarchive.nationalarchives.gov.uk/+/www.hm-treasury.gov.uk/stern_review_report.htm. Accessed 15 April 2012

Thompson, D. (1995) *The Concise Oxford English dictionary*, Oxford: Oxford University Press

Thompson, M.T. and Sieber, J. (2011) 'Climate tipping as a noisy bifurcation: A predictive technique', *IMA J Appl Math*, 76: 27–46

Tickner, J. (ed.) (2003) *Precaution, environmental science, and preventive public policy*, Washington, DC: Island Press

Torgerson, D. (1999) *The promise of green politics environmentalism and the public sphere*, Durham, NC: Duke University Press

UNFCCC (1992) *United Nations framework convention on climate change*, Geneva: United Nations Office at Geneva, FCCC/GEN/23 B, http://unfccc.int/resource/docs/convkp/conveng.pdf. Accessed 7 May 2011

van Wensveen, L. (2000) *Dirty virtues: The emergence of ecological virtue ethics*, Amherst, NY: Humanity Books von Bertalanffy, L. (1971) *General systems theory: Foundations development applications*, London: Penguin

Walter, K., Zimov, S., Chanton, J., Verbyla, D. and Chapin III, F. (2006) 'Methane bubbling from Siberian thaw lakes as a positive feedback to climate warming', *Nature*, 443: 71–5

WCED (1987) *Our common future*, Oxford: Oxford University Press

Webster, M., Forest, C., Reilly, J., Babiker, M., Kicklighter, D., Mayer, M., Prinn, R., Sarofim, M., Sokolov, A., Stone, P. and Wang, C. (2003) 'Uncertainty analysis of climate change and policy response', *Climatic Change*, 61: 295–320

Weinberg, A. (1986) 'Science and its limits: The regulators dilemma', in National Academy of Engineering, *Hazards, technology and fairness*, Washington, DC: National Academy Press

White, L. (1967) 'The historical roots of our ecological crisis', *Science*, 155: 1203–7

White, M. (1999) *Properties of materials*, New York: Oxford University Press

Williams, M. (1998) 'Feyerabend, Paul Karl', in Craig, E. (ed.) *Routledge encyclopedia of philosophy*, London: Routledge

Williams, R. (1992) 'Transformation of scientific data into policy relevant information', in Lykke, E. (ed.) *Achieving environmental goals: The concept and practice of environmental performance review*, London: Belhaven

Wilson, G. and Bryant, R. (1997) *Environmental management: New directions for the twenty-first century*, London: UCL Press

WMO (1999) *El Niño/La Niña update*, No. 8, February, World Meteorological Organization, www.wmo.int/pages/prog/wcp/wcasp/documents/WMO_ElNino_Feb1999.pdf. Accessed 8 May 2011

Worrall, J. (1989) 'Why both Popper and Watkins fail to solve the problem of induction', in D'Agostino, F. and Jarvie, I. (eds) *Freedom and rationality: Essays in honor of John Watkins*. London: Kluwer

Worrall, J. (1998) 'Lakatos, Imre', in Craig, E. (ed.) *Routledge encyclopedia of philosophy*, London: Routledge

Wynne, B. (1996) 'May the sheep safely graze? A reflexive view of the expert-lay knowledge divide', in Szerszynski, B., Lash, S. and Wynne, B. (eds) *Risk, environment and modernity: Towards a new ecology*, London: SAGE

3   Discourse analysis
Brundtland and management

3.1 Introduction

This section will set the scene for the rest of the chapter before Section 3.2 conducts a discourse analysis of the WCED (1987) report in detail, particularly noting ethical and epistemological assumptions, along with discussion of political processes including citizen participation. Section 3.3 discusses responses to the WCED report before Section 3.4 draws this analysis together. Thereafter, the remaining chapters look at the practice and theory of sustainable development since the WCED report. The focus of the examination of the sustainable development literature will be to identify:

- when limitations of knowledge or epistemological difficulties are significant;
- what the ethical assumptions are, particularly inconsistencies in ethical assumptions;
- discussion of politics, especially, what models of policy-making are proposed, particularly what notions of participation are indicated.

The results of the discourse analysis in this chapter and the next are that policy at least sometimes acknowledges something of the limits to human knowledge of the Earth System presented in Chapter 2, but tends to ignore it for practical purposes. The ethical assumptions of sustainable development policy literature are predominantly the materialist utilitarianism of economics but rights language and to an extent virtue language is present in this policy, if scant in application. Participatory approaches to policy are the dominant explicit discourse, even if market-based approaches are virtually as common and there is no indication of how the pluralism implicit in participatory approaches is to be reconciled with the typical imposition of utilitarian ethics, through economics and market approaches. The lack of practical working through epistemological limitations and participation, in the sustainable development literature, appear to be the key reasons why a near business-as-usual status quo has been maintained and societies are hardly any more sustainable now than upon the 1987 release of *Our Common Future*. If readers wish to gain a more nuanced understanding of this conclusion about sustainable development discourse or need to be convinced by the evidence, then they should continue through the next two chapters. If readers are happy to accept the above summary, they can move on to the analysis in Chapter 5 of whether the Earth System can be managed and safely pushed to its limits, in order to maximise economic growth.

There are many books, articles and chapters that outline sustainable development and the problems implicit in the term; Lélé (1991), Reid (1995), Pezzoli (1997), Mebratu (1998), Jacobs (1999) and Benton (1999) are particularly useful. This section will now review the history of the term before its popularisation by the WCED.

Reid (1995, 24–55) and Trzyna (1995, 7–8) provide histories of sustainable development since the mid-twentieth century and Mebratu (1998, 494–8) looks back into prehistory and suggests that before the 'Western' 'Enlightenment' most forms of human knowledge contained 'a strong component of living in harmony with nature and with one another. This is the logical essence of what we, today, call sustainability' (Mebratu, 1998, 517–18).

Facets of the current concept of 'sustainable development' have numerous origins:

- The population and food supply concerns of Thomas Malthus (Mebratu, 1998, 498–9).
- Environmental and ecological literature particularly since the 1960s (Reid, 1995, 24–35).
- The 'anarchism' epitomised by 'small is beautiful' (Schumacher, 1974) and appropriate technology (Mebratu, 1998, 499–500).
- Recognition of the political significance of international pollution (Reid, 1995, 35–6).
- The 1972 United Nations Conference on the Human Environment in Stockholm (Mebratu, 1998, 500–1; Reid, 1995, 36–8).
- The promotion of economic and industrial development as a key or the key aim for all national governments since at least the mid-twentieth century (Sachs, 1993, 4–6).
- That this aim for 'development' has unintended social and environmental consequences (Reid, 1995, 44–53; Sachs, 1993, particularly 4–8).

By the time of the World Conservation Strategy (IUCN, 1980), the phrase 'sustainable development' had enough value that the Strategy 'closes with a section entitled "Towards Sustainable Development"' (Reid, 1995, 40). Even as early as this, issues with prediction and sustainable development had been identified: 'We cannot predict what species may become useful to us' (IUCN, 1980 in Reid, 1995, 41). In reviewing these early initiatives, Reid (1995, 42) notes that sustainable development proposals that emphasise ecological concerns and their relationship to economics and politics typically neglect to say clearly what are the (often implicit) changes called for in economics and politics, or how they can be identified, let alone how to achieve them. Reflecting on early initiatives, Reid argues that less industrialised countries were concerned about the even greater global injustice, (global) ecologically sustainable development policies might bring: implying that political naivety by environmentalists and epistemological issues are a key reason for these concerns (Reid, 1995, 42–3).

At about the same time as the World Conservation Strategy (IUCN, 1980), the Brandt Report or Independent Commission on International Development Issues (ICIDI, 1980) dwelt on problems that had been identified in development processes, particularly that 'development' had not benefited 'the broad masses of poor people' (ibid., 24). It is also worth mentioning that ICIDI (ibid., particularly 12, 24, 49) calls into question the materialistic, philosophical assumptions implicit in much 'development' policy.[1] Indeed, it perhaps promotes rights and virtue ethics (ibid., particularly 12 and 49) over the economistic utilitarianism present in much 'development' policy. The ICIDI analysis also highlighted that the economies of nations in the 'South' were harmed by more powerful 'interests' and 'structures' (Reid, 1995, 48–9), and this still appears the case today. However, Reid (ibid., 48, 50–2) argues that the ICIDI proposals were naive and were inconsistent with its analysis of problems of development initiatives. In particular, they failed to make adequate arguments for why global common interest should be put ahead of individual national interests, and why the common interests of people within nations should be put ahead of the individual interests of those with power within nations. According to Reid, there was also a lack of discussion about how these issues should be addressed; even about how effective 'rational' debate might be started on these issues, among the powerful.

The International Union for Conservation of Nature (IUCN) continued its moves to integrate environmental and development concerns, at its 1986 conference in Ottawa, for 'practical and moral' (ibid., 53) reasons, suggesting that environment and development are inseparable. This was to be expected as by this time the global consultation process of the WCED was already in full flow.

Redclift (1987) was completed before the final version of the WCED report was published (ibid., 12–14), though in discussing the work of the WCED Redclift (ibid., for example 14, 204) does imply that without a change in values little progress towards sustainable development will be achieved. Redclift's analysis tends not to discuss values directly; instead, it is focused on 'radical structural reform … of the international economic system' (ibid., 14; cf. Jamieson, 1992; Padilla, 2004; Smith, 2003, 29–51).

3.2 WCED

It was the process of producing *Our Common Future* (WCED, 1987), more widely known as the Brundtland Report, which particularly brought the sustainable development concept to sufficient prominence to bring about the United Nations Conference on Environment and Development (UNCED), the 1992 Earth Summit in Rio de Janeiro (CSD, 1997, paragraph 3). It appears that the WCED also largely set the agenda for this summit and other future work on sustainable development (e.g. EU, 2001, 2; 2006, 2).

As such a central document in the development of sustainable development ideas, a detailed discourse analysis of the content of the WCED report is worthwhile. This analysis will also highlight the range of issues that are involved in sustainable development; which, with the interconnected nature, also illustrated further increases the difficulties raised for conventional policy-making, because of the limitations of human knowledge. This section will look at the process of the WCED, the specification given to the WCED, the report's 'definitions' of sustainable development, the benefits and problems that the WCED associate with existing forms of 'development' and the solutions the report suggests to this set of problems. This analysis will particularly highlight discussion of epistemology, ethics and participation in the WCED. This examination will enable us to see how this particular – and particularly important – piece of intergovernmental sustainable development literature deals with the issues of prediction and control and of ethical approaches in this context, raised in the previous chapter.

WCED: *process, specification and 'definition'*

The report was produced to 'propose long-term environmental strategies for achieving sustainable development' (WCED, 1987, ix) after 'public hearings ... on five continents' (ibid., xiii). The report was commissioned by the UN General Assembly, who gave the WCED

> three objectives: to examine the critical environment and development issues and to formulate realistic proposals for dealing with them; to propose new forms of international cooperation on these issues that will influence policies and events in the direction of needed changes; and to raise the levels of understanding and commitment to action of individuals, voluntary organizations, businesses, institutes and governments.
>
> (Ibid., 3–4)

Through their deliberations and public hearings, the WCED focused on the observation that much 'development' makes more people 'poor and vulnerable while at the same time degrading the environment. How can such development serve next century's world of twice as many people relying on the same environment?' (ibid., 4). Benton (1999, 205–6) even argues that a 'structural feature' of numerous large 'development' projects is brutality to those without power, by those with power and that these projects result in dislocation from many of the things held most dear.[2]

The 'definition' of sustainable development by the WCED, which is most commonly highlighted, is: 'Sustainable development is development that meets the needs of the present without compromising the ability of future generations to meet their own needs' (WCED, 1987, 43, see also 8, 40 and 44).

It has been difficult to get effective action to coalesce around this definition, at least where there is tension between the justice issues implicit in 'needs', environmental issues implicit in 'future generations' and development as economic growth.[3] Perhaps the clearest suggestion given about how to resolve any tensions is in a quotation 'hidden' on page 293 of their report:

> Humanity ... exists and is supported within the world of nature ... literally ... When, therefore, we optimistically declare that economic development and environmental maintenance can go along hand in hand, this qualifier must immediately be added: only if the maintenance of the ecosphere is made the first priority. Economic development must be secondary.
>
> (Stanley Rowe reproduced by the WCED, 1987, 293)

Indeed, Lélé (1991, 614, see also 616–18) argues that 'economic growth by itself leads to neither environmental sustainability nor removal of poverty'. Even the OECD only '*suggests* that economic growth contribute directly to poverty reduction' (OECD, 2001, 213, emphasis added).

There are epistemological issues implicit in the definition, in particular how to know what has to be done to ensure that future generations can meet their own needs and what forms of development current and future generations want. These epistemological difficulties could be a key reason why progress towards sustainable development has not been as the WCED hoped. Lack of clarity about ideas such as 'needs', 'progress', 'sustainability', 'cost and benefits' (e.g. WCED, 1987, 43), the ethical and political ideas underpinning the notion of sustainable development and issues usually collected under the general description of 'political economy' may be other important factors. Greater progress towards sustainable development may have been achieved if more attention had been paid to

- the concept of 'needs', in particular the essential needs of the world's poor, to which overriding priority should be given; and
- the idea of limitations imposed by the state of technology and social organization on the environment's ability to meet present and future needs.

(Ibid., 43)

This quotation follows directly from the preceding 'definition' of sustainable development. The WCED recognise the contested nature of 'needs' as a concept, and although they do not explore this in detail, they give a reasonable indication here, later on the same page and at WCED (ibid., 54–5) of what they mean in the report by this for practical policy-making purposes.[4] The second bullet implies connections between 'technology', 'social organization' and limits to the levels of stress that the environment can withstand. For practical policy-making processes, it is not clear that the WCED present methods that can identify the connections or limits. However, they do make it clear that they believe that connection and limits are important. Perhaps the closest they come to suggesting methods for identifying limits is where they write that many limits 'will manifest ... in ... rising costs and diminishing returns' (ibid., 45). However, they offer no suggestions for identifying 'suddenly' (ibid., 45) crossed limits. This 'epistemological shortfall' is potentially a profound problem for any putative Baconian efforts to control or manage the Earth System for human benefit.

As noted in the previous chapter, 'management' is a key 'modern' policy response to this situation (and will be examined in Chapter 5). This was not explicitly specified as a response in the WCED, though the general tenor of the report (ibid., 8, 75–6, 240, 250) is in favour of global management. In addition, management is mentioned explicitly in numerous other places in the Brundtland Report and is implicit in the overall approach taken by the WCED. Jamieson (1992, 142–6) would question whether this assumption by the WCED is based on adequate foundations and this is a concern I share. Indeed, trying to operationalise Earth System management may have been a key reason for lack of progress to sustainable development.

WCED: *benefits and problems of development*

The major environmental issues and major successes and failures of (economistic utilitarian) development policy are recorded by the WCED (1987, 2–3). These successes include reduced infant mortality, increased human life expectancy, greater food production and increased numbers who are literate and attending school. 'Failures' of 'development' recorded here are that there are more people in absolute terms who are hungry, illiterate, without clean water, without adequate shelter, without sufficient fuel wood and the gap between the rich and the poor is increasing and appears likely to continue to increase. Environmental problems, which appear to have been caused largely by particular forms of development and could threaten development, or even threaten species 'including the human species' (ibid., 2) are suggested to include desertification (see ibid., 125–8 for details), acid rain, climate change, stratospheric ozone depletion and toxic substances, all of which can affect provision of sustenance to humans. Issues that the WCED thinks are important enough to dedicate chapters to are

- the international economy;
- population and human resources;
- food;
- species and ecosystems;
- energy;
- industry;
- urban development;
- global 'commons';
- security.

Let us consider some of these areas in turn to establish the report's position as far as epistemology, ethics and decision-making are concerned. The international economy is both an 'issue' and will need to be considered as part of any 'solution' to the questions posed by sustainable development and will therefore be considered separately. Economics and other themes that need to be part of the solution will be considered in more detail in later sections. Significant aspects of these themes will be noted with respect to the above specific issues in the relevant sections. Where appropriate, note will be made of policy related progress in addressing the issues discussed.

WCED: *population and food*

Demographics is obviously a key question for the WCED. However, the report places as much emphasis on ethical, more particularly justice, questions of the 'rich' using more than their fair share of the carrying capacity of the Earth System (for example ibid., 44, 55–7, 95–116). Indeed, it is made clear that the Commission make an ethical assumption that people can be an asset not a liability (ibid., 109–116). The WCED makes an ethical and pragmatic argument (ibid., 98–9, 118–144) that producing enough food for projected populations would be relatively easy if there were 'changes in food habits', that is if people ate less meat, etc. This could connect with the ethical virtue of moderation. More important for the WCED than food supply are political and ethical issues of food distribution, terms of food trade, providing the means for the poor to efficiently produce food if they want to, stocks in case of crop failure, government intervention, and questions of levels of stress to the Earth System from human activity. The report (ibid., 241) also argues that unplanned urban development has effects on food production potential. The WCED (ibid., 122–3) argue that causes of problems of insecure food supply include subsidies that favour farmers in industrialised countries, which some notions of justice would consider unjust. Brundtland (ibid., 144) suggests that 'we have the knowledge we need to conserve our land and water', and barring any major Earth System change the WCED appear correct, so it is perhaps political will that is the main bottleneck.

The WCED (ibid., 57–8, 130–7, 137–8) further suggest that agriculture, forestry, agroforestry and fishing should creatively use ecological reality rather than aim for maximum short-term profits. Once again this is perhaps an indication that they favour virtuous stewardship rather than economistic utilitarian management. That creative use of land for agriculture, forestry and agroforestry should be suited to local conditions such as topology, erosion susceptibility, soils, water availability, farming knowledge and appropriate use of chemicals, organic materials and natural pest control. Use of water for fishing and aquaculture should be within the ecological limits of that water. This has clear parallels with permaculture (Mollison, 1988) and it suggests the importance of local knowledge as well as centralised 'expertise'. The WCED (1987, 140) argue for improved 'productivity of inputs' by using organic material, wind and solar power for energy supply, particularly in areas where electricity is not readily available; these measures are to include efficient irrigation pumps, with emphasis again on local control independent of centralised 'bureaucracies'. They also suggest systems that use industrial agrochemicals efficiently (thus less dependence on centralised industrial production) and safely (ibid., 140). The WCED argue that agricultural research needs greater focus towards helping poor farmers on marginal land (ibid., 138–9). This would be about 'fairer' distribution of 'wealth' rather than maximising 'industrial' agricultural production; though asking why poor farmers are on marginal land and who is on the best land would have been worthwhile. The WCED (ibid., 139) question the ethics of control of genetic resources by private commercial organisations. In this connection, Lélé (1991, 617) argues that the WCED analysis of the environmental effects of the 'green revolution' promotes confusion when seen alongside their advice about organic methods, chemical fertilisers and pesticides.

Drawing on an egalitarian notion of distributive justice, the WCED suggest (1987, 141–3) land reform and respecting rights of 'subsistence farmers ... pastoralists and nomads' (ibid., 142), and preferential assistance for the rural poor by administrations rather than to rich landowners. They recommend opportunities in non-agricultural work in rural areas such as services and small-scale manufacturing (ibid., 142–3).

These suggestions appear to be based on deontological and virtue ethic notions of justice as well as respect for the intrinsic value of local communities rather than on an assumption of maximising global material wealth. Suggesting a virtue of moderation, the report notes that: 'Sustainable global development requires that those who are more affluent adopt life-styles within the planet's ecological means' (ibid., 9, see also 44). This is an issue that it seems still can barely be seriously addressed (e.g. AHRB/ESRC, 2006; Brook Lyndhurst, 2006; Dauvergne, 2010; Defra, 2003; Fuchs and Lorek, 2002; Holdsworth and Steedman, 2005; Hounsham, 2006; Jackson and Michaelis, 2003; Steedman, 2005, particularly 4; UNEP, 2004; Uzzell *et al.*, 2006). It is interesting that much of this sustainable consumption literature is implicitly working towards greater moderation of fulfilment of desires or temperance, but finds it difficult to acknowledge this, or speak in explicitly normative terms. It is not clear whether this is because of 'liberal' political assumptions about neutrality between notions of the good life or because presenting reduced consumption in moral terms is ineffective, at least, from governments who are not perceived to be acting effectively themselves in reducing their own consumption. It is also interesting that this literature does not emphasise the Aristotelian/Thomist assertion that living virtuously (including temperance) promotes happiness in the virtuous; this suggests that a materialist utilitarian assumption is common in this sustainable consumption literature. The reasons sustainable consumption is only starting to be seriously addressed by government are not clear but one possibility is that it was assumed that this would be democratically unpopular, so everything else has been tried (perhaps particularly facilitating technology improvements) in the hope that people would choose sustainable lifestyles spontaneously. The WCED demonstrate an awareness of these types of difficulty, when the report refers to 'painful choices [that] will have to be made. Thus, in the final analysis, sustainable development must rest on political will' (WCED, 1987, 9).

In terms of our general themes, overall, discussions of population and food in the WCED perhaps tend to favour unspecified notions of virtue ethics, perhaps with specific rights emphasised to help achieve a virtue notion of justice. Maximising global economic utility appears a lower priority than fairer distribution of wealth to the poor. Greater respect for and understanding of 'local' knowledge is an implicit epistemological and participatory suggestion.

WCED: habitat and species loss

The WCED (ibid., 147–52, 165–6) argue that urgent action is required to reduce loss of habitat and species for economic, 'moral, ethical, cultural, aesthetic, and purely scientific reasons' (ibid., 13, see also 147), claiming that this is a 'prerequisite for sustainable development' (ibid., 166). They make 'epistemological' suggestions that there are critical thresholds in forest systems and connections between climate change, habitat and species loss (ibid., 152) and that causes of habitat and species loss include pressure from human populations as well as irrational and short-sighted government policies (ibid., 152–8). The report (ibid., 157–9) suggests integrated and participative processes, which take into account all relevant factors, to address these causes of loss of habitat and species. They add detail to the economics (ibid., 155–164), arguing for pragmatic reasons that in order for the industrial nations to gain the benefit of the wealth of genetic resources in the 'third world', rural people in those nations need to 'realize some of the economic benefits of these resources' (ibid., 157, see also 160). This would be in addition to the 'justice' of such rewards for rural people. The WCED (ibid., 162–3) make suggestions about international arrangements to reduce loss of habitat and species. They suggest initiatives at the national level (ibid., 163–5), and here (ibid., 165) they imply the epistemological assumption that it is better for decisions to be made collectively and consciously, rather than unwittingly, as the sum of individual choices. An issue that they note repeatedly (ibid., particularly 147–8, 155–6, 218) is that loss of varieties (both wild and cultivated) as well as species involves losing the variety of genetic resources required to respond to crop diseases and changes in environmental conditions. It can be argued that this is because of 'difficulties' in predicting what future 'genetic resources' will be needed, for material human 'welfare'.

To summarise, the WCED tend to focus on economic reasons for addressing habitat and species loss, though they do note less instrumental reasons. They further suggest that focusing on 'property rights' for local people is more just and will be more effective at gaining participation of local people in providing their knowledge. They suggest diversity as a response to difficulties in prediction.

WCED: energy and climate change

The WCED (ibid., 168–202, particularly 172) argue that energy supply is significant for sustainable development for reasons including resource consumption and availability, climate change, pollution, acidification, risks of nuclear accidents and the proliferation of nuclear weapons. They also suggest (ibid., 202) a policy prescription, that decisions about energy should be deliberate rather than left to short-term pressures.

The report (ibid., 173–4, 176–7, 188, 196–202) suggests that energy efficiency is the most important and cost-effective response to these problems, making practical (ibid., 196–200) and economic suggestions (ibid., 200–1). The WCED (ibid., 196–8) argue, perhaps from a 'justice' perspective, that energy efficiency and income distribution are often related. Brundtland (ibid., 59) notes connections, by arguing that energy efficiency will affect 'policies in urban development, industry location, housing design, transport systems, and the choice of agricultural and industrial technologies'.

They also advocate renewable energy (ibid., 59, 192–6); however, they importantly note that 'fuelwood and hydropower also entail ecological problems' (ibid., 59). The WCED highlight 'high levels of hidden subsidies for conventional fuels' (ibid., 195) as a barrier to renewable energy, among other regulatory and market issues that need to be addressed. There have been initiatives to address subsidies for conventional fuels, though UNEP/IEA (2002) argues these have not been as effective as they might have been.

The WCED (1987, 181–9) are deeply ambivalent about nuclear energy, particularly because of 'unresolved problems' (ibid., 189). Among these are epistemological problems, for example around knowing whether waste disposal sites will be stable for thousands of years. Equally, they are clear about the issues, hazards and risks that go along with many forms of renewable energy (ibid., 189–96, especially 193–4) such as shortages of fuel wood and ecosystem destruction from large hydropower schemes. Epistemological problems appear less of an issue with renewable energy sources, particularly given the greater 'ease' there is in obtaining empirical evidence of drawbacks from renewable rather than nuclear energy, as they tend to be of smaller scale, and repeatable 'experiments' with these problems are likely to cause more localised harm. Looking at issues with fossil fuels, the WCED note GHGs, regional (acidification) and local pollution. The WCED reviewed the climate change research that was current when the report was compiled, noting the difficulties for policy presented by limitations in knowledge:

> The effects of warmer oceans on marine ecosystems or fisheries and food chains are … virtually unknown. There is no way to prove that any of this will happen until it actually occurs … wait until significant climate change is demonstrated, it may be too late for any countermeasures to be effective against the *inertia*.
>
> (Ibid., 176, emphasis added)

It is worth noting how little has changed since the report was published. They then argue that if this is added to the difficulties in international negotiations, this will make addressing climate change very difficult. The WCED (ibid., 176) suggest improved science, international policies to reduce GHGs and strategies to minimise damage from any climate change, 'backed by a global convention if necessary'. This appeared to be based on advice from the 1985 meeting at Villach involving the World Meteorological Organization, the UN Environment Programme and the International Council of Scientific Unions (ibid., 175–6). A process of improved science has been established in the IPCC. The UNFCCC (1992) and Kyoto Protocol (1997) are the current state of legal instruments and frame practical action.

Given the level of uncertainty and the epistemological difficulties implicit in their description of climate change, the development of a strategy for making decisions with such poor knowledge might have been a good recommendation; or at least a recommendation for such research. A reason why a recommendation of this form was not made can perhaps be found when, in tension with their comments on the previous page quoted above, they suggest climate 'research to reduce scientific uncertainties' (WCED, 1987, 177). It may be possible to reduce uncertainties from a purely scientific perspective, but if 'there is no way to prove that any of this will happen until it actually occurs' (ibid., 176) then science cannot be of determinate use to policy-making. This book attempts to clarify the epistemological problems implicit in sustainable development and make some suggestions about how they might be addressed. It is worth noting that one of the contributors to the WCED process, talking about the effects of pollution on forests, is recorded as saying: 'It is a very difficult task for ecologists to foresee what changes are going to be because the systems are so complex' (ibid., 179). If it is very difficult to foresee the effects of stress on a forest, then prediction of the effects of stress on the Earth System may be impossible, given that the Earth System is made up of numerous connected forests, seas, deserts, etc. Similarly, in reflecting upon acidification, the WCED (ibid., 180) make the epistemological point that the effects of acidification can interact with other stresses, in damaging reinforcement. They also suggest that some causes are difficult to prove but prevention appears economic, for those where the evidence is reasonably clear (ibid.).

Overall, the discussions of the WCED on energy indicate the difficulties of making policy on the assumption of prediction of consequences. Thus, rather than 'run-up' policies designed to take us to the limits of (unknowable) thresholds, then, moderation should perhaps be the watchword. This ethic seems more in keeping with the epistemological context in which we find ourselves, than economistic utilitarianism.

WCED: *industry*

The WCED report (ibid., 206–19) notes the benefits and environmental issues that industry has brought about, arguing that industry 'is perhaps the main instrument of change that affects the environmental resource bases of development' (ibid., 329). The report importantly notes that information economies need (manufacturing) industry (ibid., 206). It states that agriculture requires input from industry (ibid., 206). However, Mollison (1988) suggests that cultivation could be very different in form from the current situation; this suggests that here the WCED were being more normative than they needed to be. The WCED suggest increasing epistemological difficulties: 'It is becoming increasingly clear that the sources and causes of pollution are far more diffuse, complex, and interrelated – and the effects of pollution more widespread, cumulative, and chronic – than hitherto believed' (WCED, 1987, 211).

They note progress that had been achieved in addressing environmental issues associated with industry (ibid., 210–17). However, even the most industrially advanced economies still depend on a continued supply of basic manufactured goods. Whether made domestically or imported their production will continue to require large amounts of raw material and energy [as well as causing emissions].

(Ibid., 217)

There is no suggestion that this progress in 'de-materialization' (ibid.) has addressed the above epistemological difficulties, with industry typically becoming less wasteful or just turning air and water emissions into solid material, only some of which is useful. Industry had not achieved the radical change needed for sustainability that the WCED (ibid., 213) called for, nor has industry achieved it to date or have plans to achieve it. The recommendations are for 'policies that inject resource efficiency considerations ... strict observance of environmental norms, regulations' (ibid., 217), so the report (ibid., particularly 217–32) does not make it clear how to achieve the radical change to industry to operate, within even questionable estimates, a 'sustainable yield' and a 'sustainable sink' of the Earth System.[5] The argument in this book is that it is the WCED's confidence in target setting that is perhaps misplaced. It is not clear what goals need to exist to achieve ecological sustainability, and so policies designed to take us up to the environment's putative 'limits of resilience' have the potential for failure built into them. Once again, it might be suggested that policies driven by the principle of moderation rather than maximisation are more appropriate for sustainability, where there are limits of prediction.

The WCED (ibid., 139, 214, 218, 230–1) are also concerned about the power of large companies dominating fields of industry, such as mining and seed production. The report argues that transnational corporations have responsibilities in their operations to assist governments in achieving sustainable development, including making the results of audits of facilities and risk assessments publicly available (ibid., 231). Brundtland appears implicitly concerned about the undemocratic effects of concentrations of power in large corporations and economistic utilitarian ethical assumptions that large stock market listed corporations are perhaps bound into.

As industry is so central to questions about sustainable development, it is worth considering some of the specifics that the WCED suggest for sustainable industrial development, progress since 1987 and reasons for that progress or lack of it. First, let us look at principles for conventions 'dealing with transfrontier pollution or management of shared natural resources' (ibid., 220). These issues have been addressed in a variety of ways:

- The 1989 *Basel Convention on the Control of Transboundary Movements of Hazardous Wastes and Their Disposal*, which has set a context in which waste minimisation is encouraged (UNEP, 2002).
- Developments of the 1972 *London Convention – Prevention of Marine Pollution by Dumping of Wastes and Other Matter*.
- International legislation covering specific water courses.

- Developments of the 1979 UNECE *Convention on Long-Range Transboundary Air Pollution*.

Overall, these have been reasonably effective in dealing with specific issues within their respective remits, in part because the science of these is relatively uncontroversial.

The WCED report (1987, 220) also discussed 'more effective use of economic instruments'. Specific suggestions include internalising environmental costs through ideas such as the polluter pays principle (ibid., 220–1) and incorporating environmental criteria into taxation and any subsidies (ibid., 221–2). Though these suggestions should help the development of industry towards greater sustainability, Common *et al.* (1993), Foster (1997), O'Connor (2002) and Smith (2003, 29–51), for example, argue that this approach is deeply problematic in practical terms and ethical terms. While discussing economics and industry, they very importantly note 'there are limits to what society can expect industry operating in competition with other industries to do voluntarily' (WCED, 1987, 220), with regulations being suggested to 'level the playing field'. As discussed in Chapter 2, Jamieson (1992, 139–46) argues that there are philosophical (epistemological and ethical) limits to the questions that economics alone can address. If we accept the arguments of Jamieson, sustainable development is an issue that economics cannot address (cf. Padilla, 2004; Smith, 2003, 29–51).

A further specific is for industry and industry bodies to be encouraged to promote good corporate environmental and social responsibility and disseminate best practice information (WCED, 1987, 222–3). It might be argued that this is a suggestion for companies to balance virtue ethics against economistic utilitarianism, by going beyond legal requirements and the need to satisfy shareholders.

A related suggestion (ibid., 59–60) is to redouble efforts to minimise pollution, emphasising anticipation and prevention over clean up. The WCED appear to make the epistemological assumption that the impact of new technologies can be anticipated. The experience of the ozone depleting properties of CFCs (Crutzen, 1996), among other examples, calls this into question.

A final broad point is advocacy that technology, 'the key link between humans and nature' (WCED, 1987, 60), needs to be indigenised by developing countries, developed to reduce its environmental impact and better address the needs of the poor, particularly in developing countries. It can be argued that this promotes making technology decisions more democratic, as the decisions are made at a more local level, conceivably by the customer and manufacturer. Beyond suggestions that policy be directed to achieve this in private and public sectors, their recommendations are vague.

The chemical industry is discussed in more detail, noting the technical benefits and economic benefits for countries 'including many developing ones' (ibid., 223), but also that the industry and 'its products, can have a particularly severe impact on the environment' (ibid.). More detail is added in the following pages, including discussion and suggestions to address the hazardous waste and industrial accidents the industry is largely responsible for. The report states that the chemical industry 'continues to generate an increasingly wider range of products and wastes whose effects, especially long-term ones, on human health and the environment are *not precisely known*' (ibid., 224, emphasis added) – a clear indication of limits to human knowledge.

This points to epistemological questions around the current regulation of chemicals. Cox and Tait (1991), Adams (1995), RCEP (2003), Weinberg (1986), Porritt (2000, 47–62, 93–4) and Shackley and Wynne (1995) suggest that it appears that the WCED understate the epistemological problems of understanding the effects of chemicals. To illustrate, the chairman of the Commission is quoted in the press release to RCEP (2003) as saying: 'Given our understanding of the way chemicals interact with the environment, you could say we are running a gigantic experiment with humans and all other living things as the subject … We think that's unacceptable' (RCEP, 2003).

That the WCED understate epistemological problems is unfortunate as they suggest the products of the chemical industry 'are built into current systems of production and the technological structure of contemporary society, and it will be a long time before these can be replaced with … inherently safer technology and systems' (WCED, 1987, 224).

Some progress has been made with inherently safer systems since then (Kletz, 2003), but it appears that the chemical industry is built into contemporary society at least as much in 2015 as in 1987. The WCED (1987, 224) indicate the scale of the task of assessing the effects of chemicals. Given the difficulty of the task of assessing the effects of chemicals, the known effects and the possible consequences indicated by the WCED, it is a little surprising that they do not even contemplate the possibility of a global society much less dependent on chemicals. They could have tried to sketch the policy implications of this, so that policymakers and citizens could make an informed choice. It is not clear that anyone has done this type of work (cf. Lee, 1993).

The WCED (1987, 226–9, 231) advocate informing neighbouring countries, workers, consumers and citizens about risk assessments of chemicals, so that they can make informed choices and participate in debates about policy decisions about products and facilities; this appears to have been 'patchy' to date and transfers responsibility from the chemical industry to others.

Importantly, the WCED (ibid., 213–14) argue that population increases cannot be absorbed as agricultural workers, suggesting this needs to be done by 'industry' even if this is 'small-scale, decentralized' (ibid., 215).[6] This appears to assume that 'industrial' agriculture is the only way to feed increased populations. Concepts such as permaculture (Mollison, 1988), though, suggest that this is a questionable assumption. The WCED also appear to assume that 'industrialism' is the only way to give people fulfilling lives through 'products and services' (WCED, 1987, 214). This is something the 'global virtue tradition' would (ethically) question and permaculture (Mollison, 1988), among others, offers a practical alternative.

To summarise, the WCED do put into question the utilitarianism that much of industrialism assumes, but perhaps place too much store in using prediction of effects as the correct method to decide limits that should be placed on industrial activity. There is some emphasis on the participation of 'community' actors in industrial decision-making.

WCED: *global commons*

The WCED (1987, 261–86) discuss managing commons, in particular the oceans, space and the Antarctic. They suggest the importance of the oceans (ibid., 262–3) noting factors causing stress to ecosystems in them (ibid., 262–4) to the point of 'possibly disrupting planetary support systems', 'complex and long lasting effects' and even questioning 'survival itself' (ibid., 264). Suggestions for 'oceans management' include:

- Improved and better implemented international agreements on reducing over-exploitation, pollution discharges and waste disposal. Efforts have been made on these in the 'London Convention' and various regional initiatives, with varying success.
- Improving data and data availability. This has been addressed through initiatives such as www.oceansatlas.org.
- Greater analysis of possible effects based on better data and developing theories.
- Addressing the differences in power of some companies and countries in relation to their use of the oceans.

(Ibid., 264–74)

Important limitations in knowledge of the oceans are noted (ibid., 266–7), which given continued contestations over fishing quotas, for example, may never be eliminated. Despite this, as indicated in the above suggestions from their section entitled 'oceans management' (ibid., 264), the WCED tend to make Baconian managerial ethical and epistemological assumptions.

To illustrate the breadth of the Brundtland notion of sustainable development, let us note that the WCED (ibid., 274–9) suggest that human use of space needs to be managed, in the common interest, in the following ways:

- Preventing the deployment of weapons in space. Particularly because of the debris testing inevitably creates, causing problems for all other uses of space.
- Using remote sensing to collect data on the Earth System. They suggest that better coordination would be worthwhile.
- Justice in use of geosynchronous orbit; this appears based on an egalitarian notion of justice.
- Regulation of 'Nuclear Power in Orbit'.

(Ibid., 277)

These worthy suggestions perhaps again make managerial assumptions; however, perhaps with more justification as these are largely based on knowledge of discrete human activities and discrete artificial systems, which might be argued are less demanding epistemologically than the Earth System.

The WCED (ibid., 279–86) argue for guarding present achievements in governing Antarctica, making suggestions about how this might be achieved in the light of 'pressures for mineral development'. Suggestions include:

- Strengthening cooperation in scientific investigation (ibid., 282–3).
- Given the practical difficulties of mineral extraction from the Antarctic, the WCED (ibid., 283–4) recommend proceeding with negotiations, to ensure that any mineral development causes minimum environmental impact and that the 'proceeds [are] equitably' shared before economic discoveries are found. The detail of what the ethical assumption 'equity' means is not clear.
- More inclusive dialogue about the future of the Antarctic.

They also raise the practical and epistemological issue that 'depletion of Antarctic fish stocks ... could have severe and *unpredictable* effects' (ibid., 281, emphasis added).

Overall, discussions of global commons demonstrate the significance of limits of epistemology and suggest that choosing economic growth over other ethical principles is normative not neutral, as is often assumed by economists.

WCED: *security*

The WCED make the practical argument that: 'Environmental stress is both a cause and an effect of political tension and military conflict. ... [for] control over raw materials ... Such conflicts are likely to increase' (ibid., 290). They discuss (ibid., 290–304) the deeply significant environmental and social causes and consequences of warfare and 'arms races', arguing that the relationships between these are poorly understood (ibid., 290). They imply that these contribute greatly to development not being sustainable in physical, practical terms, but also suggest that these 'may stimulate an ethos that is antagonistic' (ibid., 294). Perhaps the most important aspect of this is the 'misdirecting of scarce resources ... The distorting effects of the "arms culture" are most striking, in the deployment of scientific personnel' (ibid., 297–8).

They analyse the reasons behind the 'arms culture' (ibid., 298–300). In order to move 'towards security and sustainable development', the WCED (ibid., 300–4) make a number of suggestions.

- The WCED (ibid., 301–2) see existing cooperative (i.e. non-market) management of environmental questions such as Antarctica as useful models that should be extended.
- The WCED (ibid., 302) suggest systems for early warning of 'thresholds' about to be crossed, that might cause environmental conflicts. They suggest that these should be operated by international organisations, which would warn any parties involved and try to help resolve the issue peacefully. For

the reasonably confined and simple examples given ('soil erosion, growth in regional migration and uses of commons that are approaching the thresholds of sustainability') this is a reasonable suggestion. However, this book argues that for many of the most important issues (e.g. climate change) and the combinations of stress on the Earth System from all environmental issues, it is not currently clear that humans have the epistemological ability to know what any thresholds are.

- Moving spending from military uses, to instead prevent environmental conflict and 'natural' disasters (ibid., 302–4).
- Continuing efforts to disarm (ibid., 304).

The issues and suggestions that the WCED discusses in detail have now been outlined. The practical measures the report suggests to promote sustainable development are vague. The argument in this book is that this may be because of epistemological limitations and the report's dominant (economistic utilitarian) ethical assumptions. I have outlined the report's epistemological and ethical assumptions in each of the issue areas discussed thus far. Now let us consider epistemology and ethics as well as associated topics such as administration, risk and law in some detail.

WCED: epistemology

The WCED (ibid., particularly 4–10) note the interlocking nature of sustainable development issues and some of the epistemological difficulties that administrations have in responding to the connectedness of unsustainability. They suggest greater integration of policy-making processes and responsibilities, particularly environment and economy, but without giving any clear ideas how this should be done.

The WCED recognise the importance of knowledge in addressing sustainable development issues (ibid., especially 10, 28–41, 133). The report typically implies that difficulties in knowledge are associated with connections between the issues implicit in sustainable development and that limitations in knowledge make moving towards sustainable development more difficult.

They importantly note 'that the ability to anticipate and prevent environmental damage requires that the ecological dimensions of policy be considered at the same time as the economic ... and other dimensions' (ibid., 10). However, they are not clear how this observation can be applied to the Earth System. For example:

- for which issues environmental damage can be anticipated;
- whether damage can be anticipated in a way that it can be prevented;
- where this damage will occur;
- how much of any damage can be anticipated;
- which policy decisions any damage is connected to.

To try to make some of these clearer, obvious environmental damage from build-ing a dam (e.g. flooding upstream) might be anticipated; however, less obvious damage from that dam (e.g. lower fish catches because fewer high nutrient sedi-ments are carried out to sea) might not be clear until after it has been built. Similarly, the WCED do not make it clear how to anticipate the environmental effects of changes in, for example, economic policy. This is less a criticism of the WCED than it is a highlighting of the epistemological difficulties implicit in sustainable development.

Brundtland indicates the significance of environmental issues:

> When the century began, neither human numbers nor technology had the power radically to alter planetary systems. As the century closes ... major, unintended changes are occurring in the atmosphere ... and in the rela-tionship among all these. The rate of change is outstripping the ability of scientific disciplines ... to assess and advise. It is frustrating the attempts of political and economic institutions ... to adapt and cope.
>
> (Ibid., 22, see also 27, 310, 313, 343)

Note the admission of epistemological difficulties by the WCED and its percep-tion of the significance of this for policy. The WCED probably overstate the possible harm from the issues they discuss when they write: 'We are unanimous in our conviction that the security, well-being, and very survival of the planet depend on ... changes, now' (ibid., 343). Unsustainable development issues might threaten the security, well-being and survival of humanity and the bio-sphere. However, it will take a change in the state of the sun into a red giant or some similarly significant event before the 'planet' is threatened.

The WCED report (ibid., 22–3) concludes its introductory chapter with vague general recommendations that perhaps point to epistemological problems about the course to proceed with, while at the same time emphasising their belief in the urgent need for action. The report extends this type of analysis, arguing that

> nature is bountiful, but it is also fragile and finely balanced. There are *thresh-olds* that cannot be crossed without endangering the basic integrity of the system. Today we are close to many of these thresholds ... the speed with which changes ... are taking place gives little time in which to *anticipate* and prevent unexpected effects ... The risks increase faster than our abilities to manage them.
>
> (Ibid., 32–5, emphasis added)

Again, the WCED suggest the crucial significance of environmental issues and limitations in human ability to understand them. Unfortunately, they do not make clear what the thresholds are, how they have been identified, how it has been ascertained that we are close to those thresholds and how long we have to 'anticipate and prevent'. It is not clear that Earth System science has identi-fied all the relevant thresholds in over twenty years since the WCED report.

Indeed, it is not clear how we can 'anticipate' 'unexpected effects' in order to prevent them. How can something that is unexpected be anticipated? Perhaps they meant 'unintended'? The WCED report indicates a key issue with management approaches in the last sentence. The report again highlights the importance of unintended consequences and the epistemological difficulties of unanticipated consequences, when they write: 'Technological developments may solve some immediate problems but lead to even greater ones. Large sections of the population may be marginalized by ill-considered development' (ibid., 44). They follow this quotation with examples, arguing: 'Today's interventions are more drastic in scale and impact, and more threatening to life-support systems both locally and globally' (ibid.).

Thresholds are suggested in the response of the climate system to greenhouse and ozone depleting gases, as well as in ecosystems, in response to pollution and poor agricultural practices (ibid., 35). However, they do not suggest how these can be identified, although the assumption is that they can be identified. But what if they cannot? In this case, policies designed to take us right up to threshold limits might be mistaken.

As well as the difficulties raised by thresholds, the report notes that connections between aspects of the Earth System are a key area where limitations of knowledge make 'managing' the Earth System more difficult. Let us consider some examples in more detail. The WCED (ibid., 3–8, 27–41, 126–7, 135–6, 147) outline the connection of major environmental issues and major successes and failures of development policy or policy in broad terms, even if it is often not immediately clear how any of this analysis can be used in policy-making. Connections, locally and globally, are suggested between poverty, political arrangements, inequality, gender issues, economic growth, trade policies, debt (often of questionable justice), aid priorities, population, housing, transport, farming, forestry, soil erosion, siltation, arms spending, famine, drought, flooding, desertification, refugees, industry, water supply, resource depletion, soil degradation, energy supply, toxic emissions, poorly controlled inappropriate subsidised agrochemicals, under-utilised organic waste, ozone depletion, species loss, habitat loss and climate change. Given this list of connections, it should be clear that management is impossible.

To make management even more difficult, Brundtland highlights the importance of connections between economies of different countries and the connection of this to the Earth System. The report also notes connections across political boundaries via systems such as rivers and atmospheric processes. As a specific example of connections, the WCED (ibid., 127–8) argue that causes of desertification are complex but include population growth, poor 'land use practices (especially deforestation), adverse terms of trade and civil strife' along with cash cropping (often encouraged by 'aid' donors), which forces subsistence communities onto marginal land.

The WCED emphasise the importance of the connections in other places (ibid., especially 11, 22, 45–9, 62–5, 67–90, 261–3), arguing that sustainable development 'will require policy changes in all countries, with respect both to their own development and to their impacts on other nations' development' (ibid., 49). They also state: 'Many of the environment and development problems that confront us have their roots in ... sectoral fragmentation of responsibility. Sustainable development requires that such fragmentation be overcome' (ibid., 63).

Further important connections of issues to themes have been noted in previous subsections, and important connections between themes will be noted in later subsections. All these connections suggest that reductive epistemological approaches are difficult in practical terms; suggesting that for many sustainable development issues such as climate change, the Earth System is the correct level of analysis. Thus, prediction and control approaches need to consider all the connected factors illustrated above to be effective. The difficulties with this can be illustrated by the current limitations of prediction of climate models and the complexity of connecting these to social systems. This, and unimagined tipping points in the Earth System, suggest that assuming humans can predict just how far we can stress the Earth System before catastrophe happens is either a very courageous or a very reckless assumption. All in all, just the connections in the Earth System mean that a predictive, management-based model of sustainable development is a fantasy.

A further area where Brundtland highlights the importance of epistemological questions is risk assessment; thus, focused discussion of this is appropriate. The WCED (ibid., 60–2) call for more thorough risk assessments. However, they assume that these techniques are adequate to ensure the environment is not 'overstressed' to the point of reaching tipping points. Chapter 2 has called this into question.

The WCED (ibid., particularly 87–9, 217–19, 230, 323–6) argue that technologies, such as renewable energy or genetic engineering, can help development be more or less sustainable, putting trust in risk assessment to decide which. This is in tension with a number of examples given by the report. First, the WCED (ibid., 185) argue that conducting risk assessments for nuclear reactors is deeply problematic. Second, they (ibid., 178–81) suggest that assessing the effects of relatively simple transboundary air pollution is deeply problematic because of the complexity of ecosystems. This is more difficult for risk assessment of complex chemicals, genetic engineering and interactions of all human produced stress to the Earth System. A third example is when the WCED (ibid., 224, 230) imply the effects of chemicals are difficult to assess, or even unpredictable, and that risk assessments only 'better identify risks' not perfectly identify risks.

All of these difficulties are primarily because of limitations of current epistemology. The report states 'the future ... will be marked by increasing risk. The risks associated with new technologies are growing ... the risks of irreversible damage to natural systems ... globally ... are becoming significant' (ibid., 323).

The report suggests using new technology to better collect and disseminate data about 'Earth change' (ibid., 323), this to be coordinated by a 'Global Risk Assessment Programme' (ibid., 325). The IPCC and UNEP (Chemicals'

Branch), among others, have since fulfilled some of this role with regard to specific issues. The WCED (ibid.) call for this programme to be authoritative, presumably to make action prompt and effective, without being clear what they mean by authoritative. Authoritative could suggest a process that is not as open (Popper, 1966) as it might be; this has been a (questionable) criticism of the IPCC. Indeed, largely unfair criticism of lack of openness of the IPCC has perhaps contributed to slow progress in addressing climate change.

As is apparent from the above discussion, epistemological questions are connected with a number of other themes; there will be further discussion of epistemology below. To summarise now though, the WCED make clear that epistemological limits mean that prediction is a problematic assumption for policy in a complex connected world but they still tend to assume prediction for policy.

WCED: *ethics*

'We have the power to reconcile human affairs with natural laws and to thrive in the process' (WCED, 1987, 1) – here the WCED imply connected ethical and epistemological assumptions. This section primarily addresses discussions of ethics; however, where necessary, note will be made of related epistemological questions. This book will argue that we have the ability to face up to the challenges described in the WCED report and respond rationally (in some sense) in a way that should help human societies to thrive, in the sense of citizens participating in the important decisions that affect their lives. However, this book argues that 'we' do not have the power of predictive understanding of the challenges of sustainable development, where this equals an ability to control the Earth System for the material benefit of humanity. This, in turn, leads to questions regarding the analytical coherence of ethical systems, to the extent that they, in practice, assume predictable consequences.

It is interesting to contrast the implicit criticism of neo-classical economics from the world faiths in Palmer and Finlay (2003) with the following from the WCED, which follows the above quotation: 'In this our cultural and spiritual heritages can reinforce our economic interests and survival imperatives' (WCED, 1987, 1). The WCED follow this by a paragraph emphasising their 'belief' in the value of economic growth to 'build a future that is more prosperous, more just and more secure' (ibid.). They then make clear that their 'hope … is conditional on decisive political action now to begin managing environmental resources to ensure both sustainable human progress and human survival' (ibid.). Note the use of the term 'belief' and of the virtue 'hope' (cf. Connelly, 2006, 70); the use of virtue language or ideas is not uncommon in the WCED (1987, particularly 1, 27–8, 41, 44, 277, 313) but with no clear discussion of the basis for virtue ethics or other forms of ethics, in relation to sustainable development. In a relevant, insightful manner, Mebratu (1998, 515–17) suggests that a common problem in the sustainable development literature is calls for a new ethic, in a way that can gain broad acceptance, without it being clear what that new ethic should be.

Hinting at one possible way forward, Mebratu (ibid., 509) suggests eco-theologians see the vice of greed as being key; this is in accord with the 'global virtue tradition'. Mebratu (ibid., 517) importantly argues that there is a connection between economic and social structures and the ethics that are widely held. If a change in dominant ethics is a good way to move towards sustainable development, then it may be that a sufficient change in ethics will also change economic and social structures sufficiently. Attfield (1994, 41–62) argues that 'Western' traditions offer hope for an adequate environmental ethic without the need to abandon those ethics for a 'new' ethic. He also questions whether a new ethic would be effective or even possible.

Also note the implicit assumption, in the preceding quotation from the WCED, in favour of management rather than coexistence and the emphasis on resources rather than pollution. This emphasis is common in the WCED. This book calls both these assumptions into question. Indeed, the report (WCED, 1987, 58–9) emphasises the importance of pollution over resource depletion. Brundtland (ibid., particularly 1, 10, 28, 35, 37, 174, 261–86, 308) assumes that 'management' is the correct way to achieve sustainable development, without first addressing the epistemological problems in their analysis, as highlighted by this chapter. This is unfortunate, as the purpose of theories of management appears typically rooted in an economistic utilitarian desire to predict and control (e.g. Sheldrake, 2003, 1–2). The WCED (1987, 261) perhaps assume that management is the only rational response (cf. Jamieson, 1992, 142–6; Padilla, 2004, 532; Smith, 2003, 29–51). Does this mean that the WCED assume that only economistic utilitarianism is rational?

The WCED (1987, 41) state their ethical 'premise that every human being – those here and those who are to come – has the right to life and to a decent life'; also 'sustainable development aims to promote harmony among human beings and between humanity and nature' (ibid., 65). The preceding two quotations are perhaps broadly what they mean when they argue: 'Human survival and well-being could depend on the success in elevating sustainable development to a global ethic' (ibid., 308). They further state: 'The case for the conservation of nature should not rest only with development goals. It is part of our moral obligation to other living beings and future generations' (ibid., 57). In contrast with neo-liberal and marketisation assumptions, the report is critical of groups striving 'for survival and prosperity with little regard for its impact on others' (ibid., 27).

Thus, the WCED are using several notions of ethics (also welfare (ibid., 108, 196) and rights (ibid., 261)) without being clear about any relationship between them. Benton (1999, particularly 203–9, 224–9) notes something of this lack of clarity in some detail and highlights its significance. Neefjes (1999, particularly 275, 278)[7] implies that individualistic values are a key cause of conflict and the unsustainable consequences of conflict.

To complicate matters further, the WCED imply that the notion of common interest is also fundamental to their understanding of sustainable development. This can be seen from the WCED (1987, particularly 46–9, 63, 254, 261, 273–4, 304) and in the title of the report *Our Common Future*. They link common interest to justice when they write: 'Inability to promote the common inter-est in sustainable development is often a product of the relative neglect of economic and social justice within and amongst nations' (ibid., 49). This still appears the case today. The WCED appear to assume some value in the notion of 'national interest' (e.g. ibid., 147) without saying how this relates to ideas such as common interest.

The legal suggestions in the WCED have epistemological, participatory and ethical components and implications; perhaps most important are the ethical aspects of rights-based ethics. The WCED (ibid., 330–4) report the detailed legal discussions that had taken place about sustainable development. This reporting includes an annex listing twenty-two legal principles (ibid., 348–51). A discussion of some of these is worthwhile, as they raise important questions for this book.

> 1. All human beings have the fundamental right to an environment ade-quate for their health and well-being (ibid., 348).

This is a laudable aim; however, given the problems of knowing what levels of stress the Earth System will withstand before the Earth System changes enough to threaten human lives, considering questions of health and well-being appears a little premature in practical terms for a legal principle.

> 2. States shall conserve and use the environment and natural resources for the benefit of present and future generations (ibid.).

A number of questions can be asked of this; let us note some examples. First, how to decide what present and future generations will consider 'benefits'? Second, does this notion of benefits imply an unreasoned assumption (given the lack of thorough discussion of ethics by the WCED) in favour of utilitarianism? As a last example, if the possibility of the Earth System changing catastrophically in response to multiple stresses cannot be dismissed, without making a universally held leap of faith, thinking about benefits may be analytically premature.

> 3. States shall maintain ecosystems and ecological processes essential for the functioning of the biosphere, shall preserve biological diversity, and shall observe the principle of optimum sustainable yield in the use of living natu-ral resources and ecosystems (ibid.).

Let us consider examples of similar questions that can be asked of this. It is not clear that humans currently know what is 'essential for the functioning of the biosphere', though deforestation, GHGs, chemicals and possibly genetically modified organisms, for example, may contribute to radically changing the nature of the biosphere. It is not clear how to know if and how much of each in combina-tion will cause a rapid change in the biosphere. Thus, this requirement is difficult to operationalise. Does it mean humans need to stop all of these activities now because we do not know where any thresholds are, or simply continue 'business as usual' in the hope that we do not cross them?

The WCED argue elsewhere (ibid., 148) that it will be impossible to preserve all biological diversity, so 'preserve biological diversity' appears too absolute for a legal principle without some other guidance.

The phrase 'optimum sustainable yield' combines an assumed knowability of threshold limits with economic utilitarianism. It implies that science or some other process can decide what an optimum sustainable yield is for a given situation. Given the contestations over fishing quotas, this is questionable even in relatively simple confined situations. If the context were extended to the Earth System, the difficulties in knowing technically what an optimum would be are huge, even if moral principles could be universally agreed for 'optimality'.

The other principles are similarly but less affected, particularly as they are more procedural and less 'substantial', covering environmental standards, collection and publication of data, assessments, consultation, international development aid, cooperation, equity, prevention of environmental harm, liability, emergency preparedness and settlement of disputes; even if many of these notions would be contested. Less difficulty in achieving such procedural principles is perhaps why something of these later principles has been implemented in the Aarhus Convention (UNECE, 1998), rather than the first three.

The WCED (1987, 331–2) make some suggestions about how nations can incorporate these principles into legal processes. They (ibid., 332–3) suggest consolidating existing and proposed legal principles into a UN charter that 'should prescribe ... interstate behaviour needed to maintain ... life on our shared planet' (ibid., 332). This appears to assume that the behaviour required to maintain life on our shared planet can be known in such a way as to be capable of codification in a legal charter. It will be clear by now that this book calls this assumption into question. Overall, legal discussions in the WCED are not a convincing way of moving towards sustainable development; the subsequent 'inconsistent' effectiveness of the application of legal instruments strengthens this argument.

As neo-classical economics is the principal practical outcome of a particular notion of utilitarian ethics, it is relevant to discuss the suggestions of economics that are part of the WCED at this point. The WCED (ibid., 67–75) outline the reasons behind the poor economic progress of some less industrialised countries. These include:

- taking on poorly advised debt, which was often poorly used, often on the advice or stipulation of lenders;
- inequalities in political and economic power;
- unfavourable trade terms;
- poor government decisions.

They do make suggestions about better distribution of wealth between nations (ibid., particularly 75–90, 230–1) but the application of these since the report has been inconsistent – in spite of the effort of developing countries for many years (ibid., 75). As well as the lack of power of poor countries, a further possible reason for this limited progress on 'fairer trade' is that the WCED did not state clearly the reasons behind this suggestion.[8] They do, however, make clear the relevance of these questions to environmental issues. Complicating these matters further, the WCED also argue that 'rapid growth combined with deteriorating income distribution may be worse than slower growth combined with redistribution in favour of the poor' (ibid., 52). In addition, they argue that sustainable development 'requires' growth 'in all countries' to be 'less material- and energy-intensive and more equitable in its impact' (ibid., see also 57). The WCED (ibid., 76–8) suggest increasing the quality and quantity of finance to 'developing' countries, particularly by the World Bank and the International Monetary Fund (IMF).

The inconsistencies in the discussions of economics by the WCED are particularly unfortunate given the centrality they place on economics in allowing development to be sustainable (cf. Jamieson, 1992; Padilla, 2004; Smith, 2003, 29–51). To expand a little, the WCED (1987, 52–4, 62–5, 67–90) argue that economic activity needs to take fully into account the ecological costs as they are 'integrated in the workings of the real world' (ibid., 62). However, Common *et al.* (1993), Foster (1997), O'Connor (2002) and Smith (2003, 29–51), for example, argue that this is problematic in practical and ethical terms. Indeed, the WCED (1987, 53–4) hint at this. It is important to note that they give examples of where 'ecological and economic concerns are not necessarily in opposition' (ibid., 62). Nonetheless, the practical problems of reconciling economics and ecological concerns remain; particularly where robust prediction of costs and benefits is difficult or impossible, or the democratic issues raised if some people are ignored who see moral concerns that they believe cannot be captured by economic cost–benefit analysis (cf. Smith, 2003, 29–51). Padilla (2004) is an important discussion of the limitations of the ability of economics, particularly in the form of cost–benefit analysis, to address climate change and by implication sustainable development. Specifically, it raises technical questions around discount rates, compensation criteria and questionable normative assumptions that systematically bias against reducing stress to the Earth System.

The WCED conclude their main discussion of economics (1987, 67–90) by suggesting that 'economic, social and environmental catastrophes' (ibid., 89) are possible, at least in the 'developing world'. They argue that economic growth in the developing world is required to avoid this and believe that economic growth is thus required in 'industrial countries', even if they argue that this needs to be focused on the benefit of the poorest and respect environmental problems. They argue that this can be achieved without catastrophic changes in the Earth System, without giving clear reasons why catastrophe will not happen. Reid is critical of the WCED in this regard, saying that they 'evade the question of how to reconcile growth with ecological limits', leading to maintenance of the economistic, utilitarian ethical status quo (Reid, 1995, 59). Again, 'tentative interest in the reorganisation of economic activity to meet prioritised human needs is swamped by the frequency of references to … conventional economic growth' (ibid., 60, see also 64–5). Reid (ibid., 65) argues that the WCED's reluctance to clearly address high levels of consumption in industrialised countries 'reveals a Northern bias' of 'comfortable Keynesian reformism'. As noted earlier, Lélé (1991, 614, see also 616–18) argues that 'economic growth by itself leads to neither environmental sustainability nor removal of poverty'.

The WCED do raise important questions about ethical assumptions for policy. However, the lack of systematic discussion of ethics and of discussion as to how ethics might fit with epistemological questions renders the report incomplete at best.

WCED: politics and participation

All of the preceding issues and themes require translation into policy, through political processes. For the purposes of this section, politics concerns questions of power to make and be involved in policy decisions, including who is involved in those decisions and what epistemological and ethical assumptions are considered legitimate in policy processes. This section will analyse the WCED discussions of politics specifically, also noting areas where political resolution of the issues and themes is important. Facets of politics that the WCED emphasise include normative questions, questions around power, questions of 'administration' and questions of participation of citizens in policy decisions. These will all be discussed to give a sense of the WCED position on this range of questions; however, it can be argued that the most substantive proposal for processes of 'sustainable' policy-making by the WCED is greater citizen participation (cf. Jacobs, 1999, particularly 34–5). Thus, the rest of the book after this chapter will emphasise discussions of participation more than other 'political' questions.

Brundtland argues that there are social justice or equity facets to many environmental issues (WCED, 1987, 35). In particular, the Commission argue that those primarily responsible for many environmental issues benefit from the benefits of industrialism, but everyone is at risk and most do not have any control. Indeed, the WCED state that 'physical sustainability *cannot* be secured unless development policies pay attention to ... equity between generations ... [and] equity within each generation' (ibid., 43, emphasis added).

The Commission (ibid., especially 27, 41, 43–4, 46–9, 59, 67–90, 141–4, 152–4, 214–15, 225–8) emphasise an equity or justice component of sustainable development in numerous places – both equity in distribution and exchange. They imply that inequity is often a cause of environmental stress, because it sets up destructive cycles where inequity makes environmental stress worse and so on (ibid., 27, 49, 67–90, 118–44, 152–4). Reid argues that the WCED 'does not include a thorough analysis of the reasons for these inequities and of the part played by the economically more powerful nations, institutions and corporations' (Reid, 1995, 63).

Reid (ibid., 129–50) follows up this criticism of the Brundtland Report by conducting an analysis of the ontological, epistemological and ethical assumptions and other conditions, which promote current forms and levels of injustice and unsustainable development more generally. He goes on to discuss ways these obstacles to sustainable development can be overcome, arguing that individuals and thus societies will need to become broadly more virtuous (ibid., 151–77). To give examples, Reid (ibid., 155) calls for 'progress' to be less focused on growth and more on 'sufficiency', and for wealth to be less focused on material possessions and more on broader quality of life questions (ibid., 161–3). Benton (1999, particularly 209–10) also notes the significance of limitations of ethical analysis by the WCED, suggesting examples of tensions in international agreements that attempted to follow the agenda set by the WCED, implying that these inconsistencies and tensions favour powerful interests. Korten (1996) and Sachs (1993)[9] also provide useful insight into these types of questions. Benton (1999, particularly 206–9) plus Reid (1995, 69–70) in his discussion of Schumacher (1974) both hint that materialist ontology and materialist utilitarian ethics are important and questionable factors in conventional ideas of development. It appears that these are currently typically imposed by power rather than agreed upon by reason. Benton (1999, particularly 207) and Reid (1995, particularly 129–50) are keen to point to non-material effects of development in complex connected social systems. Reid (ibid., 70–88) reviews alternative models of development that offer alternative visions and values of development that are more compatible with greater social justice and reduced stress to the Earth System.

The WCED (1987, 40) do argue that the notion of 'development' is often understood in too narrow a sense, perhaps implying that it is too often associated overly with economic growth. However, when the report (ibid., 43) suggests that 'development' is 'economic and social' progress, they put an emphasis on the economic development component of social development that appears at least to be in tension with other parts of the report. This is an illustration of a general tendency within the WCED to a lack of clarity about the place of economic growth in sustainable development. This book suggests that a key reason for this lack of clarity is epistemological difficulties in knowing the relationship between economic activity and stress to the Earth System, as well as the unpredictability of the effects of changes in technology. Padilla (2004), Smith (2003, 29–51), Jamieson (1992), Sachs (1993) and his contributors, Reid (1995), Korten (1996) and the 'global virtue tradition' call into question an over-emphasis on economic growth in policy-making.

The WCED (1987, 49–52) do clarify in the following sense the significance of economic development in sustainable development, when it emphasises that it is needed in the 'developing' world to provide for the needs of poor people. In this, they make questionable assumptions about the possibility of redistribution within countries, without adequately addressing connections of this to questions of the distribution of wealth between countries.

The above has indicated something of the interaction between power and normative questions for sustainable development. Now let us consider the Commission's analysis of the administrative difficulties of addressing sustainable development and the suggestions that they make.

The difficulties administrations have in dealing with issues that cross institutional compartmentalisation are noted by the WCED (ibid., 9–10). One issue is where one department or organisation addresses its primary responsibility but creates other problems; for example, a department of energy succeeds in supplying required levels of electricity, but creates acid rain. Another issue is where environment departments are assumed to solve all environment problems on their own, without the cooperation of wider society; thus, in the previous example, solve acid rain without the assistance of the energy department.

Brundtland recommends comprehensive, holistic or transdisciplinary approaches to address these types of issue. However, they do not give particularly concrete advice about how institutions should implement this. The standard organisational theory response to these types of issues is to assemble cross-disciplinary teams (e.g. Tidd *et al.*, 2001, 335). Faber *et al.* (1998, 199–202) and Gibbons *et al.* (1994) do give some indications of the benefits and issues of this approach. A further issue of cross-disciplinary teams is that one form of problematic compartmentalisation is often replaced with another.

One possibility would be, as the WCED (1987, 314) perhaps imply, if sustainable development were in some sense to parallel economics (or even replace economics) as a central concern of the vast majority of organisations. The questioning of economistic utilitarianism by the global virtue tradition and alternative perceptions of economics based on different assumptions, such as putting the economics of Adam Smith back into the context of his other (ethical) thought, may be important here. Ecological economics (e.g. Daly and Cobb, 1990; Faber *et al.*, 1998) and other 'economic' thought that questions materialist utilitarian assumptions (e.g. Bokare, 1993; Braybrooke and Mofid, 2005; Pesch, 2002–3; Schumacher, 1974; Siddiqi, 1981) may also provide some insights. Approaches using the above insights, among others, might replace the ethic of economistic utilitarianism with the 'sustainable ethic' that the WCED call for (1987, particularly 308).

The WCED (ibid., 308–42) attempt to set out what sustainable development means for institutions, particularly United Nations institutions, on the basis that: 'The real world of interlocked economic and ecological systems will not change; the policies and institutions concerned must' (ibid., 310) but progress since then has not been encouraging.

The report also argues that both industrial and industrialising countries will be harmed by ecological problems and that both types of country need to be involved in addressing the inequality that is wrong in itself and a key cause of ecological problems (ibid., 308–9). To achieve this, the WCED (ibid., 309) assert that 'past patterns' will have to change profoundly. Their core suggestion is that the institutions need to be concerned with sources rather than effects (ibid., 310–19). In this regard they state:

> All agencies of government, of international organizations, and of the major private-sector institutions … must be given a mandate to pursue their traditional goals in such a way that those goals are reinforced by a steady enhancement of the resource base … of the small planet we all share.
>
> (Ibid., 312)

A number of thoughts need to be considered about this criterion for organisational design. Again, the WCED are focusing on resources and appear to ignore pollution and other forms of stress to the Earth System. This makes a doubtful assumption, as questions such as climate change are at least as important as resource avail-ability (cf. Faber *et al.*, 1998, 42–4). There is no mention of if and how questions of equity are to be brought into the mandates of organisations; this would lead to normative consequences. Brundtland does not appear to offer concrete advice about what altering mandates means in practice or how to achieve the alterations. Further, the technical and ethical questions about substitutability of 'resources', or capital, are far from resolved (e.g. Ekins, 2003, 150–3). Nonetheless, the WCED are suggesting that rather than the dominance of economistic utilitarianism 'man-dates', there needs to be greater balance between economistic utilitarianism and other forms of ethics, such as global virtue tradition.

The suggestions about how international cooperation might be fostered are vague (WCED, 1987, 41, 261–86, 312–13), beyond some specific suggestions about the oceans, outer space and Antarctica. In particular, the reasons why nations should look beyond national interest are not made clear. This is presum-ably towards some form of common good, or at least, given the potential harm to all nations, that national interest and common interest are closer than is typically assumed by individual nations.

To bring questions of power, institutional change and participation together, the WCED appear correct when they say that 'the changes required involve all countries, large and small, rich and poor' (ibid., 11, similarly 22, 40), even if larger changes are required by those with greater responsibility for the current situation. The WCED suggest the key areas that sustainable development will affect are 'the exploitation of resources, the direction of investments, the orien-tation of technological development, and institutional change' (ibid., 46). From this, it is clear that there are many existing interests that may not be immedi-ately keen on changing their plans. The WCED (ibid., 46–9, 67–90) recognise the importance of power for the issues they are trying to address. However, they do not make clear how this should be tackled. Although this question is beyond the scope of this book, a few indications are worthwhile. If, as Wissenburg (1998, particularly 204) argues and Reid implies (1995, particularly 176–7), it is ultimately citizens that hold power over democratic governments, companies and even 'the market', then it is in the hands of citizens to decide whether development becomes more or less sustainable. More specifically, whether socie-ties become more or less equal and how much societies risk stressing the Earth System to see whether it will collapse.

It is probably relatively 'rich' citizens in industrialised countries who consume more, who have most power, as individuals and in the 'example' they set for those who are only now gaining significant ability to pursue consumerism. Reid (ibid., particularly 176–7), Korten (1996, particularly 261–8, 277–91, 325–8), Daly and Cobb (1990, particularly 400), Rolston (Engel and Engel, 1990, par-ticularly 70–1), the 'global virtue tradition' and O'Neill (1993) suggest or imply that a change towards a less material, instrumental set of ontological and ethical assumptions is needed, with broadly more virtuous ethical assumptions being a possible candidate. To the extent that this type of change happens should make questions of power and sustainable development easier to negotiate. To illustrate, Connelly (2006, 49, 52) suggests that widespread ecological virtuousness might lessen the need for environmental policy-making.

The report (WCED, 1987, 47–8) reflects on political processes of participation, arguing that 'commons' community control of land has been more successful at minimising environmental issues than 'enclosure' into private property, even if commons community control is typically less productive in the short term. They indicate that self-interest is an important factor in the problems of development, before suggesting this can be compensated for by measures such as laws and taxes imposed by administrations. However, they argue: 'Most important, effective participation in decision-making processes by local communities can help them articulate and effectively enforce their common interest' (ibid., 47, see also 63).

Brundtland indicates that, beyond the local level, these types of issues are both more important and more difficult to resolve, often because 'political jurisdiction and areas of impact do not coincide' (ibid., 47), suggesting international cooperation as one way to address this. The report (ibid., 48) argues that at the international level, economic interactions and power are similarly important.

It is not clear how the WCED reconcile the call for international cooperation with suggestions (ibid., 63) for local participation in a decentralised 'management of resources'. The concept of subsidiarity might help but, for global issues, good coordination may be more important than decentralisation. The WCED (ibid., 231) argue that responsibility for sustainable development ultimately rests with national governments, even in 'developing countries'.

The Commission (ibid., 65) indicate other broad political process solutions, in addition to mutual self-interest, to allow development to be more sustainable. Reid is scathing when he says of these: 'Their magnitude and scope – in effect a major overhaul of established systems ranging from national politics to international trade and finance – are matched only by the absence of any guidance as to how they might be achieved' (Reid, 1995, 61). It may be too strong to say that the WCED do not offer any guidance, but the other suggestions of the WCED appear largely dependent on its first suggestion: 'a political system that secures effective citizen participation in decision-making' (WCED, 1987, 65). Bruntland's authors are not very clear about how to improve participation; they do argue that to assure the poorest 'get their fair share ... Such equity would be aided by political systems that secure effective citizen participation in decision making and by greater democracy in international decision making' (ibid., 8).

The WCED (ibid., particularly 9, 21, 23, 47, 63–5, 133–4, 136–7, 143) imply that participation is an essential or even the most important (ibid., particularly 65) component of sustainable development,[10] but without giving clear indication of how this might be achieved. They suggest 'public inquiries' for 'large-scale projects' to help draw 'attention to different points of view', referenda for particularly important decisions (ibid., 63–4) and that 'free access to relevant information and the availability of alternative sources of technical expertise can provide an informed basis for public discussion' (ibid., 64).

Specifically with regard to 'empowering vulnerable groups' (particularly 'indigenous populations'), the WCED (ibid., 114–16) make a number of suggestions, including that educational institutions and health facilities should be provided before economic development, presumably to help address differences in power (ibid., 116). The reason for this appears to be 'a just and humane policy' (ibid., 115) and that these are 'the only cultures that have proved able to thrive in these environments' (ibid.).

The report frequently emphasises the need for comprehensive or holistic approaches (for example ibid., 67–90, 144, 158–9, 310–43). The discussion of the international economic system (ibid., 67–90) is reasonably comprehensive in technical terms, but does little to suggest how epistemological difficulties can be addressed, or describe the moral basis for the suggested changes in the international economic system. Alternative possible moral starting points for the exchange of goods to economistic utilitarianism, such as egalitarian virtue schemes, may be more effective than the articulation by the WCED. As should be clear from the above, discussions of changes to political processes in the WCED are hardly clear and systematic.

If the WCED could not offer a detailed blueprint (ibid., 2) it would be folly for this book to try. Instead, it is hoped that the analysis here helps to identify the key issues in sustainable development and that this will provide some indications of possible ways to more effective comprehensive approaches. Chapters 4 to 6 will add insight from policy responses, environmental management responses and theoretical responses to the WCED and sustainable development more generally, to the analysis of the WCED in this chapter. Chapter 7 will build on this analysis, suggesting possible ways forward with regard to epistemological and ethical questions. Chapter 8 then suggests how participation may help to address epistemological problems along with adding legitimacy and promoting greater cooperation with any 'decisions'. This discussion will begin where the WCED (ibid., particularly 9, 21, 23, 47, 63–5, 133–4, 136–7, 143) ends: the argument that improved participation is an essential component of sustainable development.

3.3 Responses to the WCED as a document

Various criticisms of specific aspects of the WCED by commentators have been noted in Section 3.2. However, it will be worth drawing out broad issues raised.

Nature (1987) applauds the intent of the WCED but believes that in an imperfect world it should have spent more effort on prioritising the issues that were raised. The key reason for this is that *Nature* assumes, and has largely been proved right to date, that without addressing the selfishness of countries and individuals it will not be possible to address all the issues described by the WCED. *Nature* implies, quite reasonably, that only the issues that can be addressed without harming the interests of the powerful will be effectively tackled, at least until a time when such self-interested behaviour is not acceptable.

Ekins (2003, 149–50) argues that the WCED chose to ignore the limits to growth thesis (Meadows *et al.*, 1972) not because evidence was not accumulating to support it, but because of difficulties in politicians 'selling it' to electorates. A key factor in the difficulties convincing electorates was probably the criticism that Meadows *et al.* did not adequately take into account that price increases encourage resource substitution. It is still not widely understood that limits to industrialism are more likely set by pollution, emissions and the stress caused to the Earth System, rather than resource constraints (Faber *et al.*, 1998, 42–4).

Given the previous discussion of the WCED, it should not be surprising that many find the WCED vague or worse (Mebratu, 1998, 503). Mebratu suggests that the consequences of this are 'acceptance of a largely undefined term as a basis sets the stage for a situation where whoever can pin his or her definition to the term automatically will win a large political battle for influence over the future' (ibid.). The key suggestion by Mebratu, in order to achieve sustainable development, is a call to strengthen 'the logical coherency within the concept' (ibid., 518). It is hoped that the analysis of the epistemological issues that surround sustainable development, in this book, may help increase logical coherence. It is also hoped that the analysis of the poor quality of ethical theory in the WCED by this book, with a highlighting of some ethical themes in the sustainable development literature, may also be useful.

Reid (1995, 63) argues that commentators on the WCED 'question its synthesis of environment, equity and economics'. These commentators include Hueting (1990) who also argues that increases in GNP are too often wrongly associated with economic sustainability, and even social and environmental sustainability. Hueting concludes (ibid., 115) 'what we need least is an increase in national income'. Lélé (1991) also highlights tensions between the WCED and calls for economic growth on the one hand and reduced stress to the Earth System and greater equity in distribution of wealth and material goods on the other. These commentators do not make particularly clear the reasons for these tensions, though Hueting (1990, 112–13) does suggest that it is normative dogma. One possible explanation is that the WCED do not explicitly suggest how to resolve the tensions between the economistic utilitarian ethical assumption that underpins calls for economic growth and other forms of ethics (perhaps particularly virtue ethics) that perhaps underpin calls for better ecological stewardship (Attfield, 1994; Barry, 1999) and equity. Calls by the WCED for wider participation in policy-making do indicate one procedural way forward. Reid (1995, 63–5) argues that the way the WCED resolved the tensions in practice for their report was that the WCED favoured economics and assumed that everything else could be worked out on that basis.

3.4 Conclusions

The immense scope, difficulty and importance of the task that is encapsulated by the phrase sustainable development should be clear from the preceding analysis.

The WCED authors summarise the ethical, epistemological, and institutional difficulties of achieving sustainable development when they write:

> The compatibility of environmental and economic objectives is often lost in the pursuit of individual or group gains, with little regard for the impacts on others, with a blind faith in science's ability to find solutions, and in ignorance of the distant consequences of today's decisions. Institutional rigidities add to this myopia.
>
> (WCED, 1987, 62)

Notwithstanding the above quotation, the dominant epistemological assumption of the WCED appears to be a Baconian predict and control managerial attitude to the Earth System. In addition, the text does display a significant emphasis on broad, integrated, comprehensive or even a transdisciplinary approach to the questions it considers. The dominant ethical assumption of the WCED appears to be economistic utilitarianism, even if some mention is made of deontological and virtue notions of ethics; however, there is no clear method of resolution for tensions between ethical schemes, and these are in tension, anyway, with the economic growth aspirations recommended by the report. The dominance of economics over virtue appears to have been the result to date, perhaps for reasons of political, economic and rhetorical power. The rhetorical power of economistic utilitarianism is perhaps primarily located in an acceptance of the contestable assertion that neo-classical economics is a 'science' or at least not normative (cf. Brawley, 2005, 140; Keynes, 1931, 372; Korten, 1996, 74–5; Stern Review, 2006, 28–31). Greater participation of citizens in policy-making is the key suggestion by the WCED for political processes; however, suggestions in the report on this subject are not clear. Progress on questions of participation is considered in more detail in Chapter 8.

The next chapter will discuss intergovernmental policy responses to the call for sustainable development that the WCED report made.

Notes

1 Porritt (2005, 317–20) is an illuminating summary of the psychological problems of materialism, when considering sustainable development questions.
2 It is important to note that Benton (1999, 211–12) argues that brutality has also been associated with 'conservation' projects.
3 This tension is made more difficult to resolve when the report contains vague statements such as: 'Sustainable development requires meeting the basic needs of all and extending to all the opportunity to satisfy their aspirations for a better life' (WCED, 1987, 44). The second part of the sentence appears to be a charter for everybody to satisfy all their aspirations, which the tone of the report overall (and the paragraph following the above quotation) suggests is not sustainable by the Earth System.
4 Reid (1995, 69–88) and Benton (1999, 203–5, 227–9), among others, insightfully explore the notion of needs.
5 It is perplexing that the WCED (1987, 217) appear to recommend 'rare metals' as a way to make development more sustainable.

6 The WCED (1987, 215) suggest 'small-scale material processing' is energy intensive, thus trade-offs may be necessary. Life-cycle analysis (ISO/FDIS 14040, 1997)) and permaculture (Mollison, 1988) may point to ways to decide where technically optimal overall distribution of production of different types of product would be.

7 A very useful examination and summary of the interaction of self-interested politics, politics for the common good, armed conflict, environmental stress, refugees situations, aid, importance of local ecosystem knowledge, participation in policy-making, etc.

8 One possibility would be to question the utilitarian basis of much international commercial activity and suggest that a virtue of (broadly Aristotelian) justice rather than libertarian justice or market ideas of justice (e.g. Nozick (1974/2002, particularly 149–82) is more appropriate. Hayward and O'Neill (1997) and Kymlicka (2002, especially 102–59) among others examine something of questions of this type. Thanks are owed to Chukwumerije Okereke for discussions on this area. Okereke (2008) includes a good review of notions of justice and how they apply to sustainable development. Paterson (1996) is a useful and relevant discussion of how notions of justice might apply to climate but also more broadly sustainable development.

9 Thanks are owed to Chukwumerije Okereke for discussions in this area.

10 Neefjes (1999, particularly 277–8) argues that efforts to improve participation are essential even in situations of conflict and refugee crisis.

References

Adams, J. (1995) *Risk*, London: UCL Press

AHRB/ESRC (2006) *Cultures of consumption – News*, Issue 5, www.consume.bbk.ac.uk/newsletter/news5.html. Accessed 14 May 2011

Attfield, R. (1994) *Environmental philosophy: Principles and prospects*, Aldershot: Ashgate

Barry, J. (1999) *Rethinking green politics: Nature, virtue and progress*, London: Sage

Benton, T. (1999) 'Sustainable development and the accumulation of capital: Reconciling the irreconcilable', in Dobson, A. (ed.) *Fairness and futurity: Essays on environmental sustainability and social justice*, Oxford: Oxford University Press

Bokare, M. (1993) *Hindu economics: Eternal economic order*, New Deli: Janaki Prakashan

Braybrooke, M. and Mofid, K. (2005) *Promoting the common good: Bringing economics and theology together again*, London: Shepheard-Walwyn

Brawley, M. (2005) *Power, money, and trade: Decisions that shape global economic relations*, Ontario: Broadview

Brook Lyndhurst (2006) *Innovative methods for influencing behaviours & assessing success: Triggering widespread adoption of sustainable behaviour*, London: Department for Environment, Food and Rural Affairs

Common, M.S., Blamey, R.K. and Norton, T.W. (1993) 'Sustainability and environmental valuation', *Environmental Values*, 2(4), 299–334

Connelly, J. (2006) 'The virtue of environmental citizenship', in Dobson, A. and Bell, D. (eds) *Environmental citizenship*, Cambridge, MA: MIT Press

Cox, S.J. and Tait, N.R.S. (1991) *Reliability, safety and risk assessment*, Oxford: Butterworth-Heinemann

Crutzen, P. (1996) 'My life with O-3, NOx, and other YZO(x) compounds (Nobel Lecture)', *Angewandte Chemie-International Edition*, 35: 1758–77

CSD (1997) *Global change and sustainable development: Critical trends*, UN Economic and Social Council, E/CN.17/1997/3, www.un.org/esa/documents/ecosoc/cn17/1997/ecn171997-3.htm. Accessed 14 May 2011

Daly, H. and Cobb, J.B. (1990) *For the common good*, London: Green Print

Dauvergne, P. (2010) 'The problem of consumption', *Global Environmental Politics*, 10(2): 1–10

Defra (2003) *Changing patterns: UK government framework for sustainable consumption and production*, London: Defra

Ekins, P. (2003) 'Sustainable development', in Page, E.A. and Proops, J. (eds) *Environmental thought*, Cheltenham: Edward Elgar

Engel, J.R. and Engel, J.G. (eds) (1990) *Ethics of environment and development: Global challenge, international response*, London: Belhaven

EU (2001) *A sustainable Europe for a better world: A European Union strategy for sustainable development*, Brussels: Commission of the European Communities – COM(2001)264 final, http://eur-lex.europa.eu/LexUriServ/LexUriServ.do?uri=COM:2001:0264:FIN:E N:PDF. Accessed 14 May 2011

EU (2006) *Renewed EU sustainable development strategy*, Brussels: Council of the European Union, http://register.consilium.europa.eu/pdf/en/06/st10/st10117.en06.pdf. Accessed 14 May 2011

Faber, M., Proops, J. and Manstetten, R. (1998) *Ecological economics: Concepts and methods*, Cheltenham: Edward Elgar

Foster, J. (ed.) (1997) *Valuing nature? Economics, ethics and environment*, London: Routledge

Fuchs, D. and Lorek, S. (2002) 'Sustainable consumption governance in a globalizing world', *Global Environmental Politics*, 1: 19–45

Gibbons, M., Limoges, C., Nowotny, H., Schwartzman, S., Scott, P. and Trow, M. (1994) *The new production of knowledge: The dynamics of science and research in contemporary societies*, London: SAGE

Hayward, T. and O'Neill, J. (eds) (1997) *Justice, property and the environment: Social and legal perspectives*, Aldershot: Ashgate

Holdsworth, M. and Steedman, P. (2005) *16 pain-free ways to help save the planet*, London: National Consumer Council

Hounsham, S. (2006) *Painting the town green: How to persuade people to be environmentally friendly*, Green-Engage, www.green-engage.co.uk/PaintingtheTownGreen.pdf. Accessed 14 May 2011

Hueting, R. (1990) 'The Brundtland report: A matter of conflicting goals', *Ecological Economics*, 2(2): 109–17

ICIDI (1980) *North–South: A programme for survival, report of the Commission*, London: Pan

ISO/FDIS 14040 (1997) *Environmental management – life cycle assessment – principles and framework*, Geneva: International Standards Organisation

IUCN (1980) *World conservation strategy: Living resource conservation for sustainable development*, Gland: IUCN

Jackson, T. and Michaelis, L. (2003) *Policies for sustainable consumption*, London: Sustainable Development Commission

Jacobs, M. (1999) 'Sustainable development as a contested concept', in Dobson, A. (ed.) *Fairness and futurity: Essays on environmental sustainability and social justice*, Oxford: Oxford University Press

Jamieson, D. (1992) 'Ethics, public policy, and global warming', *Science, technology and human values*, 17: 139–53 (also in Light, A. and Rolston III, H. (2003) *Environmental ethics: An anthology*, London: Blackwell)

Keynes, J-M. (1931) *Essays in persuasion*, London: Macmillan

Kletz, T. (2003) 'Inherently safer design – its scope and future', *Process Safety and Environmental Protection*, 81(B6): 401

Korten, D. (1996) *When corporations rule the world*, West Hartford: Kumarian Press

Kymlicka, W. (2002) (2nd edn) *Contemporary political philosophy: An introduction*, Oxford: Oxford University Press

Kyoto Protocol (1997) *Kyoto Protocol to the United Nations Framework Convention on Climate Change*, Geneva: United Nations Office at Geneva – FCCC/CP/1997/L.7/Add.1, http://unfccc.int/resource/docs/cop3/l07a01.pdf. Accessed 14 May 2011

Lee, K. (1993) 'To de-industrialize is it so irrational?', in Dobson, A. and Lucardi, P. (eds) *The politics of nature*, London: Routledge

Lélé, S. (1991) 'Sustainable development: A critical review', *World Development*, 19: 607–21

Meadows, D., Meadows, D., Randers, J. and Behrens, W. (1972) *The limits to growth: A report for the Club of Rome's project on the predicament of Mankind*, New York: Potomac Associates

Mebratu, D. (1998) 'Sustainability and sustainable development: Historical and conceptual review', *Environmental Impact Assessment Review*, 18: 493–520

Mollison, B. (1988) *Permaculture: A designers' manual*, Tyalgum, NSW: Tagari Publications

Nature (1987) 'Defining half a problem', *Nature*, 327: 1–2

Neefjes, K. (1999) 'Ecological degradation: A cause for conflict, a concern for survival', in Dobson, A. (ed.) *Fairness and futurity: Essays on environmental sustainability and social justice*, Oxford: Oxford University Press

Nozick, R. (1974/2002) *Anarchy, state and utopia*, Oxford: Blackwell

O'Connor, M. (2002) 'Reframing environmental valuation: Reasoning about resource use and the redistribution of sustainability', in Abaza, H. and Baranzini, A. (eds) *Implementing sustainable development: Integrated assessment and participatory decision-making processes*, Cheltenham: Edward Elgar/UNEP

OECD (2001) *Sustainable development: Critical issues*, Paris: Organisation for Economic Co-operation and Development

Okereke, C. (2008) *Global justice and neoliberal environmental governance: Ethics, sustainable development and international cooperation*, Abingdon: Routledge

O'Neill, J. (1993) *Ecology, policy and politics: Human well-being and the natural world*. London: Routledge

Padilla, E. (2004) 'Climate change, economic analysis and sustainable development', *Environmental Values*, 13: 523–44

Palmer, M. and Finlay, V. (2003) *Faith in conservation: New approaches to religions and the environment*, Washington, DC: World Bank, http://go.worldbank.org/3L9IDQNFO0 or www.arcworld.org/books_resources.asp. Accessed 9 May 2011

Paterson, M. (1996) 'International justice and global warming', in Holden, B. (ed.) *The ethical dimensions of global change*, Basingstoke: Macmillan

Pesch, H. (2002–3) *Teaching guide to economics*, Lewiston, NY; Lampeter: Edwin Mellen Press

Pezzoli, K. (1997) 'Sustainable development: A transdisciplinary overview of the literature', *Journal of Environmental Planning and Management*, 40: 549–601

Popper, K. (1966) (5th edn) *The open society and its enemies*, London: Routledge and Kegan Paul

Porritt, J. (2000) *Playing safe: Science and the environment*, New York: Thames & Hudson

Porritt, J. (2005) *Capitalism as if the world mattered*, London: Earthscan

RCEP (2003) *Chemicals in products: Safeguarding the environment and human health – reducing the risks from chemicals*, London: Royal Commission on Environmental Pollution

Redclift, M. (1987) *Sustainable development: Exploring the contradictions*, London: Routledge

Reid, D. (1995) *Sustainable development: An introductory guide*, London: Earthscan

Sachs, W. (ed.) (1993) *Global ecology*, London: Zed Books

Schumacher, E.F. (1974) *Small is beautiful: A study of economics as if people mattered*, London: Abacus

Shackley, S. and Wynne, B. (1995) 'Global climate change: The mutual construction of an emergent science-policy domain', *Science and Public Policy*, 22(4): 218–30

Sheldrake, J. (2003) *Management theory*, London: Thomson

Siddiqi, M. (1981) *Muslim economic thinking: A survey of contemporary literature*, Leicester: Islamic Foundation

Smith, G. (2003) *Deliberative democracy and the environment*, London: Routledge

Steedman, P. (2005) *Desperately seeking sustainability?* London: National Consumer Council

Stern Review (2006) *Stern Review on the economics of climate change*, http://webarchive. nationalarchives.gov.uk/+/www.hm-treasury.gov.uk/stern_review_report.htm. Accessed 15 April 2012

Tidd, J., Bessant, J. and Pavitt, K. (2001) (2nd edn) *Managing innovation: Integrating technological, market and organizational change*, Chichester: John Wiley

Trzyna, T. (1995) *A sustainable world: Defining and measuring sustainable development*, Sacramento: International Center for the Environment and Public Policy, California Institute of Public Affairs

UNECE (1998) *Convention on access to information, public participation in decision-making and access to justice in environmental matters*, Geneva: UNECE, www.unece.org/env/pp/ documents/cep43e.pdf. Accessed 14 May 2011

UNEP (2002) *Draft Strategic Plan for the implementation of the Basel Convention*, Geneva: UNEP, www.basel.int/meetings/cop/cop6/english/3e.pdf. Accessed 14 May 2011

UNEP (2004) 'Stumbling blocks on road to green consumption', *UNEP's Sustainable Consumption Newsletter*, Issue 56, www.unep.fr/scp/publications/scpnet/pdf/scpnet56. pdf. Accessed 14 May 2011

UNEP/IEA (2002) *Reforming energy subsidies*, Paris: UNEP/IEA, http://apps.unep.org/ publications/index.php?option=com_pub&task=download&file=-Reforming%20 Energy%20Subsidies-2002150.pdf. Accessed 8 February 2015

UNFCCC (1992) *United Nations framework convention on climate change*, Geneva: United Nations Office at Geneva, FCCC/GEN/23 B, http://unfccc.int/resource/docs/convkp/ conveng.pdf. Accessed 16 May 2011

Uzzell, D., Muckle, R., Jackson, T., Ogden, J., Barnett, J., Gatersleben, B., Hegarty, P. and Papathanasopoulou, E. (2006) *Choice matters: Alternative approaches to encourage sustainable consumption and production*, London: Department of the Environment, Food and Rural Affairs

WCED (1987) *Our common future*, Oxford: Oxford University Press

Weinberg, A. (1986) 'Science and its limits: The regulators dilemma', in National Academy of Engineering, *Hazards, technology and fairness*, Washington, DC: National Academy Press

Wissenburg, M. (1998) *Green liberalism*, London: UCL Press

4 Discourse analysis
Do governments want to manage the earth? Yes!

4.1 Introduction

This chapter continues the discourse analysis of the previous chapter, of the epistemological difficulties, lack of agreement on ethics, internal inconsistencies and proposals for participation of the intergovernmental sustainable development literature, by examining key post WCED documents produced by the UN, the EU and the OECD. This examination comprises Sections 4.2–4.4, before Section 4.5 draws the analysis together. This will provide a sedimented view of how policymakers have responded to questions around sustainable development, in particular what the typical epistemological and ethical assumptions are and which policy processes are promoted.

4.2 From UNCED to WSSD

The United Nations Conference on Environment and Development (UNCED) happened in June 1992 in Rio de Janeiro in Brazil. It was convened on the authority of the UN General Assembly resolution 44/228 of 22 December 1989. This resolution expresses the basis for calling for the UNCED because UN members

> [were] deeply concerned by the continuing deterioration of the state of the environment and the serious degradation of the global life-support systems, as well as by trends that, if allowed to continue, could disrupt the global ecological balance, jeopardize the life-sustaining qualities of the Earth and lead to an ecological catastrophe, and recogniz[e] that decisive, urgent and global action is vital to protecting the ecological balance of the Earth.
>
> (UN, 1989)

The resolution then outlines problems of environment and development, along with approaches to be taken, in similar terms to the WCED (1987). The UNCED meeting had five main formal outcomes: (1) the Rio Declaration; (2) the Climate Convention; (3) the Convention on Biological Diversity; (4) the Forest Principles; and (5) Agenda 21. These will each be analysed and outlined to give a sense of the assumptions and content of these key sustainable development documents.

The Rio Declaration

The Rio Declaration (1992) sets out twenty-seven principles, picking up many of the key themes of the WCED and putting them into diplomatically acceptable language. An early paragraph in the declaration suggests an ontological assumption with epistemological implications by 'recognizing the integral and interdependent nature of the Earth, our home'. The meaning of this is not particularly explicit but appears to imply that the Earth System is the key 'unit of analysis' for sustainable development. Principle 1 contains utilitarian and anthropocentric ethical assumptions: 'Human beings are at the centre of concerns for sustainable development.'

Principle 2 starts: 'States have … the sovereign right to exploit their own resources', but Palmer and Finlay (2003) indicate that the 'global virtue tradition' would call into question an ethical assumption of exploiting nature in an instrumental economistic utilitarian sense.[1]

Principle 3 does perhaps indicate some limited notion of stewardship: 'The right to development must be fulfilled so as to equitably meet developmental and environmental needs of present and future generations'. The use of the term 'equitably' perhaps implies a virtue notion of justice rather than libertarian justice or market ideas of justice.[2]

Principle 4 appears to articulate an epistemological and normative assumption: 'In order to achieve sustainable development, environmental protection shall constitute an integral part of the development process and cannot be considered in isolation from it.' The next principles have a similar tone but are more specific, emphasising cooperation, priority for the poor, 'unsustainable patterns of production and consumption' and 'participation of all concerned citizens'. Principle 12 in discussing international trade makes a reasonably clear assumption in favour of economistic utilitarianism. The next principles address liability and 'transfer' of harmful substances.

Principle 15 describes the 'precautionary approach' in a way that has been widely used since 1992. It is interesting to contrast the widespread use of the principle on precaution with the level of use of other principles such as those that call for 'eradicating poverty' or to 'reduce and eliminate unsustainable patterns of production and consumption'. For example, versions of precaution have been implemented in legislation, whereas the 'eradication of poverty' struggles to get beyond rhetoric, despite huge popular movements pressing to address this issue.

Overall, there is much emphasis on participation of citizens generally and marginalised groups in particular in sustainable development decision-making. There is an epistemological emphasis on the connection of issues. With regard to ethics, there is a mix of economistic utilitarian assumptions and other unspecified forms of ethics with no clear method of resolution of tensions. As with the WCED, this last point probably means that the most powerful advocates of their ethical position will tend to have their assumptions accepted, where there is conflict.

The Climate Convention

The Climate Convention outlines an international response to climate change, calling for 'stabilization of greenhouse gas concentrations in the atmosphere at a level that would prevent dangerous anthropogenic interference with the climate system' (UNFCCC, 1992, Article 2). So right at the core of United Nations Framework Convention on Climate Change (UNFCCC) is an apparent assumption that humans can predict the level of GHGs that are dangerous, in order to avoid this and *manage* the risk or even the planet. Further examination of this Convention is relevant:

> The Parties should take precautionary measures to anticipate, prevent or minimize the causes of climate change and mitigate its adverse effects. Where there are threats of serious or irreversible damage, lack of full scientific certainty should not be used as a reason for postponing such measures, taking into account that policies and measures to deal with climate change should be cost-effective so as to ensure global benefits at the lowest possible cost.
>
> (Ibid., Article 3, principle 3)

There appears (UNFCCC, 2005) to be no clear agreed method to negotiate any tensions between taking action to minimise the effects of climate change and minimising (presumably) economic costs. At least one reason for this may be the epistemological difficulties in knowing the level of emissions that will cause dangerous climate change, as recent efforts in this regard demonstrate (Rapid Climate Change, 2006; Schellnhuber *et al.*, 2006, e.g. 20–1[3]). In the absence of clear methods to negotiate such tensions, it is unsurprising that economic costs appear to have been given priority. UNFCCC (1992) Article 3, principle 4, calls for climate change initiatives to be integrated with sustainable development issues. The UNFCCC states its epistemological assumptions in the following way: 'To further the understanding and to reduce or eliminate the remaining uncertainties regarding the causes, effects, magnitude and timing of climate change and the economic and social consequences of various response strategies' (ibid., Article 4, paragraph 1(g)). But what if 'reducing or eliminating … remaining uncertainties' is a chimerical objective? The UNFCCC (1992) does not appear to contemplate how to address climate change if uncertainties are not being eliminated or reduced sufficiently, to have significant practical benefit; as Chapter 2 indicates. UNFCCC (ibid.) Article 6, paragraph (a)(iii) does call for 'public participation in addressing climate change and its effects and developing adequate responses' which may help from an 'open society' (Popper, 1966) perspective. The difficulties in knowing what will cause dangerous climate change are perhaps one key reason why more concrete plans to address climate change were not agreed.

Since 1992, the most significant development in policy response to climate change is the Kyoto Protocol of 1997, which was a development within the UNFCCC (1992). The protocol does not reflect on the difficulties of knowing what will cause climate change, it simply tries to facilitate modest, somewhat politically acceptable, reductions in GHG emissions and maintenance of sinks for such gases. The closest that the UNFCCC comes to epistemological considerations is a call to reduce uncertainty (ibid., Article 10, paragraph (d)). It will be clear by now, that this book's argument is that the UNFCCC may be starting in the wrong place. The Kyoto Protocol (1997) is more interesting with regard to ethics, as in Article 10 it considers questions of responsibility between nations via 'common but differentiated responsibilities', which implies a 'common good', 'egalitarian' flavour of ethics.[4]

In sum, the Climate Convention says little of significance about epistemology, ethics and participation. This is perhaps most important with regard to epistemology, given the limitations that climate science had and still has with regard to predicting the future climate.

The Convention on Biological Diversity

The Convention on Biological Diversity (CBD) states early on that difficulties of knowledge are a significant limitation 'upon which to plan and implement appropriate measures' (CBD, 1992, preamble). This phrase perhaps indicates that the CBD makes Baconian assumptions. The preamble proceeds, 'noting that it is vital to anticipate, prevent and attack the causes of significant reduction or loss of biological diversity at source' (ibid.).

There appears to be little analysis of the causes of reduction of biodiversity in the CBD, or efforts to address them; however, the WCED (1987, particularly 147–66) suggests that the key sources of reduction in biodiversity include:

- clearing land for many types of 'development';
- ignorance of the effects of actions, such as that clearing rainforest typically yields very poor quality agricultural land;
- poverty, such that clearing rainforest or poaching is better in the short term than letting your family starve;
- industrial development causing pollution;
- greed, such as clearing rainforest in order to own the land and then making no attempt to make productive use of it;
- subsidies for activities such as clearing rainforest that is not then used;
- poor or corrupt application of regulations.

The CBD next indicates precaution when it suggests further consequences of limitations of knowledge 'that where there is a threat of significant reduction or loss of biological diversity, lack of full scientific certainty should not be used as a reason for postponing measures to avoid or minimize such a threat' (CBD, 1992, preamble). The CBD goes on to highlight particular questions of justice with regard to 'indigenous and local communities', women and biodiversity by 'recognizing that economic and social development and poverty eradication are the first and overriding priorities of developing countries' (ibid.).

This appears to assume that economic development is required for poverty eradication, which the United Nations Commission on Sustainable Development (CSD) (1997, paragraphs 15 and 16) plus Blanke and Burdick (2005) call into question. The CBD does not appear to address any tensions between justice for indigenous people and whether their perceptions of poverty are the same as 'modern' notions of poverty (see also CBD, 1992, Article 8, paragraph (j)). The preamble continues:

> Aware that conservation and sustainable use of biological diversity is of critical importance for meeting the food, health and other needs of the growing world population, for which purpose access to and sharing of both genetic resources and technologies are essential.
>
> (CBD, 1992)

This appears to treat any claims by indigenous cultures to protection of their land, biodiversity that lives there and their way of life, as secondary to materialist utilitarian concerns about the rest of the global human population. These utilitarian ethical assumptions are made clearer in the final paragraph of the preamble and Article 1, among other places. The rest of the Convention (ibid.) sets out broad guidelines for how biodiversity should be protected (Articles 3–21), regulation of commercial access to 'genetic resources' (Article 15), technology transfer (Article 16), regulation of biotechnology (Articles 8, paragraph (g) and 19) and legal framing requirements (Article 2, 22–42). With regard to biotechnology, the Convention appears to assume that hazards from biotechnology can be predicted and contained or managed. However, difficulties in knowing what biodiversity should be preserved and how to do it are perhaps key reasons why measures that are more concrete were not agreed. (N.B. these assumptions have ethical as well as scientific components.)

Again, though admitting difficulties in predicting, to allow management, the CBD tends to assume that this is the appropriate approach to questions of biodiversity. It also tends to assume economistic utilitarianism, and participation is focused on nation states rather than citizens.

The Forest Principles

The Forest Principles (UN, 1992, emphasis added) are principles for 'the *management*, conservation and sustainable development of all types of forests'. This stated purpose of the Principles suggests largely economistic utilitarian ethical assumptions, which are echoed during the rest of the document. Indeed, the preamble, paragraph (g), puts 'economic development' before 'the maintenance of all forms of life' in sentence construction, perhaps suggesting ethical priority of the former over the latter.

The preamble, paragraph (c), states: 'Forestry issues and opportunities should be examined in a holistic and balanced manner.' The use of the term holistic suggests an epistemological assumption. The intention of the term 'balanced' is not clear; however, it could be taken to imply a broadly Aristotelian virtue ethics approach, without making particularly clear what the extremes are or what the balance should be.

The first two principles have broadly similar epistemological, ethical and policy-making assumptions to the Rio Declaration. One variation is Principle 2b that suggests forests fulfil 'spiritual needs'. Principle 3c adds 'integrated and comprehensive' as epistemological suggestions.

Principle 5a makes suggestions about how 'indigenous people' can be allowed to maintain their culture, presumably within existing forests. However, the principle appears to make the ethical assumptions that these 'indigenous people' must 'perform economic activities', and property rights are required even if these are in tension with these indigenous cultures. Principle 5b calls for the full participation of women in decisions related to forests. Principle 6 details the various benefits forests offer to humans so these can be taken into account in (economic?) decisions. Principles 7 and 9–15 outline the context in which it is suggested forest (utilitarian) *management* processes will need to operate to be successful. These principles have similar epistemological and ethical assumptions to the Rio Declaration. One thing that the Forest Principles indicate more clearly is a tension between an ethical assumption of economistic utilitarianism and promotion of participation in policy decisions of groups who might not share those ethical assumptions.

Agenda 21

Agenda 21 (1992) is the key broad detailed text that resulted from the UNCED; although not legally binding it has been described as '"soft" law' (Robinson, 1992, v). It does appear to form a key guide to policymakers trying to implement sustainable development (cf. Reid, 1995, 186), particularly at the local level, with local Agenda 21 initiatives. The following discussion analyses in detail the chapters of Agenda 21 that raise epistemological and ethical questions or contain discussions of participation.

Chapter 1 of Agenda 21 sets the broad scene of the document and sustainable development. The second paragraph indicates an unsurprising epistemological assumption where it talks of a 'need to take a balanced and *integrated* approach to environment and development questions' (1.2, emphasis added).[5] Once again, the use of the term 'balanced' perhaps implies an Aristotelian virtue ethical assumption, though it is not clear what the balance or extremes are.

Chapter 2 of Agenda 21 discusses 'International Cooperation to Accelerate Sustainable Development in Developing Countries and Related Domestic Policies'. This is largely concerned with increasing economic growth but the emphasis is on facilitating this in 'developing countries', probably more clearly than the WCED (1987). It appears significant that this is the first substantive chapter of Agenda 21 and appears to implicitly assume that an economistic utilitarian ethic should be the foundation of sustainable development. To complicate this analysis, there are hints of other ethical frameworks, for example, discussion of 'cooperation and solidarity' (2.1) may not simply be a means of ensuring economic growth. The specific suggestions in the chapter are broadly:

- more just trade arrangements;
- making trade and environment mutually supportive;
- providing adequate financial resources to developing countries;
- encouraging economic policies conducive to sustainable development.

Note the economistic tenor of these. A closer examination will illustrate difficulties with Agenda 21. More just trade arrangements are discussed (2.5–2.17) particularly suggesting removal of terms of trade that discriminate against 'developing' countries. Agenda 21 is not clear what the call for greater justice is based on. For example, is this based on utilitarian notions, fear of conflict, some notion of justice broadly similar to the virtue of Aristotle, or a combination of such factors?

'Making trade and environment mutually supportive' (2.19–2.22) includes Agenda 21 making the contestable statement 'an open, multilateral trading system … contributes to an increase in production and incomes and to lessening demands on the environment' (2.19). The basis of this assumption is not clear and literature such as CSD (1997, paragraphs 15 and 16) and Blanke and Burdick (2005) call this assumption into question. This is not to say that all trade is bad for the environment, just to call into question whether all trade organised by particular market structures is indeed sustainable. There is nothing in the rest of the section that suggests these types of question have been addressed, nor broader questions of when trade and reduced stress to the Earth System are mutually supportive. The approach of the section is underpinned by an assumption that trade will continue in broadly the same way as the current situation, so the section is largely concerned with how obviously essential environmental regulations can be implemented, without affecting trade too much.

'Providing adequate financial resources to developing countries' (2.23–2.30) focuses around addressing debt issues, without addressing the poor advice from lenders or even requirements for loans to be spent on projects with poor returns for borrowers and which benefited industries in countries providing loans (Adams, 1995; WCED, 1987, 67–75). The suggestions appear focused on encouraging capitalist financial structures in debtor nations.

'Encouraging economic policies conducive to sustainable development' (2.31–2.40) makes further suggestions to try to encourage free market capitalism, presumably based on particular utilitarian ethical assumptions, though there is some meagre acknowledgement of tensions between this form of capitalism and sustainability (both social and environmental), without making a serious attempt to resolve these tensions.

'Combating poverty' is the topic of Chapter 3, emphasising that initiatives to address poverty need to be integrated in a way that is hugely ambitious from the viewpoint of the knowledge requirements. To illustrate, integration is suggested for initiatives to address 'greater equity in income distribution' (3.1), just trade, environmental policies that give a high priority to those resources that poor people use to provide for themselves,

> demographic issues, enhanced health care and education, the rights of women, the role of youth and of indigenous people and local communities and a democratic participation process in association with improved governance ... strengthening employment and income-generating programmes.
>
> (3.2–3.3)

This range of simultaneous policy questions sets a hugely ambitious agenda. The chapter even allows for 'food self-sufficiency' (3.8l) and the 'integration of traditional methods of production that have been shown to be environmentally sustainable' (3.8m) which those in favour of market economics and industrialism might call into question.

'Changing consumption patterns' is the subject of Chapter 4, which extends the analysis of the significance of consumption in the WCED, emphasising under consumption by many of the world's poorest (4.5) as well as excessive consumption by much of the rich segment of the world population (4.5). It emphasises the importance of achieving sustainable consumption (4.9, 4.13) in a way that has not been reflected in government action since the UNCED. It assumes that sustainable levels of consumption and stress to the Earth System can be identified (4.10e) without making clear the processes that can achieve this. Agenda 21 (4.17) suggests that sustainable consumption will be achieved by changes in technology (4.10, 4.18–4.19), changes in policy and by reinforcing 'values that encourage' it. Most of the effort since the UNCED appears to have been on technology and policy change rather than value change. With regard to policy change, Agenda 21 suggests principles for minimising waste (4.19) and makes suggestions about encouraging green consumerism, for example by eco-labelling (4.20–4.26).

Global virtue tradition would help to promote moderation (or temperance) of consumption as a virtue and greed as a vice. Greater cooperation by governments with organisations encouraging sustainable values might have been more effective than efforts to date. It appears that attempting to change consumerist values has been too difficult to reconcile with liberal notions of not promoting a vision of the good life, for governments to make many efforts in this regard. Alternatively, it may be too counter to the industrialism vision of the good life held by governments for them to embrace many initiatives that question industrialism.

Epistemological and participatory ideas are the focus of Chapter 8: 'Integrating environment and development in decision-making'. It recommends to this end (8.3) a 'broader range of public participation', that 'countries ... develop their own priorities' (8.4) 'taking account of ... linkages', to 'ensure ... coherence', and 'ensuring transparency'. The chapter (8.5) includes a hugely challenging specification for sustainable development decision-making processes, considering the scope of the issues involved:

a. Analysis should stress interactions and synergisms; a broad range of analytical methods should be encouraged so as to provide various points of view.

b. Adopting comprehensive analytical procedures for prior and simultaneous assessment of the impacts of decisions, including the impacts within and among the economic, social and environmental spheres; these procedures should extend beyond the project level to policies and programmes; analysis should also include assessment of costs, benefits and risks.

It is not clear that any tools of the form called for in paragraph 8.5 have been developed for even small projects let alone 'policies and programmes' or the huge interconnected questions that make up the global sustainable development issue. Agenda 21 does not appear to have recognised the significance of the epistemological questions raised by the WCED and appears to assume that some expert centred neo-platonic[6] 'philosopher king' (Palmer and Finlay, 2003, 16; Popper, 1966, Vol. 1) response is the correct one. Given the epistemological difficulties surrounding sustainable development, a more 'open society' (Popper, 1966) approach, such as outlined in Chapter 2, may be more appropriate.

A symptom of this Baconian approach is that Agenda 21 (8.6–8.7) suggests that comprehensive indicators[7] and national strategies may help to integrate sustainable development decision-making. It goes on (8.8) to suggest that the 'scientific community ... should intensify efforts to clarify the interactions' within sustainable development. If there have been comprehensive efforts of this type, their results are not obvious or widely known. The chapter (8.9–8.12) goes on to call for the need to consider environment and development in an integrated manner to be taught to all citizens and for techniques developed for integrated analysis to be taught widely in the education system and to policymakers. It (8.11) argues that systems to engage citizens 'should establish mechanisms for facilitating a direct exchange of information and views with the public'. These 'systems' still appear only to be at an experimental stage at the moment.

Changes to legal systems to promote integrated decision-making are the next subject of Chapter 8. Here, Agenda 21 appears to set great store by legal systems achieving sustainable development without offering obvious answers to the questions raised by the legal discussions of the WCED in Chapter 3. It is interesting to note that the legal system is suggested 'as a normative framework for economic planning and market instruments' (8.13) without a thorough discussion of the ethical basis for any legally codified economistic normative notion of sustainable development. Changes to economic systems are subsequently discussed (8.27–8.28) with internalisation of costs and market principles being promoted, without the issues highlighted with these approaches by authors such as Common *et al.* (1993), Foster (1997), O'Connor (2002) and Smith (2003, 29–51) being clearly addressed.

'Protection of the atmosphere' is the subject of Chapter 9, with the first section of the chapter specifically looking at 'addressing the uncertainties: improving the scientific basis for decision-making'. Agenda 21 states (9.6) that predictive scientific understanding of the atmosphere and human interactions with it is needed. Prediction appears to be the underlying epistemological aim of the section and chapter.

'Environmentally sound management of biotechnology' is considered in Chapter 16. Paragraphs 16.1–16.28 discuss applications of biotechnology, suggesting that biotechnology can largely 'solve all the problems of the Third World' (Ho, 1999, 34), specifically by addressing food and raw material supply (16.2–16.10), 'improving human health' (16.11–16.19) and environmental protection (16.20–16.28). The suggestions include intelligent use of existing organisms (e.g. integrated pest control, using brewing concepts to produce raw materials, waste treatment, perhaps organic agriculture and even permaculture (Mollison, 1988)), as well as creating novel organisms using recombinant DNA techniques. Unfortunately, the chapter does not distinguish between these approaches, either in descriptions of application, risk assessment or the epistemological abilities required to understand them. In discussing medical technology, Agenda 21 calls for 'research to assess the comparative social, environmental and financial costs and benefits of different technologies for basic and reproductive health care within a framework of universal safety and ethical considerations' (16.14). Agenda 21 does not make clear what 'universal safety and ethical consideration' are, should be or how they can be established, though the way costs and benefits are discussed at the beginning of the sentence does suggest an assumed universality of a particular strand in utilitarian ethical thought.

'Enhancing safety and developing international mechanisms for cooperation' and 'enabling mechanisms for the development and the environmentally sound application of biotechnology' are discussed in paragraphs 16.29–16.45. The suggestions about risk assessment of biotechnology (16.29–16.36 and 16.39c) are vague beyond building on existing methods. This is unfortunate as there is no discussion of the adequacy of existing initiatives, indicating that adequacy is assumed. It is also unfortunate given the 'faith' earlier sections of the chapter put on these 'safety' recommendations. Chapter 16 appears to be much more concerned with promoting biotechnology on the basis of assumed 'net' benefits, than assessing any risks, although any net benefits are still controversial for recombinant DNA techniques (e.g. Food Standards Agency, 2005; GM Nation, 2003). In point of fact, paragraph 16.3g admits the need to 'improve capabilities in basic and applied sciences and in the management of complex interdisciplinary research projects'. This perhaps admits limitations of knowledge for biotechnology. Indeed, as noted towards the end of Section 2.2 of this book, there is a significant amount of literature that might be interpreted as suggesting that assessing the risks of recombinant DNA technologies is problematic. Arguments in this book about the limitations of science throw further doubt on the current ability to assess the risks from techniques that perhaps increase the likelihood of horizontal gene transfer and the self-replication of any products of such DNA transfer.

The chapter then emphasises: 'The environment is threatened in all … components … and all the interactions between the components of biodiversity and their sustaining habitats and ecosystems' (16.20). The emphasis on interactions is followed up by the suggestion (16.29) to consider interactions in discussions of risk assessment of biotechnology. This is a suggestion that has been formally implemented (e.g. EU, 2001a); however, it does not appear to have been thoroughly applied (e.g. ACRE, 2006), probably because of epistemological difficulties in doing so.

This is followed by calls for the 'widest possible public participation and taking account of ethical considerations' 'on principles to be applied on risk assessment and management' (16.30) without discussing what are to be considered 'valid' forms of ethics in detail. Only vague suggestions about principles for public participation are described and it is not established that 'management' of the Earth System is possible (cf. Jamieson, 1992, 142–6).

Suggestions for participation of 'major groups' are discussed in Chapters 23–34 of Agenda 21, though citizens who do not fall into those groups appear only to have input via local authorities. Let us consider some of the suggestions for participation now. Chapter 23 discusses 'strengthening the role of major groups'. These groups are:

- women;
- children and youth;
- indigenous people;
- non-governmental organisations (NGOs);
- local authorities;
- workers and their trade unions;
- business and industry;
- scientific and technological community;
- farmers.

'The need for new forms of participation has emerged' (23.2) discusses the logic of the need for participation, without outlining principles for how participation should happen. Chapter 8 of this book will explore how this might be fleshed out.

Given the epistemological focus of this book, let us note the statement that 'indigenous people' have 'a *holistic* traditional scientific knowledge' (26.1, emphasis added) and the sustainability of many of those societies. This appears to be an area little studied in a way that has had significant policy impact. It is also illuminating to contrast this with the effects of reductive Western science and technology, particularly when Agenda 21 appears to want to impose utilitarian (Baconian?) ethical ideas on indigenous people. To illustrate this ethical imposition, 'increasing the efficiency of indigenous people's resource management systems, for example, by promoting the adaptation and dissemination of suitable technological innovations' (26.5c ii).

'Strengthening the role of non-governmental organizations' is discussed in Chapter 27 of Agenda 21. It is not very clear what is meant by NGOs.[8] It appears to include environment and development NGOs, but criteria for consideration as an Agenda 21 NGO is not clear. This is a concern, given the access to policy-making and the role in implementation of sustainable development that the chapter recommends for NGOs. The potential for 'unpleasant' or at least undemocratic NGOs, particularly if they can obtain political power, is a concern that is not addressed by the chapter. Bass *et al.* (1995, 83–9) make some suggestions that may help address this concern. Local authorities' initiatives in support of Agenda 21 are outlined (28); in particular, how local authorities can implement practical measures, facilitate local participation and promote sustainable development. However, little specific advice is given on how participation should be encouraged or institutionalised, even if there is a little more than in the WCED.

A reformist approach to the role of business and industry to facilitate reducing stress to the Earth System is promoted, rather than the radical change called for by the WCED (1987, 213). This was perhaps based on the assumption that research into the 'internalization of environmental costs into accounting and pricing mechanisms' (30.9) would be adequate to ensure sustainable development. Research in this area has proved contentious for many reasons (Ekins, 2003, 150–3); difficulties in knowing the level of stress the Earth System will stand mean that these questions may never be satisfactorily resolved. Agenda 21 (30.18) calls for entrepreneurs to adopt 'stewardship' and 'implement sustainable development policies'. The use of the term stewardship is not discussed, but may be interpreted as a call for a virtue ethic approach (Barry, 1999) including balancing profit against reducing stress to the Earth System.

The discussion of how the 'scientific and technological community' can facilitate sustainable development states (31.1) that greater interdisciplinary work needs to be encouraged along with greater listening to the general public about how science and technology should develop for the benefit of society (similarly at various points throughout Chapters 31 and 35 of Agenda 21). The same paragraph also emphasises that 'the independence of the scientific and technological community to investigate and publish without restriction and to exchange their findings freely must be assured' (31.1) before going on to emphasise that science cannot be assumed to provide final answers or certainty. Paragraph 31.2 asserts that policymakers believe that they should set the policy frameworks for science for sustainability, which appears in tension with the previous quotation (cf. Shackley and Wynne, 1995). Agenda 21 does not appear to engage with the question of whether this limits the openness, and thus problem-solving capabilities, of science for sustainability.

This discussion raises questions such as how to negotiate questions of the limits that society should put on science and what guidance there should be to science from society. It seems clear that societies have the obligation to prohibit scientific experiment, such as on live humans without informed consent, that go beyond accepted behaviour in that society. The alternative appears to turn experiment into a neo-religious totalising ideology. The broader question of guidance to science from society is probably even more complex, other than to say that it is probably unavoidable, if only by funding decisions. However, if as Shackley and Wynne (1995) suggest, the answers policymakers want limit the answers that scientists look for and provide, then this could significantly limit the potential effectiveness of science at addressing unsustainable development from an 'open society' (Popper, 1966) viewpoint. It is possible that Chapter 31 of Agenda 21 makes the assumption that policymakers, because of representative democratic legitimacy, guide science beyond funding decisions and other 'unavoidable' constraints. However, advocates of post-normal science (Ravetz and Funtowicz, 1999) among others (e.g. Wynne, 1996) suggest that a more open (Popper, 1966) approach, perhaps based in deliberative or discursive democratic (Dryzek, 2000, v–vi) justifications, may be more 'effective'. Something of these issues will be picked up in Chapter 8.

Agenda 21 suggests that ethics could be addressed by 'strengthening and establishing national advisory groups on environmental and developmental ethics, in order to develop a common value framework between the scientific and technological community and society as a whole, and promote continuous dialogue' (31.10). It is unclear as to whether specific study of the ethics of environment, development, science and technology or a broader study of the ethics of environment and development is being called for. It is also important to note that Agenda 21 sees addressing these questions in a structured manner as an option. Given the significance of applied ethics for the WCED, and to a lesser extent in Agenda 21, it is surprising that there is no direct discussion of the theoretical basis for any applied ethics, particularly given relevant literature such as Engel and Engel (1990) and IUCN/UNEP/WWF (1991). Similarly, there is no discussion of how ethical theory insights might be brought to bear to support sustainable development. Agenda 21 (23.1) states that 'critical to the effective implementation … of Agenda 21 will be the commitment and genuine involvement of all social groups'. It is then surprising that there is no discussion of how implicit support for sustainable development by the 'global virtue tradition', including the world religions, might be encouraged to provide practical support – particularly as this had already been indicated in Engel and Engel (1990).

Agenda 21 appears to make no effort to consider a role for religious groups in promoting sustainable development, unless they are classified as NGOs. Given the moral authority that religious groups command for many people, as well as the political power and the on-the-ground facilitation abilities of many religions (Palmer and Finlay, 2003), this appears a little short sighted. The depth of ethical theory that is part of many religions is at least one reason why treating religions as different from 'NGOs' appears wise. Any exclusion would be particularly unfortunate given the considerable encouragement and practical action for sustainable development that the world religions have given and the huge effects they could have (cf. Palmer and Finlay, 2003). One might ask how will sustainable development be turned into a global ethic without the active cooperation of the world religions?

Overall, there is little indication of how the limitations in theories of knowledge highlighted in this book should be addressed, nor of a willingness to tackle such issues, even though they have been recognised to some extent. As outlined above, the situation with ethical questions is a little better.

The first sentence of Agenda 21's chapter specifically on science suggests a utilitarian instrumental ethical assumption towards science and the Earth System: 'This chapter focuses on the role and the use of the sciences in support-ing the prudent management of the environment and development' (35.1). The use of the word 'prudent' is interesting; it is not clear whether it is meant in the sense of the virtue of prudence, e.g. Aquinas, or the perhaps more limited utilitar-ian sense (Rosen, 2003, 56, 77–8, 119, 121, 126–8).[9] However, given the context of the rest of the sentence, a more utilitarian interpretation appears more likely, specifically, the use of the term management and the assumption that manage-ment is possible (cf. Jamieson, 1992).

It is then noted that the 'Earth system' is made up of interlocked systems. It suggests that science can provide 'a more accurate estimate ... of the carrying capacity of the planet Earth and of its resilience under the many stresses placed upon it by human activities' (35.2). It should be clear that this is a Baconian assumption, both (1) ethically in the sense of wanting to use the Earth in a utilitarian and economistic sense – to its limits, plus (2) assuming that these limits can be known before they are crossed. From the discussion of abrupt climate change policy responses in Chapter 2 (e.g. POST, 2005) it should be clear this Baconian approach is still almost exclusively the approach of policy. The paragraph proceeds to suggest that this can be achieved with 'technologi-cal' means without addressing the deeper epistemological issues raised by this book. Indeed, the following paragraph alludes to the deeper epistemological difficulties highlighted by this book where it implies that the Earth System contains 'complex systems that are not yet fully understood and whose con-sequences of disturbances cannot yet be predicted' (35.3, see also 35.5, 35.6b, 35.6c). It suggests the 'precautionary approach' as one possible resolution to this situation but does not go significantly beyond this.

Suggestions for 'education, public awareness and training' to encourage what is assumed to be a more 'sustainable epistemology' include that 'cross-disciplinary courses could be made available to all students' (36.5i). The Agenda goes on to say that 'countries ... could strengthen or establish national or regional centres of excellence in interdisciplinary research and education in environmental and developmental sciences, law and the management of spe-cific environmental problems' (36.5j). This is a laudable aim and to an extent reasonable; however, given Jamieson (1992, 142–6), it is questionable how sustainable the epistemological and ethical assumptions 'management' rests on are. This chapter of Agenda 21 makes quite a specific 'open' suggestion about how participation in decision-making should take place: 'At the national and local levels, public and scholastic forums should discuss environmental and development issues, and suggest sustainable alternatives to policy mak-ers' (36.5k). The chapter also argues that 'programmes at a post-graduate level should include specific courses aiming at the further training of decision mak-ers' (36.5l). This does not make clear whether courses should simply educate 'decision makers' in the facts of sustainable development or engage them with broader questions, such as whether conventional ways of making decisions are adequate for sustainable development.

The chapter proceeds to discuss increasing public awareness: 'The objective is to promote broad public awareness as an essential part of a global education effort to strengthen attitudes, values and actions which are compatible with sustainable development' (36.9). This statement appears a little premature as neither the WCED (1987), Agenda 21 nor the other official documents that came out of the UNCED make clear what 'attitudes, values and actions which are compatible with sustainable development' are. Perhaps the most concrete result in that regard is that these documents make clear what social trends of action are unsustainable, in particular increased stresses to the Earth System and high levels of poverty. Clear discussions of sustainable attitudes and values are not easy to identify in these documents, if they exist. The mention of values in Agenda 21 are typically financial values or 'personally held values', which suggests that Agenda 21 makes an assumption that values do not need to be arrived at in an inter-subjective fashion. The level of agreement among global virtue traditions about possible 'sustainable' values suggests that a subjective assumption may be too simplistic. It may be that a large majority of the population of the world could indeed agree on sustainable values, with a significant minority disagreeing with these and among themselves but nonetheless the unsustainable values of conventional economics and consumerism are promoted and even imposed by political elites. Agenda 21 continues its discussions of increasing public awareness by making practical suggestions (36.10). Importantly, the first of these is that raising awareness should be by involvement in policy decisions.

Agenda 21 makes various suggestions about environment and development training: 'Training programmes should promote a greater awareness of environment and development issues as a two-way learning process' (36.12). This echoes earlier emphasis on sustainable development being participative in quite a concrete way. The section emphasises the need for training at all levels from job-specific to managerial, professional and policy-making. This appears to have been resisted by some groups such as economists that are very important for questions of sustainable development (Common, 2003). Resistance of economists to considering ecological questions may be based on reasons such as an implicit understanding of the difficulties that economics has in 'internalising externalities' and that ecological science questions the materialist utilitarian normative framework of much economics.

'Information for decision-making' (40) discusses knowledge for sustainability, e.g. 'bridging the data gap' and 'improving information availability'. The section on deficiencies in data is motivated by such gaps 'seriously impairing the capacities of countries to make informed decisions concerning environment and development' (40.2). As well as simply informing decisions, the suggestions in the chapter also imply a Baconian desire to understand nature in a predictive sense, in order to control it to fulfil human physical needs and wants; in particular, the way in which the concept of management is used (cf. Jamieson, 1992, 142–6). Paragraph 40.22 focuses on the 'production of information usable for decision-making'; however, this is more concerned with providing existing information in forms more suited to decision-making, than addressing the types of epistemological issue raised in this book.

Overall, Agenda 21 indicates that participation should be used for reasons of openness (Popper, 1966) as well as acquiescence to decisions. The ethics favours the utilitarianism typical of the documents already discussed, if perhaps raising more questions about this than the WCED. Similarly, the epistemology tends to assume prediction while raising significant questions about the possibility of this.

Reactions to the UNCED

In order to see particularly if existing reactions to the UNCED are similar to the analysis of this book, let us consider the following published reactions. Benton among others is scathing about the practical benefits of the UNCED: 'The agreements reached contain few legally binding targets, and the vast division of interest between different nation states and regions led to a reduction of much of the text to the status of pious rhetoric' (Benton, 1999, 223).

Mebratu suggests that the preparations for the UNCED may have been more important than the results of the conference itself. In particular, the preparation of national reports 'covering current national environmental and developmental aspects and drawing up an action plan for promoting sustainable development within the national context' (Mebratu, 1998, 502). In particular because preparation of these reports 'in most countries, involved participation of major stakeholders down to the grassroots level. This process took the concept of sustainable development to every corner of the world' (ibid.).

OECD (2001, 111–12) implies that in spite of vagueness, the UNCED was important in outlining international principles around which action and participation can coalesce.

Overall, the UNCED documents tend to make implicit economistic utilitarian ethical assumptions, but ethics is barely explicitly discussed. Baconian predict and control epistemological assumptions are common, though again typically implicit. The suggestions for participation are an improvement on the WCED, though not particularly comprehensive, necessarily 'open' (i.e. they often assume that the 'elite' knows best), nor has implementation been, shall we say, universal.

Earth Summit+5

Five years after the UNCED, the UN conducted a major review of progress in the implementation of Agenda 21. Their overall conclusions were:

> Positive: growth in world population is slowing, food production is rising, the
> majority of people are living longer and healthier lives, and environmental
> quality in some regions is improving.

Negative: the growing scarcity of fresh water, loss of productive agricultural land and downward spiral of poverty for many threaten to undermine these gains and cause collapse of local economies.

Overall: global catastrophe is not imminent, but business-as-usual is not likely to result in sustainable development – that is, a desirable balance of economic growth, equitable human development and healthy, productive ecosystems.

(Critical Trends, UN, 1997)

The source that appears to be given is a document by the CSD (1997 paragraph 15). If the sentence from paragraph 15 had been quoted it would have read: 'Global catastrophe does not *appear* to be imminent' (ibid., emphasis added). Thus to say so definitely that 'global catastrophe is not imminent' is not simply based on the reference given, and does not appear to take into account well publicised research such as Rahmstorf (1994, 1995).

The CSD (1997, paragraph 12) does suggest that nuclear war, 'fossil fuel exhaustion', population pressures and industrial pollution have become less of a concern, in part because of policy interventions. However, it notes that new issues of deep concern have been brought to the fore, suggesting the importance of limits to current epistemology. The CSD (ibid.) suggests the 'overall situation is more complicated, more surprising and, generally, more positive than anticipated' than that described by Meadows *et al.* (1972) and similar. The CSD then highlights uncertainty and perhaps suggests that development of the idea of 'scenarios' is an admission that Baconian prediction and control of the Earth System is currently impossible. They state that there are trends that threaten 'catastrophic collapse of local economies ... these threats are real and near-term; they already affect millions of people' (CSD, 1997, paragraph 14). Thus, the UN (1997) document's exclusions of discussion of catastrophe from sustainable development debate would appear to have very real consequences for at least some people. The CSD (1997, paragraphs 15 and 16) calls into question whether economic growth will necessarily lead to a better life for all. The introduction concludes by stating that 'history shows that many negative trends can be reversed given agreement on clear objectives' (ibid., paragraph 14). For many of the key issues of sustainable development, climate change being a good example, 'agreement on clear objectives' has not been possible for reasons including uncertainty in the science of the issues. If agreement on clear objectives cannot be reached for the network of issues that cause unsustainable development because of epistemological difficulties, then we perhaps need to examine assumptions that mean clear objectives are needed for political action. Baconian prediction and control plus economistic utilitarianism are key assumptions that should be reconsidered.

Further illustrating the significance of epistemological difficulties for policy, the CSD (ibid., paragraph 4) highlights that policy integration has been difficult to implement, particularly because of difficulties in trading off conflicting objectives. The same paragraph calls for better 'means' of addressing these decision-making difficulties, suggesting a need for means to 'prioritize measures according to severity of the problem and the time required for policy to take effect' (ibid.). Chapter 2 suggests that prioritising, by employing utilitarian numerical methods of assessing severity, is and will remain difficult. A morphological approach such as Charlesworth (1998) (cf. Bostrom, 2002) may better help to facilitate democratic debate about key priorities for global governance. Chapter 2 also suggests that determining the time when policy needs to be applied to achieve the required results is also deeply problematic, given the hundreds of years of inertia in the climate system, as one component of the Earth System. After unpacking these issues, it appears that the CSD (1997, paragraphs 4 and 6) makes Baconian predict and control assumptions. This indicates the importance of the epistemological issues that this book draws out. The CSD (ibid., paragraph 4) suggests that unpacking the ethical assumptions surrounding sustainable development questions may improve debate about how to 'reconcile different interests'. It should be noted that talk of 'interests' might indicate a utilitarian assumption, so a more plural and effective approach might be to talk of respecting and addressing different ethical assumptions.

The CSD (ibid., paragraph 5) introduces the concept of 'pressure-state-response' as a 'widely accepted' concept for use in integrated environmental assessment. The pressure-state-response concept appears to be very useful as a means of visualising and prioritising sustainable development issues, even if it does not resolve the epistemological issues highlighted in this book.[10]

The key recommendations of the CSD are:

- increased investment in ... basic education and health care;
- the encouragement of clean and efficient technologies;
- pricing reform which begins to internalise ... social and environmental costs.

(Ibid., paragraphs 215–17)

These are laudable aims, but the second and third arguably assume that Baconian predict and control epistemology will be adequate to achieve sustainable development. This is despite the CSD (ibid., paragraph 218) noting that historically 'efficiency gains ... have been more than offset by the volume of economic growth'; this is often known as the rebound effect (Sorrell, 2007). The last recommendation perhaps also assumes that economistic utilitarianism will be adequate to achieve sustainable development, even though work such as Common *et al.* (1993) had already called into question the effectiveness, in practice, of initiatives to internalise environmental costs into consumer prices. Indeed, the CSD (1997, paragraph 217) highlights the political problems of introducing 'new taxes and the phase-out of subsidies'.

Overall, the CSD (1997) and the UN (1997) suggest that some progress had been made since the UNCED but for many issues rhetoric had and remained much more forthcoming than action. Perhaps the area where there had been the most significant change was in participation. The following was offered as an indication of the level of participation, even if the quality of any participation is not clear: '150 countries have established national councils on sustainable development or similar bodies ... Over 1,800 cities and towns have drawn up a local Agenda 21 based on the Rio document' (UN, 1997).

WSSD Johannesburg in 2002

The World Summit on Sustainable Development (WSSD) was held in Johannesburg in 2002. The brochure for the summit (UN, 2001) echoes many of the themes of earlier documents. The foreword makes clear that progress in achieving sustainable development had not been as effective as the UN Secretary General had hoped. He called for the summit to be 'an opportunity to rejuvenate the quest to build a more sustainable future' (ibid., 1). It is interesting to note the UN Secretary General concludes by calling 'to put in place a new ethic of global conservation and stewardship' (ibid.) (cf. Attfield, 1994, particularly 13–62; Barry, 1999).

The *Report of the World Summit on Sustainable Development* (UN, 2002) opens with a 'political declaration'; in the first point of this 'the representatives of the peoples of the world ... reaffirm our commitment to sustainable development' (ibid., 1). In the second, it states: 'We commit ourselves to building a humane, equitable and caring global society, cognizant of the need for human dignity for all' (UN, 2001, 1). This sentence suggests a set of largely virtue ethical assumptions, particularly in the use of the term caring. Points 3 to 7 of the declaration proceed to indicate a sense of moral imperative for sustainable development in terms more of common good than individual good; similar sentiments appear in other places in the declaration. Points 11 to 15 outline the environment and development challenges that the world faces, ending with an intriguing use of a Biblical allusion, to the pivotal importance of charity or love:

> 15. We risk the entrenchment of ... global disparities and unless we act in
> a manner that fundamentally changes their lives the poor of the world may
> lose confidence in their representatives and the democratic systems to which
> we remain committed, seeing their representatives as nothing more than
> sounding brass or tinkling cymbals.
> (UN, 2002, 3; cf. 1 Corinthians 13:1 King James Version)

This could be seen as a call for a change from the current economistic utilitarian ethical assumption, that appears to drive the increase in disparity between rich and poor, to a neo-Christian virtue ethic not dissimilar to that articulated by Aquinas, as 'sounding brass or tinkling cymbals' refers to those without 'love' or 'charity'. Palmer and Finlay (2003) plus Connelly (2006, 70) suggest that seeing some notion of love or charity as a virtue may be acceptable to most of the 'global virtue tradition'. Virtue language appears in other parts of the declaration.

The report presents a plan intended to speed progress towards sustainable development, which is worth analysing. The notion of good governance, which had not received prominent treatment in UN sustainable development literature already discussed, is emphasised early on in the plan (UN, 2002, 8). Given the lack of systematic consideration of ethics and sustainable development in prominent UN literature on sustainable development, the following quotation is a little perplexing: 'We acknowledge the importance of ethics for sustainable development and, therefore, emphasize the need to consider ethics in the implementation of Agenda 21' (ibid., 9). Ethics of sustainable development is identified as an issue 'to be considered' (ibid., 103) implicitly for research in the 'summary of the partnership plenary meetings' (ibid., 87), but this does not give ethics the priority the earlier quotation (ibid., 9) suggests.

The recommendations for 'changing unsustainable patterns of consumption and production' (ibid., 13) are broadly similar to the policy discourse documents already analysed. They assume the epistemological issues that surround industrialism can be solved. This is in spite of the difficulties already experienced by, for example, the EU eco-label scheme as discussed in the next chapter. Indeed, the brief proposals about addressing levels of consumption generally are as vague as earlier documents;[11] presumably, because it was not diplomatically acceptable to grasp the nettle of reducing consumption or because of materialist utilitarian ethical assumptions. This is despite the fact that the global virtue tradition typically sees moderating consumption as a good in itself for individual humans and societies, let alone for the sake of the Earth System. Lack of governmental action to reduce consumption appears to assume that reducing stress to the Earth System by increasing efficiency of technology will be sufficient to achieve sustainable development. This is in tension with the analysis of the CSD (1997, paragraph 218) on the rebound effect noted earlier. Indeed the next section of the report discusses 'protecting and managing the natural resource base of economic and social development' (UN, 2002, 20) and starts with 'human activities are having an increasing impact on the integrity of ecosystems that provide essential resources and services for human well-being and economic activities' (ibid.). This suggests that more than greater efficiency will be needed to reduce stress to the Earth System to sustainable levels, even without the epistemological questions raised by this book.

Discussion of tourism includes the phrase 'non-consumptive tourism' (ibid., 33). This is perplexing as all tourism other than local cycle and walking tours[12] consumes at least the energy required for transport. The UN (ibid.) refers to a 'Global Code of Ethics for Tourism as adopted by the UN World Tourism Organization' (UNWTO). This code of ethics (UNWTO, 2001) is largely focused on a laudable, more equitable distribution of material wealth from tourism and the minimization of cultural and ecological harm of tourism, rather than a broader consideration of if and how tourism can reflect the ethical assumptions of local populations. There is though a degree of pluralism to the code of ethics: utilitarian, rights and virtue ethics ideas and language are all used, even if there is no discussion of the relationship between them. There is a tendency to favour economic utilitarianism and the rights of individuals to be tourists; however, discussion of moderation of use of tourist facilities (e.g. ibid., Article 3, paragraph 4) does have a virtue character. It is interesting to note that page 3 of the UNWTO lists various international agreements relevant to tourism, including the CBD (1992), but does not note the significance of tourism to the UNFCCC (1992).

Overall, there is little consideration of ethics, uncertainty and epistemology by the report of the WSSD. Discussions of participation tend to be aspirational rather than reporting success or practical.

Seyfang (2003) suggests reactions to the WSSD included anger and disappointment, particularly at the lack of political will to turn good intentions into action, and especially with regard to 'consumption patterns in the north, [and] international trade'. Reasons for lack of political will to address sustainable development may well include uncertainty about the consequences of human stress to the Earth System and that economistic utilitarian ethical assumptions make it difficult to take action to address over-consumption, without clear evidence of short-term harm (cf. Jamieson, 1992; Padilla, 2004).

The WSSD was characterised by much talking but little listening, fatigue and little clear idea what the purpose of the event was, according to Wapner (2003, 1–3). He notes (ibid., 3) significant concrete targets, but lack of plans about how to achieve them. With significance for reconciling tensions between utilitarian and virtue ethics, he suggests that the partnerships organised at the WSSD were hopeful, that is unless they 'convert public-spirited initiatives into merely commercial endeavors' (ibid., 4). Relatedly, Wapner (ibid., 5–6) argues that many in the 'North', particularly the US, were keener advocates of economic globalization as compatible with sustainable development than at the UNCED. He importantly notes (ibid., 5), in a change from the UNCED, that 'much of the South is increasingly concerned with environmental issues', particularly in order to provide for 'the poor'. Significantly from the viewpoint of comparing legal and deontological approaches, he (ibid., 6–8) argues that although there is more environmental legislation and bureaucracy than there was during the UNCED, overall the Earth System was more stressed in 2002 than in 1992. He attributes this primarily to a change of attitude by the US and the lack of seriousness with which the international community treats environmental questions in practice (particularly funding) in comparison with trade questions. Wapner (ibid., 8–10) concludes by calling into question the value of the term sustainable development as perhaps suggesting an overambitious agenda. However, as he himself argues, there is a need to consider environmental and social injustice issues in an integrated way, particularly as the causes of both are often similar. Thus, in tellingly virtue language, Wapner (ibid., 10) notes 'bad governance, violent conflict ... wasteful and unmindful affluence, inappropriate technology, accelerated population growth and worldviews that see nature as a realm separate from human life to be forever exploited in the name of satisfying human desires'.

Assessing UN sustainable development initiatives

The UN has been pivotal in developing and taking forward the idea of sustainable development. Its reports inform decisions and it organises the global meetings to facilitate turning sustainable development rhetoric into plans. Lack of speed in turning rhetoric into reality appears to be more down to the choices of nations rather than lack of effort by the UN. That Rio+20 was even less inspiring or effective than the WSSD (Adelman, 2013) reinforces this. However, lack of substantial efforts by the UN to address questions of ethics, epistemology, policy-making under condition of uncertainty and participation may also be key factors in slow progress. Let us now consider something of the efforts of the European Union to move towards sustainable development, as these have perhaps been the largest concerted effort so far.

4.3 EU sustainable development strategies

The EU is perhaps the largest economy with some diversity in approaches to environment and development questions that has seriously endeavoured to reduce stress to the Earth System. EU initiatives on environment and development often refer to sustainable development, and have done so for some time; some of these will be discussed in the next chapter. However, it was only in 2001 that an EU wide strategy was proposed.[13] A discussion of this 2001 strategy and the 2006 strategy in this section will be informative in respect of applying the concept of sustainable development to policy-making without discussing hundreds of national approaches and myriad local Agenda 21 initiatives.

2001 EU sustainable development strategy

The specific origins of the 2001 EU strategy for sustainable development were:

> At its meeting in Helsinki in December 1999 the European Council invited the European Commission 'to prepare a proposal for a long-term strategy dovetailing policies for economically, socially and ecologically sustainable development' … [as] part of the EU preparations for [the WSSD].
>
> (EU, 2001b, 2)

The 'vision' (ibid.) of sustainable development that the EU offers had to have the environmental component 'tacked' back on to the social and economic components (ibid.). A key practical component of this vision is 'environmentally-friendly technologies' to decouple 'environmental degradation and resource consumption from economic and social development' (ibid.). However, the strategy does not make clear how this will be achieved, so this appears to be a leap of faith rather than a clear 'management' plan. The strategy focuses 'on a small number of problems which pose severe or irreversible threats' (ibid., 3).[14] These being identified as climate change, poverty, an aging population, biodiversity loss, increased waste, soil degradation, congestion and that: 'Severe threats to public health are posed by new *antibiotic-resistant strains of some diseases* and, potentially, the *longer-term effects* of the many *hazardous chemicals* currently in everyday use; threats to *food safety* are of increasing concern' (ibid., 4, emphasis in original).

The EU proceeds to outline the key reasons it perceives for lack of success in addressing these issues:

> Attempts have been made at many levels of government and society to address them. Initiatives such as local Agenda 21 have proved to be an effective means of building a consensus for change at local level. However, these efforts have so far had only limited success due to the difficulty in changing established policies and patterns of behaviour, and in bringing the responses together in a co-ordinated way.
>
> (Ibid.)

Thus, the key issues are structures (established policies) in which people operate, the difficulty of changing these in a way that promotes sustainable development and 'patterns of behaviour'. The phrase 'patterns of behaviour' is quite reminiscent of Aristotelian virtue ethics, which are about developing patterns of good behaviour. This and 'green' literature such as Connelly (2006), Sandler and Cafaro (2005), van Wensveen (2000), Benson (2000, 67–83), Hursthouse (2000), Barry (1999), Dobson (1998, 236–7, 262) and O'Neill (1993) and the rest of the 'global virtue tradition' suggest that a virtue approach may be effective at facilitating and encouraging sustainable patterns of behaviour. However, if 'established policies' or ethical assumptions on which policy-making are based encourage 'unsustainable' 'vices', such as greed, then there are likely to be tensions between policies and any efforts to facilitate 'sustainable virtues' (cf. Sandler and Cafaro, 2005). If wanton consumption and greed are unsustainable vices then to the extent that policy-making is based on promotion of wanton consumption and greed, policy is likely to promote unsustainable development.

Conventional economics, typically used as perhaps the key foundation of most policy-making, may make something close to these assumptions. Direct discussion of the ethical underpinnings of conventional economics is rare; however, Keynes (1931, 372) provides an eloquent description of the ethical (and theological?) assumptions of economic practice:

> For at least another hundred years we must pretend to ourselves and to every one that fair is foul and foul is fair; for foul is useful and fair is not. Avarice and usury and precaution must be our gods for a little longer still.

In defence of Keynes, if the above is seen in context, it is clear that Keynes is acutely aware of the problems of greed and other vices; he advocates economic growth to provide for human needs, not wanton consumption. He may well have been horrified to see the way his ideas have been used to help produce the current economic system, particularly the difference in wealth between the richest and poorest in the world. More thought by Keynes about how to ensure that avarice would become accepted as foul again after 100 years might have been worthwhile.

Korten (1996, 74–5) argues that the ideas of Adam Smith have similarly been 'betrayed'. To the extent that policymakers assume that economic cost–benefit analysis is the preferred way to make policy, which Smith (2003, 29–51) argues they often do, this might be argued to be based on some form of collective avarice or greed, which 'spills over' into individual behaviour.[15] Thus, it may be that the assumptions of policy-making need to change in order to promote sustainable patterns of behaviour. As noted in Section 2.4, the global virtue tradition does see greed as a vice and does promote moderation of desire for material possessions (or temperance) as a virtue. This suggests that if policy-making were to assume greed and wanton consumption as bad rather than good, this could be more democratically popular than is typically assumed. Problems would come especially if governments promote sustainable virtues when this is in tension or even in contradiction with their own policy-making assumptions, and the actions of political leaders and civil servants. Problems would also come if people who live by greed and wanton consumption are seen to unjustly 'free ride' (Jasay, 1989) on 'virtuous' people who moderate their consumption and seek the common good rather than individual wealth. Hence, any change to 'sustainable virtue' policy assumptions would probably be effective to the extent that it included all nations.

The EU proceeds to echo something of these sentiments (EU, 2001b, 4–5), their summary being: 'Tackling these unsustainable trends and achieving the vision offered by sustainable development requires *urgent action*; committed and farsighted *political leadership*; *a new approach to policymaking*; widespread *participation*; and *international responsibility*' (ibid., 4, emphasis in original).

Their call for urgent action is based in the inertia in the Earth System, society and policy decisions. That is, once 'capital' is invested in particular ways of doing things, it is often difficult to make changes; also it can take decades or centuries for the results of stress to the Earth System to be seen. Political leadership is advocated for some notion of common good: '*Political leadership is essential* ... Changes to policy must be made in a fair and balanced way, but *narrow sectional interests must not be allowed to prevail* over the well-being of society as a whole' (ibid., 4–5, emphasis in original). The use of the term 'interests' here is perhaps important, as it could imply a criticism of self-interest or greed. However, the new approach to policy-making they advocate (ibid., 5) does not reflect this, beyond putting responsibility on 'citizens and businesses'. Instead, it focuses on better coordination of policy. It is not clear whether this was a deliberate decision or a lack of 'vision'. In arguably virtue terms, the EU (ibid., emphasis in original) states it should be:

> A *responsible partner in a globalised world* ... [particularly] ... *by putting its own house in order* ... As EU production and consumption have impacts beyond our borders, we must also ensure that all our policies help prospects for sustainable development at a global level.

The strategy goes on to make proposals that are more detailed. The first of these is around improving 'policy coherence' (ibid., 6); particularly by more comprehensive assessments of the full effects of policies on the environment, society and the economy. In this, they identify uncertainty of outcomes of human actions as a key question. Their response to this lack of certainty is the

> precautionary principle, lack of knowledge must not become an excuse for lack of action or for ill-considered action. Risk and uncertainty are a part of life. The role of science and research is to help identify the nature of the risks and uncertainties we face, so as to provide a basis for solutions and political decisions. Policy makers have a responsibility to manage risk effectively, and to explain its nature and extent clearly to the public.
>
> (Ibid., 6)

Their characterisation of 'science and research' is quite reasonable. However, although it is ultimately in some sense policymakers who make decisions about socially decided risks, these decisions need not be of the perhaps implicitly utilitarian management variety – a virtue-based stewardship approach is an alternative. As participation is such a key part of sustainable development, it is unfortunate that public involvement is envisaged to be only as passive receivers of information; this is not in the spirit of previously discussed UN sustainable development literature. For such important issues, which are of genuine concern to many people, some vision of genuine open participation would appear better. The EU proceeds to highlight particular areas, such as subsidies for agriculture, where greater policy coherence is required. Indeed, they highlight removing subsidies for unsustainable activities as the key way of 'getting prices right' (ibid., 7).

The next proposal discussed in some detail is 'invest in science and technology for the future'. Here, the EU states: 'Without these investments, adjustment to sustainable development will have to happen much more through changes in our consumption patterns' (ibid.). Investment in developing technologies that cause less stress to the Earth System while providing equivalent function is worthwhile. However, the above quotation appears to assume humans can know the level of stress the Earth System will withstand, before it alters radically, which was called into question in Chapter 2. If we cannot know what stress the Earth System will withstand, a better (more rational?) response may be to invest in more sustainable technology and reduce over-consumption with equal vigour.

The EU devotes quite a long section to 'improve communication and mobilise citizens and business' as their main discussion of the participation component of sustainable development. First, they note citizens' distrust of policymakers and their scientific advisers because these are perceived to be 'driven more by narrow sectional interests than the wider interests of society' (ibid., 8). Their response: 'An open policy process ... allows any necessary trade-offs between competing interests to be clearly identified, and decisions taken in a transparent way' (ibid.). Popper (1966) suggests that openness could go beyond transparency of trade-offs.

The EU argues that greater transparency 'may lengthen the time taken to prepare a policy proposal, but should improve the quality of regulation and accelerate its implementation. The views of those from outside the Union should also be sought' (EU, 2001b, 8). They proceed to argue that sustainable development will need citizens to feel they can make a difference through their own actions as well as openness of policy-making. For the strategy, the ability to make a difference is to be encouraged through continuing local Agenda 21 initiatives and developing more effective initiatives in the education system to foster '*a sense of individual and collective responsibility*, and thereby encouraging changes in behaviour' (ibid., emphasis in original) – an implicit call for moderation. The section concludes with suggestions to encourage corporate social responsibility, noting proposals for making EU policy-making more open, and a reiteration of calls for education systems to 'help develop wider understanding of sustainable development' (ibid., 9). Lack of more concrete proposals for participation by citizens, particularly in policy-making, is unfortunate given the importance of this in sustainable development literature and the lack of trust by citizens in policymakers (for many, specifically of the EU).

Discussion moves on to particular targets based on the 'policy principles' (ibid.) already described. The proposals are admirable but it is far from clear that the proposals will adequately address the issues identified by the EU, particularly given the epistemological issues suggested in this book. The document spends a significant amount of time considering how the strategy will be implemented and reviewed in the context of the EU as an organisation.

Overall, it is not clear how the strategy will meet the challenges of sustainable development it identifies. Its ethical and epistemological assumptions are unclear and inadequate to address the issues it identifies: it appears in favour of predictive epistemology; and economistic utilitarianism tends to be the favoured ethical response. Discussions of participation indicate that participation is seen as important to sustainable development; however, proposals tend to be about informing citizens of reasons for decisions rather than encouraging citizens to become involved in deliberations.

2006 EU sustainable development strategy

The 2006 EU sustainable development strategy starts by paraphrasing the WCED (1987) 'definition' of sustainable development. It then states that sustainable development

> is an overarching objective of the European Union ... It is about safeguarding the earth's capacity to support life in all its diversity and is based on the principles of democracy, gender equality, solidarity, the rule of law and respect for fundamental rights, including freedom and equal opportunities for all. It aims at the continuous improvement of the quality of life and wellbeing on Earth for present and future generations.
>
> (EU, 2006, 2)

Thus, the strategy is nothing if not ambitious and broad in its scope. They go on to state that for the EU, 'the main challenge is to gradually change our current unsustainable consumption and production patterns and the nonintegrated approach to policy-making' (ibid.); we will see how this is unpacked below. In specifically discussing environmental protection, the EU indicates that this should 'prevent and reduce environmental pollution and promote sustainable consumption and production to break the link between economic growth and environmental degradation' (ibid., 3). The strategy does not make clear how this can be done. It does perhaps imply a predictive approach to policy when it states: 'All EU institutions should ensure that major policy decisions are based on proposals that have undergone high quality Impact Assessment (IA), assessing in a balanced way the social, environmental and economic dimensions of sustainable development' (ibid., 7).

The strategy states 'key challenges' (ibid.) for which it makes extensive if rather vague proposals, including:

- Climate change – the emphasis in these proposals is on meeting already agreed emission targets and improving technology, rather than questioning the sustainability of activities implicated in the consumption of fossil fuels.
- Transport – the emphasis of these proposals is on technology change, changing choices of modes of transport and perhaps reducing the need for travel through improving logistics 'planning' and fiscal incentives. Promoting sustainable 'consumption' of transport is only addressed indirectly in these ways, with fiscal approaches assuming that environmental harm can be given financial valuations even though Common *et al.* (1993), Foster (1997), O'Connor (2002) and Smith (2003, 29–51), for example, have all questioned such approaches. The assumption that environmental harm can be given financial valuation is common throughout the strategy.
- Sustainable consumption and production – discussions in the 2006 strategy appear to focus on changing technologies to allow consumption to continue as normal.
- Conservation and management of natural resources – although this does emphasise reducing stress to the Earth System, it implicitly assumes that levels of stress that components of the Earth System withstand can be effectively predicted, for example 'Maximum Yield in Fisheries' (EU, 2006, 13). The recommendations also include 'reuse and recycle' (ibid.); the term 'reduce' which is normally suggested as a higher priority in the motto 'reduce, reuse, recycle!' (e.g. Scott and Schiffler, 2004) is notable by its absence.
- Public health – proposals perhaps include the implicit assumption that risk assessment of 'genetically modified food and feed' (EU, 2006, 16) can adequately predict and control 'possible long term effects on human life and health, animal health and welfare, environment and consumer interests' (ibid.). This might be questioned in the light of epistemological issues highlighted in this book.

- Global poverty – the EU state their 'overall objective' for addressing global poverty 'to actively promote sustainable development worldwide and ensure that the European Union's internal and external policies are consistent with global sustainable development and its international commitments' (ibid., 20).

Proposals include implementing existing aid and trade agreements; however, there is no mention (even vague and platitudinous) made of the effect that subsidies of EU agricultural produce have on sustainable development in lower income countries, even if subsidy reduction is mentioned in general proposals about economics (ibid., 24).

The strategy then discusses overarching systemic proposals, perhaps intended to try to make initiatives to address sustainable development more integrated and coherent. The first of these is 'Education and training … Education is a prerequisite for promoting the behavioural changes and providing all citizens with the key competences needed to achieve sustainable development' (ibid., 22). What the behavioural changes are is not clear from the strategy; however, the EU website which outlined sustainable development policies perhaps hints at this:

> Sustainable development will not be brought about by policies only: it must be taken up by society at large as a principle guiding the many choices each citizen makes every day, as well as the big political and economic decisions that have ramifications for many. Realising this vision requires profound changes in thinking, in economic and social structures, and in consumption and production patterns.
>
> (Europa, 2006)

One objective of this book has been to give an indication of the levels of profundity of the changes and to indicate what the changes might be, at least more than the EU (2006) or Europa (2006), though these might hint at a need for (a virtue of) moderation by citizens. The strategy does make more explicit some of the rights it feels are needed for sustainable development by referring to the Aarhus Convention (EU, 2006, 26).

Discussion of research and development as a theme suggests that it should 'promote inter- and transdisciplinary approaches involving social and natural sciences and bridge the gap between science, policy-making and implementation' (ibid., 23) along with emphasising a desire for technology to solve much unsustainability and probably assuming that financial valuation can adequately reflect environmental costs.

Overall, it is not clear how the strategy will meet the main challenges it identifies of changing current unsustainable consumption and production patterns and effectively integrating approaches to policy-making. Nor are its ethical and epistemological assumptions clear or clearly adequate to address the issues it identifies. It appears in favour of predictive epistemology; the precautionary principle and prevention are mentioned vaguely as a response to uncertainty (ibid., 5).

Economistic utilitarianism tends to be the favoured ethical response. Discussions of participation indicate that participation is still seen as important to sustainable development; however, proposals are 'vague'.

That the 2011 and 2013 EU reports on progress against the strategy are 'mixed' and contestable plus that success or failure in achieving the strategy is attributed closely to economic development indicates the limits of economistic sustainability policy. The view that progress is contestable can be illustrated, as although GHG emissions have reduced over the defined periods, this is relative to the aim of the strategy rather than the aim that climate science suggests is necessary. The final words on this can be left to the EU itself:

> Overall, keeping in mind that almost half of the headline indicators of the EU SDI [Sustainable Development Indicator] set are moving in a moderately or clearly unfavourable direction, more efforts seem to be needed to put the European Union on the path to sustainable development.
>
> (2013, 28)

4.4 OECD 2001

The OECD (2001) reviews sustainable development theory and practice. It is perhaps the most recent theoretical and practical document that attempts, to some extent, to be authoritative about sustainable development. The WSSD was much more concerned with practical action, for which the OECD (2001) appears to have formed a significant intellectual context.

'Economic, Environmental and Social Trends' are reviewed (ibid., 11–27) with the conclusion being that the effects of economic activities raise deep epistemological questions: 'With inappropriate incentives … *economic activities* can lead to pressures that risk reaching *critical thresholds* … [and] inducing *irreversible effects*' (ibid., 27, emphasis added). In that chapter, the OECD also argues that poor coordination is harming efforts to move towards sustainable development. They imply that continuing large inequalities between countries and the absolute poverty of large portions of the human population (ibid., 22–3) are also harming efforts to move towards sustainable development.

They note the significance of uncertainties, admitting 'limits in our understanding' and that there are '*small but non-negligible probabilities of catastrophic break-down* in the long-term' (ibid., 45, emphasis added). They are not clear why catastrophe will be in the 'long-term', nor do they show how to arrive at robust probabilities that are useful to policy-making, given 'limits in our understanding'.

Unsurprisingly, the OECD (ibid., e.g. 35, 47) makes economistic utilitarian assumptions with regard to sustainable development. They state that

> an important challenge for governments is to better incorporate sustainability concerns into economic policies, since economic objectives play a dominant role in day-to-day policy formulations and in the priorities of many voters and of most policy makers. For this to happen, the concept

of sustainable development has to be more strongly anchored into standard economic discourse and into the practice of government policies.

(Ibid., 35)

Note that the OECD implies that 'sustainability concerns' should be subservient to economics on the basis of not specifically reasoned assumptions of some unspecified proportion of citizens, and the assumptions of policymakers who have perhaps been enculturated into making economistic utilitarian calculations (cf. Jamieson, 1992; Padilla, 2004; Smith, 2003). The OECD does not make clear the evidence for their assertion. Palmer and Finlay (2003, xi) note that Wolfensohn states that 'two thirds' of the citizens of the world belong to one of eleven world religions. These religions (Palmer and Finlay, 2003) appear not to favour dominance of economistic utilitarian assumptions; thus, these citizens, if they considered their assumptions thoroughly, might articulate different priorities for different ethical positions. Palmer and Finlay imply that alternative assumptions might give higher priority to forms of virtue ethics over economics. These virtues include seeing moderation of consumption as a virtue and greed as a vice (ibid.). If environmentalists and members of trade unions who question economics as the dominant aim of policy, perhaps in favour of some notion of justice, were added, then it is likely that the majority of citizens globally will question the assumption of the OECD.

Measurement of sustainable development is discussed with the report noting that this is a 'significant challenge' (OECD, 2001, 55). However, it only notes issues around additional long-term requirements in comparison to existing statistics and that issues cross national boundaries in ways that the subjects of existing statistics typically do not (ibid.). They do not discuss whether and how measurement is a distraction, if sustainable development faces the types of epistemological and practical issues highlighted in this book, such as the possibility of thresholds in the Earth System that cannot be known until they are crossed. This epistemological assumption of the value of measurement appears (e.g. ibid., 72–3) to be based on Baconian predict and control managerial assumptions (see Chapter 2) as well as the contribution indicators can make to public debate.

Economistic utilitarian and Baconian managerial predict and control assumptions appear to importantly affect their approach to 'taking a longer-term view' (ibid., 105), where they assume that 'risk' 'management' is an adequate response to unsustainable development issues. As we saw in Chapter 2, Jamieson (1992, 142–6) would call into question human abilities to 'manage' risk in the long-term. The OECD is quite explicit about the need to predict 'the capacity of governments to address longer-term issues effectively depends on their ability to predict future trends and emerging issues' (OECD, 2001, 105). They then go on to note various practical issues in obtaining the required information and turning this into action. This section of OECD (2001) does not address the broad epistemological issues highlighted in this book.

A good overview of the importance of participation of citizens in sustainable development and current participation practice is provided by the OECD (ibid.,

103–5). Here, they make the useful suggestions that national governments need to make the participation processes for decisions implemented through the 'WTO, IMF World Bank and OECD' (ibid., 103) and similar institutions start earlier, and with the basis and form of participation more clearly specified to prevent 'the final outcome from being captured by sectoral interests' (ibid., 105). They proceed to conduct a useful discussion of institutional and decision-making innovations for sustainable development nationally (ibid., 105–11) and internationally (ibid., 111–20). Organisations reviewed include national governments, UN organisations, the OECD, the World Trade Organization (WTO), the World Bank, the International Labour Organization (ILO), the World Health Organization (WHO), the EU and the North American Free Trade Agreement (NAFTA).

The effectiveness of policy instruments in addressing sustainable development is reviewed (ibid., 127–49). Types of instrument reviewed are command and control, economic, liability, compensation, education, voluntary approaches plus management and planning. Key conclusions include that policy frameworks should better reflect linkages between unsustainable development issues without becoming too complex. It is argued that there are deep problems using economic cost–benefit analysis for sustainable development. In spite of this, they appear to recommend this and 'greater use of economic instruments' (ibid., 148) generally (cf. Smith, 2003, 29–51). Quite reasonably, they promote the removal of subsidies that promote unsustainable development and for tax reform that promotes sustainable development. Although they recognise limited empirical evidence of effectiveness, they advocate experimentation in the creation of markets in tradable permits. The OECD is much more explicit about the potential benefits than problems of tradable permits. They state that 'improving economic efficiency is a common rationale of intervention in all areas' (OECD, 2001, 149); they are not clear what this means but, depending upon definitions, it is conceivable that very economically efficient industrial systems are also very inequitable and cause large amounts of stress to the environment.

A review of whether technological developments have been moving toward sustainable development (ibid., 157–75) suggests a mixed picture, as 'rebound effect[s]' (ibid., 171) and similar phenomena mean that gains from technical innovation are often not as positive as hoped. Their review seriously calls into question the faith in technology of von Weizsäcker *et al.* (1998) and the World Business Council on Sustainable Development (WBCSD, 2000, especially 12); further, it suggests that technology alone will not allow industry to achieve the radical change needed for sustainability (WCED, 1987, 213). The OECD does make suggestions to improve the sustainability of technology development (OECD, 2001, particularly 174–5), but they do not offer clear and robust processes that will guarantee the radical change that the WCED believed was necessary.

The relationship between international trade, investment and sustainable development is examined (ibid., 213–34). It is argued that international trade and investment are good for economic growth but can contribute to environmental and social problems if the proper policies are not in place. They imply that terms of trade still need to be changed so that they do not discriminate against the poorest (ibid., 219, 234).

The implications of sustainable development for poorer (non-OECD) countries are considered (ibid., 243–65). The report agrees with the WCED that the challenges are typically quite different for these countries. They conclude that there are some trade-offs between poverty reduction and environmental protection, as well as win–win opportunities. The OECD calls for coherent international strategies to minimise the trade-offs and maximise the win–win opportunities. They do not consider whether there needs to be trade-offs between economic growth and income distribution as the WCED (1987, 52) implies. Indeed, there is little direct discussion of the relationship between economic growth and environmental sustainability in this chapter at all. Perhaps the OECD simply makes the economistic utilitarian assumption that economic growth is intrinsically good (cf. Jamieson, 1992). They end their chapter with the hope that global political will and effective policies in poor countries are coming together to address extreme poverty, but they are less clear about ecological sustainability.

Questions of natural resource management are considered (OECD, 2001, 273–97), noting the epistemological significance of uncertainties in this regard (ibid., particularly 273, 293–4). A number of broad recommendations are made (ibid., 297). First to address market failures and public goods; here they tend to assume that the best approach is private property rights, though they do allow 'co-operative approaches'. The OECD is not clear about the particular notion of private property it means; however, given the tone of the rest of the report, it is perhaps reasonable to assume that they seek to promote notions of private property that support free market capitalism (cf. Hoppe, 2006; Munzer, 1998 [2003][16]). Until there is clear evidence that free markets are the best way to minimise stress to the Earth System, such promotion is ideological. Many 'free market environmentalists' (e.g. Anderson and Leal, 1991) do argue that establishing property rights means that owners will take better care of their property. However, there are a number of objections to this, including that 'nature' has intrinsic or non-utilitarian 'value'. Most importantly for this book, with complex global systems that contain difficult to identify thresholds, it is not clear that the total number of permits to pollute can be identified for allocation. To the extent that promotion of free markets is based on economistic utilitarian ethical assumptions, it is also normative. Consumerism is perhaps typically associated with free markets and the production and consumption associated with consumerism are probably key causes of stress to the Earth System; for example, atmospheric carbon dioxide concentrations (IPCCWG1, 2001, 6). At least some aspects of the global virtue tradition promote notions of property that are less absolute, less focused on maximising wealth and more focused on communal well-being rather than personal affluence (e.g. Palmer and Finlay, 2003, 122, 140). Another recommendation is to research non-market natural resource values such as the value of biodiversity. This again appears to make contestable economistic utilitarian ethical assumptions (cf. Jamieson, 1992; Padilla, 2004; Smith, 2003, 29–51).

In discussing climate change, the OECD (2001, 303–25) emphasises the epistemological significance of the connection of this issue to many others and 'the long time horizons and uncertainty surrounding' climate change (ibid., 303).

The latter in particular means that it is difficult for policymakers to respond with economic cost–benefit analysis and planning approaches. This echoes the epistemological questions raised by this book and suggests that alternatives to the ethics of the maximisation of utility may be appropriate. They also imply questions of justice, because industrialised countries are the key cause of climate change but poor countries will probably suffer most from any ill effect. The report recommends large GHG emission reductions in the short term and makes suggestions about how this can be realistically achieved within existing policy-making frameworks. The section concludes (ibid., 325) that 'technical and social innovation ... could lower emissions ... and enhance economic growth in developing countries and globally in the long term'. They do not consider moderation of consumption in detail, again apparently making an economistic utilitarian ethical assumption.

Discussing transport, the OECD (ibid., 367–91) argues for nationally and internationally coordinated technical and taxation changes including taxation of aviation fuels (ibid., 387). In addition, they argue that governments should educate citizens about the effects of travel and 'develop a sense of shared responsibility and accountability for more sustainable transport' (ibid., 390). This is an example of where the OECD looks as though it is promoting some notions of the common good (i.e. 'shared') and an ethic of duty associated with it (i.e. 'responsibility and accountability') and perhaps an unspoken moderation.

The OECD (ibid., 397–420) argues convincingly that agriculture is crucial to sustainable development. In summary, their recommendations for this subject are first, quite reasonably, to reduce subsidies 'to farm in environmentally damaging ways' (ibid., 420). Making unargued utilitarian ethical and ideological assumptions, they propose markets are the correct response to stress to the Earth System. Specifically, they propose finding ways of rewarding farmers for the non-market benefits they bring to society and provide signals that discourage stress to the Earth System from agriculture, i.e. policies should 'work *with* and not *against* market signals' (ibid., 420, emphasis in original). Notwithstanding the deeper questioning of market approaches earlier in this book, where markets do operate, adjusting markets to achieve aims determined by other means is reasonable. The report proposes that citizens should be encouraged to choose more sustainably farmed and distributed agricultural products. Again this is reasonable and in some sense promoting virtue, but also ideologically putting the emphasis on consumers, when if one product is clearly more sustainable than another, then means such as legislation banning less sustainable products should be considered. At a more fundamental level than implied in the OECD report, if consumers in OECD countries were encouraged to moderate desires for meat, exotic and low cost food, this would be in line with what the report recommends.

Progress of manufacturing in moving towards sustainable development, particularly changes in environmental impact, is reviewed (ibid., 429–48). The report argues that 'overall, the manufacturing sector in OECD countries ... from 1980 to 2000 ... reduced its pollutant emissions and resource input despite a greater than 50% increase in production output' (ibid., 429). It is not clear whether the

50 per cent figure is an increase in economic value (inflation adjusted or not) or some form of measure of physical output. Also, they do not make it clear (e.g. ibid., 442, 445) whether these improvements have involved the movement of high impact raw material processing to non-OECD countries, that are no longer included in the figures for that reason. In addition, they add that if individual sectors are considered, a more complex picture emerges, with some improving more than others. The picture they present for pollution intensity (ibid., 442–3) is also complex, with suspended solids being reduced by 20.3 per cent but toxic chemicals increasing by 4.2 per cent. Their statements of improvement are all the more questionable when they suggest that data for some effects of manufacturing is 'insufficient or even unavailable' (ibid., 429). Note the epistemological problems these questions raise for predictive management of 'industry'. Looking at the broader point that the OECD is making about efficiency gains, an assumption that sustainable development policies can be built on this basis is called into question by unresolved issues around the rebound effect. That is consumers saving money by greater efficiency and then spending the money saved on extra other consumption (cf. ibid., 171; see also Binswanger, 2001; Dimitropoulos and Sorrell, 2008).

Raising epistemological questions, the OECD (2001, 443–6) argues that the environmental impact of services and their relationship to manufacturing is not well understood. The OECD (ibid., 445–6) does not make clear that the WCED concerns that current information economies need manufacturing industry (WCED, 1987, 206) have been addressed. Again, the evidence presented in this book suggests that epistemological issues are key in this. Moderation of consumption of products and services should reduce stress to the Earth System whatever the stress associated with them is.

The OECD (2001, 446–8) makes a number of suggestions for sustainability improvements to manufacturing, including: (1) 'eco-efficiency' (WBCSD, 2000); (2) environmental management systems such as ISO 14001 and the Eco-Management and Audit Scheme (EMAS); (3) reporting of 'environmental, economic and social performance'; (4) linking investment with 'sustainability rating systems for enterprises'; (5) 'market-based environmental policies', 'economic instruments' and 'voluntary agreements'; and (6) integration with other relevant policy fields such as innovation. Most of these have broadly managerial assumptions – for example, discussion of environmental management systems, 'efficiency', 'reporting' and 'rating'. The information presented by the OECD suggests manufacturing management changes since the WCED had not achieved the radical change needed for sustainability (WCED, 1987, 213), nor do the trends or suggestions look promising in that regard. The next chapter will examine the effectiveness of industrial 'environmental management' in more detail.

Spatial planning is the subject of the final chapter (OECD, 2001, 453–72). Their suggestions about this and the need to consider these issues in sustainable development are very worthwhile; however, these do jar with the laissez-faire free market tone of much of the rest of the report and they still have a predict and control flavour (e.g. ibid., 457). The fact that, unbidden, an organisation dedicated to economic development recognises some limits to economistic approaches when considering questions of environment and development speaks volumes.

To summarise, the OECD (2001) does sometimes note something of the epistemological issues of sustainable development highlighted earlier, particularly in Chapter 2, but they tend to gloss over these and do not offer clear robust resolutions. They tend to make economistic utilitarian ethical assumptions, though they do tend to see some value in other assumptions such as cooperation (ibid., 297) and shared responsibility (ibid., 390), that some would find to be in tension with free market economic assumptions. Their discussions of participation are quite helpful; however, there is little depth to them and scant discussion of the literature on the subject.

4.5 Conclusions

This chapter has reviewed some key policy responses to the notion of sustainable development outlined in the WCED (1987). There are many more, including national sustainable development plans and more local Agenda 21 plans. Reviewing all these is clearly beyond the scope of this book. It is hoped that the preceding analysis is adequate as a review of some of the key documents that set the context in which national and local sustainable development plans are situated.

From the intergovernmental literature reviewed, it is clear that issues identified by the WCED (ibid.) as needing to be addressed in sustainable development have not been well resolved so far, and it is not clear that current proposals will adequately address current unsustainable development. There is little analysis of the reasons for lack of progress on sustainable development in this intergovernmental literature; for example, UN (2002, 1) motions vaguely in the direction of lack of political will, action and 'responsibility' and perhaps even implies too much selfish individualism. Europa (2006) and the EU (2006) perhaps imply similar reasons but do not conduct significant analysis. The analysis of this chapter suggests the following reasons for continued unsustainable development:

- Epistemological models used to try to understand unsustainable development as a connected set of policy issues are not clearly adequate for prediction and control approaches to policy. Discussion of epistemology in the policy documents is limited. Policy processes that are less dependent on prediction should be more effective.
- There is tension and inconsistency in the ethical assumptions made in the policy documents. Discussion of appropriate ethical schemes for sustainable development is scant in the policy documents reviewed. Utilitarian approaches dominate but rights-based ethics are quite common and there is also a flavour of virtue. Given the above epistemological limitations, ways should perhaps be considered to use ethical models less dependent on prediction, perhaps particularly virtue ethics.

- Proposals for citizen participation are both vague and tend to be aimed more at informing citizens than aimed at involving them in decision-making.

The next chapter will now consider environmental management responses to sustainable development to gather an impression of how the environmental sustainability component of sustainable development has been tackled in practice. Environmental management is the dominant practical response to unsustainable development and I suggest it is rooted in Baconian predictive controlling epistemological assumptions and economistic utilitarian ethical assumptions.

Notes

1 James (1986, 4), Hay (2002, 105–6), Sandler and Cafaro (2005, 163) and Palmer and Finlay (2003) each provide specific relevant material that indicates significant contestation of the anthropocentric nature of Principle 1 of the Rio Declaration, adding something like stewardship as a balance to sovereignty. The term 'exploit' perhaps has particularly Baconian economistic utilitarian associations. Attfield (1994, particularly 41–62) is a useful discussion of the historical development and significance of such ideas. This is not to say that nations do not have the right to exploit, simply that this right can be contested and perhaps should be justified in the context of sustainable development discourses and unpredictability rather than simply assumed.
2 See Chapter 3, endnote 8.
3 It is interesting that the focus of discussion of 'solutions' to climate change in Schellnhuber *et al.* (2006) is on technology.
4 Thanks are owed to Chukwumerije Okereke for discussion on this last point.
5 Each paragraph of Agenda 21 is numbered and the pages are not so for clarity references will be to paragraph numbers. Within this section, references to paragraphs are simply referenced by paragraph numbers in brackets e.g. (1.1) for Agenda 21, 1992, paragraph 1.1.
6 The example given by Palmer and Finlay and discussion by Popper suggests this type of attitude can even become violently intolerant.
7 Indicators are also assumed to have value in numerous chapters of Agenda 21. The value of indicators is discussed in Chapter 6.
8 For those concerned that environmental NGOs are the preserve of Western neo-imperialists, it is worth noting that the WCED highlight that the Nairobi-based Environment Liaison Centre had 230 NGO members, 'the majority from developing countries' (WCED, 1987, 327).
9 Utilitarian notions of prudence are perhaps closer to shrewdness or foresight, which for Aquinas are part of prudence along with other parts, such as caution.
10 See OECD (2003) for a more recent discussion of the pressure-state-response concept.
11 That is change the T (technology) component rather than the A (affluence or per-capita consumption) component of I=PAT; see Chapter 6 for more detailed discussion of I=PAT.
12 Even these will consume extra food resources and shoe leather or cycle parts.
13 The legal status of the EU strategy is not straightforward (Steurer, 2005, 5, footnote 3).
14 It is possible that focusing on a small number of issues was in order to make the task of 'management' more manageable.
15 Cf. Clayton and Radcliffe (1996, particularly 168–83, 239–40).
16 The discussion of the property theories of Hume and Bentham by Munzer (1998 [2003]) are particularly relevant.

References

ACRE (2006) *General advice on notifications for import and marketing of* GM *maize grain*, London: Defra

Adams, J. (1995) *Risk*, London: UCL Press

Adelman, S. (2013) Rio+ 20: Sustainable injustice in a time of crises, *Journal of Human Rights and the Environment*, 1: 6–31

Agenda 21 (1992) *Agenda 21*, www.un.org/esa/dsd/agenda21. Accessed 16 May 2011

Anderson, T. and Leal, D. (1991) *Free market environmentalism*, Boulder, CO: Westview Press

Attfield, R. (1994) *Environmental philosophy: Principles and prospects*, Aldershot: Ashgate

Barry, J. (1999) *Rethinking green politics: Nature, virtue and progress*, London: SAGE

Bass, S., Dalal-Clayton, B. and Pretty, J. (1995) *Participation in strategies for sustainable development*, London: International Institute for Environment and Development, http://pubs.iied.org/7754IIED.html. Accessed 6 February 2015

Benson, J. (2000) *Environmental ethics: An introduction with readings*, London: Routledge

Benton, T. (1999) 'Sustainable development and the accumulation of capital: Reconciling the irreconcilable', in Dobson, A. (ed.) *Fairness and futurity: Essays on environmental sustainability and social justice*, Oxford: Oxford University Press

Binswanger, M. (2001) 'Technological progress and sustainable development: What about the rebound effect?', *Ecological Economics*, 36(1): 119–32

Blanke, M. and Burdick, B. (2005) 'Food (miles) for thought: Energy balance for locally-grown versus imported apple fruit', *Environmental Science and Pollution Research*, 12(3): 125–7

Bostrom, N. (2002) 'Existential risks: Analyzing human extinction scenarios and related hazards', *Journal of Evolution and Technology*, 9(1)

CBD (1992) The convention on biological diversity, www.cbd.int/convention/text. Accessed 16 May 2011

Charlesworth, M. (November 1998) 'What are the most important issues facing our species?', *Green Politics Newsletter*

Clayton, A. and Radcliffe, N. (1996) *Sustainability: A systems approach*, London: Earthscan

Common, M. (2003) 'Economics', in Page, E.A. and Proops, J. (eds) *Environmental Thought*, Cheltenham: Edward Elgar

Common, M.S., Blamey, R.K. and Norton, T.W. (1993) 'Sustainability and environmental valuation', *Environmental Values*, 2(4): 299–334

Connelly, J. (2006) 'The virtue of environmental citizenship', in Dobson, A. and Bell, D. (eds) *Environmental citizenship*, Cambridge, MA: MIT Press

CSD (1997) *Global change and sustainable development: Critical trends*, UN Economic and Social Council, E/CN.17/1997/3, www.un.org/esa/documents/ecosoc/cn17/1997/ecn171997-3.htm. Accessed 14 May 2011

Dimitropoulos, J. and Sorrell, S. (2008) 'The rebound effect: Microeconomic definitions, extensions and limitations', *Ecological Economics*, 65(3): 636–49

Dobson, A. (1998) *Justice and the environment: Conceptions of environmental sustainability and theories of distributive justice*, Oxford: Oxford University Press

Dryzek, J. (2000) *Deliberative democracy and beyond: Liberals, critics, contestations*, Oxford: Oxford University Press

Ekins, P. (2003) 'Sustainable development', in Page, E.A. and Proops, J. (eds) *Environmental thought*, Cheltenham: Edward Elgar

Engel, J.R. and Engel, J.G. (eds) (1990) *Ethics of environment and development: Global challenge, international response*, London: Belhaven

EU (2001a) 'Directive 2001/18/EC of the European Parliament and of the Council of 12 March 2001 on the deliberate release into the environment of genetically modified organisms and repealing Council Directive 90/220/EEC', *Official Journal of the European Communities*, L 106/1–38

EU (2001b) *A sustainable Europe for a better world: A European Union strategy for sustainable development*, Brussels: Commission of the European Communities – COM(2001)264 final, http://eur-lex.europa.eu/LexUriServ/LexUriServ.do?uri=COM:2001:0264:FIN:EN:PDF. Accessed 14 May 2011

EU (2006) *Renewed EU sustainable development strategy*, Brussels: Council of the European Union, http://register.consilium.europa.eu/pdf/en/06/st10/st10117.en06.pdf. Accessed 16 May 2011

EU (2011) *Sustainable development in the European Union: 2011 monitoring report of the EU sustainable development strategy*, Luxemborg: EUROSTAT, http://ec.europa.eu/eurostat/en/web/products-statistical-books/-/KS-31-11-224. Accessed 25 October 2014

EU (2013) *Sustainable development in the European Union – Key messages – 2013 edition*, Luxemborg: EUROSTAT, http://ec.europa.eu/eurostat/en/web/products-statistical-books/-/KS-02-13-237. Accessed 25 October 2014

Europa (2006) *EUROPA > European Commission > Environment > Policies > Sustainable Development*, http://ec.europa.eu/environment/eussd. Accessed 28 June 2006

Foster, J. (ed.) (1997) *Valuing nature? Economics, ethics and environment*, London: Routledge

Food Standards Agency (2005) *Safety assessment of genetically modified foods research programme* (G02), http://tna.europarchive.org/20120620180604/www.food.gov.uk/multimedia/pdfs/g02report. Accessed 8 February 2015

GM Nation (2003) GM *nation? The findings of the public debate*, London: HMSO, DTI/Pub 6914/0.5k/09/03/NP. URN 03/1292

Hay, P. (2002) *Main currents in Western environmental thought*, Bloomington: Indiana University Press

Ho, M-W. (1999) (2nd edn) *Genetic engineering – dream or nightmare? Turning the tide on the brave new world of bad science and big business*, Dublin: Gateway

Hoppe, H-H. (2006) (2nd edn) *The economics and ethics of private property*, Auburn, AL: Ludwig von Mises Institute

Hursthouse, R. (2000) *Ethics, humans, and other animals: An introduction with readings*, London: Routledge

IPCCWG1 (2001) *Climate change 2001: The scientific basis*, Cambridge: Cambridge University Press

IUCN/UNEP/WWF (1991) *Caring for the Earth: A strategy for sustainable living*, Gland: The World Conservation Union, United Nations Environment Programme, World Wide Fund For Nature, https://portals.iucn.org/library/efiles/documents/CFE-003.pdf. Accessed 16 May 2011

James, A. (1986) *Sovereign statehood: The basis of international society*, London: Allen & Unwin

Jamieson, D. (1992) 'Ethics, public policy, and global warming', *Science, Technology and Human Values*, 17: 139–53 (also in Light, A. and Rolston, III H. (2003) *Environmental ethics: An anthology*, London: Blackwell)

Jasay, D. (1989) *Social contract, free ride: A study of the public goods problem*, Oxford: Clarendon Press

Keynes, J-M. (1931) *Essays in persuasion*, London: Macmillan

Korten, D. (1996) *When corporations rule the world*, West Hartford: Kumarian Press

Kyoto Protocol (1997) *Kyoto Protocol to the United Nations Framework Convention on Climate Change*, Geneva: United Nations Office at Geneva – FCCC/CP/1997/L.7/Add.1, http://unfccc.int/resource/docs/cop3/l07a01.pdf. Accessed 16 May 2011

Meadows, D., Meadows, D., Randers, J. and Behrens, W. (1972) *The limits to growth: A report for the Club of Rome's project on the predicament of mankind*, New York: Potomac Associates

Mebratu, D. (1998) 'Sustainability and sustainable development: Historical and conceptual review', *Environmental Impact Assessment Review*, 18: 493–520

Mollison, B. (1988) *Permaculture: A designers' manual*, Tyalgum, NSW: Tagari Publications

Munzer, S. (1998 [2003]) 'Property', in Craig, E. (ed.) *Routledge encyclopedia of philosophy*, London: Routledge

O'Connor, M. (2002) 'Reframing environmental valuation: Reasoning about resource use and the redistribution of sustainability', in Abaza, H. and Baranzini, A. (eds) *Implementing sustainable development: Integrated assessment and participatory decision-making processes*, Cheltenham: Edward Elgar/UNEP

OECD (2001) *Sustainable development: Critical issues*, Paris: Organisation for Economic Co-operation and Development

OECD (2003) *OECD Environmental indicators: Development, measurement and use*, Paris: Organisation for Economic Co-operation and Development, www.oecd.org/dataoecd/7/47/24993546.pdf. Accessed 16 May 2011

O'Neill, J. (1993) *Ecology, policy and politics: Human well-being and the natural world*. London: Routledge

Padilla, E. (2004) 'Climate change, economic analysis and sustainable development', *Environmental Values*, 13: 523–44

Palmer, M. and Finlay, V. (2003) *Faith in conservation: New approaches to religions and the environment*, Washington, DC: World Bank, http://go.worldbank.org/3L9IDQNFO0 or www.arcworld.org/books_resources.asp. Accessed 9 May 2011

Popper, K. (1966) (5th edn) *The open society and its enemies*, London: Routledge and Kegan Paul

POST (2005) *Rapid climate change*, www.parliament.uk/briefing-papers/POST-PN-245.pdf. Accessed 6 February 2015

Rahmstorf, S. (1994) 'Rapid climate transitions in a coupled ocean-atmosphere model', *Nature*, 372: 82–6

Rahmstorf, S. (1995) 'Bifurcation of the Atlantic thermohaline circulation in response to changes in the hydrological cycle', *Nature*, 378: 145–50

Rapid Climate Change (2006) *Rapid climate change: International science conference*, 24–27 October, Birmingham, www.rapid.ac.uk/rapid/rapid2006. Accessed 8 February 2015

Ravetz, J. and Funtowicz, S. (1999) 'Post-normal science: An insight now maturing', *Futures*, 31(7): 641–6

Reid, D. (1995) *Sustainable development: An introductory guide*, London: Earthscan

Rio Declaration, The (1992) *Rio Declaration on environment and development*, www.unep.org/Documents.multilingual/Default.asp?DocumentID=78&ArticleID=1163. Accessed 16 May 2011

Robinson, N. (ed.) (1992) *Agenda 21 and the UNCED proceedings*, New York: Oceana

Rosen, F. (2003) *Classical utilitarianism from Hume to Mill*, London: Routledge

Sandler, R. and Cafaro, P. (eds) (2005) *Environmental virtue ethics*, Lanham, MD: Rowman & Littlefield

Schellnhuber, H-J., Cramer, W., Nakicenovic, N., Wigley, T. and Yohe, G. (eds) (2006) *Avoiding dangerous climate change*, Cambridge: Cambridge University Press

Scott, N. and Schiffler, A. (2004) Reduce, reuse, recycle! An easy household guide, Totnes: Green Books

Seyfang, G. (2003) 'Environmental mega-conferences: From Stockholm to Johannesburg and beyond', *Global Environmental Change*, 13: 223–8

Shackley, S. and Wynne, B. (1995) 'Global climate change: The mutual construction of an emergent science-policy domain', *Science and Public Policy*, 22(4): 218–30

Smith, G. (2003) *Deliberative democracy and the environment*, London: Routledge

Sorrell, S. (2007) *The rebound effect: An assessment of the evidence for economy-wide energy savings from improved energy efficiency – a report produced by the Sussex Energy Group for the Technology and Policy Assessment function of the UK Energy Research Centre*, UK Energy Research Centre ISBN 1-903144-0-35, www.blakealcott.org/pdf/Rebound_Report_UKERC.pdf. Accessed 16 May 2011

Steurer, R. (2005) *Strategies for sustainable development as policy integration processes?* Workshop paper at 'Environmental policy integration: Defining and developing the state of the art', 21–22 March, University of East Anglia, Norwich, UK

UN (1989) *United Nations conference on environment and development*, A/RES/44/228, www.un.org/documents/ga/res/44/a44r228.htm. Accessed 16 May 2011

UN (1992) *Non-legally binding authoritative statement of principles for a global consensus on the management, conservation and sustainable development of all types of forest*, A/CONF.151/26(Vol.III), www.un.org/documents/ga/conf151/aconf15126-3annex3.htm. Accessed 16 May 2011

UN (1997) Five years after Rio: Where do we stand? United Nations Department of Public Information – DPI/SD/1910, https://unic.un.org/aroundworld/unics/en/whatWeDo/productsAndServices/publications/index.asp?callPage=home&category=4. Accessed 16 May 2011

UN (2001) *Johannesburg Summit 2002*, United Nations Department of Public Information – DPI/2233, www.un.org/jsummit/html/brochure/brochure12.pdf. Accessed 16 May 2011

UN (2002) *Report of the world summit on sustainable development*, New York: United Nations – A/CONF.199/20

UNFCCC (1992) *United Nations framework convention on climate change*, Geneva: United Nations Office at Geneva, FCCC/GEN/23 B, http://unfccc.int/resource/docs/convkp/conveng.pdf. Accessed 16 May 2011

UNFCCC (2005) *Summary report on topics covered at the workshops on mitigation of climate change*, Geneva: United Nations Office at Geneva, FCCC/SBSTA/2005/INF.5, http://unfccc.int/resource/docs/2005/sbsta/eng/inf05.pdf. Accessed 8 February 2015

UNWTO (2001) *Global code of ethics for tourism*, New York: United Nations

van Wensveen, L. (2000) *Dirty virtues: The emergence of ecological virtue ethics*, Amherst, NY: Humanity Books

von Weizsäcker, E.U., Lovins, A.B. and Lovins, L.H. (1998) *Factor four: Doubling wealth – halving resource use. The new report to the Club of Rome*, London: Earthscan

Wapner, P. (2003) 'World Summit on sustainable development: Towards a post-Jo'burg environmentalism', *Global Environmental Politics*, 3(1): 1–10

WBCSD (2000) *Eco-efficiency: Creating more value with less impact*, Geneva: World Business Council on Sustainable Development

WCED (1987) *Our common future*, Oxford: Oxford University Press

Wynne, B. (1996) 'May the sheep safely graze? A reflexive view of the expert-lay knowledge divide', in Szerszynski, B., Lash, S. and Wynne, B. (eds) *Risk, environment and modernity: Towards a new ecology*, London: SAGE

5 Environmental management responses to sustainable development

5.1 Introduction

In the two previous chapters, key intergovernmental sustainable development literature has been analysed for its epistemological and ethical assumptions along with discussions of participation. This chapter will examine the effectiveness of managerial epistemological assumptions in practical initiatives, to see if 'management' practice can transcend the 'knowledge' difficulties already identified, particularly in Chapter 2. This chapter will also note discussion of ethics and participation in such managerial literature, before Chapter 6 considers academic (theoretical) sustainable development literature. At which point the discussion of epistemology and ethics will have been broadened. Chapter 7 addresses ethics directly and Chapter 8 considers questions of participation in some detail.

Even if the reader is happy to accept the limitations of managerial approaches to environmental issues, the discussion of managing ecosystems in this section and of life cycle assessment in a later section will be worthwhile reading to illustrate just how profound these limitations are and are likely to remain. Readers who still have faith in the ability of environmental management to maximise economic growth up to the limits of the Earth System should consider all the evidence presented here, in order to refine their theology for this faith.

There are at least three areas of human activity where the term 'environmental management' is appropriate:

- Management of human environments in buildings, e.g. air conditioning.
- Management of 'natural' environments, e.g. park rangers, game wardens. The WCED implies that this is an appropriate response to the Earth System as a whole. For example, 'the underlying unity of the oceans requires effective global management' (WCED, 1987, 264). Chapter 2 explored the appropriateness of this for the Earth System, arguing that an assumption in favour of global management makes a large leap of faith in human abilities.
- Efforts to reduce the environmental effects of human activities, e.g. industrial effluent treatment.

The first is of little direct relevance to this book, other than the resources used and pollution caused by such efforts. The second is relevant as a key response to minimise the 'symptoms' of unsustainable development, and it has received discussion in relation to Earth System science literature in Chapter 2. It will receive a more direct treatment shortly. The third is perhaps the primary response to prevent the 'causes' of unsustainable development – e.g. minimise stress to the Earth System. An emphasis on prevention is common in sustainable development governmental literature (e.g. ibid., 59–60, 284) and efforts to reduce stress on the Earth System from industrialism will receive most attention in this chapter. It is worth repeating that the WCED believed that industry 'is perhaps the main instrument of change that affects the environmental resource bases of development' (ibid., 329).

5.2 Managing ecosystems

There are significant amounts of literature on managing ecosystems and environments. Calow's *Encyclopaedia of Ecology and Environmental Management* (1998) does not contain entries for ethics, epistemology or participation. Discussion of all the literature on managing environments is beyond the scope of this book; however, the following texts do have some discussion of epistemological and normative questions with regard to managing environments.

An interesting and relevant attempt to develop new approaches to environmental management that acknowledges many of the epistemological difficulties highlighted in this book is proposed by Costanza *et al.* (1992). It emphasises that attempts to manage the Earth System are based on questionable assumptions (ibid., 37), management as control is futile (ibid., 93), prediction is inexact and insisting on prediction is unreasonable and 'lends support to avarice' (ibid., 227–8). This last remark helpfully and astutely connects epistemology and ethics. Costanza *et al.* (1992) and similar literature may hold some insights that will help in reducing stress to the Earth System; however, it tends to reinforce the hypothesis that the Earth System cannot be controlled for human benefit. Costanza *et al.* (ibid., 157–69) is a chapter looking specifically at thresholds in ecosystems and criteria for them, in particular at how threshold criteria can be constructed. First, it considers 'socially constructed' criteria, typically based on 'political' judgements made on empirical evidence for confined ecosystems. Second, it discusses threshold criteria it labels 'scientific'. It labels these scientific as these criteria are for specific ecosystems, where ecological science can be more confident of being effectively prescriptive, based on empirical evidence from past stress to ecosystems. Neither of these approaches robustly addresses the epistemological issues with finding thresholds in the Earth System, as highlighted by this book.

Some recent *Environmental Management* journal articles that point to epistemological difficulties around environmental management include Duinker and Greig (2006), Edvardsson (2004), Hamed and El-Beshry (2004) and Preston (2002); these note issues of uncertainty, including around thresholds. Indeed, Alexander

(2001), a retiring editor of *Environmental Management*, remarks that the founding editor of the journal believed 'environmental management signified stewardship: not control of nature ... care and respect' (ibid., 701). This again suggests potentially important connections between epistemology and ethics. Alexander (ibid.) goes on to state 'many environmental problems and solutions have unexpected repercussions', which is a key possible epistemological reason why prevention of environmental problems is better than cure, and prediction and control is a questionable approach to 'management' of 'the environment'.

There is little in recent issues of the journal to support an assumption that even at a reasonably local level nature can be predicted and controlled for human benefit in a Baconian way. It is unfortunate that these practitioners have not been able to convince governments and key policymakers that the Earth System cannot be made to conform to human desires.

In considering management of ecosystems, Ludwig (2001) declares 'The Era of Management is Over', primarily for epistemological reasons, but he also implies that the ethical assumptions implicit in 'management' need to be made explicit and debated, rather than assumed and imposed by policymakers.

From the specific perspective of sustainable development, Jacobs (1999, 22) argues that some critics of the concept of sustainable development believe that 'acceptance of the concept by environmental groups is ... a fatal co-option into technocratic "global management" sideshows designed not to disturb the fundamental processes of capital accumulation'. It should be clear by now that this book would suggest changes to the status quo. This would include reducing stress to the Earth System from the capital accumulation of current industrialism. What is particularly relevant in the light of earlier discussion of Bacon's *New Atlantis* in Section 2.5 is a criticism of the connection between the promise of 'global management' and 'capital accumulation'.

These difficulties with managing ecosystems mean that, beyond the scale of a large farm, private property is problematic as humans will have profound difficulties managing anything larger. As national parks demonstrate, a patchwork of private large farm-sized pieces of land can be adequately coordinated. As markets are typically based on the assumption of private property, this raises questions about markets operating beyond the farm scale – e.g. national parks are often a mixture of private property and government administration.

5.3 Industrial management responses to environmental issues

In the past few decades, companies and other organisations have come under significant new pressure from public sentiment, customers, legislators and investors to reduce the harmful impacts that they have on the environment. This chapter now looks briefly at the historical context of current efforts by industrial management to address environmental issues, before discussing some key concrete current initiatives that aim to reduce the environmental impacts of industrial societies. The initiatives discussed will include ISO 14001, EMAS and life cycle assessment.

The primary purpose of these discussions of responses to environmental concerns in industrial societies is to attempt to show the significance of the assumptions behind these initiatives. This is, first, to examine whether the epistemological assumptions underpinning such approaches are likely to be adequate for 'management'. Second, to illuminate questions of whether ethical assumptions underpinning currently dominant accounting, financial and economic theory and practice are adequate to ensure, or at least allow, sufficient technical resolutions of environmental issues. That is, it can be suggested that all individual known, human created environmental issues can probably be technically resolved if certain known things are done or not done[1] by humans. Hence, the question of whether humans can and will achieve environmental sustainability can perhaps be characterised as depending on the social context of technical decisions. This is the reason why an idea such as sustainable development is needed, because sustainable development recognises that the social context to environmental problems needs to be considered and probably addressed to adequately deal with those environmental problems.[2] Perhaps the most important aspect of this social context is that giving up particular levels of certain industrial activities, which appears required for environmental sustainability, depends upon social agreement. Currently, the social context of industrial activities appears to be mediated primarily[3] by accountancy, financial and economic theory and practice or 'economics' for short.[4] So a key question is: does economics encourage, or even allow, environmental issues to be adequately technically addressed?

5.4 A brief history of industrial environmental management

Environmental concerns about industrial activities, at least in the form of public health concerns, probably originated as soon as the first possible effects of industrial pollution were identified. So dating the start of environmental concerns about industrial activities probably depends on the chosen definition of 'industrial'. If the pollution associated with the production of artefacts from the Bronze Age onwards, and the pollution problems of early mining and timber shortage problems in Britain since the Tudor period, are defined as craft environmental problems, or at least pre-industrial problems, then the beginning of the industrial revolution in Britain marks the beginning of industrial environmental problems.

Early industrial management responses to environmental concerns probably reflected the localised nature of early industry (Ponting, 1993, 360–2). So some owners and managers of industrial facilities will have genuinely tried to minimise the amounts and effects of any pollution produced and used resources as efficiently as possible, or tried to use alternative resources (i.e. coal and coke rather than wood and charcoal). Minimum use of scarce resources and efficient use of all resources was probably always pursued for financial reasons, even if pollution was ignored. Indeed, efficient use of resources is probably pursued more diligently where labour resources are relatively less expensive than material resources (i.e. typically early in industrialisation). Other owners and managers may simply have made sure that they and their families lived far enough away from the pollution.

Industrial management theory and practice was probably specific to each organisation until about 1911, when F.W. Taylor published *The Principles of Scientific Management* and Henry Ford introduced moving assembly lines in 1913. Since then, most industrial management theory and practice has either been developments of, or reactions to, these ideas. In addition there have been many more specific trends and fashions in management theory and practice that need not detain us here. The concrete beginnings to current initiatives by industrial management to address environmental issues can be located in management systems, and particularly quality management systems. Management systems are those that are put into place by the management of organisations, which are aimed at allowing their organisation to be systematically managed. Quality management systems are management systems aimed at assuring particular levels of quality of performance by organisations.

The origins of both management systems and quality management systems were probably in military practices. Most quality management systems were and are produced to a 'standard'. These standards are aimed at guiding and approving the development and implementation of these management systems. Initially, there was a variety of 'standards' such as the British Standard BS 5750 and a wide variety of company specific standards, to which both companies and their suppliers were expected to conform (TC 176, 2000). This created unnecessary duplicated work for suppliers to different companies and markets. This has been largely resolved by the production of the international standard ISO 9000 by the International Standards Organization (ISO). ISO 9000 is generally used in combination with any additional specific requirements for particular customers or markets.

The basic process used by many management system standards can be described as a continual improvement cycle of the following form:

1   Decide what the aims are.
2   Decide the best way to achieve those aims.
3   Specify what needs doing.
4   Try to do it.
5   Check whether it is being done and whether it is achieving the aims.
6   Re-evaluate the aims, and whether the ways being used to attempt to achieve the aims are the best ways available.
7   Repeat the cycle from point 3.

Based on then-existing experiences of management systems in general, of quality management systems in particular, and experience of environmental auditing plus health and safety risk assessment, the British Standards Institute developed an environmental management systems standard BS 7750: 1994. This and subsequent standards (ISO 14001 and EMAS) are environmental management system (EMS) standards aimed at guiding and approving the efforts of organisations, particularly companies, to introduce documented management systems that aim to reduce environmental impacts. That is, they aim to manage human activity by implementing some level of control of human actions on the (quite reasonable) assumption that if certain actions are taken then certain predicted immediate results will typically occur. The ISO developed an equivalent international standard ISO 14001: 1996, which replaced BS 7750. It might be argued that ISO 14001: 1996 is a less exacting standard than BS 7750: 1994 as ISO 14001: 1996 has less demanding requirements on the maintenance of registers of environmental effects and legal requirements. ISO 14001: 1996 does, however, put more emphasis on emergency preparedness and response than did BS 7750: 1994.

5.5 ISO 14001

ISO 14001 is the environmental management systems standard of the ISO. The basic approach taken by ISO 14001 is a continual improvement cycle notionally starting with an organisation developing an environmental policy. An overall programme for continuous improvement is prepared by identifying the 'environmental aspects'[5] of the organisation, often by an environmental audit, along with any 'legal and other requirements' that apply to the organisation. From this information, specific 'objectives and targets' are developed and turned into broad 'environmental management programmes'.[6]

Once these programmes have been developed, the notional next phase is 'implementation and operation'. This means implementation of the programmes and operation of any environmental management practices, such as testing effectiveness of pollution control equipment. This is notionally followed by a 'checking and corrective action' phase. ISO 14001 completes the continual improvement cycle with a requirement for a 'management review'. An initial continuous improvement cycle is now notionally completed and the environmental policy should be revised in line with results of the other steps in the continuous improvement cycle. In practice, the process is not normally as simple and linear as this description or the standard suggests. For example, there is a requirement for specifying 'responsibilities' in the 'implementation and operation' phase of the standard; however, in practice, deciding responsibilities for implementing any 'programmes' from the preceding 'planning' phase is usually closely linked to developing those 'programmes'. So activities will often cross between clauses of the standard.

ISO/TC 207 is the Technical Committee (TC) of the ISO responsible for developing environmental management standards, including ISO 14001. The explicit 'principles' that are used by ISO/TC 207 when developing all ISO 14000 series of standards are stated on their website.

- They must result in better environmental management.
- They must be applicable in all nations.
- They should promote the broad interests of the public and the users of the standards.

- They should be cost effective, non-prescriptive and flexible, to allow them to meet the differing needs of organisations of any size worldwide.
- As part of their flexibility, they should be suitable for internal or external verification.
- They should be scientifically based.
- And above all, they should be practical, useful and useable.

(TC 207 FAQ, 2004)

A key overall goal of ISO 14001 can also be found on the ISO/TC 207 website where it states: 'By providing a framework for improved environmental performance they will be contributing to one of the key purposes of environmental management standards: they will be contributing to the goal of sustainable development' (TC 207 About, 2004).

This webpage then goes on to describe the 'background' to the formation of ISO/TC 207. The key features are that 'in August of 1991, the ISO ... formally established the Strategic Advisory Group on the Environment' (ibid.). After the establishment of the Business Council for Sustainable Development in preparation for the UNCED of 1992, 'this council went to the ... international standards organizations to see what they were doing in the area of environmental management and to encourage them to become more active' (ibid.). The reasons for the desire for international standards can be discerned from the following quotation: 'Any work proposed had to ensure a common approach to environmental management that would enhance both business and environmental performance, and facilitate trade' (ibid.).

Thus, ISO 14001 probably assumes economic growth and trade are 'good' (presumably based on economistic utilitarian ethical assumptions), and compatible with ecological sustainability. Further matters of principle within the ISO can also be observed:

> There had been some discussion as to whether the environmental management standards should be developed under the Quality Management Technical Committee, TC 176. It was determined, however, that environmental concerns were not subordinate to quality concerns; but were of separate and equal importance. Their integration was recommended.
>
> (Ibid.)

Thus, environment and quality are assumed to be of equal importance, but both perhaps less important than economic growth.

Evaluation of ISO 14001: 1996 against sustainable development

ISO 14001 is aimed at improving the environmental performance of organisations. From the broader perspective of sustainable development, there are important benefits, limitations and assumptions of ISO 14001: 1996. The important benefits of ISO 14001 include that it can be used by organisations to help reduce their environmental impacts. It can also give an incentive to those organisations that will attempt to address environmental issues only where they will gain competitive advantage or maintain a competitive position.

The important limitations of ISO 14001 include first that bureaucracy is generated. Second, there is some environmental impact from operating an environmental management system. More paperwork is often generated. Third, although continual improvement is required, the rate of improvement is not assessed. How close an organisation is to best practice is also not necessarily assessed.

Another limitation is that whether the organisation is or is not moving towards environmental sustainability or sustainable development is not assessed. A key reason for this is that it is not yet clear what environmental sustainability or sustainable development are in order to allow assessment against these criteria. However, it does appear that ISO 14001 does put at least as much emphasis on the economic development aspect of sustainable development, in comparison to other social considerations and to environmental issues.

The important assumptions that can be suggested to be implicit in ISO 14001 include first an assumption that sufficient companies and organisations will voluntarily take part to allow or achieve environmental sustainability or sustainable development. This adoption appears not yet to have happened on a very wide scale. Semi-official figures for July 2003 (Tsujii, 2003) suggest that there are thousands of ISO 14001 certifications.[7] Taking the country with the largest number of certifications to ISO 14001, which is probably the most favourable example for ISO 14001, Japan had 12,392 ISO 14001 certifications (ibid.) out of over 600,000 manufacturing companies and about 4,000 large manufacturing companies (MITI, 1999).

Second, there appears to be an assumption that the contexts in which companies and organisations operate can, and will, allow them to improve environmental performance sufficiently. What is sufficient? There is a need for a concept such as environmental sustainability, or in a wider social context, sustainable development, to guide society to produce answers for organisations in industrial societies to use. It is significant that ISO 14001: 1996 does not define the levels of environmental performance that organisations should achieve; it simply requires 'continual improvement'. This seems reasonable, but at least some of this 'continual improvement' can be continual improvement purely in the operation of the 'bureaucracy' of the environmental management system, rather than reductions in environmental harm caused by the organisation. Part of the reason for this is that it is impossible with one standard to cover adequately every type of organisation. In some sectors of industry, there have been moves to address environmental performance levels for those sectors, for example the chemical industries' 'responsible care' scheme (ICCA, 2008). However, as previously mentioned, ISO 14001 does not require organisations to try to identify what environmental sustainability or sustainable development means for them. Probably the main reason for this is that there is not yet agreement, or even a credible process by which agreement can be reached, about what is meant by environmental sustainability and sustainable development in technical terms. Probably the key reason for this is the epistemological limits of the science of many key environmental problems. Epistemological limits mean, for example, that thresholds in systems cannot be robustly predicted.

A further assumption appears to be that economics will allow and ensure sufficiently environmentally sustainable practices. This appears to be a questionable assumption because currently dominant economic theory does not appear to take sufficiently into account the reality of the ecological context in which it operates.

There is, perhaps, an implicit assumption in ISO 14001 that the types of organisation, which will have an ISO 14001 system, will be those that operate the best environmental options in their sector. This can be called into question when operators of nuclear power stations have ISO 14001 (British Energy, 2001).

There is an assumption that pressure from customers and/or consumers will cause sufficient numbers of companies to introduce ISO 14001, and operate it in a way to reduce significantly the environmental harm of their operations. This appears *not* to be happening on a wide scale.

MacDonald (2005) is an interesting and useful article that details attempts to use 'The Natural Step' (2011) as a model of principles to guide ISO 14001 systems to sustainable development. However, the article avoids difficult questions of ethics and epistemology highlighted in this book, particularly by glossing over them and stating that the following is beyond the scope of the paper: 'Before commencing with implementation of ISO 14001 ... all stakeholders [should] begin with a common understanding of sustainability and its requirements' (ibid., 5).

Beyond this, discussion of sustainable development and ISO 14001 appears common but is of even more limited depth (cf. Starkey and Welford, 2001). Operation of ISO 14001 systems should help to move towards sustainable development; however, the standard perhaps makes questionable Baconian ethical and epistemological assumptions without obviously taking account of the questions around knowledge limitations raised by this book.

5.6 EMAS

EMAS is an EU Council Regulation (EEC) No 1836/93 of 29 June 1993 that has very similar aims to ISO 14001. This is demonstrated by the EU Commission Decision (97/265/EC on 16 April 1997) to recognise ISO 14001 as fulfilling the EMAS regulation, as long as the ISO 14001 'certification' of the site has been carried out by 'accredited' certifiers and additional criteria are also fulfilled.

The EMAS website suggests that it is intended to extend and complement legislative approaches to address environmental issues (EMAS FAQ, 2001). The website then goes on to discuss the part that the idea of sustainable development plays in the reasons for the regulation.

The goal of sustainable development ... calls for the use of a wider range of tools for environmental policy ... 'We need instruments which:

- promote information, awareness and commitment with citizens and in the business community;
- give the right incentives for environmental improvements in the market place; and
- ensure the integration of the environment into other policies.'

At the level of the European Commission such an instrument is already evident in EMAS.

(Ibid.)

This suggests that any economic development component of sustainable development is seen as more important than other social aspects of sustainable development or environmental sustainability aspects. The validity of this assumption can be questioned both because economistic utilitarianism is perhaps globally only a minority assumption and because physical Earth System and epistemological limitations mean that economic growth cannot be guaranteed.

Evaluation of EMAS against sustainable development

EMAS is aimed at improving the environmental performance of sites of industrial activity. From the broader perspective of environmental sustainability or sustainable development, the important benefits, limitations and assumptions of EMAS are similar to those of ISO 14001. An additional benefit of EMAS is

the company must ... adopt a company environmental policy ... which, in addition to providing for compliance with all relevant regulatory requirements regarding the environment, must include commitments aimed at the reasonable continuous improvement of environmental performance, with a view to reducing environmental impacts to levels not exceeding those corresponding to economically viable application of best available technology.

(Council Regulation (EEC) No 1836/93 of
29 June 1993 (EMAS) Article 3)

This requirement for the company policy will not necessarily rapidly be converted into widespread action at the industrial site.

The assumption of EMAS that is different from ISO 14001 is that public scrutiny will ensure sufficiently sustainable practices; this appears a questionable assumption, at least where local and wider populations and pressure groups do not take a direct interest in the environmental implications of industrial sites.

In addition, the assumption that sufficient companies and organisations will voluntarily take part to allow or achieve environmental sustainability or sustainable development is equally questionable for EMAS. Semi-official figures for July 2003 (Tsujii, 2003) suggest that there are thousands of EMAS sites. Taking the country with the largest numbers of EMAS sites (the only one with more than

1,000 sites), which is probably the most favourable example for EMAS, Germany had 2,364 EMAS sites (ibid.) out of over 3 million companies (Branchenbuch, 2000). Note that any company might consist of more than one site. Wenk (2005) makes clear that since 2001, there has been a downward trend in EMAS registrations.

It is worth noting that ISO 14001 is less prescriptive than EMAS. As EMAS had already been published before ISO 14001 was finalised, it is possible that a less prescriptive standard was deliberately developed, in order to allow more organisations to be given credit for efforts that they were making to reduce their environmental impacts. A more cynical interpretation might be that an easier standard was developed so that less committed organisations could gain a 'green badge'.

As for ISO 14001, there is perhaps an implicit assumption in EMAS that the types of site that will have EMAS will be those that operate the best environmental options in their sector. Similar to ISO 14001, this can be called into question when nuclear power stations have EMAS (EMAS Help Desk, 2003). Discussion of sustainable development and EMAS appears common but of quite limited depth (cf. Starkey and Welford, 2001). Operation of EMAS systems should help to move towards sustainable development; however, the potential drawbacks are the same as those with ISO 14001: the regulation perhaps makes questionable Baconian ethical and epistemological assumptions without grappling with the questions around epistemological assumptions raised by this book.

Requirements in EMAS for more information to be publicly available than with ISO 14001 should allow greater possibilities for participation of citizens in policy-making processes.

5.7 Life cycle assessment

Life cycle assessment is a possible component of environmental management systems, though not required by either ISO 14001: 1996 or EMAS. In the context of environmental management systems, the particular aim of life cycle assessment is to compare the environmental impacts of alternative materials, energy sources and designs of process and product, in order to attempt to choose the best options. The basic methodological approach used in life cycle assessment is that the environmental impacts of the materials, products, processes, etc. are assessed and if possible compared for the whole life cycle or some defined part. That is, assessment is typically made of impacts from the extraction of raw materials and energy resources, via transport, conversion, use, maintenance, etc. through to final disposal or recycling. The term 'cradle to grave' is often used to illustrate the concept of life cycle.

It is worth noting at this stage that life cycle assessment can be a very helpful broad heuristic perspective, as well as a specific technique of collecting and assessing data. To clarify, using the perspective of life cycle assessment is essential in many circumstances (though probably not sufficient or complete) to try to gain an adequate understanding of the interaction of human societies and the rest of the world, whether applied to limited industrial contexts or broad, society-wide research. This is something that appears not to have been explicitly addressed by those who consider environmental philosophy in general and epistemology in particular. Life cycle assessment as a technique and a perspective will be discussed in this chapter.

The ISO has also developed standards for life cycle assessment in addition to developing ISO 14001, the environmental management system standard. The life cycle assessment standards are all in the ISO 14040 series and describe life cycle assessment as a specific technique for collecting and analysing environmental data. There are other texts and methods of describing life cycle assessment but ISO 14040 and the associated standards are or are becoming the essential starting point. It should be noted that there exist other approaches, which include consideration of social impacts as well as environmental impacts. The following explanation of life cycle assessment as a specific technique is based on the structure and content of these ISO standards in general, and ISO 14040 in particular, as this describes the overall process in sufficient detail for present purposes.

The broad process of life cycle assessment is described by ISO 14040 in terms of the following stages:

1   Definition of goal and scope.
2   Life cycle inventory analysis.
3   Life cycle impact assessment.
4   Life cycle interpretation.
5   Reporting.

These are often not tackled in a simple linear fashion, with cycles and iterations within the above general structure likely.

Before starting a life cycle assessment study, ISO 14040 says that 'the goal and scope of an LCA study shall be clearly defined and consistent with the intended application' (ISO/FDIS 14040, 1997, Section 5.1). ISO 14040 then specifies that 'the goal of an LCA study shall unambiguously state the intended application, the reasons for carrying out the study and the intended audience, i.e. to whom the results of the study are intended to be communicated' (ibid., Section 5.1.1). The reasons for this circumspection appear to be that there have been significant numbers of occurrences of controversy when different life cycle assessment studies have come to opposite conclusions about broadly similar subjects. So, for example, studies connected to aluminium producers suggested that the lighter weight of aluminium-based car bodies means that these have a lower environmental impact; but studies connected to steel producers suggested that the latest lightweight steel bodies have a lower impact, because of lower energy use and pollution problems connected with the production of steel compared to aluminium (ENDS Report, 1994, No. 233, 24–6). Minimising these types of issue is a significant concern throughout the ISO life cycle assessment standards. However, these issues still raise epistemological issues for policy processes based principally on predicting stress from technology and policy options. Key components of the scope of the study that 'shall be considered and clearly described' are:

- the 'function and the functional unit';
- the 'system boundaries';
- the 'data quality requirements';
- where a comparative study is being undertaken, methodological issues associated with that comparison shall be considered and explicitly addressed;
- where a 'critical review' or explicit discussion of quality of the life cycle assessment study is required, the methods to be used are to be made clear in the scope of the study 'as well as who conducts the review'.

(ISO/FDIS 14040, 1997, Section 5.1.2)

The vagueness of these requirements and lack of clarity about how epistemological issues will be overcome only lead to further concerns about relying on life cycle assessment as a basis for policy. Life cycle inventory analysis is the stage where an inventory of the impacts over the life cycle is collected and collated:

Inventory analysis involves data collection and calculation procedures to quantify relevant inputs and outputs of a product system. These inputs and outputs may include the use of resources and releases to air, water and land associated with the system.

(Ibid., Section 5.2.1)

This is followed by life cycle impact assessment, which 'is aimed at evaluating the significance of potential environmental impacts using the results of the life cycle inventory analysis' (ibid., Section 5.3). Typically, this is the stage where implicit value judgements most importantly take place, such as the relative concern that should be given to different harms from different pollutants (e.g. carcinogen or neurotoxin). It can be suggested that these value judgements should be made more explicit, to be made more open to ethical and political debate. The next stage is life cycle interpretation, which will often take the form of conclusions and recommendations based on the life cycle inventory analysis and life cycle impact assessment, for example what to do about pollutants. Again, implicit value judgements that should be open to critical ethical and political debate are quite typical here. The final stage of life cycle assessment is reporting; the following indicates the factors that are important in reporting:

The results of the LCA shall be fairly, completely and accurately reported to the intended audience. The type and format of the report shall be defined in the scope phase of the study.

The results, data, methods, assumptions and limitations shall be transparent and presented in sufficient detail to allow the reader to comprehend the complexities and trade-offs inherent in the LCA study. The report shall also allow the results and interpretation to be used in a manner consistent with the goals of the study.

(Ibid., Section 6)

Again, this indicates the limitations and difficulties of even the most comprehensive and time-consuming processes for technical analysis of relatively simple components of our industrial civilisation.

The above is an adequate description of life cycle assessment as a specific technique for collecting and assessing data. The broader heuristic potential of life cycle assessment springs both from the benefits that it brings to analysis of environmental and connected issues, and from the limitations of analysis that it exposes, which then have epistemological implications. Before explicitly addressing the heuristic potential of life cycle assessment, let us consider the origins, benefits and limitations of the technique, in order to draw out its heuristic potential. There are differences between the stages of life cycle assessment so let us separate the stages for discussion.

As can be seen from the preceding ISO 14040-based description of life cycle inventory analysis, one set of influences on life cycle assessment is systems analysis in general, and input–output analysis in particular. Indeed, the Society of Environmental Toxicology and Chemistry traces the roots of life cycle inventory analysis in the following way (Fava *et al.*, 1991, 3): 'One of the first publications to report the calculation of cumulative energy requirements for the production of chemical intermediates and products was that of Harold Smith at the World Energy Conference in 1963.'

Life cycle inventory analysis adds to input–output analysis the requirement to consider all relevant inputs and outputs over the whole life of the system or systems being analysed. In other words, an effort is made to consider all of the factors defined as relevant. So one alternative that has lower environmental impacts, for example, while it is being manufactured, might have higher environmental impacts at other times, e.g. while the materials were being obtained, while being used and at subsequent disposal. Thus, the alternative that has lower environmental impacts during manufacture might be judged to have higher impacts over the two whole life cycles. Alternatively, if the impacts during manufacture are more important than those at other times, the alternative with lower manufacturing environmental impacts might be judged to be better over the two life cycles.

An important assumption in life cycle inventory analysis is of the effectiveness of division and summation of problems to allow solutions to be generated. This is probably less of an issue at this life cycle inventory analysis stage, than at the later life cycle assessment stage. The reason for this is that life cycle inventory analysis establishes levels of impact of human activity, and human activity is often created by division and summation, whereas the later life cycle inventory assessment stage deals with impacts on non-human nature. For 'nature', divisions are artificially imposed on non-artificial reality, with these reductionist divisions often being inadequate or problematic (cf. Lemons, 1996).

The whole life cycle assessment process builds on life cycle inventory analysis. Most of the remaining stages identified by ISO 14040 simply use widespread academic and business reporting processes and ideas, with the exception of life cycle inventory assessment.

First in assessment, ecological and medical sciences are used to identify the issues that are important and need to be considered. Second, ecological and medical sciences are used to try to understand the relationships between the inputs and outputs identified in the life cycle inventory analysis, and any problems these cause. There is a variety of ways of assessing the levels of effect; these generally involve taking each identified issue and using scientific disciplines, such as toxicology and climate research, to assess the significance of these levels of effect. For example, levels of pollution of water are assessed against the ability of the watercourse into which the pollution is discharged to break down the pollution. A further, more problematic, example is the discharge of persistent toxic chemicals. These can be assessed against the known effects that they will have in the immediate vicinity of their discharge, but the effects that they will have over a longer period, while they are transported over longer distances and come into contact with other chemicals, is more difficult to determine.

There remains at least one significant 'technical' issue with conducting life cycle inventory assessments. This issue is the need to reconcile (probably incommensurate or at least only morally comparable) different categories of effect. So one option might cause lower levels of one type of pollution (e.g. GHG emissions) over its whole life cycle and another might cause lower levels of another type of pollution over its whole life cycle (e.g. toxic emissions). There then remains the problem of how to try to compare these types of pollution. If the different types of pollution cause different types of effect, and for both types of pollution there is uncertainty about the levels of harm, significance of harm and significance of different causes of that harm, then comparisons are difficult if not impossible. This issue may just undermine *all* technical attempts to resolve environmental issues. Ethical aspects of issue comparison will remain to be resolved, even if technical aspects of comparisons can be resolved. Ethical comparisons will probably remain difficult and contested. To give a simplified illustration of an ethical comparison issue, how should the cancer-causing properties of benzene from unleaded petrol be compared with the nerve toxin properties of leaded petrol?[8] It might be possible to avoid the issue of comparison in some circumstances, if it is possible to synthesise a better solution than any of those originally assessed, using the results of the life cycle assessment as inspiration. That is try to develop a solution that minimises all types of environmental and connected issues. This is often not technically possible, at least in the short to medium term.

One important intrinsic assumption in life cycle inventory assessment is similar to that for life cycle inventory analysis; specifically that division and summation of problems to allow solutions to be generated is effective. This is probably more of an issue during assessment than analysis. An additional important assumption is that we can know the important effects of actions in order to make decisions. All the remarks made in this book regarding the capacity to predict and control complex interconnected interaction, throw this assumption into doubt.

The problems that the EU has had in developing eco-labels using a life cycle assessment approach (ENDS Report, 1995, No. 240, 28–9) indicate the difficulties of conducting and getting agreement about the results of life cycle assessments. All of these issues with life cycle assessment hint at the problems of *all* efforts to address environmental problems technically. The problems the EU has in developing eco-labels has given politicians and civil servants concrete experience of current epistemological limits with regard to environmental issues. These types of question are noted throughout this book. This practical experience may help the issues identified by this book to be taken up by civil servants and politicians.

The preceding discussion has drawn out the heuristic potential of a life cycle perspective. This can be broken down into, first, the potential of a life cycle perspective to allow more robust analysis (though not necessarily robust enough) of environmental and connected issues. Second, the difficulties of conducting life cycle assessments, that are widely agreed, point to the practical limits of current epistemology. This gives clues as to where epistemological research is required and may point to epistemological issues that are newly identified, or at least not widely discussed. In addition, the difficulties of getting agreement on life cycle assessment-based eco-labels (ENDS Report, 1995, No. 240, 28–9) point to the political importance of taking into account different vested interests.

Evaluation of life cycle assessment against sustainable development

In broad terms, life cycle assessment appears more socially neutral than ISO 14001 and EMAS in that the effects that life cycle assessment has on society and the environment depend more upon how life cycle assessment is deployed. That said, as a technique and a heuristic approach, it is certainly an important tool in efforts to try to allow development to be more sustainable. In the long term, the contribution that a life cycle approach makes to epistemology may be more important in allowing development to be more sustainable, than does life cycle assessment as a specific technique. This can take at least two forms; first by highlighting areas where research might improve existing epistemology and, second, and perhaps more importantly, at least in the short term, by highlighting that Baconian predict and control assumptions are questionable.

Of the techniques identified for this book, life cycle assessment is arguably the most thorough technique for analysing the impacts of technology options, notwithstanding its limitations or later discussion of ecological footprinting. It can be argued that any ecological assessment of technology that does not use a heuristic life cycle approach, even if it does not conduct a detailed life cycle analysis, is not as thorough as it might be, and questions can be raised about any conclusions drawn. This includes political theory based on ecological footprinting (e.g. Dobson, 2003, 83–140; 2006, 502–14; cf. Beekman, 2004).

Let us now turn to other management-oriented initiatives that are being used to try to address environmental and connected issues related to industrial societies.

5.8 Other initiatives

In order to set in context the initiatives that have just been analysed, this section will discuss possible relationships between ISO 14001, EMAS, life cycle assessment and other initiatives, such as legislation, ecological footprinting, pollution control, cleaner technologies, design for the environment and industrial ecology. First these other initiatives will be described and analysed.

Legislation

Legislation is an obvious 'tool' for governments to 'manage' stress to the Earth System from industry. It has been used to address environmental issues, primarily by specific actions associated with specific industrial activities being required. For example, when disposing of waste, companies in the UK must follow specified legal procedures. As alluded to when discussing the EMAS scheme (itself enacted under an EU regulation), legislation has been used for many years by governments with significant success but the limits of legislation, as an approach to making industrial activities more environmentally sustainable, appear to be not far away. Reasons for this include that legislation tends to have unsubtle effects and many environmental issues have subtle (or at least diffuse) causes as well as being complex and riven with epistemological difficulties that can make specifying legislation difficult. For some issues, epistemological difficulties lead to contested science, which perhaps tends to lead to difficulties with social acceptability.

For these and ideological reasons, there is a tendency to move towards market mechanisms, fiscal interventions and voluntary agreements. These appear spurred by economistic utilitarian ethical assumptions and knowledge of the difficulties that governments have micro-managing societies. Perhaps in response to this neo-liberal move, the notion of ecological virtue appears increasingly popular among political theorists who consider environmental questions. This virtue turn also appears spurred by an awareness of the diffuse causes of many environmental issues, which makes legislation difficult and may make 'virtuous behaviour' desirable whatever the (ethical) motivation for such behaviour (cf. Connelly, 2006). It is also perhaps spurred by awareness that epistemological limitations mean that 'expert' policymakers cannot manage societies for minimum ecological impact.

Ecological footprinting

Ecological footprinting (Wackernagel and Rees, 1996) is a technique for visualising life cycle analysis type data for larger, more generalised systems by developing an estimate of the geographical scale of the environmental impacts of, for example, a country. Wackernagel and Rees (ibid., 15) estimate that the ecological footprint of Holland is approximately 15 times its own geographical area. Ecological footprinting is not currently widely used in industry but is a useful technique for communicating an indication of levels of stress to the Earth System from (industrial) societies, perhaps to aid democratic participation. The technique has similarities to life cycle assessment except it tends to be less concerned with detailed specific technical assessments and is more policy focused. Its methodological focus is a concern with the amount of land required to support a particular activity both to provide resources and sinks for any pollution produced. Ecological footprinting is complementary to life cycle assessment, as it perhaps deals better with resource inputs than life cycle assessment has traditionally done, given how much life cycle assessment practice has been influenced by environmental toxicology. Ecological footprinting can also produce more rapid, policy focused insights. Current practice of ecological footprinting is less effective at dealing with pollution issues (for example, how can its methodological assumption address persistent toxic pollution that no amount of land can successfully ameliorate?) and its less specific nature hides some of the epistemological issues that there are with scientific knowledge of environmental issues. Life cycle analysis and ecological footprinting might better utilise the methodological approaches of each other.

Pollution control equipment

Pollution control equipment is equipment used to stop pollution leaving an industrial site and reaching the wider environment. Examples include effluent treatment facilities and filters on emissions to air. Requirements for pollution control were common early legal requirements. However, pollution control equipment generally moves pollution from one medium (often liquid or gaseous) to another (often solid). This move between media might be better environmentally overall, but often simply moves an environmental problem from one place to another. More recently there have been moves in legislation towards more integrated pollution controls such as the UK 'Integrated Pollution Control' legislation (Environmental Protection Act of 1990) and the EU 'Integrated Pollution Prevention and Control' (IPPC) directive (96/61/EC). These are aimed at minimising overall pollution from a process. However, this appears effective only for processes with known problems where alternatives are available that are judged to contain or prevent pollution better. This brings us to our next type of initiative.

Cleaner technologies

Cleaner technologies are technologies that are designed from the outset to eliminate environmental problems, particularly the pollution problems that pollution control equipment is intended to control. A technique such as life cycle assessment is needed in order to decide whether one technology is cleaner than another. Cleaner technology is adopted because of both legal requirements such as the IPPC and where payback periods on operational savings are adequate to justify any additional capital outlay according to the financial and accounting criteria placed on the process under consideration. This last point hints at a limitation of cleaner technologies, that is, in a market economy cleaner technologies will only tend to be adopted when 'economic'. Cleaner technologies also face epistemological and normative issues in deciding which is cleaner.

Design for the environment

'Design for the environment' is a collective term for a broad range of approaches. A reasonable way of characterising the range of approaches is to say that they lie across a spectrum. At one end of the spectrum are approaches that believe that the best available techniques of design analysis such as life cycle assessment are needed to analyse designs in detail to assess their relative environmental impacts. At the other end of the spectrum are approaches that, recognising the difficulty and complexity of life cycle assessment, use a few or even one rule of thumb. These rules of thumb might be as simple as making a product's packaging recyclable. There appears to be no widespread legal requirement to use design for the environment. However, design for the environment is the industrial management response that best matches policy concepts, such as ecological modernisation (Weale, 1992; Hajer, 1997) and *Factor Four* (von Weizsäcker et al., 1998). Ecological modernisation appears to be the dominant policy framework of governments of industrialised countries concerned with addressing ecological issues. Design for the environment and ecological modernization all suffer from the same limitations as life cycle assessment as discussed earlier. In addition, design for the environment and perhaps ecological modernisation tend to hide the limitations of 'technological-fix' (including epistemological limitations) solutions to unsustainable development in a way that life cycle assessment does not. Indeed, life cycle assessment tends to expose the limitations of a 'technological-fix' approach.

Industrial ecology

Industrial ecology is a concept where outputs from one process are designed to be inputs to other processes (Ayres and Ayres, 1996). This concept has considerable value but, even if adequately integrated industrial processes can be developed and the energy to drive these processes comes from 'good'[9] renewable energy sources, there will remain the demanding issue of the land or ocean space required to provide the energy to drive these renewable energy sources, including energy to adequately recycle any products. Whether the surface area of the earth can provide sufficient renewable energy for large-scale industrial activity, grow enough food for large human populations and leave some room for land that is not solely for human purposes, is open to question.

5.9 Relationship between initiatives

From the description of ISO 14001 and EMAS, it is clear that these are quite similar; indeed, it is quite possible for an organisation to have both. Life cycle assessment, design for the environment, ecological footprinting, cleaner technologies and industrial ecology can be added to environmental management systems beyond the requirements of ISO 14001 or EMAS. Ecological footprinting has broader uses beyond industry, as does legislation. It is important to note that legislation is an important part of the context to the operation of industries, including when it specifies pollution control equipment. Environmental management systems can identify opportunities to use pollution control equipment beyond legal requirements, if cleaner technologies are not yet available.

Do these initiatives taken together mean that current efforts to address the environmental issues related to industrial societies can transcend the epistemological limitations already highlighted in this book? The analysis here suggests many reasons to suspect that for the foreseeable future this is a large and contestable assumption – no for now. This, in turn, may lend weight to the WCED's (1987, 213) suggestion that a radical approach to making industry sustainable is needed. Indeed, given the stakes involved, it might be argued that it is more reasonable to attempt to minimise stress to the Earth System rather than predict the level of stress it will withstand. This is the alternative strategy suggested by the findings of this book. Rather than seeking to develop policies that take us to the unknowable thresholds of environmental limits, threatening unsustainable environmental stress in the process, policy should aim at the moderation of consumption, production and waste. That is, less industrial activity and negative economic growth may be a price worth paying for many more important things in current civilisations. Perhaps essential to achieving democratic assent and cooperation in any such endeavour are maximising genuine participation in such decisions and questioning (philosophically and with illustrations) materialist economistic utilitarian ethics.

5.10 Theoretical analysis of changes required to industrial societies

There is literature that looks at questions around changes to industrial systems for environmental reasons, even if it does not tend to directly consider the epistemological questions raised by this book. A review of all this literature is beyond our scope here; however, there are some important texts that are worth brief mention and are representative of much of this literature.

Factor Four (von Weizsäcker *et al.*, 1998) is a high-profile discussion focused on increasing resource productivity by a factor of four, which gives many examples of possible improvements when measured in narrow ways. However, the technical suggestions in *Factor Four* can be criticised, in particular for not having an adequate life cycle approach, even heuristically. This means that some solutions might be more resource efficient in one way, but less so in others. It also means that some of the suggestions may create as many other problems as they aim to solve. For example, in discussing cars they suggest the use of lightweight composites as the main body materials without detailed discussion or references about the effects of these materials in comparison to existing materials when the vehicle is disposed of.

More generally, the emphasis of *Factor Four* is on improving resource efficiency rather than addressing waste and pollution production. This is a questionable objective. The main reasons for this are that it is less clear that resource shortages will cause critical thresholds in the Earth System to be crossed (cf. Steffen *et al.*, 2004, 36) and resource shortages are dealt with reasonably adequately by economic supply and demand dynamics, neither of which is the case with pollution and waste. Indeed, for all their emphasis on resource productivity, von Weizsäcker *et al.* note that it may be 'the absorptive capacity of the earth for all the pollutants and wastes' (1998, 258) that is critical to unsustainable development. Faber *et al.* (1998, 42–44) also suggest it is waste and pollution problems that are more important than resource issues. That said, as von Weizsäcker *et al.* (1998, xxii) point out, there is a direct connection between resource use and pollution. However, unless tested by something like life cycle assessment, their assumption that reducing resource use will adequately address pollution appears unproven.

As well as technical suggestions, *Factor Four* makes some of the same observations as this book. In particular, it is critical of contemporary economic structures and the philosophical assumptions that underpin these (ibid., 143–209, 271–99). It argues there is urgency with regard to addressing unsustainable development (ibid., 211–68). Further, it suggests that efficiency gains will not be enough (ibid., 258, 269, 292–3), particularly given that the advertising industry (and much popular culture) can probably create infinite wants. Sachs (1993, 14–17) echoes this point. Sachs also echoes the WCED (1987, 206) and points to deeper criticisms of techno-optimistic approaches to sustainable development when he writes:

> Those who hail the rising information and service society as environment-friendly, often overlook the fact that these sectors can only grow on top of the industrial sector and in close symbiosis with it ... Efficiency without sufficiency is counterproductive; the latter must decide boundaries of the former.
>
> (Sachs, 1993, 15–17)

Sachs also suggests that this is a supra-rational belief when he writes:

> However, the rambling development creed impedes any serious public debate on the moderation of growth ... the development syndrome has dangerously narrowed the social imagination in the North as well as in the South. As the North continues to set its sight on an infinite economic future, and the South

cannot free itself from its compulsive mimicry of the North, the capacity for self-mobilized and indigenous change has been undermined worldwide.

(Ibid., 17)

Evidence for the importance of these types of criticism can be seen in that the icon of high technology, 'silicon valley', is heavily polluted, particularly by the electronics industry (SVEP, 1999; SVTC, 1999).

It is suggested that the current context of technical initiatives, especially when the initiatives take place within companies, is probably accountancy practice. Such practice is therefore potentially a primary limit on what can be done or not done to address industrial environmental issues. In particular, much current accountancy practice means initiatives are expected to repay costs and start saving money within as little as six months. The primary cause of accountancy practice having such short-term timescales appears to be that most companies are expected to pay dividends and report profits at least annually – often every quarter – because of pressure from speculative investors and the current structure of (global) capital (Korten, 1996, 185–206).

The historical reasons for the development of the financial context in which companies operate are complex, but can perhaps be traced to dominant ethical assumptions within Anglo-Saxon countries and that these countries currently appear to be increasingly culturally dominant within the world. Von Weizsäcker *et al.* (1998, 139–42, 289–99) and Korten (1996, 261–8) suggest similar analyses. Indeed, Korten argues that materialist epistemological assumptions of modern science, neo-classical economics and modernity more generally are closely related to the operation of dominant financial structures. This is connected to seeing the creation of the maximum amount of money as the highest aim that societies should have. Korten suggests that this is manifest through the 'born to shop' ethos promoted by contemporary market economies and that this leads to dissatisfaction not happiness (ibid.; cf. Jackson and Michaelis, 2003, 61). This has important implications for ethics and sustainable development.

The social context of industrial management appears to be mediated primarily by neo-classical economics (Korten, 1996, 185–214). Other important factors probably include legislation, consumer and pressure group influence, and social moral norms. Let us consider whether current neo-classical economics will currently ensure, or at least allow, adequate technical resolutions of environmental and connected issues.[10] Much research in environmental economics, ecological economics, environmental political economy and environmental politics suggests the contrary (e.g. Costanza *et al.*, 1992; Faber *et al.*, 1998). Von Weizsäcker *et al.* (1998, 278–99) also argue to the contrary. They (ibid., xxvi–iii) give examples of how contemporary economic structures unjustly militate against taking action to address environmental issues and have questionable moral and philosophical underpinnings (ibid., 271–99). In particular, von Weizsäcker *et al.* (ibid., 139–42) suggest that finance structures tend to favour investment in resource use rather than resource efficiency, which is linked with a tendency to subsidise non-renewable energy production by a huge amount, even by so called 'free market' governments (ibid., 153–4). It is worth noting in the light of discussion of ethical assumptions that von Weizsäcker *et al.* also suggest that current market economies encourage the 'seven deadly sins' or encourage classical vices (ibid., 143). Korten (1996, 185–206) argues current financial systems are economically, socially and environmentally unsustainable, to the point of 'endangering the well-being of every person on the planet' (ibid., 206). Rees (1999, 113–15) claims there are typically abstractions within conventional economic theory that strongly promote unsustainable development. He highlights the following: production of maximum material goods does not mean maximum happiness, people do not behave like *homo economicus* and that land is not ethereal or a 'free good'.

The next question suggested is can economics and other social context factors be altered sufficiently to deal with the reality of the ecological context in which they, industry and the rest of society operate? A full answer is beyond the scope of this book. However, given the epistemological difficulties highlighted throughout, the difficulty of deciding which if any options will not lead to infinite costs suggests that economic cost–benefit analysis is deeply problematic (cf. Berkhout *et al.*, 2003, 22–3). Less consequentialist decision processes will probably be more analytically robust. To give an example, the 'global virtue tradition' sees moderation of consumption as good for individuals, societies and the Earth System, without predicting completely the consequences of such moderation.

5.11 Conclusions

Chapter 2 suggested that Earth System management or prediction and control for the benefit of humans is beyond human ability and the review of environmental management literature in Section 5.2 strengthens this argument, though there are ideas that suggest that this cannot be ruled out forever, purely on epistemological grounds. That is, prediction and control of the Earth System may become possible if there are huge intellectual leaps. However, the global virtue tradition suggests it might always be ethically unacceptable to the majority of humans to predict and control the Earth System purely for human material benefit.

All of the technical initiatives discussed above to address the ecological effects of industry are worth doing and something like them is essential if the environmental impacts of industrial societies are to be reduced. However, it is far from clear whether, in their current form and disconnection from wider social processes (in particular other processes attempting to make development more sustainable), they will be sufficient to ensure or even allow environmental sustainability, within their sphere of application.

As discussed in the sections devoted to ISO 14001, EMAS and life cycle assessment, there is often perhaps an assumption by policymakers that these and other essentially technical initiatives will be sufficient to ensure or at least allow industrial societies to become environmentally sustainable. This is a questionable assumption given that epistemological difficulties with prediction and control of the Earth System are far from being clearly addressed by the environmental management practices reviewed.

It is worth clarifying about the limits of management. Where a system can be robustly predicted or monitoring and steering 'controls' have been demonstrated to be effective on a repeatable basis, then management is effective; beyond this, stewardship, which is more humble, is the best that can be hoped for.

Chapter 6 now considers broad theoretical responses to sustainable development, broadening out our discussion of epistemology and ethics, before Chapter 7 considers ethics and Chapter 8 considers questions of participation directly.

Notes

1 This does not mean that all environmental or even all human created environmental problems can be technically resolved at the same time, simply that particular types of human created environmental problems can be resolved on an individual basis. It appears that humans not doing things that cause environmental problems is more important and, socially at least, more difficult than doing additional things to reduce environmental problems.

2 To expand a little, it can be suggested that the choices societies make affect the environments that societies inhabit; equally, the environment that societies inhabit affects the choices they make. 'Environment that societies inhabit' means physical environment ('built' and 'natural'), technical environment, moral environment, epistemological environment, etc.

3 Legislation and public pressure do exclude some activities but the choice between the remaining activities is probably made primarily by accountancy, financial and economic practices. These might be short-term accounting considerations or longer-term market share considerations.

4 The description 'accountancy, financial and economic theory and practice' will be replaced by the term economics from now on, as this appears to be what is meant if people use the term and are not referring to the academic discipline.

5 Terms in quotation marks in this section are taken from ISO 14001: 1996.

6 'Environmental management programmes' can be described as the plans intended to achieve the 'objectives and targets'.

7 The method for arriving at these figures is not clear. Thus, it should be noted that these might be companies or parts of companies. For example, a company consisting of many sites might only have one of those sites with ISO 14001 but still be counted among these figures as having ISO 14001. Alternatively, a company with hundreds of sites might have five sites with ISO 14001 and each of these sites might be counted individually.

8 In this case this appears to have been resolved by regulators by the particular type of pollution control technology used for petrol engines. That is, catalytic converters have been introduced to minimise the levels of a range of pollutants. Catalytic converters are not compatible with leaded petrol, so the unleaded alternative has been chosen without resolving the original issue. However, catalytic converters are associated with higher fuel consumption and hence higher levels of carbon dioxide production. Carbon dioxide emissions from transport are suggested to be one of the main contributors to climate change, which is an environmental issue that many would say is more important than the rest of the environmental problems that catalytic converters resolved.

9 'Good' renewable sources of energy means *at least* that the devices generate more energy than the amount of fossil and nuclear energy they require to produce (cf.

Knapp and Jester, 2000). Other environmental issues such as persistent toxic chemicals also need to be taken into account via life cycle assessment or similar.

10 Note that many of the issues connected to environmental issues are social; often, technical solutions may not be appropriate.

References

Alexander, D. (2001) 'Farewell remarks from the retiring Editor-in-Chief', *Environmental Management*, 28(6): 701–2

Ayres, R.U. and Ayres, L.W. (1996) *Industrial ecology towards closing the materials cycle*, Cheltenham: Edward Elgar

Beekman, V. (2004) 'Environmental utilization space between science and politics', *Journal of Agricultural and Environmental Ethics*, 17(3): 293–300

Berkhout, F., Leach, M. and Scoones, I. (2003) (eds) *Negotiating environmental change: New perspectives from social sciences*, Cheltenham: Edward Elgar

Branchenbuch (2000) http://english.branchenbuch.com. Accessed 2 February 2004

British Energy (2001) *Safety, health and the environment review 2000–2001*, www.british-energy.com/environment/she/she_2001/shereview.pdf. Accessed 2 February 2004

Calow, P. (1998) *The encyclopedia of ecology and environmental management*, Oxford: Blackwell Science

Connelly, J. (2006) 'The virtue of environmental citizenship', in Dobson, A. and Bell, D. (eds) *Environmental citizenship*, Cambridge, MA: MIT Press

Costanza, R., Norton, B. and Haskell, B. (1992) *Ecosystem health: New goals for environmental management*, Washington, DC: Island Press

Dobson, A. (2003) *Citizenship and the environment*, Oxford: Oxford University Press

Dobson, A. (2006) 'Citizenship', in Dobson, A. and Eckersley, R. (eds) *Political theory and the ecological challenge*, Cambridge: Cambridge University Press

Duinker, P. and Greig, L. (2006) 'The impotence of cumulative effects assessment in Canada: Ailments and ideas for redeployment', *Environmental Management*, 37(2): 153–61

Edvardsson, K. (2004) 'Using goals in environmental management: The Swedish system of environmental objectives', *Environmental Management*, 34(2): 170–80

EMAS FAQ (2001) *Frequently asked questions*, http://europa.eu.int/comm/environment/emas/tools/faq_en.htm. Accessed 2 February 2004

EMAS Help Desk (2003) UK EMAS 'Registered Sites', http://europa.eu.int/comm/environment/emas/pdf/sites/uk_en.pdf. Accessed 2 February 2004

ENDS Report (1994) Steel and aluminium industries battle over car market, London: Environmental Data Services

ENDS Report (1995) New EC timetable for eco-labelling programme, London: Environmental Data Services

Faber, M., Proops, J. and Manstetten, R. (1998) *Ecological economics: Concepts and methods*, Cheltenham: Edward Elgar

Fava, J.A., Denison, R., Jones, B., Curan, M.A., Vigon, B., Selke, S. and Barnum, J. (eds) (1991) *A technical framework for life-cycle assessment*, Brussels: Society of Environmental Toxicology and Chemistry

Hajer, M. (1997) *The politics of environmental discourse: Ecological modernisation and the policy process*, Oxford: Oxford University Press

Hamed, M. and El-Beshry, M. (2004) 'Uncertainty analysis in dissolved oxygen modeling in streams', *Environmental Management*, 34(2): 233–44

ICCA (2008) *Responsible care status report (2008 edition)*, International Council of Chemical Associations, www.icca-chem.org/ICCADocs/ICCA%20-%20Responsible%20Care%20_English.pdf. Accessed 18 May 2011

ISO/FDIS 14040 (1997) *Environmental management – life cycle assessment – principles and framework*, Geneva: International Standards Organization

Jackson, T. and Michaelis, L. (2003) *Policies for sustainable consumption*, London: Sustainable Development Commission

Jacobs, M. (1999) 'Sustainable development as a contested concept', in Dobson, A. (ed.) *Fairness and futurity: Essays on environmental sustainability and social justice*, Oxford: Oxford University Press

Knapp, K. and Jester, T. (2000) 'An empirical perspective on the energy payback time for photovoltaic modules', *Solar 2000 conference*, Madison, WI, 16–21 June, www.ecotopia.com/apollo2/knapp/PVEPBTPaper.pdf. Accessed 18 May 2011

Korten, D. (1996) *When corporations rule the world*, West Hartford, CT: Kumarian Press

Lemons, J. (ed.) (1996) *Scientific uncertainty and environmental problem solving*, Cambridge, MA: Blackwell

Ludwig, D. (2001) 'The era of management is over', *Ecosystems*, 4(8): 758–64

MacDonald, J. (2005) 'Strategic sustainable development using the ISO 14001 Standard', *Journal of Cleaner Production*, 13: 631–43

MITI (1999) *Preliminary report of the basic survey on commercial and manufacturing structure and activity in 1998: Overview of small- and medium-size companies of commerce and industry of Japan*, MITI, www.meti.go.jp/english/statistics/tyo/syokozi/pdf/h2c5s1ae.pdf. Accessed 2 February 2004

Natural Step (2011) *The four system conditions*, www.naturalstep.org/the-system-conditions. Accessed 11 May 2011

Ponting, C. (1993) *A green history of the world: The environment and the collapse of great civilizations*, London: Penguin

Preston, B. (2002) 'Indirect effects in aquatic ecotoxicology: Implications for ecological risk assessment', *Environmental Management*, 29(3): 311–23

Rees, W. (1999) 'Scale, complexity and the conundrum of sustainability', in Kenny, M. and Meadowcroft, J. (eds) *Planning sustainability*, London: Routledge

Sachs, W. (ed.) (1993) *Global ecology*, London: Zed Books

Starkey, R. and Welford, R. (2001) *The Earthscan reader in business and sustainable development*, London: Earthscan

Steffen, W., Sanderson, A., Tyson, P., Jäger, J., Matson, P., Moore III, B., Oldfield, F., Richardson, K., Schellnhuber, H-J., Turner, B.L. and Wasson, R. (2004) Global change and the Earth System: A planet under pressure, Berlin: Springer-Verlag, Executive Summary, www.igbp.net/download/18.56b5e28e137d8d8c09380001694/1376383141875/Springer+IGBP+Synthesis+Steffen+et+al+%282004%29_web.pdf. Accessed 9 May 2011

SVEP (1999) *Water quality watershed health in serious condition*, Silicon Valley Environmental Partnership, www.mapcruzin.com/svep/water_quality.htm. Accessed 18 May 2011

SVTC (1999) *SVTC cumulative exposure project (CEP) maps*, Silicon Valley Toxics Coalition, http://mapcruzin.mobi/svtc_cep. Accessed 18 May 2011

Taylor, F.W. (1911) *The principles of scientific management*, New York: Harper & Brothers

TC 176 (2000) *About TC 176*, International Standards Organization, www.iso.org/iso/home/standards_development/list_of_iso_technical_committees/iso_technical_committee.htm?commid=53882. Accessed 2 January 2004

TC 207 About (2004) About TC 207, International Standards Organization, www.tc207.org/About207.asp. Accessed 2 July 2004

TC 207 FAQ (2004) Frequently asked questions, International Standards Organization, www.tc207.org/faq.asp?Question=9999. Accessed 2 February 2004

Tsujii, K. (2003) *The number of ISO14001/EMAS registration of the world*, ISO World, www.ecology.or.jp/isoworld/english/analy14k.htm. Accessed 2 February 2004

von Weizsäcker, E.U., Lovins, A.B. and Lovins, L.H. (1998) *Factor four: Doubling wealth – halving resource use. The new report to the Club of Rome*, London: Earthscan

Wackernagel, M. and Rees, W. (1996) *Our ecological footprint: Reducing human impact on the Earth*, Canada: New Society Publishers

WCED (1987) *Our common future*, Oxford: Oxford University Press

Weale, A. (1992) *The new politics of pollution*, Manchester: Manchester University Press

Wenk, M. (2005) *The European Union's eco-management and audit scheme (EMAS)*, Dordrecht: Springer

6 Sustainable development theory

Moving from management to stewardship

6.1 Introduction

Chapter 5 argued that practical environmental management cannot currently overcome or transcend the epistemological limitations of prediction and control of the Earth System discussed in Chapter 2. These assumptions are typically implicit in intergovernmental sustainable development literature discussed in Chapters 3 and 4. The same goes for ethical assumptions: economistic utilitarianism can legitimate potentially dangerous policy design that will take us towards thresholds in the Earth System that are currently unknowable due to the complexity of the Earth System.

To recap, the broad approach of the book is to compare official sustainable development policy documents and sustainable development theory, in order to identify and suggest possible alternative or even improved epistemology, ethics and policy-making processes. The latter part of this process starts in earnest here. This chapter will consider theoretical responses to sustainable development in high-income countries,[1] in particular to open up discussion beyond environmental management practice and intergovernmental discussions of sustainable development. Chapter 2 discussed important indications of alternative approaches, specifically the 'open society' (Popper, 1966), Palmer and Finlay (2003) and, most specifically relevant, Jamieson (1992); this chapter will consider a broader range of ideas. Section 6.2 will consider theoretical responses to sustainable development, in particular the epistemological and ethical ideas used in these, to look for potential responses to epistemological limitations and ethical contestations. Section 6.3 will examine theory that more specifically considers epistemological questions and sustainable development. Section 6.4 will analyse ideas that more specifically consider ethical questions and sustainable development. Section 6.5 will draw these discussions together. Chapter 7 will propose possible improvements to the ethical basis of sustainable development, before Chapter 8 addresses questions around citizen participation in sustainable development decision-making in greater detail than in this chapter.

Before considering more specifically sustainable development policy ideas, a brief discussion of more general policy theory will provide useful context. There is a diffuse understanding of the significance of limitations of knowledge for policy, even if there is little engagement with the depth of difficulties described in Chapter 2. Relevant literature is noted throughout this book. Exceptions that do wrestle directly with profound difficulties in prediction are 'post-normal' science (Ravetz and Funtowicz, 1999), the growing literature on 'wicked problems' (e.g. APSC, 2007; Brown et al., 2010; Ritchey, 2011) and the precautionary principle. It is not clear that any of these fields offer significantly better explicit 'solutions' than Popperian participative policy but they are fields that may develop helpful responses to making policy in an unpredictable world; the precautionary principle is discussed later in this chapter.

With ethics, the picture is largely simpler with little discussion of ethics in the broad policy literature. Policy theory and practice tends to assume its ethical aim is economic, materialist, utilitarian and consequentialist (Hill, 2009; Hogwood and Gunn, 1984; Hudson and Lowe, 2009; John, 2011; Jones, 1994; Pressman and Wildavsky, 1984; Rose, 2005; Torgerson, 1999) or simple financial minimisation of costs and maximisation of benefits. Tullock (2006), Theodoulou and Cahn (1995), Castles (1999), Sabatier (2007) and Peters and Pierre (2006) do complicate this picture, but they do not appear to have developed robust, widely agreed models of how policy-making chooses between different forms of ethics. The key suggestion by Lindblom (1968), which is broad enough to apply to ethics, is that policymakers, at all levels in administration, respond to influence from the media, political party allegiance, bureaucratic allegiance, personal moral positions, pressure groups, public opinion, etc.

6.2 Broad theoretical responses

There is an extensive literature that addresses sustainable development questions. The following is intended to give a broad overview of the literature most relevant to the questions being explored in this book, to see how this points beyond the intergovernmental literature already analysed.

One common orienting framework is provided by the distinction between 'strong' and 'weak' sustainability. Daly (1992) and Ekins (2003, 150–3) characterise those who advocate weak sustainability as making the assumption that more 'natural capital' can be replaced by 'manufactured and human capital' than is suggested by those who advocate strong sustainability. Ekins writes of the assumptions of advocates of strong sustainability: 'Substitutability of manufactured for natural capital is seriously limited by such environmental characteristics as irreversibility, uncertainty and ... "critical" components of natural capital which make a unique contribution to welfare' (ibid., 151).

It is worth noting that for Ekins, this debate is framed by the utilitarian or even economistic utilitarian notion of 'welfare'. Some advocates of strong sustainability call into question how widely utilitarian ethics should be applied by suggesting that some or all of 'nature' has 'intrinsic' value that goes beyond the utility that it provides to humans. Reid (1995, 41–2) notes tensions between materialist and utilitarian arguments for sustainable development and those rooted in seeing ecosystems as having value beyond what material benefits can be obtained from them. More relevant to this book is the belief that there are critical or essential aspects to the Earth System and that irreversibility and uncertainty are important ideas that are relevant to human knowledge of the Earth System and its components.

Ekins argues that even from a utilitarian 'welfare' point of view, strong sustainability is more robust than its weak counterpart as it is analytically a more 'falsifiable' (Popper, 1972) assumption than weak sustainability, because for weak sustainability

> there may be insuperable difficulties in performing the necessary monetisation and aggregation ... the numbers ... cannot shed any light on the question whether the assumption of commensurability and substitutable capitals was justified in the first place. In assuming away any differences at the start, there is no way of establishing later on whether such differences were important.
>
> (Ekins, 2003, 151–2)

It is also important to note that Ekins (ibid., 152) argues that loss of natural capital will have a greater tendency to be irreversible. In considering the Earth System and substitutability, Ekins concludes: 'If our current development is unsustainable, it is because it is depleting some critical, non-substitutable components of the capital base on which it depends' (ibid., 153).

In discussing weak and strong sustainability, Ekins (ibid., 150) implies that the weak sustainability aimed at by many national governments assumes achieving economic growth while reducing all types of stress to the Earth System, which Ekins sceptically states would be 'unprecedented'. He then argues that recent environmental destruction is also unprecedented (ibid., 166), but suggests that there are policy options that will 'increase economic output, while improving the environment: removing environmentally damaging subsidies, increasing take-up of already competitive, environmentally benign technologies, and ecological tax reform' (ibid., 167).

From an 'ecological modernisation' perspective, Ekins appears broadly correct; however, it is important to note that thorough technical comparisons of different technological options, such as life cycle assessment (ISO/FDIS 14040, 1997), often find that each technology is better in some ways but worse in others. That said, there do appear to be significant technologies that are broadly, though not unquestionably, more benign than alternatives – renewable energy technologies being a good candidate. So economic policy options can be improved in regard to the level of environmental harm, but it is not clear that they can be sufficient to ensure ecological sustainability, and economic approaches may still promote unsustainable attitudes (cf. Berglund and Matti, 2006; Jamieson, 1992; Padilla, 2004; Smith, 2003, 29–51).

Ekins (2003, 153–5) argues that ecological sustainability issues are different in character than economic and social sustainability. Most importantly for this book, he implies that because of complexity, scientific uncertainty and thresholds, parts of the Earth System essential for human civilisation or complex life could end up being 'sacrificed for economic or social benefits, without appreciation of the wider implications' (ibid., 155). Unfortunately, Ekins (ibid., 155) also implies that levels of stress to the Earth System before thresholds are crossed can be 'estimated' without making clear how. We have already seen how this objective is cast into doubt by the complexity of the Earth System. Once again, polices based on 'thresholds' may be misguided. This assumption also affects his discussion of technology and policy options (ibid., 166–7), though he does note the difficulty of the task, suggesting ten-fold technical improvement and politically difficult changes are required. He also suggests that recent progress is not encouraging as regards the potential for 'compatibility between economic growth and environmental sustainability' (ibid., 167).

Discussing indicators of sustainable development, Ekins (ibid., 155–65) argues that the key limitation of indicator schemes that seek to use 'a common unit (normally money) … is that it is often either impossible, or very difficult or very controversial, to convert all changes … to … any … common numeraire' (ibid., 156). This would make this type of indicator deeply problematic in pluralistic societies, though it might be better than only using existing economic indicators; arguably less controversial would be

> a range of indicators intended to cover the main issues … related to sustainable development … unless all the indicators are moving in the same direction … it is impossible to say whether … sustainable development is being approached or not.
>
> (Ibid.)

So as we can see, Ekins still highlights problems with these types of indicator (cf. Adger, 2006, 274–5). In addition, both these types of indicator also have the problem of difficulties knowing what caused the indicator or indicators to move in a sustainable or unsustainable direction.

As part of his discussion of indicators, Ekins (2003, 158–60) uncritically discusses conceptions of human capital and social capital. However, these can be criticised as dehumanising utilitarian conceptions that treat humans as little more than cogs in the great machine of industrialism. In this discussion, Ekins at least appears to treat human achievements such as art, music, literature, philosophy, architecture, compassion and all the 'nobler' aspects of humanity as having no 'value' other than increasing the economic performance of the global economy. I have no essential objection to people having that value system. There are those, though (cf. Palmer and Finlay, 2003), who find such a diminished (sub-human (Lewis, 1963, 15–32)) view of humans tragic and deeply worrying. Even if it is difficult to find academic literature that directly questions the notions of human capital and social capital, there is literature critical of specific studies using these ideas. In pluralistic societies, it is not clear on what basis such economistic utilitarian ethical assumptions should be imposed.

Ekins is more critical of proposed indicators and their ability to adequately reflect environmental questions, though he does still consider this largely in instrumental materialistic utilitarian terms. He hints at epistemological difficulties in identifying critical natural capital, levels of stress the Earth System will withstand and quantifying 'cultural considerations' (Ekins, 2003, 163–5), but appears to proceed to assume that such poorly based indicators are still a good route to sustainable development. The logic of this is not clear but is perhaps based on the assumption that it is better to have ecological indicators as well as economic indicators. An analytically more robust response might be, first to conclude that, despite huge efforts spent on developing indicators, no satisfactory scheme has been found and, second, to question the value of using indicators as a policy tool to be aimed at, rather than simply as measures of problems. Thus, it is perhaps better to argue that both GNP and 'sustainable development indicators' (ibid., 156) should have much less rhetorical power in policy-making than they do now (cf. Jamieson, 1992; Padilla, 2004; Smith, 2003, 29–51). Ashok Khosla[2] also calls into question the value of indicators:

> How do we measure ... areas which constitute sustainable development? How do we put numbers or colours or other descriptors to these indicators of the quality of life or well-being? One answer to that is perhaps, do we need to? Another question we must address is: Are there indicators that are not amenable to quantification? And if we do try to quantify them, do we fall into the same trap as the economists have fallen into for the last one hundred and fifty years – that is, in believing that only things that have numbers mean anything? Clearly this is not the route to take ... we must not lose the forest for the trees.
>
> (Trzyna, 1995, 9)

Khosla goes on to indicate the policy process he prefers:

> I think it is the ... decision-making processes of society, and the transparency and participation of these decision-making processes that are more likely to lead to better solutions for development than simply a methodology that can be put into a computer which will churn out the results.
>
> (Ibid.)

This view will be discussed in more detail in Chapter 8. Ekins begins to conclude his analysis in his review of the concept of sustainable development by reflecting on the difficulties governments have in surviving without economic growth. Notwithstanding questions that might be raised with the example of reduced carbon dioxide in Russia since communism, he importantly suggests that 'there is very little evidence that economic recession leads even to environmental improvement ... The danger is that ... a society faced with a choice between economic growth and environmental sustainability will continue to choose the former' (Ekins, 2003, 167). Here, Ekins does not consider reasons why societies

will continue to choose economic growth. One possible reason is the economistic utilitarianism he himself seems to assume. The 'global virtue tradition' offers
an alternative that appears more likely to choose environmental sustainability
over economic growth as it is less rooted in materialist instrumental assumptions.
Virtue, including moderation, appears more rational if Ekins is correct when he
writes, 'eventually, of course, environmental degradation will make economic
growth unachievable ... leaving the society to cope with both economic and
environmental disintegration' (ibid., 167–8). In conclusion, Ekins summarises
the preceding analysis writing that

> societies can make the shift to environmentally sustainable development,
> but the changes are being resisted ... If ... the biosphere and climate are
> resilient, this will not matter. But if gloomier predictions come to pass, these
> wasted years and this generation, which knew what to do, but could not
> muster the necessary political will to do it, will be held responsible.
>
> (Ibid., 168–9)

Given the epistemological difficulties highlighted in this book, it may be claiming too much to say that 'this generation ... knew what to do', beyond that we
do have a good idea that reducing stress on the Earth System would be prudent
(ambiguity intended). It is hoped that this book provides some pointers to how
this reduction in stress to the Earth System might be achieved.

A useful typological review of the then existing sustainable development and
environmental sustainability literature is provided by Dobson (1998). In this, he
argues that

> the principle motivation behind any conception or theory of sustainable
> development is human interest in human welfare. Sustainable develop-
> ment is, therefore, an anthropocentric notion in a way that environmental
> sustainability need not (but may) be ... conceptions of environmental sus-
> tainability entertain a broader potential community of recipients [of justice].
>
> (Ibid., 61)

This book does advocate sustainable development; however, as should be clear
this is not based purely on human interest or human welfare, particularly if
welfare implies economistic utilitarianism. This book advocates sustainable
development on the assumption that human societies will continue to exist and
hence 'development' of those societies will continue even if (only if, perhaps)
there is a choice by those societies for less consumerist lifestyles, which cause
less stress to the Earth System. The 'global virtue tradition' would see this as a
positive development of societies. This alludes to a further issue that this book
would take with the statement made by Dobson,[3] that is, he appears to assume
that development is broadly economic development, which is reasonable given
the typical notion of development used in the sustainable development literature. Nonetheless, a more critical engagement at this point in his argument may

have been worthwhile (cf. Goulet in Trzyna, 1995, 45–57). This book does not assume human interests are always paramount either. Attfield (1994, particularly 13–62) indicates how the historical notion of stewardship did not assume anthropocentric human interests as always paramount, and how this stewardship could underpin a notion of sustainable development.

Sustainable development does appear, quite reasonably, to assume that it is humans that are making decisions about development, and what is required to sustain any developments. However, this book suggests that it is not clear how humans can identify all significant critical thresholds, thus how humans can identify 'critical natural capital' and 'irreversible nature' in the terminology of the typology by Dobson (1998). This suggests a less consequentialist (and less deontological?) approach than that described by Dobson. Attfield (1994, particularly 13–62) also indicates that some historical notions of stewardship and the justice implied in these notions see different communities (including non-humans) owed justice in different ways. Attfield further suggests that these notions of stewardship can include communities due justice that are at least as broad as Dobson's environmental sustainability and that notions of justice can be based on virtue ethics as well as consequentialist and deontological ethics.

Helping to orient the sustainable development debate, Jacobs (1999, 23–6) argues that, like concepts such as democracy, liberty and social justice, sustainable development has two levels: there are core ideas that are constituent parts of the concept, and a second level where meaning of the component ideas is contested. He argues that the following are the core components of sustainable development and outlines how they have been used and contested in sustainable development discourse:

1 Environment–economy integration: ensuring that economic development and environmental protection are integrated in planning and implementation.
2 Futurity: an explicit concern for the impact of current activity on future generations.
3 Environmental protection: a commitment to reducing pollution and environmental depredation and to more efficient use of resources.
4 Equity: a commitment to meeting at least the basic needs of the poor of the present generation (as well as equity between generations).
5 Quality of life: a recognition that human well-being is constituted by more than just income growth.
6 Participation: the recognition that sustainable development requires involvement of all groups or 'stake-holders' in society.

(Ibid., 26–7)

Jacobs (ibid., 27, 29–30) argues that bringing this broad range of ideas together into a concept that has such 'widespread endorsement' (ibid., 30) makes sustainable development deeply significant. Thus, 'disagreements over the "meaning of sustainable development" are not semantic disputations but *are* ... substantive political arguments' (ibid., 26, emphasis in original). He (ibid., 27, emphasis in original) is keen to claim that '*Agenda 21* (the global action plan for sustainable development signed by 173 national governments at [UNCED])' gives 'authority' to treat participation as having value in its own right. For the WCED, 'participation was primarily regarded as a means to the substantive ends represented by the first five core ideas' Jacobs (ibid.) claims. This is important for this book, but it may be more accurate to say that the WCED saw participation as intrinsically valuable for sustainable development and a useful means to an end. Indeed, it may be that Agenda 21 treated participation too much as an end in itself to deflect attention from difficult environmental questions, rather than seeing participation as being a good when bound into the whole that makes up sustainable development.[4] To give an example that might clarify, courage is a virtue for Aristotle, but Aristotle would want to see courage deployed for the sake of justice not extortion.

The notion of participation is an important issue and aspects of this will be considered in more detail in Chapter 8. In the meantime, the following is offered as an indication. Giving participation intrinsic value can be based on a variety of ontological assumptions about the nature of human persons such as they have freewill or intrinsic dignity. However, a stronger argument of the value of participation in the context of this book will be that while humans do not know what is required to prevent catastrophic unsustainable development, maximising participation should maximise:

- participation as a good in itself for the above intrinsic arguments;
- the problem solving capacity of societies from an 'open society' (Popper, 1966) viewpoint;
- informing citizens of the consequences of their actions;
- 'buy-in' or at least acquiesce any 'solutions', both those facilitated by governments and other organisations, and the solutions that individuals and households have to implement themselves (cf. ibid., 42–3). If this includes the maximum possible reduction of material standards of living, in consumerist 'classes', this will hopefully minimise stress to the Earth System.

Obviously maximising participation will cause stress to the Earth System in itself from the activities associated with participation. Citizens can themselves make decisions about whether they judge particular participation is worth the related stress to the Earth System, but it is not clear that there is a better 'system' than this available to make this trade-off.

Of the core ideas he identifies, Jacobs argues that

> sustainable development is evidently *not* the path of development which has been followed by the global economy … in signing *Agenda 21* … countries … accepted that sustainable development *does* represent a new trajectory for development … the new discourse has changed the nature … of political activity and debate on these issues.
>
> (Ibid., 27–8, emphasis in original)

Jacobs further argues 'that governments have felt obliged to do *something*' (ibid., 28, emphasis in original) to move towards sustainable development, pressure groups have been able to use commitments such as Agenda 21 leverage (cf. Benton, 1999, 211) and policy-making organisations have been trying to learn how to apply sustainable development in practice.

Some examples of where Jacobs (1999, particularly 29, 31–9, 40–5) notes the significance of unresolved questions about ethical and political assumptions for sustainable development are:

- whether 'the environment' has value only in the sense that it can provide economic benefits to humans, whether it has value for non-economic benefits it provides to humans or whether it has intrinsic value for its own sake as well; how to resolve any conflicts between these positions;
- whether economic growth (economic utilitarianism) or industrialism is a good in itself, or even the key good for policy, or whether there other more important goods (typically other notions of liberty than economic liberty; rights or virtues);
- whether justice is based on strict application of current legal property rights or, noting past injustice and current inequality of economic and political power, whether some more egalitarian form of justice should be sought, or whether the best possible stewardship (however defined) should be the aim;
- the value of citizens participating in the policy decisions that affect their lives;
- what should be included in the notion of sustainable development?

In the absence of determinate answers to these questions, perhaps discursive participation is the best way to resolve them. This will be discussed further in Chapter 8.

In his discussions, Jacobs does not question the epistemological assumption of much sustainable development literature that the limits of stress to the Earth System can be determined (ibid., particularly 23–4, 27, 29, 31–2, 40–5). He does perhaps hint at these problems (ibid., 23–4, 29, 40) and hints at part of a possible political resolution when he says that development has not been sustainable in recent decades (ibid., 27). Thus, it may be possible to get agreement that current and projected levels of stress to the Earth System appear unsustainable and should be reduced. This leaves 'simply' the question of by how much and by what methods.

Jacobs characterises environmental protection contestations using the strong and weak sustainability ideas previously outlined (ibid., 31–2). He also characterises contestations around equity, the scope that sustainable development should have and participation (ibid., 32–8). As these are important questions that have not been directly addressed so far let us do so now.

With regard to equity, he notes that those who have done well out of the inequalities of the current system are often less keen to address this aspect of sustainable development, though some 'Northern NGOs' (ibid., 33) have done some campaigning on this issue in 'the North'. Equity is one way that Jacobs suggests some want to extend the scope of sustainable development beyond simple environmental concerns, others include gender issues, the importance of participation, a range of quality of life issues that go beyond income[5] and respect for diversity of societies. Jacobs, importantly, is keen to point out that 'technocratic' (ibid., 37) environmentalism could be in danger of not respecting this diversity of societies.

It is clear that the broad understanding of sustainable development that Jacobs indicates would be a 'new goal' (ibid.) for politics. Jacobs implies that this is a key reason why in 'most Northern countries, the debate about sustainable development is conducted entirely within the environmental field' (ibid., 35) such that in Britain 'a huge "National Strategy"… went unremarked' (ibid., 36). About participation, Jacobs (ibid., 34) argues that where 'governments … adopt … a "top-down" interpretation of … participation … such participation is required … in the implementation … not in deciding objectives … Governments decide objectives, using expert knowledge … "participation" frequently becomes a disguise for government inaction'.

This is an important observation, particularly so as it suggests a connection between basing policy on expert knowledge and inaction. To expand on this, it appears:

- typically governments use experts to design policy;
- typically, with regard to sustainable development, experts decide that ultimately it is citizens who need to change their actions and attitudes to achieve sustainable development, including so that governments can do their part without being voted out of office;
- Dryzek (1990, 116) suggests that typically citizens assume that experts and administrations know what is best with regard to policy questions.

Thus, there may be a 'stand-off' with experts expecting governments to 'encourage' citizens to become sustainable and citizens expecting experts and governments to put policies in place that will achieve sustainability. We will perhaps have to go through a process where citizens learn that experts cannot achieve sustainability until a point where citizens take responsibility for their own actions and vote for governments that will put structures in place that allow greater sustainability (cf. Hounsham, 2006, particularly 64, 130, 141)

The more 'experts' freely admit that they cannot tell governments how to achieve sustainability, because they do not know the levels of stress the Earth System will withstand before 'catastrophic' changes will take place to the Earth System, the sooner perhaps more citizens will take responsibility for reducing their personal stress on the Earth System and vote for necessary societal changes. However, in the face of uncertainty about consequences, citizens will perhaps do that only to the extent that they have indications that 'global society' is moving away from a dominant ethic and practice of economic growth at any cost to an alternative ethic and practice where sustainable development is a key component.

It is not clear how this can be achieved (cf. Heyd, 2003), but if the ecological virtue ethics implicit in Palmer and Finlay (2003)[6] were to be presented in such a way that leaders of the most powerful nations and global institutions felt the need to respond, a debate might be started that sufficiently captured the public and administrative imagination that moving towards ecological sustainability might occur more rapidly. Indeed, the global virtue tradition might so capture public imagination that leaders of nations and institutions are encouraged by citizens to seriously address the equity component of sustainable development. This might happen if leaders of the economically powerful nations and powerful economic institutions were to admit that their ethical assumptions of economic growth at any cost ('economic utilitarianism') had turned greed from a public virtue into a public vice (cf. Bishop, 1995). This is perhaps required before there is any hope of corrupt national leadership, often associated with very inequitable government of many of the poorest nations, being replaced by governments that govern more for the benefit (common good?) of all citizens of those countries.

Indeed, this type of transformation in global ethics might even help to reduce 'global terrorism' by reducing resentments at injustice and the unquestioning purveyance of economic growth as the key good of societies. It might even isolate terrorists who would commit acts of violence out of hatred or greed by reducing the injustice felt by the wider populations who currently support terrorists (cf. Al Moumin, 2011).

Discussing 'bottom-up' approaches to participation, Jacobs (1999, 34–5) emphasises ordinary citizens being more involved in setting objectives and deciding how to achieve them rather than simply being involved in 'doing their bit' in practical action. Something that perhaps unifies the contestations Jacobs identifies as outlined above is between those whose ethical assumption is that the dominant aim of policy is nearly always to maximise welfare in the form of economic utility (money), and those who hold that other ethical positions should be given greater weight.

Assuming that indicators can be used to make an assessment of the 'vibrancy of communal life' and other less tangible aspects of sustainable development, Jacobs (ibid., 41–3) appears to put an uncritical trust in an empirical epistemology. The literature describing the model of indicators that Jacobs offers is no longer readily available; these appear to have been replaced by a broader range of indicators (Defra, 2010). It is not clear that these can adequately capture aspects of communal life whose 'value' is arguably completely beyond measurement if it is lived to its fullest. The closest is perhaps a measurement of levels of volunteering but one perspective is that the love of parents for their children is the most important 'facet' of 'communal life' and it is far from clear how that can be measured accurately.

This lack of criticality of empiricism by Jacobs is unfortunate (cf. Pezzoli, 1997, 571) given the epistemological and ethical questions raised around indicators in this book. Jacobs proceed to note that 'GNP … is clearly inadequate' (Jacobs, 1999, 41) but fails to consider that if one type of indicator is inadequate because of the perverse effects that it has had on societies, will other forms of indicator simply compound these problems, particularly if the most important 'components' of communal life cannot be measured?

It is worth noting the implicit reductive epistemology assumed by Jacobs and other advocates of indicators. This is not to say that measuring environmental stress, social problems and social progress is of no use, because these are essential to inform democratic debate, as Jacobs rightly points out. However, Jacobs and many other supporters of indicators appear to assume that they can be used to 'manage' societies and the Earth System by 'trial and error' or Baconian 'predict and control' (cf. Jamieson, 1992, 142–6). That is, apply a policy, see what happens and adjust the policy in the light of the result. This makes at least two questionable assumptions. First, it assumes that policy can be carried out as an isolated experiment, when most policies are, at least, intellectually connected via reflective processes and physically via the Earth System. Jacobs appears to admit at least a broad connection of the economy and the environment. Second, it assumes that society and the Earth System have not changed whilst you are doing your 'experiment', such that when you apply your revised policy there would be an expectation that it would work in a similar way to the first iteration. It is quite possible that society and/or the Earth System will be in a quite different state when the revised policy is applied. Thus, any results are quite unpredictable.

A useful relevant treatment of environmental ethics is provided by Brennan (2003). This includes arguing that environmental ethics has been focused on securing legal or moral consideration for non-human facets of the Earth System, with little consideration of whether this is the correct mode of engagement with environmental ethics (ibid., 17–19, 21–2). The emphasis on securing legal consideration is presumably because courts are the dominant way of resolving different views in practice, particularly in the US. Emphasis on securing moral consideration for non-humanity was presumably a response to the human-centred ethics of modernity. Brennan (ibid., 19–21) records various ways this (re-)extension of consideration of non-humanity has been attempted.

The important political and ethical distinction between consumer and citizen are explored by Brennan (ibid., 24–5). Further, he (ibid., 21, 25) appears to argue that most contemporary environmental philosophers agree that the operation of economic systems, particularly beyond the bounds of its competence, is a key cause of environmental damage, apparently without systematic philosophical attempts to identify what the boundaries of economics should be.

Brennan (ibid., 26–31) also notes that questions, including epistemological and ethical questions, around expertise, risk and uncertainty are 'relatively unexplored by environmental philosophers but of considerable practical importance' (ibid., 26; cf. Parker, 2014). Brennan (ibid., 27) suggests that 'Adam Smith's *homo economicus* was a prudent and rational calculator of likely future contingencies', which indicates that economic utilitarianism is fundamentally based on the notion of prediction. He then outlines the current practical difficulties with prediction and environmental issues (ibid., 28–9) in a broadly similar way to this book. In this, he highlights the importance of optimistic or cautious assumptions, offering 'only' Socratic probing as a tool to resolve questions of which of these to adopt.

Epistemological work by Wynne and others is reviewed by Benton (2003, 62–3); specifically he examines the social, particularly policy, context to environmental science and the effect that this context has on scientific conclusions. He notes that there are ambivalent results of this work in motivating concrete action to address issues. In particular, Benton (ibid., 63) discusses credence this work gives to optimistic readings of climate change science, that there will be little harm from human activities, thus justifying (oil) business as usual. He suggests that these ideological readings of climate science by vested interests ignore analytically equally valid pessimistic readings that harm could be much worse than is generally assumed. This book attempts to indicate ways that decisions can be made that adopt a less ideological, more realistic, assumption that takes both extremes into account.

To clarify, if we consider the question of climate change in terms of potential outcomes, we will note that if optimistic outcomes are considered, the best we can hope for is perhaps greater material wealth (given current inequitable market systems, unequally distributed) and potentially greater ability to control the Earth System or at least better abilities to react if things do go wrong. If pessimistic outcomes occur, millions or billions of humans will have to live in privation, we will lose the current global civilisation, the human race could become extinct and, at worst, all complex life forms on earth will disappear. The level of stress on the Earth System from human activity is probably the determining factor humans can 'control'.

A relevant review of economic thought as it applies to sustainable development is presented by Common (2003, 78–96), in particular by drawing out ethical and epistemological implications. He argues that environmental questions were central to the 'classical' economics of Adam Smith and particularly Thomas Malthus (ibid., 84). It is claimed (ibid., 84–5) that with the advent of neo-classical economics, little attention was given to the 'role of the environment in relation to economic activity'. This was the case until the 1970s when considerations of natural resource availability were taken up (ibid., 85–6). These considerations were largely separated from economic issues around pollution and amenity, taken up at the same time, and both are largely ignored by mainstream economics (ibid., 86–7). He implies (ibid., 87) that mainstream economics is even more likely to ignore more recent ecological economics, which attempts to integrate questions of resources, pollution, amenity and distribution with standard neo-classical economics concerns.

Common (ibid., 85) states that economic growth became the 'holy grail' of economists after the Second World War. Common develops this line of argument:

> Adam Smith ... now mainly known for his *doctrine* of the 'invisible hand' ... the idea that allowing individuals to pursue their own self-interest through market transactions promotes the general good ... in its modern form it is one of the central ideas of economics. It can be shown that, given certain

conditions, if everything that is of interest to anybody is traded in competitive markets, then the outcome will be ... it will not be possible to change
things so as to make somebody feel better off except at the cost of making
somebody worse off.

(Ibid., 88, emphasis added)

Common argues that based on this, economics, despite typically claiming otherwise, becomes prescriptive or normative even though in practice this means large
inequalities in 'wealth and income'. This discussion implies that conventional
economics also embodies materialist utilitarian ethics and ignores calls for greater
justice such as those from the world religions (Palmer and Finlay, 2003).

The analysis goes on to discuss recognised situations in which the above
assumptions of economics do not apply, such as nobody has private property
rights over the atmosphere. Common (2003, 88–91) outlines the suggestions
that mainstream economists have to deal with these issues, particularly when
constructing forms of trading system, before he criticises these from technical and
ethical perspectives.

The technical criticisms include epistemological difficulties, particularly
around knowing the level of stress the Earth System will withstand. Common
(ibid., 90–1) does point to one partial resolution of this question when he discusses tradable permits that could start from current levels of emission and
reduce them; however, there still remains questions of the rate at which they
need to be reduced and to what level. I would argue that something akin to
Aristotle's virtue of temperance is a better approach to reduce stress to the
minimum for a society alongside its other goals, if we cannot know the maximum we can safely go up to.

The ethical criticisms are of the implicit materialist utilitarianism of mainstream economics, favouring instead a process of deliberation by citizens
(ibid., 91) and implicitly plurality of ethics (utility, rights and virtue). In the
same paragraph, Common argues for precaution as a response to 'pervasive uncertainty about how natural systems work'. It is not clear whether Common sees this
as an ethical or technical response or a combination of these.

In explicitly considering sustainable development, Common (ibid., 91–5)
states that few economists 'found much to quarrel with' in the WCED (1987)
before implying this was based on the economic perspective of the WCED. In
particular, he emphasises the substitutability assumed by the WCED, discussed
earlier in this chapter in relation to the notions of strong and weak sustainability.
Common (2003, 94) argues in this regard that a paper by Hartwick (1977) 'has
had a profound influence on the way economists think about sustainable development', before highlighting that there are important technical and normative
assumptions in acceptance of substitutability.

In conclusion, it is argued (Common, 2003, 95–6) that addressing ecological issues and sustainable development requires insights from many disciplines
beyond economics, highlighting politics and natural science. He poses the question about how reduced material wealth can be made compatible with democracy

without attempting to answer the question. One possible suggestion being canvassed in this book is for the 'global virtue tradition' to be highlighted as an alternative or at least a complement to the materialist utilitarian ethics that is currently dominant in government and commercial institutions.

From Wilkinson (2003), we can draw out epistemological and ethical insights provided by legal studies. The successes and failures of law at addressing environmental issues are presented by Wilkinson (ibid., 102–16):

- Improved air and water quality where appropriate laws have been implemented and enforced.
- Success in endangered species protection where that can be achieved by limiting trade in the species or products derived from that species and where it can be achieved by protecting specific areas of habitat from 'development'.
- Stratospheric ozone layer protection.

An important connection of these issues is that, if there is political will, it is quite clear what should be done to achieve protection and the science behind these judgements is fairly uncontested; that is, there are no significant epistemological issues. Wilkinson contends that environmental law has been less successful in delivering effective:

- enforcement and implementation;
- adequate response to climate change;
- fisheries protection.

Epistemological issues or at least contested science have played a part in the lack of success in addressing climate change and fisheries protection because those who want to continue to stress nature more than the majority of scientists suggest is wise, use dissenting scientists to justify continuing business-as-usual. Wilkinson also importantly claims (ibid., 116–18) that existing environmental law may reinforce existing social inequalities and entrench 'capitalist consumer-driven … modern western life'. Further important suggestions are made (ibid., 116): first, that environmental laws have had a cultural effect beyond their direct consequences, in particular changing attitudes and even moving ethical assumptions away from concern with humans towards increased concern for non-humanity; and, second, raising the political profile of environmental issues.

A common approach to sustainable development questions in the literature is the I=PAT Commoner/Ehrlich 'equation' (Ekins, 2003, 167) and variations. One definition is from Daily and Ehrlich:

> The impact (I) of any population can be expressed as a product of three characteristics: the population's size (P), its affluence or per-capita consumption (A), and the environmental damage (T) inflicted by the technologies used to supply each unit of consumption.
>
> (1992, 762)

A useful discussion of this concept that draws out many of the implications of the equation is conducted by Reid (1995, 112–23). The equation does appear to indicate broadly what needs to be done in practical terms to reduce stress to the Earth System and is commonly used to imply that stress to the Earth System should be reduced. However, it does not eliminate questions of the level of impact the Earth System will withstand or which technologies will cause least stress to the Earth System. The difficulties of this last point were discussed in the preceding chapter of this book, particularly with regard to life cycle assessment.

The above survey gives an indication of broad responses to sustainable development, and the frequent discussion of epistemological and ethical questions in this literature suggests their importance for sustainable development. This is an important step beyond the intergovernmental sustainable development literature discussed in previous chapters. The next section will consider literature that addresses epistemological questions around sustainable development more directly.

6.3 Epistemological responses

A report of a workshop 'Sustainable development: epistemological challenges to science and technology' (Modvar and Gallopín, 2005) outlines many of the epistemological issues raised by this book. It also makes many similar suggestions, in particular the recommendation for more open (Popper, 1966) participative processes to address sustainable development.

The Committee on the Applications of Ecological Theory to Environmental Problems (1986) includes early discussion of epistemological difficulties around environmental problems. This demonstrates that some of the epistemological difficulties highlighted in this book were known many years ago, which raises questions about if and when epistemological difficulties will be overcome to allow robust prediction for policy.

Lélé (1991, 613) is critical of the characterisation of key problems associated with sustainable development, the analysis of those problems, content and structures of the proposed solutions and responses to 'incomplete knowledge and uncertainty', giving examples from international trade, agriculture and tropical forests (ibid., 616–18). Given the emphasis Lélé (ibid., 613) puts on questions of 'incomplete knowledge and uncertainty', it is surprising that he does not clearly highlight these issues nor explore the implications, beyond perhaps implying that the issues need to be made explicit to enable debate.

Respecting ignorance and uncertainty (Gibson, 1992, 158–73) outlines a broadly similar analysis of the limits to human knowledge for sustainable development policy as indicated by this book. Based on this analysis, he suggests that it is vital that these limits be recognised and considered in policy-making. More specifically, he makes a range of useful suggestions, including addressing what is 'clearly unsustainable … and [increasing] efforts to make socio-ecological systems more resilient and adaptable in the face of surprises' (ibid., 165). Themes in the suggestions include open, iterative, network policy processes that prepare for the worst case and promote adaptable, diverse technologies less dependent on centralised support.

Another of the relatively few discussions of sustainable development that looks directly at epistemological issues is provided by Mebratu (1998). This includes discussion of how different types of institution and theoretical perspective view the concept of sustainable development, suggesting unsurprisingly that businesses are primarily concerned with efficiency (ibid., 503–12). Second, that eco-feminism is concerned with 'the critical correlation between the domination of nature and the domination of women, with the connection of the subjugation of women' (ibid., 506). Third, that eco-socialism believes sustainable development will be achieved through 'ecologically oriented socialist development' (ibid., 507). Fourth, that eco-theologians have used less anthropocentric inspirations from within and beyond their own traditions to argue that greed is an ecological vice with humility, detachment and gratitude being ecological virtues (ibid., 509). Fifth, that environmental economics attempts to achieve sustainable development, by internalising externalities to give (more) accurate prices to reflect environmental harm. Lastly, that 'ecological' perspectives highlight interconnections of natural systems and are more or less critical of the epistemological assumptions behind 'deterministic interventions' by humans (ibid., 511). This analysis brings Mebratu (ibid., 513) to propose that the correct epistemological assumption is 'interaction between the parts and the whole'; however, his analysis of epistemology and sustainable development goes a little deeper than this.

Viederman (Trzyna, 1995, 36–43) is a relevant treatment of epistemological questions and sustainability. It emphasises problems of predictive knowledge, but argues that this does not mean that we do not know what to do, implying that reducing stress to the Earth System is the correct response (ibid., 39). He then states that 'economics ... is increasingly being recognized as part of the problem' (ibid., 39), which probably implies that economistic utilitarian ethical assumptions operationalised through conventional economics is a key part of unsustainable development. Viederman goes on quite reasonably to contend that economic systems 'are human constructs' (ibid., 39) that can be changed. He (ibid., 40) advocates humility, precaution and reversible decisions. He does not make clear how to ensure their decisions or the effects of decisions are reversible and he does not resolve issues of inertia in the Earth System. Viederman (ibid., 40–1) also implies that historically the political economy of science has tended to promote unsustainability and that scientists have a moral responsibility to be more vocal about the limits of science with regard to Earth System stress, with which I concur. Some valuable suggestions are then made (ibid., 42–3) about how science and history can be better used to promote sustainability.

An analysis presented by Ekenberg et al. (2001) claims that conventional (utilitarian) methods of risk evaluation are problematic when frequency of damage is rare but potentially catastrophic. They suggest focusing on thresholds, but are not clear how these can be identified.

Epistemological difficulties around key sustainable development issues and policy-making via participatory democracy are discussed by Pellizzoni (2003). In this, he argues that bureaucratic policy-making is ineffective in responding to radical uncertainty (or unpredictability). However, he also makes clear that certain types of participatory technology assessment are also problematic, in particular because the incommensurability of common ontological, epistemological and ethical assumptions makes agreement difficult or impossible. This is an important criticism. However, there are alternative participatory models that Pellizzoni does not discuss. These include discursive democracy (Dryzek, 1990, 2000), which should be better at responding to unpredictability because it is rooted in recognition of epistemological limits (Dryzek, 1987), and it emphasises the transformative possibilities of discourse in a variety of ways. That is, it allows the possibility and provides 'space' for people to examine their assumptions, and even if they do not change their own assumptions, at least to better respect the assumptions of others.

A very similar analysis of epistemological difficulties to this book is outlined by Stirling (Berkhout *et al.*, 2003, 37–47), particularly around risk assessment and technology assessment more generally. This is a useful chapter that brings together an impressive number of insights from social science that are relevant to the question of technology assessment but also the broader questions considered in this book. In the context of the focus of the chapter by Stirling, broadly he recommends precautionary approaches balanced by technology foresight along with the recommendation that the validity and value of plurality of assumptions be brought together in forms of participative decision processes (ibid., 48–63).

To try to respond to these problems more concretely in the context of this book, it appears that all major sets of ontological and epistemological assumptions should be able to agree that the Earth System is unpredictable. They may also be able to agree that in practice human stress on the Earth System *could* cause the end of industrial human civilizations, or worse, in a decade (given the level of uncertainty and that there is no analogue to the current situation of the Earth System), or it may take thousands of years or even may never happen. The key question is probably then how to respond, perhaps specifically whether to be cautious or confident in the face of this uncertainty. Ethical assumptions perhaps then come to the fore. A choice to be confident and 'ignore' the risks of catastrophe might be based on greed and a desire for wanton consumption. To ask groups and individuals what their ethical and epistemological choices are based on would be reasonable and could be worthwhile in discussions of policy. It is likely that some may continue to hold that greed and wanton consumption are virtues; however, when confronted with how unpredictable the Earth System is and the evidence of past rapid change in the Earth System, it seems likely that more will assume that greed and wanton consumption are vices than currently do so. 'The Natural Step' (Natural Step, 2011) and permaculture (Mollison, 1988) are reasonable practical responses at the global and local levels to a desire to minimise stress to the Earth System.

'Green Critiques of Science and Knowledge' (Hay, 2002, 120–52) is an overview that indicates more concern with whether science should be used to control 'nature' than whether it can be used to control the Earth System. Anti-democratic possibilities of privileging of knowledge of approved scientists is emphasised (ibid., 128) particularly when it is taken into account that the value-free nature of science is contested. The importance of uncertainty and chaos in green critiques of putting unquestioned faith in science is highlighted (ibid., 129–31). Phenomenological epistemology from a green point of view is discussed by Hay (ibid., 142–5, 150–1). This is interesting, but it is not clear from the description how this process can inform ethical schemes; this may be because of a lack of vision by myself and may be worth further research.[7]

There is other research that engages with epistemological questions around environmental questions, even if it does not address them directly. This includes the vast amounts of literature that discuss the precautionary principle and risk 'management' with regard to sustainable development. A complete review of all this literature is beyond the scope of this book, but it is hoped that the following provides a reasonable overview of the most relevant literature.

Tickner (2003) provides a relevant treatment of precaution from a range of authors. The first chapter (ibid., 3–16) echoes much of the analysis of this book including: 'This type of uncertainty, called indeterminacy … cannot be readily reduced' (ibid., 5). In harmony with this book, it also notes questions around prediction, fragmentation, 'latent periods' (ibid., 4), complex causal relationships including multiple stresses (ibid., 4–6), difficulties conducting isolated experiments (ibid.), narrow hypotheses (ibid., 5), ignoring what cannot be quantified (ibid., 6) and ignoring much uncertainty (ibid., 6–7). Tickner (ibid., 7) proceeds to argue that questionable assumptions about these questions have been institutionalised in environmental policy structures. Valuable suggestions are made about methods for science and policy that can better address current Earth System knowledge. However, it is not clear that any of the suggestions offer robust predictive approaches; if anything they support the broad thrust of this book – perhaps particularly where he writes: 'As citizens and purveyors of knowledge, environmental scientists have a social responsibility to sound an alarm when irreversible or serious effects may occur but are not immediately apparent' (ibid., 16).

Outlining 'precautionary assessment', Tickner (ibid., 265–77) provides a valuable positive constructive vision of the precautionary principle, which appears a significant improvement on the logic of conventional risk assessment processes, even if it may require significantly more effort in some cases. The suggestions appear to borrow quite a lot from intellectual virtues such as (Thomist) prudence and moral virtues such as temperance in satisfying immediate desires. Tickner (ibid., 277) perhaps implies this; however, he suggests that precautionary assessment will require changes in policy-making processes, without looking at the ethical principles that underpin policy-making. The suggestions do not address the inability to predict, or 'ignorance', in any obvious direct way, but may point the way to some practical ways forward, as long as they do not foster assumptions that they are an adequate 'bureaucratic' response. O'Brien (ibid., 279–94) offers a broadly similar positive vision of precaution or 'forecaring' (ibid., 279).

Other contributors to Tickner (2003) are also relevant; Kaiser argues that unpredictability in policy questions means that democratic participation in those decisions is called for (ibid., 47–50). Brown (ibid., 141–54) discusses precaution and climate change; in this he makes valuable suggestions about how difficult to quantify possible effects, can be communicated. However, he appears to assume that 'all plausible effects' (ibid., 141, see also 153) can be identified, when experience suggests that ignorance of possible effects is common in the history of human decision-making, until the effects have occurred.

Discussion of genetically modified organism (GMO) regulation by Barrett and Lee (ibid., 157–70) broadly agrees with the tone of this book. Gee and Stirling (ibid., 195–210) note the importance of questions around prediction (ibid., 195) and appear to suggest (ibid., 196) that precaution is a key response without making clear how it is an adequate response to limitations of prediction. Their discussion (ibid., 200–8) is perhaps as useful a set of policy suggestions for responding to uncertainty around environmental issues as is found in the literature reviewed for this book. Specifically they suggest a number of valuable ideas that should make risk management more robust; these include a recommendation to 'reduce the general use of energy and materials via greater eco-efficiencies so as to reduce overall burdens, thereby limiting the scale of future surprises' (ibid., 201).

This has clear parallels with calls in this book to reduce stress to the Earth System. In specifying that this should be achieved by eco-efficiencies, it is perhaps more based on economistic utilitarian ethics and techno-optimistic epistemology than it need be. If means of reduced stress were to be specified, then examples such as eco-efficiency and simpler lifestyles could have been given, in a way that was clearly intended not to be exhaustive. The suggestions by Gee and Stirling (ibid., 200–8) are useful; however, if applied to existing risk management they would require significant extra risk assessment and regulatory effort, at least in the short term. This effort may well be worthwhile; it is difficult to judge without being able to predict outcomes. It is not clear that the suggestions analytically can eliminate 'ignorance' or the problem of induction. Thus, it still appears analytically valid to highlight Baconian predict and control assumptions as problematic when applied to the Earth System, as appears to be assumed by sustainable development policy literature, particularly in the form of typical economic models.

A good outline of how different subjects use different scientific methods, past failures of scientific methods, questionable typical scientific assumptions, how some issues of sustainable development are connected and strategies to address surprises is provided by Levins (ibid., 355–68). However, none of the strategies guarantee prediction or effective elimination of ignorance; this suggests the continued validity of questioning Baconian prediction and control assumptions. Levins (ibid., 362–4) criticises the economistic utilitarian ethical assumptions of industrial science and suggests open (Popper, 1966) democratisation to 'mobilize the collective intelligence of our species', and it could simultaneously be a method to help resolve differences of opinion about ethical assumptions.

A call for scientists to be clear ('truthful', 'honest') that science cannot currently or in the foreseeable future tell us what safe levels of stress from industrial activity are, is important. She also calls for scientists to advocate democracy as the response to this limitation in science. I concur with both suggestions. We shall explore democratising policy in Chapter 8.

Tickner (2003) concludes with the collective 'Lowell statement on science and the precautionary principle'. This is interesting for a number of reasons. First, it agrees with much of the tone of this book, particularly with regard to the limits of human knowledge of the Earth System. Second, even though it makes very little direct reference to difficulties in prediction or ignorance, it implies that assuming Baconian prediction and control is deeply questionable. Third, it makes a fairly unequivocal normative assumption in favour of an 'economically sustainable future' (ibid., 383). If science wishes to be non-normative or, perhaps more possible, more neutral between different ethical assumptions, then economistic utilitarianism is perhaps an unfortunate (unspoken) organising framework to use, particularly as it assumes prediction. Given the difficulties in prediction alluded to in the statement and book, criticism of ethical assumptions that assume prediction would have been worthwhile.

A useful systematic analysis of key policy questions around notions of the precautionary principle by Turner and Hartzell (2004) includes discussion of problems of knowledge and ethical questions. They eloquently illustrate why the precautionary principle is not helpful as a decision tool, even if they make the questionable assertion (ibid., 457–8) that economics is the only way to resolve questions of trade-off. Indeed, their discussion is perhaps contradictory in this regard, particularly when they suggest that the precautionary principle can serve as a 'banner that signifies ... shared reservations about economic cost–benefit analysis' (ibid., 459).

The 'ordinary meaning' of precaution is compared by Sandin (2004) to the use of precaution or the precautionary principle in policy situations. An important part of the analysis by Sandin (ibid., 467–72) for this book is the discussion of how epistemological assumptions, particularly around standards of proof, affect the decisions about whether to be cautious or confident in the face of uncertainty. Sandin does not propose a clear resolution to these questions, but he does imply that choices made often tie ethical and epistemological assumptions together. To give a simplified example, those who make materialist utilitarian ethical assumptions tend to assume that current epistemology is sufficient to control the environment.

An interesting discussion that connects epistemology and ethics in the context of sustainable development is provided by O'Connor (2000); particularly, discussion of valuation and how different epistemological assumptions are connected to different valuation tools that can be used for policy-making (cf. Carolan, 2004). As part of this discussion, different normative assumptions are teased out in a way that perhaps suggests that different policy tools are chosen depending on normative assumptions and the outcomes that are likely from the choice of those tools: 'Every method of research enquiry carries "normative" as well as "epistemological" pre-dispositions' (O'Connor, 2000, 178). The article does suggest some intriguing possible ways forward for policy approaches that recognise and address contested epistemological and ethical assumptions. However, it does not directly discuss different types of ethical assumption – utility, rights, virtue – even if they are mentioned. If the use of different ethical assumptions is made more explicit, this may be a better starting point for policy processes, than only making different epistemological assumptions clear.

Valuable epistemological 'tools' are indicated by Chapman (2002); these are based on a discussion of virtue and the work of Aldo Leopold and Henry David Thoreau. There is some discussion of virtue ethics; however, more important for this book is the discussion of virtue epistemology. Specifically, Chapman (ibid., 136) makes explicit that a recognition of ecological science and broader ecological ideas means that 'practical wisdom' has to be extended beyond human society to encompass 'the environment'. Based on this, he advocates worthwhile ways that minimising stress to ecosystems can be visualised using a non-instrumental ethical response to nature; specifically mentioning 'temperance' (ibid., 138) with regard to consumption.

A review of 'Science, uncertainty and participation in global environmental governance' literature by Bäckstrand (2004) discusses participation as a response to difficulties in understanding the Earth System. It emphasises the contested nature of such approaches and does not directly consider any ethical implications of epistemological questions around predicting the Earth System.

Scientific Uncertainty and Environmental Problem Solving is discussed by Shrader-Frechette (1996), specifically considering examples of where common assumptions will tend to give results that are too confident in human abilities, particularly to predict and control.

A recent valiant direct engagement with sustainability and epistemology (Tapio and Huutoniemi, 2014) illustrates the difficulties faced and the fact that these are unlikely to be resolved soon – suggesting the need to go beyond epistemology and predictive approaches.

The preceding is a reasonable survey of the literature that considers epistemological questions around sustainable development. This reinforces the hypothesis that we cannot currently successfully use predict and control epistemology with the Earth System. It is important to note that much of this literature links epistemology and ethics quite closely, typically implying or arguing that less stress to the Earth System or at least subsystems is needed. Let us now consider more pointedly ethical literature around sustainable development.

6.4 Ethical responses

This section considers theory that discusses ethical responses to questions around sustainable development. Let us start by considering authors who specifically connect questions of epistemology and ethics in the context of sustainable development. The next chapter will go beyond existing approaches to propose what is hoped will be a better ethical basis for sustainable development, when the Earth System is not predictable.

Let us first return to Shrader-Frechette (1996, 23–35) noting that she links ethical responses to 'decision-theoretic uncertainty involving potentially catastrophic consequences', arguing for a form of maxi–min that seeks to avoid 'the worst possible consequences of all options' (ibid., 24) rather than 'expected-utility ethics' (cf. Langhelle, 1999; Lemons and Brown, 1995, 21). That is, she advocates caution not utilitarianism, perhaps based on some notion of virtue ethics that is not clearly articulated.

In *Sustainable Development: Science, Ethics and Public Policy*, Lemons and Brown (1995, 275–6) argue for a precautionary approach as a response to the types of uncertainty highlighted in this book. Unfortunately, the precautionary approach that they advocate only means 'the burden of proof should be … shifted to those who propose … activities … [it] means that … science … [should] identify useful indicators of environmental and human health change rather than to make precise predictions' (ibid., 1995, 276). With questions such as climate change, this might be a reasonable response to the limitations of science. However, it is not clear how this version of precaution can help citizens or policymakers make decisions as 'proof' is difficult to come by and the use of any indicators can be questioned if there are hundreds or thousands of years of inertia in the Earth System and thresholds that might mean abrupt changes in less than a decade. Despite engaging usefully and perhaps heroically with ethics and indicators, Fredericks (2013) does not eliminate these types of issue with indicators or other issues with indicators noted earlier in this chapter.

Moving on to literature that less clearly connects epistemology and ethics but considers sustainable development issues and ethics, Steffen and Tyson (2001, 3) state their opinion of the relationship between Earth System science and ethics:

> Ethics of global stewardship and strategies for Earth System management are urgently needed. The inadvertent anthropogenic transformation of the planetary environment is, in effect, already a form of management, or rather mismanagement. It is not sustainable. Therefore, the *business-as-usual* way of dealing with the Earth has to be replaced – as soon as possible – by deliberate strategies of good management.

Academic literature around ethics and sustainable development, conservation and the environment tends to focus on broad questions of appropriate attitudes to nature (e.g. deep ecology) or more specific questions, such as:

- exploitive 'development' (e.g. poor people tend to get exploited by rich powerful organisations);
- environmental (in)justice (e.g. poor people tend to live in polluted environments);

- moral considerations owed to future generations;
- moral consideration of non-human nature (e.g. animal rights);
- questions around indigenous cultures and peoples.

Or 'environmental ethics has been most concerned with ... whether nature is directly morally considerable itself, rather than ... because it is appreciated and needed by humans' (Light and Rolston, 2003, 2). Schmidtz and Willott (2002) also suggest that much environmental ethics has been occupied with more particular questions, such as extending rights beyond humans and levels of consumption.

This section will attempt to address the challenge set by Steffen and Tyson (2001, 3) above and will only tangentially address questions that are not implicit in the quotation above by Steffen and Tyson. Before that, it is worth noting that they appear to assume in the above quotation (ibid.) that global stewardship means global management. However, as already noted in Chapter 2 where this and similar literature considers limits to human abilities to predict, the emphasis is on reducing stress to the Earth System from humans, rather than predicting and controlling the Earth System. The following is an analysis of the literature that considers some of the broader ethical questions of particular relevance to this book.

IUCN/UNEP/WWF (1991) 'Caring for the Earth: A strategy for sustainable living' is an important strategy in regard to sustainable development generally and ethical questions around the subject in particular. It is similar to the WCED (1987) in that it makes ethics central to its objectives but does not conduct a clear discussion of ethics of sustainable development, at least in any philosophical depth. It states a number of principles without being explicit about how they are derived:

> Respect and care for the community of life.
>
> Improve the quality of human life ... Economic growth is an important component of development, but it cannot be a goal in itself, nor can it go on indefinitely.
>
> Conserve the Earth's vitality and diversity.
>
> Minimize the depletion of non-renewable resources.
>
> Keep within the Earth's carrying capacity ... Precise definition is difficult, but there are finite limits to the 'carrying capacity' of the Earth's ecosystems.
>
> Change personal attitudes and practices.
>
> Enable communities to care for their own environments.
>
> Provide a national framework for integrating development and conservation.
>
> Create a global alliance.
>
> (IUCN/UNEP/WWF, 1991, 9–11)

These principles mix virtue, deontological and utilitarian language without making relationships clear. The emphasis may be on virtue, perhaps particularly in conceptions of justice, but rights also figure strongly in the strategy. As should be clear from the quotation, the strategy is critical of economistic utilitarianism and aware of poor human abilities to understand stress to the Earth System. IUCN/UNEP/WWF (ibid., 12) then states:

> The nine principles outlined in this chapter are far from new. They reflect values and duties – especially the duty of care for other people, and of respect and care for nature – that many of the world's cultures and religions have recognized for centuries. The principles also reflect statements that have appeared in many reports about the need for equity, for sustainable development, and for conservation of nature in its own right and as the essential support for human life.

This suggests that the principles were derived by distilling the wisdom of those who the authors considered wise, a broadly Aristotelian approach to determining ethics. The strategy goes on to state some assumptions in the form of a 'framework' for a sustainable ethic:

> Every human being is a part of the community of life, made up of all living creatures. This community links all human societies, present and future generations, and humanity and the rest of nature. It embraces both cultural and natural diversity.

> Every human being has the same fundamental and equal rights, including: the right to life, liberty and security of person; to the freedoms of thought, conscience, and religion; to enquiry and expression; to peaceful assembly and association; to participation in government; to education; and, within the limits of the Earth, to the resources needed for a decent standard of living. No individual, community or nation has the right to deprive another of its means of subsistence.

> Each person and each society is entitled to respect of these rights; and is responsible for the protection of these rights for all others.

> Every life form warrants respect independently of its worth to people. Human development should not threaten the integrity of nature or the survival of other species. People should treat all creatures decently, and protect them from cruelty, avoidable suffering and unnecessary killing.

> Everyone should take responsibility for his or her impacts on nature. People should conserve ecological processes and the diversity of nature, and use any resource frugally and efficiently, ensuring that their uses of renewable resources are sustainable.

Everyone should aim to share fairly the benefits and costs of resource use, among different communities and interest groups, among regions that are poor and those that are affluent, and between present and future generations. Each generation should leave to the future a world that is at least as diverse and productive as the one it inherited. Development of one society or generation should not limit the opportunities of other societies or generations.

The protection of human rights and those of the rest of nature is a worldwide responsibility that transcends all cultural, ideological and geographical boundaries. The responsibility is both individual and collective.

(Ibid., 14)

These all appear quite reasonable and uncontentious except for those who believe that 'nature' has only instrumental value for humans or are committed to economistic utilitarianism. It is worth highlighting that the injunction that 'people should ... use any resource frugally' seems to be derived from virtue notions such as temperance. They state further assumptions developing the ethic quoted immediately above:

The ethic is founded on a belief in people as a creative force, and in the value of every human individual and each human society. It recognizes the interdependence of human communities, and the duty each person has to care for other people and for future generations. It asserts our responsibility towards the other forms of life with which we share this planet. It also recognizes that nature has to be cared for in its own right, and not just as a means of satisfying human needs.

An ethic is important because what people do depends on what they believe. Widely shared beliefs are often more powerful than government edicts. The transition to sustainable societies will require changes in how people perceive each other, other life and the Earth; how they evaluate their needs and priorities; and how they behave. For example, individual security is important, but people need to understand that it will not be attained solely (or even largely) through indefinite growth in their personal level of consumption.

(Ibid., 13)

It is worth highlighting the view that 'widely shared beliefs are often more powerful than government edicts'. This indicates that the IUCN/UNEP/WWF believe some notion of virtue is more central to addressing sustainable development than laws, market-based instruments or other economic initiatives. They then summarise the reasons for wanting to promote 'the ethic of living sustainably':

We need to re-state and win support for the ethic of living sustainably because:
- it is morally right;

- without it the human future is in jeopardy; poverty, strife and tragedy will increase;
- individual actions are, perhaps for the first time, combining to have global effects; and since these worldwide problems arise from today's conflicting aspirations and competition for scarce resources, the ethical principles enabling us to resolve them must also be agreed globally;
- no major society yet lives according to a value system that cares properly for the future of human communities and other life on earth.

(Ibid., 13)

These appear quite reasonable and are a good summary of reasons why this book puts significant emphasis on ethical questions around human relations to the Earth System. For example, the connections drawn between 'individual actions', 'global effects', 'ethical principles' and global agreement are all themes picked up in this book as needing to be addressed to allow sustainable development or reduce 'jeopardy' to the 'human future'. The strategy goes on to make an important but apparently unusual strategic observation:

Establishment of the ethic needs the support of the world's religions because they have spoken for centuries about the individual's duty of care for fellow humans and of reverence for divine creation. It also needs the backing of secular groups concerned with the principles that should govern relationships among people, and with nature. Such alliances will be timely and right even if the first purposes of religions and humanist groups are not the same as those of this Strategy.

(Ibid., 13)[8]

Similar strategic ideas are still not commonly discussed, perhaps in part because the US Evangelical Environmental Network (creationcare.org), although mainstream, has not been able to minimise the impact of the vocal climate sceptics around the Republican Party. The strategy explores further what an ethic of living sustainably might mean:

An ethic defines both rights and responsibilities. Thus each human individual has a responsibility to respect the rights of others. Statements of human rights, and especially the Universal Declaration of Human Rights, have played an important part in defending the individual from subjugation in the name of some 'common good'. The need to defend individual rights is a [sic] great as ever. At the same time, concerted action is required to protect and preserve common needs and shared resources. The obligations of individuals must be emphasized just as much as their rights.

(Ibid., 13)

This description of the tension between individual rights and common good is important and perhaps gives a reasonable indication of how the tension should be resolved in the context of sustainable development. The strategy continues by indicating a key role that the virtue of care has to play in a sustainable ethic:

> People in many societies need to change their attitudes towards nature, because it can no longer meet their demands or withstand their impacts. We have a right to the benefits of nature but these will not be available unless we care for the systems that provide them.
>
> (Ibid., 13–14)

Key components of the attitude to nature that need to change are probably the Baconian assumptions: first, that more control of nature is better and, second, that prediction and control of nature has no practical limits. The strategy indicates some reasons to disagree with these Baconian assumptions:

> Moreover, all the species and systems of nature deserve respect regardless of their usefulness to humanity. This is the central message of the World Charter for Nature and the Declaration of Fontainebleau. This belief also links many religions and non-religious groups.
>
> (Ibid., 14)

The profundity and huge scope of the task of promoting sustainable ethics in a global society is then indicated:

> Winning support for the ethic for living sustainably will require action on a broad front. It is not enough to publicize and teach the new approach, because well-informed people do not necessarily take the right decisions. Since value systems determine how people pursue political, legal, economic or technological goals, values associated with the ethic must pervade all spheres of human action if it is to succeed.
>
> (Ibid.)

More specific actions are recommended; develop, promote and implement the world ethic for living sustainably but also 'establish a world organization to monitor implementation of the world ethic for living sustainably and to prevent and combat serious breaches in its observation' (ibid., 17). The emphasis in the suggestions within these categories is on making the processes as inclusive as possible and recognising existing expertise and authority in the area of sustainable ethics and its implementation.

Echoing suggestions in the WCED (1987), the strategy discusses 'improving the quality of human life'. This includes suggesting indicators to give a more rounded view of the quality of human life than GNP. There is no discussion of whether such 'empirical' methods can analytically be assumed to be effective in a situation where human knowledge has significant limitations. In discussing 'Conserving the Earth's vitality and diversity' (IUCN/UNEP/WWF, 1991, 27–42), the strategy advocates 'prudence' (ibid., 28), precaution (ibid., 29–30) and reducing stress to the Earth System among other actions. 'Keeping within the Earth's carrying capacity' (ibid., 43–51) argues:

> Sustainability will be impossible unless human population and resource demand level off within the carrying capacity of the Earth. If we apply to our lives the rules we seek to apply when managing other species, we should try to leave a substantial safety margin between our total impact and our estimate of what the planetary environment can withstand. This is the more essential because while we know that the ultimate limits exist we are uncertain at exactly what point we may reach them. It is important to remember that we are seeking not just survival but a sustainable improvement in the quality of life of several billion people.
>
> (Ibid., 43)

The review of recent Earth System science in Chapter 2 suggests that we may have already exceeded the carrying capacity of the Earth System, or at least our estimates of them are not so robust that we can dismiss the possibility that inertia in 'natural' and social systems will inevitably carry us across them, let alone allow a 'substantial safety margin'. However, we do not know that for certain and at least some 'deontological' and virtue ethic schemes can still operate effectively even if it appears that cataclysm is inevitable. Fortunately, we are not at that stage; Earth System science suggests we exist in a situation where rapid cataclysm cannot be ruled out but is not inevitable. The margins of error are huge, which perhaps gives greater space for 'moral courage' than if the amount of stress the Earth System will withstand could be specifically identified.

The strategy states that 'it is unrealistic to expect people willingly to reduce' (ibid., 43) their material standard of living. However, the medical profession and the global virtue tradition among others suggest that reducing at least some types of consumption will be good for individuals as well as the Earth System. It is reasonable to assume many people would be able to muster sufficient temperance to reduce consumption if their lives depended on it (cf. recovering addicts). The much more difficult question is whether many or most people will be able to reduce their consumption when they are clear that the future of industrial civilisation (at least) *may* depend on this reduction.

Discussion moves on to numerous reasons and suggestions to encourage greater equity, reduced levels of per capita stress to the Earth System and reduce human population growth, including tackling consumption and population in an integrated way. They indicate that technical and ethical choices (ibid., 49) about the best technologies are difficult to make.[9]

What the chapter 'keeping within the Earth's carrying capacity' does not do is show how the Earth's carrying capacity can be identified robustly. Instead, it sets about suggesting how stress to the Earth System can be reduced. This is quite reasonable, but also a further indication that it is problematic to identify the carrying capacity.

Chapter 6 of the strategy, 'Changing personal attitudes and practices', emphasises informing and educating rather than challenging unsustainable attitudes and practices or ethics, perhaps on the basis of a 'liberal' assumption that consumerist values cannot be challenged directly. The 'global virtue tradition' suggests that policy based on moderation of consumption may be more democratic than is typically assumed. 'Enabling communities to care for their own environments' emphasises decentralised participatory decision-making based on local understanding and empowerment of local communities.

Chapter 8, 'Providing a national framework for integrating development and conservation', emphasises integrated laws and policies, including economic policy, that take better account of the services nature provides to humans. It makes some useful suggestions in this regard, though many of them are based on predict and control assumptions of a type that this book would call into question. They state 'the market ensures that society works within the rules and standards as efficiently as possible' (ibid., 65); this is very salient. If we do not know what rules, standards or limits on stress to the Earth System markets must work within, then this questions assumptions that markets are effective social decision-making tools. Societies emphasising the virtue of temperance (among broader virtue schemes) should in principle cause less stress to the Earth System than those emphasising markets.

'Creating a global alliance' makes clear that key sustainable development issues are global in a way that calls into question the value of notions of political sovereignty and criticises global economic structures and models of and practice of 'development' imposed on poorer countries. It then sets out some principles for 'a true partnership for sustainability' (ibid., 78) before identifying some specific actions that the international community should take, including 'Prepare and adopt a Universal Declaration and Covenant on Sustainability' (ibid., 81) based on the ethics outlined in Chapter 2 of the strategy.

The reaction in the academic and policy community to this strategy appears to have been muted. For example, the discourse on a world ethic for living sustainably called for by the strategy does not appear to have materialised in the way hoped for in the strategy; the 'Earth Charter' and associated earth dialogues, Palmer and Finlay (2003) and the 'Alliance of Religion and Conservation' out of which Palmer and Finlay (ibid.) grew, perhaps being the most concrete demonstrations of such activities.

The Earth Charter (2000) is an important development supported to some extent by governments around the world; it is in the vein of the ethics of sustainability discussed in IUCN/UNEP/WWF (1991). The discussions of economics in the Earth Charter suggest that it assumes that survival, rights and virtue are all more important than economics. Indeed, the preamble is clearly critical of current economic systems. It also appears to be critical of economistic utilitarianism when it writes: 'Fundamental changes are needed in our values, institutions, and ways of living' (Earth Charter, 2000, 1). The discussions of rights in the Earth Charter only mention property rights once, this in the context of 'the duty to prevent environmental harm and to protect the rights of people'. The other eleven times that rights are mentioned are of the form of the notion of rights broadly taken in the Universal Declaration of Human Rights. Discussion of 'care', 'solidarity', 'gratitude' and 'humility' (ibid.) implies virtue, as perhaps do the following principles from the charter:

1 Respect Earth and life in all its diversity.
2 Care for the community of life with understanding, compassion, and love.
3 Build democratic societies that are just, participatory, sustainable, and peaceful.
4 Prevent harm as the best method of environmental protection and, when knowledge is limited, apply a precautionary approach.

(Earth Charter, 2000)

Furthermore, discussion in principle 7 of the notions 'Act with restraint' and 'Adopt lifestyles that emphasize the quality of life and material sufficiency in a finite world' suggest that a virtue approach is also important alongside rights in the Earth Charter.

Both IUCN/UNEP/WWF (1991) and the Earth Charter (2000) engage with the ethical discourse called for in the WCED (1987) and significantly improve the level of that discourse in regard to the WCED and the intergovernmental sustainable development literature discussed in Chapter 4. Perhaps the greatest weakness with IUCN/UNEP/WWF (1991) and the Earth Charter (2000), both strategically and philosophically, is that they do not engage directly in any depth with the global virtue tradition.

Two broadly governmental/NGO discussions of ethical responses to sustainable development have now been interrogated for how they might respond to difficulties in predicting the Earth System. These are broadly critical of economistic utilitarianism. By way of potential contrast, let us examine at least some literature that one might expect will make economistic utilitarian assumptions and might respond to these types of question. The World Bank environment strategy (World Bank, 2001) climate change appendix and a WTO trade and environment background document (WTO, 2004) sidestep the issue of stress to the Earth System. WTO (1997) discusses environmental Kuznet curves and admits that 'some environmental problems – including carbon dioxide and nitrogen oxide emissions – worsen as income increases'; carbon dioxide emissions appear to be a key stress to the Earth System. Unsurprisingly, these documents do indeed make economistic utilitarian ethical assumptions and discussion of rights tends to focus on property rights rather than broader notions of rights. Similarly, as discussed in Chapter 2, the Stern Review (2006) illustrates the difficulties that economistic utilitarianism has in responding to difficulties in prediction of the consequences of industrial emission of GHGs. The picture is similar for OECD (2001) discussed in Chapter 4.

Turner and Pearce (1993) is an interesting academic environmental economic paper, as it holds economistic utilitarian assumptions and more cautious ethical assumptions in tension. For example, 'uncertainty dictates caution … irreversibility also dictates caution' (ibid., 181). It is then suggested that there are 'no man-made substitute[s]' for 'some ecological assets' (ibid.). Deep problems with putting economic values on ecosystems, let alone the Earth System or more limited critical ecological 'assets', are pointed out. It is argued that markets need at least some virtuous people from whom selfish 'homo economicus' people can profit (ibid., 191). Even with this deep but not exhaustive list of incompletely resolved problems with economistic utilitarianism, Turner and Pearce still favour economistic utilitarianism, even if they advocate some not insignificant improvements to conventional economic policy practice. It appears that little academic economic literature has picked up directly upon the questions raised by Turner and Pearce (1993). Some ecological economics literature (e.g. Faber *et al.*, 1998, 205–29) does pick up on the themes of this book, particularly the significant limitations of current epistemological assumption in economics and policy. However, the resolutions it suggests are not compelling and perhaps because of this, mainstream economics tends to ignore ecological economics and the questions it raises (Common, 2003). Hanley and Aktinson (Berkhout *et al.*, 2003, 77–104) follow directly on from the chapter by Stirling (ibid., 33–76) which outlines levels of human ignorance about the effects of human actions on the Earth System, even if it is not couched in those terms. It is interesting that there is virtually no recognition of such difficulties by Hanley and Atkinson despite being in the same volume.

Porritt recognises something of the ethical issues around economistic utilitarianism (e.g. Porritt, 2005, 85–6, 190–4, 317–20) and something of the significance of epistemological questions (e.g. ibid., 85–6; cf. Harrison, 2013; Porritt, 2000). However, it still suggests that 'capitalism' can be reformed without making clear how these ethical and epistemological issues can be addressed.

This brief survey of broadly economic literature indicates that economics has difficulties addressing the types of ethical questions highlighted by this book, and typically chooses to ignore such questions, perhaps because it has sufficient policy-making power that it can simply ignore such inconvenient questions (or should that be 'inconvenient truth'?).

There is more non-economic academic literature that picks up on the ethical questions highlighted by this book. Chapter 2 indicated some of this literature; a broader sketch is now in order, starting with the literature that is critical of the ethics of conventional economics, often on the basis of epistemological difficulties.

Brennan (1992) considers questions of moral pluralism but primarily succeeds in criticising cost–benefit analysis and sketching a view of the broad questions around pluralism without a clear resolution. When considering a Gaian version of Earth System science, Margulis (1999, 143) wisely writes:

> To me, the human move to take responsibility for the living Earth is laughable – the rhetoric of the powerless. The planet takes care of us, not we of it. Our self-inflated moral imperative to guide a wayward Earth or heal our sick planet is evidence of our immense capacity for self-delusion. Rather, we need to protect us from ourselves.

A valuable discussion of 'Environmental risks, uncertainty and intergenerational ethics' by Ekeli (2004) includes discussion of situations where ignorance makes it impossible to predict harm. Ekeli goes on to argue that the 'standard of knowledge with regard to the future consequences of our actions ... [are] ... *scientifically based harm scenarios* ... that can be made the subject of systematic investigation and critical discussions' (ibid., 431, emphasis in original). Given the contested nature of science, issues such as the problem of induction and (being slightly facetious) that theology can be 'the subject of systematic investigation and critical discussions', it is not clear that this suggestion for standards of knowledge is particularly helpful. This is particularly so as Ekeli does not make clear how to choose between different scientific discourses or paradigms; e.g. the IPCC and the critics of the IPCC, beyond 'wait and see', 'worst case' and 'democracy' (ibid., 440–1). Ekeli discusses other possible objections to his argument, including those based on 'faith in human ingenuity' (ibid., 432). Overall, the broad thrust of the argument accords with this book, though Ekeli only explicitly considers utilitarian and deontological ethics and some of his difficulties might have been overcome if he had considered well-developed systematic virtue schemes.

The analytical and practical limitations of economistic utilitarian assumptions, where it is difficult to predict consequences, are illustrated by Howarth (1998). With regard to climate change, this includes: 'Catastrophic outcomes are known to be possible, neither the costs, the benefits, nor even the underlying physical mechanisms can be reliably gauged' (ibid., 251). He then muses unconvincingly about the possibility of using precautionary approaches to respond to this, before arguing for '*sustainability as resources rights*' (ibid., 254, emphasis in original). Howarth notes that this is based on 'Kantian or deontological ethics' (ibid., 251); however, he gives no obvious indication of how to achieve this beyond implying that humans stop all industrial activity now. Indeed, he perhaps implies that a huge reduction in human populations is also called for by this form of deontological ethics. The less absolute nature of virtue ethics can support moderation of desire for the benefits of industrialism as a virtue (cf. Engel and Engel, 1990; Palmer and Finlay, 2003; Sandler and Cafaro, 2005), which should make implementation easier than a more absolutist deontological ethics of this form. Both virtue ethics and the deontological ethics implied by Howarth appear to analytically respond better to unpredictable consequences than utilitarianism. The emphasis on resources rather than other aspects of sustainable development is a significant limitation of the analysis by Howarth.

Munda *et al.* (1998) conduct 'a comparison between cost–benefit analysis and multicriteria decision aid'. Importantly for this book, the analysis locates this comparison (ibid., 228, 237) in recognition of limitations of human knowledge, arguing that cost–benefit analysis is operating beyond its sphere of competence given current levels of human knowledge, and they seem to suggest the same is the case for 'multicriteria decision aid'. They more clearly conclude that it is difficult to conduct multicriteria decision aid without the assumptions (including normative?) of those facilitating the analysis affecting the results. They then argue that multicriteria decision aid should still be subject to rational 'political' participatory democratic 'peer-review'.

Given the direction of this book, the review by Trzyna (2001) of efforts to bring something other than economistic utilitarian ethics into policy-making is useful. This review is not very encouraging; however, he does not analyse the ethical underpinnings of typical current policy-making processes. Thus, his talk is of bringing (non-economic) ethics into decision-making rather than of seeing how different ethical schemes would affect decision-making, which probably leaves non-economic ethics in a weaker position in policy decisions and rhetoric. That is, Trzyna still allows economics the rhetorical power of giving the impression that it is not normative. This book argues that maximising economic growth is one ethical scheme among a plurality – indeed, an irrational ethical scheme in the context of an unpredictable fragile Earth System.

Jasanoff connects epistemological difficulties with conventional economics. To illustrate, discussions of the precautionary principle state that 'utilitarian calculus of risks and benefits is harder to sustain than in the context of localized pollution problems … [because] uncertainties loom larger' (Jasanoff, 2001, 332).

One final broad ranging example should allow a sufficiently deep understanding of the queries that are raised about the Baconian ethics of conventional economics for sustainable development. Porritt (2000, e.g. 13–16, 24–5, 99, 104, 120, 135; cf. Davidson, 2000) suggests that much of the environmental movement would call into question economistic utilitarianism founded on technological control of 'nature'.

If the discussion above is taken together, it should be clear that the Baconian, materialist utilitarianism of conventional economics is widely questioned and could be said to be irrational in the face of an unpredictable Earth System. It should also be clear that virtue responses are leading contenders as more rational and democratic alternatives. Detailed discussion of virtue and an unpredictable Earth System will be the subject of the next chapter.

6.5 Conclusions

This chapter has conducted an analysis of sustainable development literature looking particularly at epistemological and ethical aspects of this literature. The review reinforces the hypothesis of earlier chapters that basing sustainable development policy on Baconian predict and control assumptions is highly questionable. The review also reinforces the hypothesis that economistic utilitarian ethical assumptions are problematic, with some form of virtue ethics appearing to be analytically the most robust alternative, but rights-based ethics are likely to have a significant part to play and some notions of consequentialism may also be a reasonable response to an unpredictable Earth System. More specific recommendations are made in the next chapter but it should be noted that any significant change in global ethics should be chosen globally by as many people and institutions as possible.

Literature that considers something of the limitations of human knowledge of the Earth System typically suggests some form of participatory democratic processes as a response for policy-making, typically assuming analysis such as that of Popper (1966) about the ability of an 'open society' to maximise 'problem solving'. Questions of what forms participatory policy-making might take will be discussed in more detail in Chapter 8. These discussions could inform decisions about processes that might also inform choices of where particular epistemological and ethical models might be used.

Notes

1 As these countries are responsible for greater per capita stress to the Earth System than other countries and those in industrialising counties who have consumerist lifestyles are generally imitating their perceptions of 'Western' lifestyles.
2 'Former IUCN Vice President and has directed INFOTERRA, the International Environmental Information System of the United Nation Environment Programme' (Trzyna, 1995, 13).
3 This discussion of Dobson (1998) oversimplifies the arguments of that book, as, for example, Dobson (ibid., 236–7, 262) does allude to virtue ethics.
4 Jacobs (1999, 35) sounds this note of caution about participation for its own sake.
5 See Jacobs (1999, 36–7, 40–1, 44) for more details.
6 Engel and Engel (1990), IUCN/UNEP/WWF (1991), the Earth Charter (2000) and Palmer and Finlay (2003) are key attempts to give a broadly global perspective of the ethics of environment and development; these will be discussed in some detail later in the next chapter. Journals such as *Environmental Ethics* tend to deal with quite specific questions from particular perspectives. This is quite reasonable, particularly given current reductive academic epistemological 'predilections'; however, this book will assume that it is not the best way to produce solutions to global problems such as unsustainable development. Indeed, by being possible to sideline as irrelevant for practical purposes, much academic environmental ethics may well be counter-productive as it leaves economistic utilitarianism unchallenged in practical political terms.
7 Kazanjian (2006) may provide some useful insights.
8 Taliaferro (Sandler and Cafaro, 2005, 160–1) makes a similar observation as well as stronger arguments for the need for environmental ethics to engage with religion. Much of the rest of the chapter is a useful treatment of philosophical questions around environmental ethics and religion, even if it might have been improved by discussion of Engel and Engel (1990), Palmer and Finlay (2003) and similar literature.
9 Discussions about minimising population growth include sufficient emphasis on education of women and natural family planning to probably be broadly acceptable to those that subscribe to all the world religions, even if some cultures would still be wary. This suggests that if a diversity of ethical perspectives is respected, questions of population control might be less problematic than is often assumed.

References

Adger, W.N. (2006) 'Vulnerability', *Global Environmental Change*, 16: 268–81
Al Moumin, M. (2011) 'How defending nature can defeat Al Qaeda', *Solutions*, 1(2), www.thesolutionsjournal.com/node/884. Accessed 27 May 2011
APSC (2007) *Tackling wicked problems: A public policy perspective*, Australian Public Service Commission, www.apsc.gov.au/publications-and-media/archive/publications-archive/tackling-wicked-problems. Accessed 26 May 2011

Attfield, R. (1994) *Environmental philosophy: Principles and prospects*, Aldershot: Ashgate

Bäckstrand, K. (2004) 'Science, uncertainty and participation in global environmental governance', *Environmental Politics*, 13(3): 650–6

Benton, T. (1999) 'Sustainable development and the accumulation of capital: Reconciling the irreconcilable', in Dobson, A. (ed.) *Fairness and futurity: Essays on environmental sustainability and social justice*, Oxford: Oxford University Press

Benton, T. (2003) 'Sociology', in Page, E.A. and Proops, J. (eds) *Environmental thought*, Cheltenham: Edward Elgar

Berglund, C. and Matti, S. (2006) 'Citizen and consumer: The dual role of individuals in environmental policy', *Environmental Politics*, 15: 550–71

Berkhout, F., Leach, M. and Scoones, I. (2003) (eds) *Negotiating environmental change: New perspectives from social sciences*, Cheltenham: Edward Elgar

Bishop, J. (1995) 'Adam Smith's invisible hand argument', *Journal of Business Ethics*, 14(3): 165–80

Brennan, A. (1992) 'Moral pluralism and the environment', *Environmental Values*, 1: 15–33

Brennan, A. (2003) 'Philosophy', in Page, E.A. and Proops, J. (eds) *Environmental thought*, Cheltenham: Edward Elgar

Brown, V.A., Harris, J.A. and Russell, J.Y. (2010) (eds) *Tackling wicked problems: Through the transdisciplinary imagination*, London: Earthscan

Carolan, M. (2004) 'Ontological politics: Mapping a complex environmental problem', *Environmental Values*, 13(4): 497–522

Castles, F.G. (1999) *Comparative public policy: Patterns of post-war transformation*, Cheltenham: Edward Elgar

Chapman, R. (2002) 'The stag-goat and the sphinx: The place of the virtues in environmental ethics', *Environmental Values*, 11(2): 129–44

Committee on the Applications of Ecological Theory to Environmental Problems (1986) *Ecological knowledge and problem-solving*, Washington, DC: National Academy Press

Common, M. (2003) 'Economics', in Page, E.A. and Proops, J. (eds) *Environmental thought*, Cheltenham: Edward Elgar

Daily, G. and Ehrlich, P. (1992) 'Population, sustainability, and Earth's carrying capacity', *Bioscience*, 42(10): 761–71

Daly, H. (1992) 'From empty world to full world economics', in Goodland, R., Daly, H. and El Serafy, S. (eds) *Population, technology, and lifestyle: The transition to sustainability*, Washington, DC: Island Press

Davidson, J. (2000) 'Sustainable development: Business as usual or a new way of living?', *Environmental Ethics*, 22(1): 25–42

Defra (2010) *Measuring progress: Sustainable development indicators 2010*, London: Defra, http://archive.defra.gov.uk/sustainable/government/progress/documents/SDI2010 _001.pdf. Accessed 19 May 2011

Dobson, A. (1998) *Justice and the environment: Conceptions of environmental sustainability and theories of distributive justice*, Oxford: Oxford University Press

Dryzek, J. (1987) *Rational ecology: Environment and political economy*, Oxford: Blackwell

Dryzek, J. (1990) *Discursive democracy: Politics, policy, and political science*, Cambridge: Cambridge University Press.

Dryzek, J. (2000) *Deliberative democracy and beyond: Liberals, critics, contestations*, Oxford: Oxford University Press

Earth Charter (2000) *The Earth Charter*, www.earthcharterinaction.org/content/pages/ Read-the-Charter.html. Accessed 19 May 2011

Ekeli, K. (2004) 'Environmental risks, uncertainty and intergenerational ethics', *Environmental Values*, 13(4): 421–48

Ekenberg, L., Boman, M. and Linnerooth-Bayer, J. (2001) 'General risk constraints', *Journal of Risk Research*, 3(1): 31–47

Ekins, P. (2003) 'Sustainable development', in Page, E.A. and Proops, J. (eds) *Environmental thought*, Cheltenham: Edward Elgar

Engel, J.R. and Engel, J.G. (eds) (1990) *Ethics of environment and development: Global challenge, international response*, London: Belhaven

Faber, M., Proops, J. and Manstetten, R. (1998) *Ecological economics: Concepts and methods*, Cheltenham: Edward Elgar

Fredericks, S.E. (2013) *Measuring and evaluating sustainability: Ethics in sustainability indexes*, Abingdon: Routledge

Gibson, R. (1992) 'Respecting ignorance and uncertainty', in Lykke, E. (ed.) *Achieving environmental goals: The concept and practice of environmental performance review*, London: Belhaven

Harrison, N.E. (2013) *Sustainable capitalism and the pursuit of well-being*, Abingdon: Routledge

Hartwick, J.M. (1977) 'Intergenerational equity and the investing of rents from exhaustible resources', *The American Economic Review*, 67(5): 972–4

Hay, P. (2002) *Main currents in Western environmental thought*, Bloomington: Indiana University Press

Heyd, T. (2003) 'The case for environmental morality', *Environmental Ethics*, 25(1): 5–24

Hill, M. (2009) (5th edn) *The public policy process*, Harlow: Pearson Education

Hogwood, B.W. and Gunn, L.A. (1984) *Policy analysis for the real world*, Oxford: Oxford University Press

Hounsham, S. (2006) *Painting the town green: How to persuade people to be environmentally friendly*, Green-Engage, www.green-alliance.org.uk/resources/Painting%20the%20town%20green.pdf. Accessed 14 May 2011

Howarth, R. (1998) 'Sustainability, uncertainty, and intergenerational fairness', in Faucheux, S., Van Der Straaten, J. and O'Connor, M. (eds) *Sustainable development: Concepts, rationalities and strategies*, Dordrecht: Kluwer

Hudson, J. and Lowe, S. (2009) (2nd edn) *Understanding the policy process: Analysing welfare policy and practice*, Bristol: Policy Press

ISO/FDIS 14040 (1997) *Environmental management – life cycle assessment – principles and framework*, www.iso.org/iso/catalogue_detail?csnumber=37456. Accessed 31 March 2015

IUCN/UNEP/WWF (1991) *Caring for the Earth: A strategy for sustainable living*, Gland: The World Conservation Union, United Nations Environment Programme, World Wide Fund For Nature, https://portals.iucn.org/library/efiles/documents/CFE-003.pdf. Accessed 19 May 2011

Jacobs, M. (1999) 'Sustainable development as a contested concept', in Dobson, A. (ed.) *Fairness and futurity: Essays on environmental sustainability and social justice*, Oxford: Oxford University Press

Jamieson, D. (1992) 'Ethics, public policy, and global warming', *Science, Technology and Human Values*, 17: 139–53 (also in Light, A. and Rolston III, H. (2003) *Environmental ethics: An anthology*, London: Blackwell

Jasanoff, S. (2001) 'Image and imagination: The formation of a global environmental consciousness', in Miller, C. and Edwards, P. (eds) *Changing the atmosphere: Expert knowledge and environmental governance*, Cambridge, MA: MIT Press

John, P. (2011) *Making policy work*, Abingdon: Routledge

Jones, B.D. (1994), *Reconceiving decision-making in democratic politics: Attention, choice, and public policy*, Chicago, IL: University of Chicago Press

Kazanjian, M. (2006) 'Ethics and phenomenology', *The internet encyclopedia of philosophy*, www.iep.utm.edu/e/eth-phen.htm. Accessed 19 May 2011

Langhelle, O. (1999) 'Sustainable development: Exploring the ethics of our common future', *International Political Science Review*, 20(2): 129–49

Lélé, S. (1991) 'Sustainable development: A critical review', *World Development*, 19: 607–21

Lemons, J. and Brown, D. (1995) *Sustainable development: Science, ethics, and public policy*, Dordrecht; London: Kluwer

Lewis, C. (1963) *The four loves*, London: Fontana

Light, A. and Rolston III, H. (2003) *Environmental ethics: An anthology*, Malden, MA: Blackwell

Lindblom, C. (1968) *The policy making process*, Upper Saddle River, NJ: Prentice Hall

Margulis, L. (1999) *The symbiotic planet: A new look at evolution*, London: Phoenix

Mebratu, D. (1998) 'Sustainability and sustainable development: Historical and conceptual review', *Environmental Impact Assessment Review*, 18: 493–520

Modvar, C. and Gallopín, G. (2005) *Sustainable development: Epistemological challenges to science and technology*. Report of the workshop 'Sustainable development: Epistemological challenges to science and technology', Santiago, Chile, 13–15 October 2004, Santiago: UN Economic Commission for Latin America and the Caribbean, www.eclac.cl/publicaciones/MedioAmbiente/3/LCL2273P/lcl2273.pdf. Accessed 7 May 2011

Mollison, B. (1988) *Permaculture: A designers' manual*, Tyalgum, NSW: Tagari Publications

Munda, G., Nijkamp, P. and Rietveld, P. (1998) 'Environmental decision making: A comparison between cost–benefit analysis and multicriteria decision aid', in Faucheux, S., Van Der Straaten, J. and O'Connor, M. (eds) *Sustainable development: Concepts, rationalities and strategies*, Dordrecht: Kluwer

Natural Step (2011) *The four system conditions*, www.naturalstep.org/the-system-conditions. Accessed 11 May 2011

O'Connor, M. (2000) 'Pathways for environmental evaluation: A walk in the (hanging) gardens of Babylon', *Ecological Economics*, 34(2): 175–93

OECD (2001) *Sustainable development: Critical issues*, Paris: Organisation for Economic Co-operation and Development

Padilla, E. (2004) 'Climate change, economic analysis and sustainable development', *Environmental Values*, 13: 523–44

Palmer, M. and Finlay, V. (2003) *Faith in conservation: New approaches to religions and the environment*, Washington, DC: World Bank, http://go.worldbank.org/3L9IDQNFO0 or www.arcworld.org/books_resources.asp. Accessed 9 May 2011

Parker, J. (2014) *Critiquing sustainability, changing philosophy*, Abingdon: Routledge

Peters, B.G. and Pierre, J. (2006) (eds) *Handbook of public policy*, London: SAGE

Pezzoli, K. (1997) 'Sustainable development: A transdisciplinary overview of the literature', *Journal of Environmental Planning and Management*, 40: 549–601

Pellizzoni, L. (2003) 'Uncertainty and participatory democracy', *Environmental Values*, 12(2): 195–224

Popper, K. (1966) (5th edn) *The open society and its enemies*, London: Routledge and Kegan Paul

Popper, K. (1972) (3rd edn) *The logic of scientific discovery*, London: Hutchinson

Porritt, J. (2000) *Playing safe: Science and the environment*, New York: Thames & Hudson

Porritt, J. (2005) *Capitalism as if the world mattered*, London: Earthscan

Pressman, J.L. and Wildavsky, A. (1984) (3rd edn) *Implementation*, London: University of California Press

Ravetz, J. and Funtowicz, S. (1999) 'Post-normal science: An insight now maturing', *Futures*, 31(7): 641–6

Reid, D. (1995) *Sustainable development: An introductory guide*, London: Earthscan

Ritchey, T. (2011) *Wicked problems – social messes: Decision support modelling with morphological analysis*, Berlin: Springer

Rose, R. (2005) *Learning from comparative public policy*, Abingdon: Routledge

Sabatier, P. (2007) *Theories of the policy process*, Boulder, CO: Westview Press

Sandin, P. (2004) 'The precautionary principle and the conception of precaution', *Environmental Values*, 13(4): 461–75

Sandler, R. and Cafaro, P. (eds) (2005) *Environmental virtue ethics*, Lanham, MD: Rowman & Littlefield

Schmidtz, D. and Willott, E. (2002) *Environmental ethics: What really matters, what really works*, New York: Oxford University Press

Shrader-Frechette, K. (1996) 'Methodological rules for four classes of scientific uncertainty', in Lemons, J. (ed.) *Scientific uncertainty and environmental problem solving*, Cambridge, MA: Blackwell

Smith, G. (2003) *Deliberative democracy and the environment*, London: Routledge

Steffen, W. and Tyson, P. (eds) (2001) *Global change and the Earth System: A planet under pressure*, Stockholm: International Geosphere-Biosphere Programme, www.igbp. net/download/18.1b8ae20512db692f2a680007648/1376383135421/science-4.pdf. Accessed 7 November 2014

Stern Review (2006) *Stern Review on the economics of climate change*, http://webarchive. nationalarchives.gov.uk/20100407172811/www.hm-treasury.gov.uk/stern_review_ report.htm. Accessed 15 April 2012

Tapio, P. and Huutoniemi, K. (2014) *Transdisciplinary sustainability studies: A heuristic approach*, Abingdon: Routledge

Theodoulou, S.Z. and Cahn, M.A. (1995) *Public policy: The essential readings*, Upper Saddle River, NJ: Prentice Hall

Tickner, J. (ed.) (2003) *Precaution, environmental science, and preventive public policy*, Washington, DC: Island Press

Torgerson, D. (1999) *The promise of green politics environmentalism and the public sphere*, Durham, NC: Duke University Press

Trzyna, T. (1995) *A sustainable world: Defining and measuring sustainable development*, Sacramento, CA: International Center for the Environment and Public Policy, California Institute of Public Affairs

Trzyna, T. (2001) *Raising annoying questions: Why values should be built into decision-making*, Sacramento, CA: California Institute of Public Affairs

Tullock, G. (2006) (Revised) *The vote motive*, London: Institute of Economic Affairs www. iea.org.uk/sites/default/files/publications/files/upldbook397pdf.pdf. Accessed 19 May 2011

Turner, D. and Hartzell, L. (2004) 'The lack of clarity in the precautionary principle', *Environmental Values*, 13(4): 449–60

Turner, R.K. and Pearce, D. (1993) 'Sustainable economic development: Economic and ethical principles', in Barbier, E.D. (ed.) *Economics and ecology: New frontiers and sustainable development*. London: Capman and Hall

WCED (1987) *Our common future*, Oxford: Oxford University Press

Wilkinson, D. (2003) 'Law', in Page, E.A. and Proops, J. (eds) *Environmental thought*, Cheltenham: Edward Elgar

World Bank (2001) *Making sustainable commitments: An environment strategy for the World Bank*, Washington, DC: World Bank, www-wds.worldbank.org/external/default/WDS ContentServer/WDSP/IB/2001/12/11/000094946_01110704111523/Rendered/PDF/ multi0page.pdf. Accessed 19 May 2011

WTO (1997) *Committee on trade and environment: Environmental benefits of removing trade restrictions and distortions – Note by the Secretariat*, New York: World Trade Organization, WT/CTE/W/67

WTO (2004) *Trade and environment at the WTO: Background document*, New York: World Trade Organisation, www.wto.org/english/tratop_e/envir_e/envir_wto2004_e.pdf. Accessed 19 May 2011

7 Ecological virtue

A better ethical basis for sustainable development than the ethics of market fundamentalism?

7.1 Introduction

Earlier chapters demonstrate that current policy incorrectly assumes that the Earth System can be predicted for practical policy purposes (cf. de Castella, 2009). They also illustrate that this assumption is linked to the instrumental, utilitarian ethics of conventional economics, with which climate policy and research is riven. That is, it is assumed that climate science can be plugged into economic cost–benefit analysis. This chapter will consider complementary ethics and epistemology in some depth. First let us remind ourselves of the ethics of conventional policy and add further detail.

Earlier discussion of the Stern Review (2006) illustrates the difficulties economics has with responding to the levels of uncertainty that there are in climate science (cf. Hof et al., 2008). Unusually for economic research, particularly applied economic research, the Stern authors make clear their ethical assumptions; economics making ethical assumptions explicit is a significant improvement in the context of this book, even if virtue is ignored by Stern. A critique of the assumptions of Stern by Spash (2007) has many parallels with the analysis of this book – in particular it emphasises the poor reasoning of the ethical assumptions of Stern and other conventional economics responses to unpredictable climate change. Spash does not consider virtue directly.

A more specifically relevant example is Tol and Yohe (2007) that addresses 'infinite uncertainty, forgotten feedbacks, and cost–benefit analysis of climate policy'. Three out of many possible responses to Tol and Yohe are: first, the worst catastrophe the authors imagine is that climate change might bring about 'negative economic growth in a region or two' (ibid., 441). Second, they consider only the economic impacts of catastrophe as they are explicitly utilitarian. This ignores that human rights, including the right to life, have a role in policy in this situation, in a way that many rights do not apply when economics is concerned only with local exchange of goods. Finally, using their own words against them, the article states:

> It is axiomatic that cost–benefit analysis can be applied to a policy decision only when uncertainty about net benefits is finite. If this condition cannot

be satisfied, then cost–benefit analysis is completely invalid and the decision-maker should turn to perspectives designed to minimize the maximum regret assigned across a wide range of plausible futures. The decision-maker, in other words, should ask analysts to determine safe minimum standards or windows of tolerable impacts.

It follows, therefore, that the discussion on how to approach the climate policy debate turns in large measure on the size of the uncertainty.

(Ibid., 430; cf. Weitzman, 2009)

In the context of the limits of prediction of the Earth System highlighted in Chapter 2, the above quotation strengthens the argument that cost–benefit analysis cannot work for abrupt climate change policy. It also points to the immorality of imposing such an approach for an issue that many people believe is more important than money (cf. Smith, 2003, 29–51).

Similar difficulties affect Settle *et al.* (2007), McInerney and Keller (2008) plus Hillerbrand and Ghil (2008). In addition, Hillerbrand and Ghil (ibid.), despite highlighting profound problems in using utilitarian neo-classical economics, recommend a version of economics by ignoring other widely held ethical schemes such as rights and virtue – despite Jamieson (1992). In addition, they make further questionable assumptions including the following. First, that addressing climate change can only come about through investing money (ibid., 2134), when it can be argued that the most effective way is for those who live substantially above subsistence to spend less, consume less and thus stress the Earth System less – that is, the ethical virtue of moderation. Second, the 'assumptions of a welfare-based approach are the most likely to be shared by people from different cultural backgrounds' (ibid., 2135). However, Sandler and Cafaro (2005), Palmer and Finlay (2003), the global justice movement, anti-capitalist movement and trade union organisations suggest that many, if not the majority of the global population, would choose moderating their consumption and greater justice (equity), in the distribution of material wealth (if not redistribution), over maximising economic growth or welfare.

A catalogue of the difficulties that economics has in addressing abrupt climate change is provided by Perrings (2003). In this, using reasonable but not completely transparent assumptions, he argues that the possibility of abrupt climate change moves the results of economic analysis of climate change from favouring adaption to favouring mitigation. He generally has a reasonable grasp of the difficulties of predicting the climate as highlighted in this book; however, his conclusions are poorly constructed for two principal reasons. First, he simply assumes that policy decisions will necessarily be made using selfish economic analysis, even if he perhaps has personal reservations about this. The second more important point is that he argues that because no country gains all the benefits of their reduced emissions, if they are being purely selfish – which is a common approach to diplomatic questions and economics – they will not and should not reduce emissions, unless all countries do the same. In fact, it might be one country's, one company's or one person's reduced emissions that

– all else being equal – stops a tipping point being crossed. Given the nature of tipping points, this could be in the immediate future and could avert cata-strophic harm to that country, company or person; we cannot know for sure. Thus, even in the economic terms that Perrings assumes, uncertainty is such that any particular reduction in emissions might increase the 'utility' of the outcome – it is just that this cannot be predicted. This is why utilitarian–consequentialist–economic approaches and ethics cannot work for climate policy when our powers of prediction are so limited. Legal/deontological approaches have similar difficulties if even targets cannot be given definitively. However, as we shall see, virtue epistemology and virtue ethics is the most widely held option that is comfortable, in philosophical terms, with making decisions in the unpredictable Earth System in which we find ourselves. Let me be absolutely clear about this – the science of the Earth System is such that it is entirely possible that a region's reduced emissions will be sufficient to prevent a regional tipping point being crossed in that region in a few years. There may have been an implicit understanding of this, when around the year 2000 Europe's resolve to reduce emissions increased, at the same time of the first prominent discussions of a tipping point in the North Atlantic bringing to Northern Europe perhaps 15°C cooling in as little as a decade.

Despite tortured reasoning and gross assumptions, the argument and particu-larly the conclusion of Broome (2010) demonstrates that it is make-believe to assume that economistic utilitarian methods will be able to put anything but fan-tasy figures into addressing catastrophic climate change in sufficient time to be 'useful'. Broome's analysis again appears unable to consider any ethics other than economics even when the difficulty of such an approach is clear. Nor is there the first thought of whether economics is globally democratic.

Further difficulties with economic approaches can be seen in van den Bergh (2010) which shows that cost–benefit analysis is irrational for climate change in its own terms, without considering the broader ethical and epistemological context in which it operates.

The discourse around geoengineering is revealing of the ethics applied to unpredictable climate change and has had recent discussion related to rapid cli-mate change. A strong philosophical case why engineering the climate cannot be done robustly because of difficulties of prediction is developed by Jamieson (1996); this also questions the utilitarian ethics of the way such engineering is presented. Schneider (1996) makes similar arguments and provides a history of geoengineering discussions that indicates that economic reasons and their under-pinning unquestioned ethical assumptions are explicitly or implicitly given as a justification for geoengineering – it is believed to be cheaper to treat the symp-toms than address the cause.[1] Similarly, apparently heavily based on early work by Schellnhuber (1998, particularly 48–127), the broader Earth System science literature tends to make predictive epistemological assumptions and econo-mistic utilitarian ethical presumptions (Newton, 1999; Schellnhuber, 2001; Schellnhuber et al., 2004; Schellnhuber and Held, 2002; Steffen et al., 2004; Steffen and Tyson, 2001).

It is hoped that this book shows, in the context of limitations in prediction, it is irrational to let cost–benefit analysis decide Earth System policy, including (abrupt) climate change policy. Thus, economics should serve humans and nature, not the Earth be the slave of money.

As discussed in Chapter 2, perhaps the most common explicit response in policy literature to concerns about abrupt or rapid climate change is a call for further research – implicitly focused on a utilitarian notion of identifying how far economic activity can push the climate system before it will break. This earlier chapter demonstrates that science cannot tell economics the tensile strength of the earth or climate system.

The most common alternative to utilitarian approaches in ethics is a deontological or rights-based approach that would typically be implemented in policy through laws. There has been a significant amount of legislation with regard to climate change at all levels, including international agreements. However, these have so far failed to produce significant reductions in carbon dioxide emissions; it can be argued that this is primarily because nations have not been prepared to promote or even barely publicly discuss moderation of consumption, despite this being clear in Rio's 1992 Agenda 21 international 'soft law'.

As seen in the last chapter, there are alternate voices to both economics and legal approaches, perhaps the most prominent is Anderson (2009, 2). He is glad of the focus brought about but sees 'the response to the Stern report as another sad indictment of societies privileging of economics over science', given the weight of science made available to policymakers for years before the Stern Review. He puts the ideological and ethical questions we face in clear terms:

> Do we continue to pay lip service to the issue of climate change, and hope future generations will understand our preference for barely-veiled hedonism over stewardship? Or are we prepared to respond genuinely to the scale of the challenge we have brought upon ourselves? ... If it is the latter, then we need to begin by revisiting the financial accounting model that has come to dominate our lives, and reestablish society's dominance over economics. Has the tripling of our economic wherewithal since the 1950s brought about a tripling in our sense of well being?
>
> (Anderson, 2009, 1)

Anderson's response to contemporary policy hegemony's 'self-delusion' is broadly in the virtue tradition discussed by this book. Let us turn to these ideas more directly now.

7.2 Relationship between types of ethics

Questions of any relationships between different forms of ethics are now relevant to our discussions. As noted in Chapter 2, there do not appear to be strong conclusions in this regard within academic literature at the moment (cf. Baron *et al.*, 1997; Brown, 2001; Hinman, 1999), thus a review of a range of literature that considers these questions in relation to environmental issues is in order.

Reviewing the then existing environmental ethics, Stone (1988) proposes a moral pluralism and suggests some ideas that need to be considered when developing such a pluralism. He does only tend to consider Kantianism and utilitarianism, posing more questions than he resolves. Responding to Stone and similar literature, Callicott (1990) raises numerous further difficulties, though again tending only to consider Kantian and utilitarian perspectives. He does allude to virtue theories, including those of Plato, Aristotle, Augustine and Aquinas; however, he dismisses these on the basis of disagreeing with some of their assumptions, apparently without testing any of these assumptions, or seeing how they fit into broader philosophical frameworks. Indeed, the description by Callicott (ibid.) of pre-Modern philosophy is mildly questionable. This is perhaps a little cavalier on his part, particularly in the light of difficulties that Kantian and utilitarian assumptions have, in doing the work he would like ethics to do. He does not assess the effectiveness of virtue ethics to do this work, nor how successful people that hold these types of assumption have been at responding philosophically to the practical questions Callicott highlights. He (ibid.)[2] proceeds to suggest a 'single moral philosophy' based on 'one metaphysics', a Darwinian concept of human–animal relations and a number of other assumptions.

Wenz (1993) perhaps starts to resolve questions of the relationship between ethical schemes when he responds to Stone and Callicott by suggesting a more nuanced notion of pluralism than either Stone or Callicott use. He criticises Stone and Callicott for discussing single (monisitic) moral theories in a way that does not accord with how these have been discussed by influential theorists normally labelled monist. Wenz argues for 'moderate moral pluralism', that is, 'a single ethical theory' that 'contains a variety of independent principles' (ibid., 69). As a justification for his position, he gives evidence that nobody uses utilitarianism (for example) in all situations, but that all people use a variety of principles.

Given earlier discussions of the 'global virtue tradition', Light (2003) is particularly useful as it revisits 'monist' and 'pluralist' questions, particularly as it aims to 'respond to practical dilemmas of forming a moral consensus around environmental issues' (ibid., 233). He suggests 'we should work within the traditional moral psychologies and ethical theories that most people already have and direct them where we can at … environmental ends' (ibid., 235).

If we assume that the above four papers are reasonably representative of environmental ethics engagement with questions of relationship between utilitarian, virtue and rights-based ethics, then these are mildly encouraging in the sense that Wenz (1993) suggests that the ethics people use do incorporate a variety of 'principles', and Light (2003) seems to see this as broadly encouraging and useful.

Beyond environmental ethics, the relationship between utility, rights and virtue appears little studied. One exception that commences with a superficial caricature of virtue ethics is Blackburn (2000). A key reason for the paucity of the analysis by Blackburn is he appears to prefer literary treatments of virtue to more philosophical ones, with the virtue scheme of Aquinas being noticeable by its absence. The paucity of the characterisation of virtue questions the conclusions that are drawn. An argument for 'unity' between utilitarian and virtue ethics for Earth System science is presented by Jamieson (2007), which may convince open-minded utilitarian philosophers of the utility of virtue ethics in the context that we find ourselves. However, something as shocking as Chapter 2 of this book may be required to cause evangelists of market fundamentalism to question their faith and stop imposing it on others as they do now. A process to consider different ethical schemes in decision-making frameworks is suggested by Velasquez *et al.* (2009). However, this does not resolve how to choose between different schemes when they are in tension as they are in the context of making policy about consumerism and sustainable development.

I would like to offer some unsatisfactory thoughts. On the basis of ontological assumptions about humans, virtues – particularly justice – decide what laws, rights and other deontological rules should apply to humans. That is, the approach that laws can promote virtue. It is also generally agreed that rights override utilitarian considerations when they come into conflict. Thus, even if it were good for the economy, people should not be executed for the money that could be made from selling tickets or pay per view television sales. For Aquinas, the limits of property rights are set by the virtue of justice – thus somebody should use property for the common good, not destroy things in mindless vandalism. Real decisions will make this more complex but to simplify, virtue determines rules and both trump utility when there is conflict. Thus, utility and cost–benefit analysis is the last thing that should be considered by policymakers, not the first.

7.3 Existing ecological virtue ideas

As outlined in Chapter 2, the global virtue tradition tends to argue that at least four virtues are 'cardinal' – i.e. pivotal – prudence, justice, moderation and courage. Virtue tradition also tends to argue that versions of the 'seven deadly sins' apply as much to environmental questions as to human relations, often arguing that consumerism wrongly inverts many of these vices, making them virtues, for example greed. Before making suggestions based on the analysis of this book, it is important to see what ideas to this end already exist. The focus of this survey is broad sustainable development concerns, rather than more specific questions such as whether nature has value beyond economic benefit that can be gained from it.

Engel and Engel (1990)[3] is a useful starting point as it sets out to fill in something of the ethical gap in the WCED (ibid., 1–2). It provides a useful illustration of how a wide variety of ethical perspectives engage with broad environment and development questions. The introduction to the volume provides a good overview of the maturing process of the idea of sustainable development and the ethical components of that maturing process.

- 'Ultimately the behaviour of entire societies towards the biosphere must be transformed' (ibid., 3, quoting the 1980 World Conservation Strategy).

- 'The United Nations General Assembly overwhelmingly adopted the World Charter for Nature ... sponsored by Zaire and Thirty Two other developing nations ... The Charter put the world body on record as "convinced that every form of life is unique, warranting respect regardless of its worth to man"' (ibid.).
- 'Willy Brandt pointed out that world development ought not to be confused with economic growth' (ibid.).
- They argue that 'there are at least five practical reasons for ... interest in ... ethics ... the role of values in human activity ... moral ideals motivate persons to care for the world around them ... clarifying the values at stake in policy decisions ... ethics is helping to resolve ... conflicts that thwart conservation and development projects ... helping to define a new social paradigm' (ibid., 6–8).
- Finally, they suggest (ibid., 15) that there is broad agreement among the diverse contributors that the correct mode of analysis of the 'ecological vision' is 'individuals-in-community'.

Engel and Engel (ibid., 9) contend that there is a 'growing consensus ... that the entire model of modern industrial development is seriously awry'. Extending this analysis they claim:

> Given the role that traditional religions have played in the course of human history to sustain complex human communities over many generations it is not surprising that in response to the overwhelming needs of our age – needs in large part created by the failures of secular society – perceptive religious leaders should discover that they have wisdom to contribute to the quest for a sustainable way of life and a responsibility to engage with others in the search for a new public environmental ethic.
>
> (Ibid., 12)

This is contestable (cf. White, 1967) but in the broad terms it uses, it appears to have some merit, in particular that many religions have perhaps helped provide guidance about human relations with 'nature' over many generations. In language, of vices that oppose virtues, Engel and Engel state:

> For the religions of the world, the moral failure of human beings to live in peace and justice with one another and the rest of creation is rooted ... in the greed, lust, selfishness and a craving for pleasure and power that are the real motivating factors behind the dominant materialistic world view.
>
> (1990, 12)

This analysis does perhaps have quite a Christian flavour, and religion is typically at least one factor in 'religious' wars and persecutions, so the analysis is naive in this regard. However, after an ongoing dialogue of over a decade, the world religions affirmed a very similar analysis in Palmer and Finlay (2003).

Broad NGO support is noted in a statement that is a good summary of unsustainable development: 'Poverty, environmental degradation and population growth are inextricably related and none of these fundamental problems can be successfully addressed in isolation' (Engel and Engel, 1990, 20). It can be suggested that it would have been more thorough to analyse whether it is population or population and consumption that are key. Nonetheless, Engel and Engel (1990) collect together a broader range of opinions on ethics around environment and development questions than any other source identified. These include feminists, writers on traditional African culture and religions, Soviet era Marxists, deep ecologists, religious writers of many shades, Latin American writers and Chinese writers. The contributors to Engel and Engel (ibid.) tend to agree with the 'global virtue tradition', particularly as outlined in Palmer and Finlay (2003) specifically in being critical of attitudes of domination and critical of seeing development purely as economic growth. Contributions that add further insights will be highlighted.

Rolston (Engel and Engel, 1990, 63–72) explores tensions between 'science-based versus traditional ethics'. Rolston notes valuable examples where ecological science can hold up a useful, critical light to traditional practices. In this analysis, he argues that 'to care about persons morally is to want them to know the truth about themselves, their society, and their illusions' (ibid., 66).

This appears sound advice for 'modern' society, its materialist consumptive assumptions, the possibility of rapid eco-cataclysm and the probable illusion of Baconian prediction and control of the Earth System, just as much as for 'traditional societies' (cf. Berkhout *et al.*, 2003, 14). Rolston also suggests areas where 'traditional ethics' are complementary to ecological science and discusses examples where traditional ethics can hold up a useful, critical light to 'modern' attitudes to the earth. Thus, Rolston (Engel and Engel, 1990, 71) argues 'the military–industrial–agribusiness nation-states in the modern West, which think themselves so cosmopolitan, can in fact be quite provincial cultures, more so than tribes and kingdoms of traditional societies'. He implies that ethics based on the assumptions of the *New Atlantis* of Francis Bacon have typically become both the key cause of an 'Earth-eating mentality' and have an intolerant attitude to non-materialist assumptions.

Sterling (ibid., 77–86) echoes key ideas of this book. It starts with a useful overview of how the 'Western world view' developed, arguing that instrumental economistic utilitarian ethics 'play a predominant yet often unrecognised role in … Westernised societies' to the point that other viewpoints are assumed 'untenable' (ibid., 79). He outlines a vision of the 'ecological world view' and makes analytical, ethical suggestions, including that the consequential ethical divisions between humans and the rest of nature are questionable given interconnections. Stressing problems of managerial approaches, Sterling argues that those who hold a mechanistic world view tend to be less aware of the consequences of their actions that are mediated through 'political and economic power', which may lead to unexpected 'sudden change' (ibid., 83).

Naess (Engel and Engel, 1990, 87–96) discusses how the 'deep ecology platform' might respond to the notion of sustainable development. A number of elements are worth highlighting. Naess is critical of industrialism and conventional development, because of their anthropocentrism, lack of ecological sustainability and the 'corrosive' effect that industrialism has when exported to 'traditional' cultures. He gives powerful examples of undemocratic developments, imposed by national governments on local communities and argues that in some Stone Age cultures, 'some fundamental aspects of life quality were at a high level – such as economic security, absence of stressful work, and lots of time for meaningful togetherness bridging the generations' (ibid., 94). Permaculture (Mollison, 1988) suggests that similar aims for quality of life may be more readily combined with at least some modern comforts than is perhaps often assumed. Naess looks at the meaning of sustainable development in more depth, arguing for both plural and compassionate humanist approaches and acknowledging tensions: 'Sustainable development today means development along the lines of each culture, not development along a common, centralized line. But faced with hungry children, humanitarian action is a priority whatever its relation to developmental plans and cultural invasion' (Engel and Engel, 1990, 95).

Naess is critical of greed and wanton consumption, in a way that accords with the global virtue tradition;[4] this includes being critical of the levels of disparity between rich and poor people. Echoing the WCED, Naess advocates non-violence and states that build-up of military might is incompatible with sustainable development. The reflection by Naess on the question of human populations highlights that levels of consumption are at least as significant as absolute numbers; nonetheless, he does advocate a reduction in global human populations over 'a thousand years ... or perhaps much less' (ibid., 92).[5] He concludes in an eminently sensible way by advocating addressing what is obviously unsustainable rather than worrying about what sustainability will be like.

Skolimowski (Engel and Engel, 1990) draws out a similarly useful strategic point, that for all the tensions in the notion of sustainable development, 'to develop or not to develop is not the question. But *how* to develop is the question' (ibid., 102, emphasis in original). That is, sustainability must recognise the reality of development of human societies.

Moore (Engel and Engel, 1990) argues that, in the 'West', domination of nature became an increasingly dominant assumption in 'Christendom' until, with the arrival of The Enlightenment, it became 'secularized and ... grew to full bloom' (ibid., 105). This does not mean that secularism is necessarily consumerist or religion non-consumerist (cf. US consumerism and the dominance of a particular strand of Protestantism in the US), just that Moore argues there was a historical congruence. He proceeds to review Christian theological insights which argue that dominion of creation should lead to stewardship rather than domination and exploitation for gratification of desires, based on notions of a creation whose value comes from its creator, not the uses humans can put it to. Relatedly, Clark (ibid., 184–5) argues convincingly that seeing nature as of only instrumental value to humans is contrary to Jewish religious teaching; this includes a valuable discussion of why 'dominion' (Genesis 1:26) should not be interpreted as domination but more likely as 'stewardship'.

Similarly, from the view point of Islam, Deen (Engel and Engel, 1990) maintains that seeing nature as of only instrumental value to humans and cruelty to animals are contrary to scripture and tradition. Deen further argues that Islam emphasises intra-generational and inter-generational justice issues as part of a broader virtue ethic scheme, including stewardship, temperance and charity. Of particular relevance for this book, Deen writes, 'even if Doomsday were expected imminently humans would be expected to continue their good behaviour' towards nature (ibid., 194).

From African perspectives, both Omari and Omo-Fadaka (Engel and Engel, 1990) argue for more local community focused approaches to sustainable development questions, including local communal management of land.

Reviewing a number of religious traditions present in China (including Christianity), Sui-cheong Chau and Kam-Kong (ibid.) emphasise agreement about the perils of possessive tendencies even for non-material 'things'. They imply that a virtue response to unsustainable development is more effective than a legal approach.

Useful feminist perspectives on the reasons for unsustainable development are provided by Pietilä and Salleh (ibid.). They both echo the analysis of Francis Bacon by Merchant (1983, particularly 80–6, 164–89), Hay (2002, 75–6, 123) and this book in being critical of desire for control. Salleh also argues that an emphasis on economic growth often disempowers women, makes life more difficult and precarious for women as well as devaluing and marginalising the values of 'typical' female activities, opinions and approaches.

Overall, Engel and Engel (1990) reinforces earlier arguments that suggest that a significant percentage of the global human population would be critical of economistic utilitarian notions of development, at least if acting as citizens rather than consumers (cf. Holden, 2002, 15–20). It also suggests these people will tend to favour virtue ethics approaches rather than alternatives.

Attfield (2003) is a very useful overview of the field of environmental ethics and effectively connects this to other disciplines relevant to sustainable development. Most importantly for this book, he defends 'biocentric consequentialism'; however, he appears to assume that all significant consequences can be known without making clear how. This is although he recognises the possibility of thresholds in the Earth System (ibid., 145) and something of the significance of uncertainty (ibid., 104, 144, 146).

More specific discussion of ecological questions and virtue ethics is now appropriate. An effective attempt to address some academic queries about environmental virtue ethics is provided by Sandler (2004). This includes arguing that preference for deontological and utilitarian ethics is tied to particular epistemological assumptions (ibid., 488–90). Specifically, he implies that the assumptions of deontology and utilitarianism are scientific in the sense that, by using appropriate deontological and utilitarian tools, individuals can in theory decide the right course of action without recourse to outside 'authorities'. He does not make clear what 'authority' can establish deontological or utilitarian tools, nor how these can be put into practice. He concludes: 'Considerable work still remains to be done before one could claim that environmental virtue ethics is a legitimate alternative to more traditional approaches to environmental ethics' (ibid., 491). This may be accurate in the 'purely academic' terms that Sandler appears to be using. However, as implied by earlier discussion in this book, if the 'global virtue tradition' is considered then the above statement appears more questionable. Specifically, the 'economics' basis of probably most policy, which sees greed and wanton consumption as virtues, would be challenged by the global virtue tradition and reversed, with both greed and wanton consumption being seen as vices. If this reverse were to happen in the consciousness of most people who are driven by the desire to consume and acquire more, this might be the single most effective change in societies, to allow them to reduce their stress to the Earth System.

As part of a useful edited volume discussing environmental virtue ethics, Cafaro (Sandler and Cafaro, 2005, 31) argues that 'any complete environmental ethics must include an environmental virtue ethics'. He reviews the life and work of Henry David Thoreau, Aldo Leopold and Rachel Carson and draws the following conclusions as 'virtues':

1 A desire to put economic life in its proper place.
2 A commitment to science combined with an appreciation of its limits.
3 Nonanthropocentrism [the moral considerability of the non-human world].
4 An appreciation of the wild and support for wilderness protection.
5 A bedrock of belief that life is good: both human and non-human.

(Ibid., 37–8)

This book clearly supports the first point. It is interesting that discussion of the second point identifies Bacon as the inspiration for utilitarian domination of nature, without clearly questioning human abilities to bend the whole of nature to our will. I am happy to assign the non-human world value beyond its utility to humans. Beyond questions of definition of wilderness, I also support the prudence of appreciating nature, again beyond utilitarian pleasure that might be so obtained. Believing that life is good is an important balance to seeing nature as a foe to be combated; however, 'reality' may be a little more complicated than either extreme. The analysis by Cafaro does add useful insights and they accord with the global virtue tradition.

A discussion of virtue and consumerism, which adds significant practical depth to earlier arguments, is provided by Wenz (2005, 197–215) (cf. Barber, 2007).[6] It argues reasonably convincingly[7] that consumerism 'relies on vices that harm both people and nature' (Wenz, 2005, 197). He illustrates environmental and social harm from consumerism with both global and local examples. The examples of harm to the global poor include increases in some causes of malnutrition, health effects of pollution, greater inequity, unjust displacement from traditional neighbourhoods resulting in poorer living and working conditions, family break up and child prostitution (ibid., 199–203). Indeed, he compares selfishness and indifference in rich consumers with German citizens in Nazi Germany (ibid., 207). Wenz (ibid., 203) further argues that 'industrial people suffer from consumerism because it perpetuates perpetual discontent, social isolation, and depression', produced by advertising creating wants, long work hours and commuting, suburban architecture, loss of family and community closeness leading to crime and less civic activity, obesity and objectification of women (ibid., 203–6). It is interesting in the light of Palmer and Finlay (2003)[8] that Wenz (2005, 197, 206–10) argues powerfully for the reaffirmation of 'traditional' virtue ethic schemes (both virtues and vices), perhaps derived from those of Aquinas, as the correct counter to consumerism. Indeed, the account by Wenz could be criticised for not giving an indication of the source of the traditional virtues he uses. Wenz (ibid., 210–2) closes with the useful suggestion that in moving to more ecological virtue, individuals should not be so extreme as to isolate themselves from society. The criticisms of consumerism by Wenz are echoed, if in less strong terms, by a number of authors in the same volume.

As part of examining questions of participation and environmental issues, Smith (2003, particularly 7–28) discusses value conflicts about environmental and connected issues. This illustrates the close link between participation and the application of ethical schemes to policy. One area where his account perhaps makes a significant confused conflation is between believing 'nature' has intrinsic value and believing that humans cannot decide between the relative merits of the effects of actions on humans and nature (ibid., 8–13). For example, Palmer and Finlay (2003) suggest that it is possible to believe that nature has (intrinsic) value beyond the instrumental benefits that humans can obtain; however, that does not mean that holding this belief determines a decision about, for example, whether a particular ecosystem can be destroyed for human benefit or not. What the religions represented by Palmer and Finlay (ibid.) tend to suggest is that gratuitous destruction for the sake of greed or wanton consumption is wrong. Smith (2003, 14, emphasis in original) goes on to say: 'According to many intrinsic value theorists, in contemporary societies we typically consider *only* the direct use value of nature.' This is probably accurate for those (policy) decisions made purely by economic cost–benefit analysis. Smith (ibid., 8–18) proceeds to highlight that there are other ways of seeing 'value' in nature in contemporary societies, even if his survey and dismissal of all forms of intrinsic valuing nature might be criticised for being less than comprehensively plural itself.

Discussing 'ethical monism' and 'value pluralism', Smith (ibid., 18–26) advocates pluralism in a convincing way. However, the particular use of the phrase 'value pluralism' by Smith (ibid., 21–4) is noteworthy as it perhaps implies a utilitarian or consequentialist assumption rather than a pluralism between different ethical frames or a broader pluralism unspecified by Smith. It is not made clear why 'value pluralism' was chosen rather than 'ethical pluralism'. Indeed, the account of value pluralism is perhaps a little confused. For example, the term 'virtue' is used in a particular way that does not obviously reflect the way in which it is used by Aristotle and similar theorists, which an account of ethical pluralism might want to mention.[9] Later chapters do paint a more complex (if more con-fusing) picture, with criticism of utilitarianism (e.g. ibid., 42–3); however, the alternatives offered, 'justice and equity', are not clarified substantially.

It is noteworthy that in this discussion, Smith (ibid., 26) appears to rule out selfish individualism and epistemological individualism as being valid within plu-ralism on the basis that they are themselves not plural.[10] It can be argued that pluralism will need to be able to cope with this individualism, even if those who declare themselves pluralist are warranted to criticise those who are individualis-tic, to the extent that this harms the plurality of a society. It can be argued that it is this selfish individualism that neo-classical economics is based on and that the operation of 'liberal capitalist' societies assumes some form of epistemological individualism (e.g. consumer sovereignty), at least. Indeed, it might be that the sub-text to the whole of Smith's book is an analysis of how policy decisions can be better based on some notion of common good rather than private good.[11]

Smith concludes his discussion of 'value pluralism and the environment' by setting out the agenda for the rest of his book by stating: 'Given that value pluralism points to there not being a single green ethical position per se, what institutional form might allow for divergent and conflicting values to be articu-lated and considered?' (ibid., 27–8). This is a worthy project with which this book is in sympathy, barring concerns about the particular use of 'value' by Smith and concerns about whether 'green ethical position[s]' are being favoured over other positions that make up plural societies; these discussions by Smith will be explored in more detail shortly. However, before that it is pertinent to note that Smith stresses the divergence of opinions in academic green theorists. It can be argued that this divergence is perhaps little greater than the divergence of opinion between academics within other ethical and political theory fields. This includes a significant diversity among liberal theorists. In defence of Smith, the diversity he presents is probably close to the diversity of opinion held by 'green activists', whereas for 'liberal activists' who are in positions of power 'the Washington consensus' is quite typically assumed in a way that many academic liberals would question. However, Palmer and Finlay (2003), supported by envi-ronmentalists and other elements of civil society, suggest that a 'liberalism', which imposes economic systems that promote greed and wanton consumption, may not be globally liberal or democratic. That Palmer and Finlay (2003) was published by the World Bank at the initiative of the then President of the bank, suggests some recognition of this. Indeed, these global counter-currents may mean that if there was genuine debate within the globally powerful countries, the populations might choose a different vision of society, particularly given the lack of engagement of the general population of those countries in existing party political activity. Thus, for the sake of practical action on the ecological and equity issues of most concern for this book, Smith might be over-emphasising the significance of differences of opinion. These differences of opinion are both between 'greens' and differences of opinion globally, and among citizens more generally, about whether 'nature' is just resources and sinks to be used for eco-nomic activity or whether nature has value beyond its economic value. This is in addition to the point that the differences he identifies might be accentuated by focusing on utilitarian values rather than on ethical pluralism.

Evidence that economic cost–benefit analysis is increasingly favoured and even imposed in (environmental) policy-making processes is offered by Smith (2003, 29–51), who argues that it is a narrow approach that does not adequately reflect the plurality of values that people apply to the environment. Similar, stronger, arguments could be made about the narrowness of cost–benefit analysis not reflecting plural ethical approaches and policy questions more generally. Smith (ibid., 32–49) argues that the forms of economics used is based on (materialist) utilitarian ethical assumptions that exclude other ethical schemes, particularly by performing opaque calculative 'rituals' that cannot be contested (ibid., particularly 46–8). He also criticises current economic methods in more technical ways, including 'an indifference to other values such as justice and equity' (ibid., 42).

Much of the rest of the environmental ethics literature, which considers such questions, appears to be critical of economistic utilitarianism. The utilitarianism of Singer is used to consider the question of suffering of animals and humans rather more directly than questions of stress to the Earth System, though he is critical of greed (e.g. Singer, 1972). The reasons why there appears little defence of economistic utilitarianism at least until recently in environmental ethics literature are not clear. However, it can be suggested that it is related to questions of power. Conventional economics (neo-classical and environmental) is typically used in policy-making (Smith, 2003, 29–51) but environmental ethics appears rarely used. This is why this book suggests that environmentalists should seek alliance with the world religions (Palmer and Finlay, 2003), anti-capitalists, trade unions and others who question economistic utilitarianism. Specifically, this would be to challenge the dominance of this ethic and bring about debate as to what ethics should be used in policy-making, rather than economics being unchallenged, most of the time in most situations. Indeed, there may be many liberal political philosophers who dislike the current practice of liberal free market societies who may wish to add their voice to calls for societies to be less organised around greed and consumerism.

To summarise, a review of a wide range of ethical literature, which considers sustainable development questions, suggests that the use of economistic utilitarian ethical assumptions is deeply questionable, with rights-based or virtue ethics being more suited to the current situation, specifically that humans cannot predict the consequences of industrialism. Indeed, the literature reviewed tends to suggest virtue ethics broadly similar to the 'cardinal virtues' and 'seven deadly sins'. Further, some versions of the virtue 'prudence' combine both consequential sub-virtues and sub-virtues that emphasise the limitations of human knowledge, humility and caution, even if the exact relationship of all these is not immediately clear.

The tentative suggestion for virtues ethics to be used by preference alongside utilitarian and rights-based ethics in responding to difficulties in predicting the effects of human stress to the Earth System will be considered. Before that let us consider literature that is more specifically critical of virtue ethics.

7.4 Questions raised of virtue

A brief description of some key criticisms of virtue ethics approaches is offered by Hursthouse (2000, 154–7). Specifically, what are the virtues and vices to use and that the terms are vague and open to interpretation. The 'global virtue tradition' suggests that for sustainable development, broad agreement about key virtues may be fairly easy to achieve. The vagueness of virtue ethics might be considered better than oversimplifying complex ethical questions by resolving them through economic methods.

A useful edited collection of 'critics' of virtue ethics is provided by Statman (1997), so let us consider some of these critical voices, starting with the introduction by the editor. Statman (ibid., 8) states that 'virtues are justified in terms of their essential role in the wellbeing of the agent', but this appears to ignore the position of Aristotle and Aquinas that might be more like 'the well-being of the agent and the communities of which they are a part'. Some hint at the possible communal nature of human flourishing is made by Statman (ibid., 23) but he does not explore this in any depth.

'Difficulties' in virtue ethics considered by Statman (ibid., 18–22) are justification, universality, applicability and the moral status of acts; let us consider these. When Statman introduces virtue ethics justification difficulties, he (ibid., 19) states that 'having rejected … justifying the virtues … as dispositions for right behaviour … [virtue ethics] seems to have … to … ground the virtues in the idea of human flourishing … or … conceive them … as … worthy in themselves'. An interpretation of Aristotle and perhaps particularly Aquinas would be that justification of virtue ethics would be in all three and they would be mutually reinforcing. Ignoring that human flourishing may have a community element appears to be at the root of the difficulties Statman (ibid.) has with justification of virtue ethics via human flourishing, as is perhaps his assumption that flourishing implies material gain. Statman (ibid., 19–20) states that all notions of human flourishing are normative. This may be true, but it is not clear that any forms of ethics do not have normative assumptions as Statman (ibid., 22) later notes. MacIntyre (1985) is suggested as leading to non-universal virtue ethics (Statman, 1997, 20); however, as a footnote suggests, this is only one interpretation of MacIntyre. On the basis of this (now assumed) lack of universality of virtue ethics, Statman argues that this causes deep theoretical and practical problems. It is later noted 'that there is wide agreement on the core norms and values' (ibid., 22–3). In addition, Palmer and Finlay (2003) suggest that something approaching universality on at least one set of crucial policy issues may be achievable with a reasonable level of effort. This holds out the possibility of a near universal structure of virtues, even if there may always be some differences in detail. It is interesting to note that in responding to this difficulty, Statman (1997, 22) writes that virtue ethics can be justified by 'cohering in the best way with our moral intuitions' without considering how our intuitions have been shaped by theorists such as Aristotle and Aquinas and their effect on societies.

A further justification issue is suggested by Solomon (ibid., 167–71), that virtue ethics have an essentially teleological nature and that both natural and theological teleology upon which virtue ethics might be based are called into question by 'modernity'. Solomon does not make clear the basis of this, which is unfortunate, as the natural teleology of Aristotle and Aquinas is perhaps more sophisticated than modern scientific critics assume (Dubray, 1912).[12] In addition, current systems theory, as well as the ecological science (e.g. Jantsch, 1980) and ecological economics (Faber *et al.*, 1998, 168–88) systems theory is used in, make successful use of limited notions of teleology. With regard to theological teleology, Palmer and Finlay (2003) suggest that for unsustainable development, multiple theological teleological bases of virtue schemes may not be as significant as Solomon suggests they are for broader ethical questions. Solomon outlines three 'internal objections' to virtue ethics raised by deontologists and utilitarians (self-centredness, action-guidance, contingency of results of actions); however, he argues that these might also apply to deontological and utilitarian ethics. Indeed, unrecognised by Solomon, Aquinas deals quite directly with the three objections and Palmer and Finlay (ibid.) suggest that agreement about action-guidance between different virtue schemes might be easier for sustainable development issues than it is for utilitarian or deontological schemes. This might mean that these objections might apply at least as much to deontology and utilitarianism as, at least, some virtue schemes.

Statman (1997, 20) states that 'no ... [practical] guidance seems to be provided by' virtue ethics. I will assume that he is talking about contemporary virtue ethics philosophical literature, as the global virtue tradition has guidance about how to apply their virtue ethics schemes. Even if we disagree with the particular schemes and guidance, this means that practical guidance is compatible with virtue ethics. Statman (ibid., 23–6) does go on to note that virtue ethics may be easier to apply, less problematic and more illuminating in practice than other forms of ethics.

When discussing the moral status of acts, Statman (ibid., 21) states: 'According to most versions of [virtue ethics] ... actions are evaluated only as manifestations of character'. However, Statman (ibid.) notes that this is not true of Aristotle;[13] thus, it appears that Statman is again being critical of contemporary virtue ethics philosophical literature, not virtue ethics schemes in general. Statman (ibid., 23) does later note that 'the evaluation of acts' is problematic for alternatives to virtue ethics.

Statman (ibid., 26–7) does implicitly raise a vital question about how to decide what are virtues and what are not virtues. He suggests that Aristotle does this primarily by considering the opinion of 'Athenian Gentlemen', which many including the present author would question. Statman does not consider the development of Aristotle by Aquinas who perhaps suggests that the 'human virtues' (prudence, justice, courage and temperance) and their systematic structure can be derived by human reason, 'independent' of revelation. More recent evidence for this 'intrinsic' nature of virtues is perhaps seen from the similarities of ethical response to environmental issues by the world religions as highlighted in Palmer and Finlay (2003). Indeed, brown capuchin monkeys appear to have an innate sense of justice (Brosnan and de Wall, 2003). This suggests that a nearly universally agreed virtue structure may be possible, and while detailed discussion of this is obviously beyond the scope of this book, it is certainly a 'vital' question. The level of agreement in Palmer and Finlay (2003) is sufficient for the purposes of this book: being critical of economistic utilitarianism and of exploiting humans and nature to fuel human greed; in a more positive vein, nine of the world faiths are recorded as advocating some form of moderation. Fortunately, there is recent literature that suggests something beyond this sufficiency. For example, van Wensveen (2005, 178–88) argues that the Western cardinal virtues[14] derived from Aristotle can be reinforced and complemented by recent neurobiology and an extensive analysis of environmental virtue, implicit or explicit in recent ecological literature. The discussion is also an eloquent illustration of how ecological virtue might work in practice in individuals.[15]

It is also worth noting that Statman (1997, 10–11, 30) suggests that virtue ethics can incorporate aspects of both rights-based and utilitarian ethics. Whether it can 'synthesise' the best aspects of both is beyond the scope of this book but may be worth further work. This is perhaps less surprising as Statman (ibid., 27–30) suggests that Kant, Hume and others that are important in 'modern' ethical systems contain more elements of virtue ethics than is typically recognised. Solomon (ibid., 165) even suggests 'any ethical theory which does not embody an account of the virtues will be importantly incomplete'. Indeed, Statman (ibid., 30) suggests that a synthesis of virtue ethics and 'alternatives' may be broadly acceptable within academia and perhaps even further afield.

'Some vices of virtue ethics' are discussed by Louden (1984) suggesting a number of issues. First, that we 'lack fully developed examples of it [virtue] in the contemporary literature' (ibid., 227). This does appear largely true, but may be the fault of contemporary literature of 1984 to thoroughly assess historical schemes. Second, that contemporary academic virtue ethics literature tends to be critical of other ethical schemes rather than suggesting positive alternatives to those other schemes (ibid.). This also appears largely true; however, a similar response to the first point can be made.

That virtue ethics is not helpful with applied ethics is the next criticism (ibid., 230). This is surprising given the applied ethics associated with the world religions and their use of virtue ethics (cf. Palmer and Finlay, 2003). He suggests (Louden, 1984, 230) rather unconvincingly that virtue ethics cannot deal well with 'tragic humans' (e.g. someone who causes significant harm even with best intentions and due diligence). He does not indicate clearly how other forms of ethics will fare better in such situations.

Louden (ibid., 230–1) suggests that 'every traditional moral community' will have rules that specify 'intolerable actions' that cannot be adequately derived from 'patterns of behaviour'.[16] His discussion of 'moral backsliding' (ibid., 231) has a similar basis. The problem here may be more to do with a philosophical assumption that particular forms of ethics are the correct ones and exclude all others, whereas ethical traditions can use virtue ethics, rules and some notion of utility. My tentative conclusions from the previous section perhaps are something that Louden (ibid., 230–1) hints at. Character change is argued by Louden (ibid., 231–2) to be a problem for virtue ethics. However, he implies the 'solution' to the 'problem' in discussing the need to 'practice' virtues.

Perhaps the most telling criticism by Louden is an observation (ibid., 232–3) of the epistemological difficulties in knowing who is a virtuous person and thus he implies what the virtues are. This has significant importance. However, similar problems perhaps affect deontological and utilitarian ethics. Indeed, this book tries to make clear that epistemological problems around understanding the Earth System mean knowing what will bring the greatest utility is deeply problematic. In addition, the level of agreement about virtue ethics for environment and development questions in the global virtue tradition suggests that an agreement on a broad set of virtues for these issues by the majority of the global population may be possible. Indeed, it may already exist, even if it is not currently clearly articulated.

Virtue ethics is accused of having a problem of 'style over substance' by Louden (ibid., 233–4) (with deontology assessed as having similar problems). He implies that ancient Greek virtue theory guarded against this in a way that contemporary virtue ethics does not, and he further implies that this is due to the Judeo-Christian heritage of contemporary virtue ethics. This perhaps suggests an 'unsophisticated' understanding of Judeo-Christian ethics, with at least some Judeo-Christian ethics containing rule-based, virtue-based and in some sense utilitarian notions of ethics.

In labelling virtue ethics utopian, Louden (ibid., 234–5) implies that rule-based ethics can deal better with complex situations. The logic of this is unclear. If virtue ethic schemes can be reduced to single figure cardinal virtues with sub-virtues and ideas that can all be applied by individuals to specific situations, without the need to have detailed rules specified, then this will be easier to achieve than in a situation where some form of 'governance' has to specify behaviour in detail. Louden goes on in the same paragraph to cite the variety of 'ethnic, religious and class groups' (ibid., 235) as another indication of utopianism by contemporary virtue theorists, in hoping to affect the moral character of real societies. Again with regard to environment and development questions, Palmer and Finlay (2003) suggest that this may be less of an issue than is typically assumed. His final 'utopian' critique of virtue ethics is of where contemporary virtue ethic theorists think of virtue ethics as an alternative to ethical rules. This appears quite reasonable, but is probably a greater reflection on contemporary virtue theorists than on historical schemes.

A final author who raises questions about virtue ethics is Slote (Baron *et al.*, 1997, 175–235) who also directly relates these to the epistemological concerns of this book. He reviews a variety of recent virtue ethics schemes and makes reference to ancient schemes. Slote does not favour any particular scheme, but he does not appear to have considered ethics such as Aquinas that perhaps answer many of the questions that Slote has, with the schemes he considers, particularly with regard to whether virtue ethics stands on its own or works with ethical 'laws'. One system that Slote (ibid., 232) considers is 'morality as benevolence' and specifically considers how this will respond to a situation when consequences are not known. He suggests morality as benevolence and consequential approaches will both be 'stymied'. However, this is probably a more significant problem for Slote as he did not explicitly consider virtue ethics schemes that have a system of virtues that complement 'benevolence' and are connected to 'universal' laws that might apply in the situation Slote considers. Thus, if a particular set of virtues is chosen, even if consequences of different actions are not clear, it may be that the action that is most virtuous is clear.

The above suggests that there are difficulties with virtue ethics; however, these appear surmountable for the reasons given above. To summarise, the 'global virtue tradition' as outlined in Chapter 2 addresses many questions around justification, universality and applicability as well as the relationship of virtue to rules. The theoretical difficulties of virtue ethics are probably not significantly greater, in general terms, than other forms of ethics. Virtue ethics does still appear, in principle, to be better able to respond to difficulties in predicting the Earth System than other forms of ethics. Or as van Wensveen writes of virtue language:

> Its internal consistency and comprehensibility are not dependent on the worldview that came into power with scientific and industrial revolutions. Given that many critics see the modern worldview as an important factor in bringing about the ecological crisis, it will be helpful to have access to a form of moral discourse that is not too much in cahoots with this worldview. Even though virtue ethics may have acquired an image of conservatism, a virtue ethic … could have surprisingly radical effects.
>
> (Sandler and Cafaro, 2005, 27–8)

We need to ask now 'which are the ecological virtues?' That is the question to which the next section will directly turn.

7.5 The virtue alternative

So far this book has brought forward a case that (ecological) virtue is one good response to an unpredictable Earth System. This section will explore what this virtue might be like.

Virtue principles and an unpredictable Earth

As noted earlier – in particular by contributors to Sandler and Cafaro (2005) – much of the existing discussion of ecological virtue is of ecological vice. This is useful in highlighting issues with existing policy processes and vice can be used in policy decisions as a way of testing options. To illustrate, policymakers might ask whether a policy will promote any of the capital vices (seven deadly sins): pride, avarice, envy, wrath, lust, gluttony and sloth.[17] However, it is not clear how these types of consideration will help generate policy options and ideas in a way that cardinal virtues might. In addition, some virtue schemes see the vices as potentially being kept in check by relevant virtues, thus the emphasis on this section is on virtue not vice.

Related to the notion of vice, Naess (Engel and Engel, 1990, 95–6) advocates addressing what is obviously unsustainable rather than being too concerned about what sustainability will be like. He is critical of greed and wanton consumption. Schellnhuber (1998, 48) does caution against such 'anti-liberal' negative approaches, but as illustrated in Chapter 2, does not propose unquestionable alternatives. The authors analysed above suggest or imply that greed and wanton consumption are vices that are harmful to individual humans, societies and the Earth System. In some sense, conventional economics is perhaps based on the assumption that these vices are virtues (cf. Keynes, 1931, 372; Korten, 1996, 74–5). It can be argued that this reversal with greed and wanton consumption being seen as virtues is a key cause of unsustainable development. The exclusivist non-stewardship[18] notion of private property, probably implicit in conventional economics, exacerbates the unsustainable tendencies of the economic practices that currently dominate globally.

What can we say that is more positive? As noted earlier, Earth System science literature often recommends stewardship, as does Barry (1999) and perhaps implicitly Attfield (1994). The global virtue tradition might also be characterised as recommending stewardship. As indicated earlier, global virtue tradition suggests that broad agreement on more specific virtues and vices might in some sense be readily globally agreed in broad terms, as an alternative to the currently dominant global ethic of economistic utilitarianism. In relation to difficulties in prediction, discussion of virtue by Socrates, Plato, Aristotle, Augustine, Aquinas, Kant (cf. Statman, 1997, 286–97), Adam Smith and John Stuart Mill among others are certainly warranted in academic circles. Further research should also involve environmentalists, trades unionists, 'anti-capitalists' and at least the religions represented by literature cited above, among others. This section will attempt to progress this discourse by outlining the best virtue response that I can, as one starting point for the use of virtue ethics in general, as a response specifically to difficulties in predicting the Earth System. Nonetheless, the level of agreement between the world religions, probably along with much of the environmental, trade union and 'anti-capitalist' movements, perhaps means that current policy-making based on economistic utilitarianism can validly and effectively be challenged with more vigour. For example, 'institutions' that are critical of economistic utilitarianism could seek to directly engage the powerful (perhaps minorities) who tend to favour economistic utilitarianism. These institutions could perhaps assist in providing avenues for the anti-capitalist movement to engage in discourse on these issues, as discourse may now be more effective than protest, particularly given isolated but high-profile violence now associated with anti-capitalist protests. It will be welcome if this helps to reduce that violence.

How might ecological virtues operate? It might be argued that virtue ethics could operate in the way that Connelly (2003) and Dobson (1993, 235; 1998: 236–7, 262; 2003, 3–4) suggest, as the internal means by which ecological citizenship is promoted beyond external actions such as taxes and regulation. Dobson's (1993, 235) statement, that 'while greens will agree that restraint is required, their belief is that self-imposed restraint is more effective and lasting than if coerced', points to the value of virtue ethics. At the collective level, if the question 'what is the virtuous thing to do?' was asked, as well as or even instead of 'what will maximise economic growth?', this should make significant difference to human activity. This would perhaps have to be done in some participative decision-making process to reflect the plurality of views rather than by 'experts' doing cost–benefit analysis. Something of what such a participative process would mean is discussed in the next chapter.

How might ecologically virtuous citizens be formed? Virtue theorists from Aristotle to MacIntyre (e.g. 1990, 128–31) believe that 'traditions' are important. Existing institutions, particularly the world religions (cf. Engel and Engel 1990; Palmer and Finlay 2003), NGOs, trade unions, other facets of civil society, perhaps some 'green' parties, schools, even 'enlightened' businesses based on service not profit, etc. could readily play a part. In addition, many of the suggestions in Bass *et al.* (1995) aimed at participation could perhaps be adapted. Literature such as Engel and Engel (1990), IUCN/UNEP/WWF (1991), Dorscht (2007), the Earth Charter (2000), Palmer and Finlay (2003), King and Vandiver-King (2008) plus Bergmann and Gerten (2010) may provide pointers and starting points for discussions. A diversity of approaches will be worthwhile, at least in the short term. Dobson (2003) and Huckle (2004) are relevant to questions of how virtuous citizens might be formed, particularly through the education system.

There are a variety of virtue schemes and opinions on virtue principles; however, I will argue that there is as much agreement in practice for these as there is for the principles of utilitarian/consequential ethics on which conventional economics is built. There is not the operational system for making decisions that there is in conventional economics and the policy processes it supports; there is some discussion later of ways forward. However, earlier chapters suggest that the assumptions of conventional economics are irrational and that economic approaches have not brought about significant reductions in GHGs in the past 20 years. Indeed, GHG emissions have increased over that period, so aiming policies to minimise emissions, balanced against other priorities rather than primarily (or even purely) aiming to maximise economic growth, are worth considering. This balanced trans-economic approach to policy would be a typical virtue perspective on policy; this is perhaps implicitly understood in society (e.g. the precautionary principle) but not typically explicitly understood or articulated. Here, I will outline virtue principles to aid the articulation and understanding of an alternative to economic growth at all costs.

The basic principle of virtue is that virtues are excellences of character learnt from the virtuous, with repeated behaviour becoming good habits or virtues.[19] Second, virtues are broadly a balance between extremes, for example courage being the virtue between the vices of cowardice and foolhardiness. Where habit is insufficient then individuals should apply the intellectual virtue of 'prudence', with the habit of this being principally deliberation based on evidence available and moral virtues to decide action. How groups might apply virtue is less examined in virtue literature but can perhaps be summarised as collective discussion replacing individual deliberation, with decisions aimed at promoting virtue but balancing other relevant ethical principles. From virtue literature such as Aristotle and Aquinas, these other ethical principles would include rights, laws and duties; they could include utility. Aristotle argued that governments should promote virtue and discourage vice, though the elitism with which Aristotle's politics is suffused is not something I support.[20] Now it is appropriate to discuss in more detail what the virtues might look like.

Much recent academic literature that discusses virtue ethics emphasises the variety of positions on virtue ethics; however, at least for practical application to environmental issues there is too much emphasis on the variety. This theoretical emphasis on variety is more on specific virtues than application to environmental issues and tends to be because of a 'reductive' approach or an unexamined assumption that different cultures will have different virtue schemes. The similarity of virtue schemes for environmental issues across cultures is examined in the next section. First, let us examine virtue principles in more detail. Much contemporary research on virtue, particularly in philosophy, tends either to simply be critical of alternatives to virtue or be reductive in the sense that it looks at one virtue or potential virtue in great detail but fails to situate that virtue in a broader virtue scheme. This detail and focus is entirely legitimate as academic practice; however, it tends to emphasise differences that theorists see with that one virtue or whether something should be considered a virtue or not. The remainder of this section will outline virtue ideas within the Western tradition emphasising similarities. The next section will explore similarities in virtue traditions across other cultural heritages as they apply to environmental issues.

As far as can be discerned at this distance in time, Socrates, Plato, Aristotle and the Stoics all subscribed to virtue schemes broadly similar to the four 'cardinal virtues': (1) wisdom or prudence, (2) courage, (3) temperance or moderation and (4) justice; even if there were schools of ancient Greek philosophy that are less clearly committed to such virtues. The virtue of wisdom or prudence is a virtue about our knowledge of the world – an intellectual or epistemological virtue. The virtue of courage is an ethical virtue that is typically seen as a balance between cowardice and foolhardiness. The virtue of temperance or moderation is also an ethical virtue about balancing consuming too much and consuming too little. This obviously applies to environmental and broader sustainable development issues but also to issues such as eating disorders. The virtue of justice is about deciding what the right thing to do is with respect to others, whether they are individuals, groups or arguably non-humans; thus, it is both ethical and political. Both individuals and groups can aim to apply or embody these cardinal virtues. There is philosophical debate about whether the likes of Plato meant virtues to be applied collectively; however, it is not clear that in practice we need to be concerned with this type of philosophical detail.

Broadly similar virtue ideas were common currency, indeed perhaps had a similar level of dominance to the current position of economics until the changes in society that led to the Salamanca School and mercantilism. These changes began to challenge the dominance of virtue ethics with more materialist and implicitly utilitarian ideas. Indeed, even with the rise of classical economics, virtue was still an important part of political economy discourse. To illustrate, Adam Smith (1776/1904, Book V, Chapter 1, paragraph 48) mentions the cardinal virtues in his discussion of justice in *The Wealth of Nations*. In *The Theory of Moral Sentiments*, Smith discusses Plato, Aristotle and particularly Stoic virtue ideas and calls virtue 'the fine polish to the wheels of society' (Smith, 1759/1790, Part VII, Section III, paragraph 5) (cf. Putnam, 2002[21]). However, it does appear that Smith perhaps had more contact with puritanical versions of Christian virtue than is fully representative of the larger body of Christian virtue philosophy (Smith, 1759/1790, Part V, Section I, paragraph 158, Part V, Section I, paragraph 213, Part VII, Section II, paragraph 74, cf. Part VII, Section IV, paragraphs 7 and 16).[22] Indeed, it may be that his meagre defence of self-love (ibid., Part VII, Section II, paragraph 84 to Part VII, Section III, paragraph 20) is limited principally because of Smith's poor knowledge of the likes of Augustine of Hippo and Thomas Aquinas. Smith's defence of self-love is poorly constructed in particular as it fails to distinguish which forms of self-love are virtuous and which are vicious.

It is important to point out that contemporary authors are emphasising the virtue character of Smith's work (e.g. Hanley, 2009) with some even suggesting that an environmental virtue ethics can be built on this (Frierson, 2006). This is not currently convincing from a practical viewpoint to address environmental questions for a number of reasons. These reasons include the unclear nature of Smith's virtue scheme, the utilitarian/consequential tenor of much of Smith's writing even about virtue (Smith, 1759/1790, Part IV, Section I, paragraphs 13, 14, 17 and 18, Part VI, Section III, paragraph 59, Part VII, Section II, paragraph 92)[23] and the lack of clarity about the relationship between utility and virtue, particularly given Smith's emphasis on utility. However, the most important problem is the small proportion of people globally who currently subscribe to Smithian virtue ideas. Nonetheless, this recent work does point to a way forward for engagement between those who hold Adam Smith as an ideologue and environmental virtue ethics.

Even as utilitarian and 'liberal'[24] a figure as John Stuart Mill, as late as 1867, discusses virtue, again this discussion is unclear and could be illegitimately construed as defending a position of 'virtue, everything on which human happiness on the largest scale depends' (Mill, 1867, 33). Despite this being a misrepresentation, certainly Mill is sympathetic to some notion of virtue and sees benefits to society – utility – in people being virtuous. Mill engages with virtue tradition in his defence of utility as the primary ethical scheme, even utility as the basis for virtue. In the light of Mill's discussion of ethics in *Utilitarianism* (Mill, 1867), he may well have been horrified for economic growth to be used as a proxy for utility in the way that it is currently used. Again, it is not clear that Mill's justification of utility as leading to happiness fully engages with all the virtue accounts then available (ibid., particularly 53–61). However, the point here is less about determining the best form or combination of ethical ideas, than establishing that even for a key utilitarian, virtue is an idea worth considering as it applies to political questions.

Alisdair MacIntyre's *After Virtue* (1985) can be seen as the touchstone of a recent revival of virtue political philosophy. In the years since then, MacIntyre appears to have developed a preference for particular virtue schemes but assumes sufficient diversity in our cosmopolitan world that he is wary of advocating any detailed virtue scheme, instead advocating resistance to the viciousness of consumerism from within varieties of tradition. The reason for this limit of ambition might be attributed to MacIntyre not fully recognising the implications of limitations of science to predict and control nature for economic cost–benefit analysis, utilitarianism and consumerism; as discussed in Charlesworth and Okereke (2010) and Chapter 2. Indeed, Palmer and Finlay (2003) suggest enough agreement in global virtue tradition to democratically challenge consumerism. Other recent virtue theorists do not go significantly beyond MacIntyre except to wrestle further with some practical applications of virtue (e.g. Walker and Ivanhoe, 2009).

What is the particular virtue scheme that so many authors have ignored since mercantilism? It is the scheme that led atheist Philippa Foot to write 'the *Summa Theologica* is one of the best sources we have for moral philosophy, and moreover that St Thomas's ethical writings are as useful to the atheist as to the Catholic or other Christian believer' (Foot, 2002, 2). That is, Thomas Aquinas's account of virtue in the second part of the second part of the *Summa Theologica* is one that systematises and extends the account of the cardinal virtues from Ancient Greece to become the most coherent and complete account of virtue known to the author.[25] The account of virtue by Aquinas (cf. MacIntyre, 2009, 88–90) will be outlined here in broad terms relevant to environmental questions, particularly abrupt climate change and with approaches to limitations in knowledge highlighted, before the next section looks in more detail at the ecological application.

First let us consider the detail that, on the basis of a wide-ranging synthesis of the literature then available, Aquinas provides about the cardinal virtues of prudence, justice, courage and temperance, before considering the wider scheme by Aquinas. To simplify significantly, Aquinas argues that prudence includes memory (knowledge of the past), understanding (knowledge of the present), shrewdness ('acquire a right estimate by oneself'), docility (learning well from others), reason (deliberating well), foresight (working towards a future good effectively), circumspection (finding ethical means to an end) and caution (avoiding future harm). In the context of the current book the last – caution – is worth considering in more detail. Part of how Aquinas describes caution is as follows:

> Of the evils which man has to avoid, some are of frequent occurrence; the like can be grasped by reason, and against them caution is directed, either that they may be avoided altogether, or that they may do less harm. Others there are that occur rarely and by chance, and these, since they are infinite in number, cannot be grasped by reason, nor is man able to take precautions against them, although by exercising prudence he is able to prepare against all the surprises of chance, so as to suffer less harm thereby.
>
> (ST, II:II:49)[26]

The first sentence is a good statement of the dominant risk management and economic approaches to policy for issues including environmental issues (Dryzek 1987, 1990; Torgerson, 1999). The second is a fair description of the situation that we find ourselves in with regard to abrupt climate change. So what is the larger notion of prudence through which we can 'prepare against all the surprises of chance'? It is not economics or rules. Later authors writing in the tradition of Aquinas state explicitly that prudence is not 'timidity or fear'. No, the tone of prudence for Aquinas (plus Aristotle and the traditions represented in Palmer and Finlay (2003)) is broadly similar to the precautionary principle; that is the virtue of prudence considers the evidence available and plays on the safe side, particularly where the only benefit of taking risks is unfairly distributed material wealth and convenience.[27]

Aquinas specifically argues that beyond the individual, prudence applies to politics and 'the conduct of the household' implying a need to consider the common good (Aquinas, ST, II:II:50). For Aquinas, 'demonstration' or 'physics' – broadly equivalent to modern empirical science – is part of understanding. It is possible that Aquinas would have distinguished between different aspects of climate science. Empirical natural science, of which the basic experimental science of climate change is an example, would perhaps be classified as understanding. The less empirical science of climate modelling and to a lesser extent paleoclimate data, such as temperatures derived from tree rings and ice cores, would perhaps be classified as variously belonging to other aspects of prudence, particularly foresight. These would all be part of prudence but might be accorded different consideration about how to be cautious, just, courageous and temperate.

Aquinas writes extensively about justice as a cardinal virtue; however, the following provides a sense (ibid., II:II:58): 'The just man gives to another what is his, through consideration of the common good ... justice is observed towards all.'

In the light of climate justice concerns and broader sustainable development questions, this can be illustrated by the sophisticated and nuanced notion of property rights of Aquinas. Aquinas holds that property rights are vital for complex societies to function effectively, but property is not to be abused but used for the benefit of the common good (cf. Fleischacker, 2004). Aquinas talks about justice in equal exchange, which the fair trade movement is attempting to address somewhat, and justice in distribution, from communities to individuals and from individuals to communities. Aquinas is not definitive about the specifics of distributive justice, in effect on the basis of subsidiarity, leaving the decision down to individual societies to make. To try to provide more specific guidance, in the context of unpredictable climate change, let me read into the account of virtue by Aquinas to identify a number of possible principles.[28] First, all people are 'equal in the sight of God'; thus, each person could be allocated equal GHG emissions. Second, that those who have historically large GHG emissions owe a debt to those who have not, particularly if science suggests that the low emitters are being or will be harmed or even disproportionately harmed.[29] Third, that those who have greater need (though this would relate to charity more than justice) could be allocated more GHG emissions. Fourth, that those with greater responsibilities may need to be allocated greater GHG emissions, at least for their professional responsibilities. Obviously, there are grave dangers of abuse of the last principle; however, it may be societies less focused on economics and laws and more on virtue would adequately hold people to account. Indeed, the recent controversies about UK MPs' expenses and loss-making bankers' bonuses, that are related to the vice of greed, provide support for this. Thus, virtue in serving the public or common good could be a criterion for allocating GHG emissions. Liberality means giving generously to others while still keeping enough to support you and your family, which is a further relevant component of justice for Aquinas. This may be helpful when trying to decide the nature of climate justice.

Also relevant is that justice is typically conceived as being between humans but it would be in the spirit of Aquinas and the contributions to Palmer and Finlay (2003) to apply a notion of justice to nature or creation.[30] This justice to nature would at least be thankful for what we receive from nature; it would see nature as having a value beyond simply the (economic) utility that we can make of nature.

Climate justice campaigns tend not to articulate the philosophical basis of their campaigns;[31] however, they appear to be based on a virtue notion of justice rather than fulfilling legal obligations or justice as maximising economic utility within society. That is, the historic producers of GHG ('The West') and larger per capita current emitters (e.g. the global middle class) are seen as having a responsibility of justice to those humans (including other high emitters) and ecosystems that may be affected by climate change. This responsibility of justice is generally discussed as those that have benefited in the present and the past from emitting GHGs have a responsibility of justice broadly as outlined above. An extra sense by which this discussion of climate justice is related to justice is that often it is through unjust trade, which though typically (though not universally) legal and arguably beneficial to global economic growth, is not just in the sense that those with more knowledge and power exploit those with less knowledge and power to benefit themselves materially. Through the institutionalisation of this exploitation since mercantilism, injustice has arguably been systematically woven into the fabric of global trade structures – hence the fair trade movement.[32] It is in large part through these colonial and post-colonial structures that 'The West' was able to gain the wealth to allow it to emit so much GHG.

If these past and present actions are injustices then the notion of restitutional justice should then apply, e.g. compensation for harm to fish from pollution. This could also apply to the ecological debt that high income countries owe to low income countries that they have exploited (Salleh, 2009; cf. www.ecologicaldebt. org). A second broad example is justice owed to people suffering ill health, which science cannot demonstrate is not related to industrial chemicals, for example cancer and asthma. A further broad example is debts owed to people increasingly affected by climate change such as in sub-Saharan Africa, Bangladesh and Small Island States.

Thus, we can see that the notion of justice for Aquinas is relevant to abrupt climate change and similar in tone to the climate justice movement, even if it does not provide an explicit grounding for that movement or a complete and incontestable account of justice.

The cardinal virtue fortitude or courage for Aquinas (see also Aristotle, *Nicomachean Ethics*, Book III, 7) includes (1) magnificence – 'accomplishment "of great and lofty undertakings, with a certain broad and noble purpose of mind,"' (2) confidence – 'that "with this the mind is much assured and firmly hopeful in great and honorable undertakings"', (3) patience – '"the voluntary and prolonged endurance of arduous and difficult things for the sake of virtue"', and (4) perseverance – '"the fixed and continued persistence in a well considered purpose"' (Aquinas, ST II:II:128). It should be clear that all of these will be needed by individuals and groups if human societies are to move from an unsustainable consumerist political economy to a sustainable 'virtuous' political economy without this move being prompted by ecological cataclysm or a 'revolution'.[33] There is discussion of aggression in Aquinas's discussion of courage – this is implicitly principally defensive rather than offensive.[34] Aquinas specifically argues that anger is a vice that is opposed to aspects of temperance. It is to be hoped that not too many more martyrs[35] will be needed to perform the principal act of courage that Aquinas discusses before a globally sustainable world ensues. Perhaps particularly through the virtue of magnificence it should be noted that virtue is not puritanical; this can be seen in that Aristotle (e.g. Gallop, 2004; Smithson, 1983) and Aquinas (e.g. Eco, 1988; cf. Fox, 2003) are not insignificant figures in the development of ideas of aesthetics, with both being noted for their eloquence. Nonetheless, as is clear in the next cardinal virtue moderation, virtues are not hedonistic. Virtues attempt to strike a good – virtuous – balance.

Aristotle (*Nicomachean Ethics*, Book III, 10 and 11) argues that temperance, moderation or partaking appropriately, applied to food, drink and sexual activity. To illustrate, for both to be healthy an athlete would eat more than someone less active. The amount and type of food consumed affects the level of stress or disturbance that a person causes to the Earth System, including GHG emissions, so this could be one factor to balance against others in an environmental virtue ethic. To give an illustration, someone who walked or cycled to work would typically consume more food; however, overall this would typically mean that less environmental stress would occur than if they had driven. Similar arguments could be developed for the environmental effects of drink and sexual activity. Aquinas discusses food, drink and sexual activity with regard to his cardinal virtue temperance but makes explicit an extension of the scope of temperance by suggesting that a virtuous person would not 'desire too many' things and that these things would be simple (cf. 'live simply that others may simply live'). It is worth contrasting this with Aquinas's virtue of magnificence that is part of fortitude. Magnificence is not related to personal consumption but to achieving broader aims. Like much in the application of virtue ethics, deciding on specifics in a situation would be about using a honed prudence to strike an appropriate balance, rather than absolute rights and wrongs. It is in the spirit of Aristotle and more clearly Aquinas to advocate a reduction in consumption of meat and animal products where it promotes personal health benefits, reduces environmental stress and allows greater efficiency, allowing more people to be fed from the same land (cf. FAO, 2006). Aquinas, some of the world religions and others would add other reasons to eat less animal products. Indeed, it would be in the spirit of this 'global virtue tradition' (e.g. Palmer and Finlay, 2003) to moderate or reduce all forms of consumption where people have enough and there may be significant impacts of over-consumption.

As part of temperance (rather than prudence), Aquinas sees humility as a virtue that is opposed to the vice of pride – 'he who wishes to overstep beyond what he is, is proud ... pride denotes something opposed to right reason'.[36] This pride could readily apply to Baconian illusions of human ability to control the Earth System, in order to maximise economic growth. Similarly, as part of temperance Aquinas argues that studiousness – moderated desire for knowledge – is a virtue that is opposed by the vice of curiosity. An example of an ecological vice of curiosity would be running a real world global warming experiment, putting ecosystems and billions of human lives at risk just for the sake of curiosity. Dr Mengele's Nazi experiments would be another example of curiosity amongst other vices.[37] Aquinas describes curiosity as knowledge leading to harm being caused to those who gain the knowledge or others, giving examples such as study preventing fulfilling duties, curiosity about 'magical arts', 'discovery ... of our neighbours faults' and 'site-seeing'. Further discussion of the last two examples is warranted. The penultimate example suggests that Aquinas would see environmental self-righteousness as a vice. The last example can be seen as a critique of hedonistic tourism, e.g. flying from London to New York for a weekend of shopping; this should be contrasted against the specific counsel that Aquinas gives for recreation or even fun as a balance to work. Indeed, Aquinas in his discussion of modesty as a part of temperance goes on to say, 'it is against reason for a man to be burdensome to others, by offering no pleasure to others, and by hindering their enjoyment', even if he does go on to further nuance and balance this discussion. Again being virtuous would be about weighing ethical virtues using prudence. Something of seeing this notion of 'curiosity' as a vice perhaps has some parallels to versions of the precautionary principle, at least about technological innovations where the harm could be very severe and the benefits are unclear.

It should be clear even from the above skating treatment that Aquinas provides a detailed account of a more or less coherent virtue epistemology and virtue ethic scheme. It can also be argued that this can help us decide (through prudence) what the right (just) thing to do is and helps the virtuous to do (through courage) the right thing and not do the wrong thing (through temperance). In addition to these, Aquinas articulates detailed descriptions of three other cardinal virtues. These are often implicit as virtues in Aristotle's account of virtue in the *Nicomachean Ethics* but Aquinas makes these explicit and details them. A useful way to think of these further virtues is that they articulate a motivation behind the 'human' virtues of prudence, justice, courage and temperance. The remaining cardinal virtues for Aquinas are faith, hope and love (cf. Connelly, 2006, 70); sometimes called theological virtues perhaps because of the discussion of these virtues by St Paul in his first epistle to the Corinthians, though given St Paul's knowledge of Greek philosophy the link with Aristotle may be stronger than the title theological implies.

Faith – 'assent of the intellect to' something unseen – is perhaps the least relevant virtue to this book but some remarks are in order. First is that given the human condition, avoiding at least one leap of faith is something difficult to achieve (cf. Faber *et al.*, 1998, 205–29). To illustrate, Chapter 2 argues that current Earth System science typically makes a leap of faith that humans can successfully control, manage or know the 'tensile strength' of the Earth System. Similarly, whatever a person's opinion on the potential harm from GHG emissions may be, as these cannot be observed directly, a certain amount of faith – at least in climate scientists – is required to form this opinion. It is also pertinent to note that Aquinas's life's work demonstrates that he saw faith and reason as complementary. For the sake of balance, it is necessary to recognise that Aquinas asserts that, for the society that he was in, heresy is worse than forgery. He then notes that forgers were at that time put to death by secular authorities and argues, that for the sake of society, if a heretic is 'stubborn' after two admonishments the heretic should be excommunicated and handed over to the secular tribunal, who would then put the heretic to death. To be absolutely clear, this is not something that I agree with.[38] To complicate this picture as discussed by DiLeo (2007), Aquinas was an advocate of freedom of conscience.[39]

Hope – 'the object of hope is a future good, difficult but possible to obtain' – set in the context of rapid climate change points to the importance of the question what is really good, e.g. material possessions or civilisation and happiness that comes through virtue. Aquinas discusses vices relevant to abrupt climate change that are related to hope, these being despair and presumption, arguing that despair is caused by sloth and leads to a vicious circle with 'covetousness' and sexual indulgence (cf. consumerism), which may have explanatory power for current and potential reactions to abrupt climate change and other environmental issues (cf. Jackson, 2002[40]). Where individuals understand that potentially despair leads to 'consumerism' or hedonism, this understanding may give individuals psychological resources to choose responses to abrupt climate change that do not make things worse. Indeed, this vicious cycle may have some explanatory power for the strength and vitriol of opposition to limiting GHG emissions in some quarters. Further, given that virtue is not about rules, a virtue approach may at least diffuse opposition to policies that are intended to reduce emissions significantly. It may even be that the discourse of virtue – that is people tend not to want to be vicious – may be the rhetorical tool that is needed to promote the questioning of climate sceptics' current position, for example, prosperity theology/rapture evangelical Christians particularly in the US and those people the world over who have greater concern for financial capital than for humans or the natural systems on which humans depend. Similar arguments can be made to the first constituency with regard to 'presumption', with Aquinas discussing presumption as humans relying beyond what is reasonable on their own power or God's power.[41]

Love or charity for Aquinas can be illustrated by the 'Golden Rule' that applies across cultures and can navigate criticisms from Kant, Bertrand Russell and G.B. Shaw (Parliament of the World's Religions, 1993; Wattles, 1996; cf. Lewis, 2001) with a typical Judaeo-Christian version being 'Love your neighbour as yourself' (cf. Rawls' 'veil of ignorance'). The discussion of love for Aquinas goes beyond this, e.g. to discuss 'Love your enemy' and what this means.[42] For Aquinas, the focus of love can be suggested as God and neighbour; however, he does argue that humans can love other creatures 'to God's honor and man's use; thus too does God love them out of charity' (Aquinas, ST II:II:25). Aquinas goes beyond stewardship of creation to something more mutual – i.e. because creation is from God, 'every creature participates in the Divine goodness, so as to diffuse the good it possesses to others' (Aquinas, ST I:106; cf. Fox, 2003).

In a way that speaks directly to all those who live above subsistence, certainly those who enjoy the benefits of consumerism, plus speaks to climate justice and sustainable development, Aquinas argues where there are individuals in extreme poverty 'or great need on the part of the common weal ... in such cases it would seem praiseworthy to forego the requirements of one's station, in order to provide for a greater need' (Aquinas, ST II:II:32). For clarity, it is necessary to return briefly to the question that was raised in earlier discussions of Adam Smith plus discussions of the vice of pride and of the virtue of temperance about what forms of self-love are virtuous and what forms are vicious. It should be clear that selfish self-love that ignores the need and feelings of others is vicious; indeed self-centredness that cares about others but is not prudent in adequately understanding their situation, while nonetheless trying to impose solutions, is not as virtuous as it might be. However, if we are to love our neighbour as our self, our neighbour is likely to want us to love ourselves.

This exposition of how the virtue theory of Aquinas might apply to an unpredictable Earth System that may include abrupt climate change is not intended to give a definitive account of how virtue might apply, rather to give an indication of the depth, coherence and relevance of virtue in this situation. Nonetheless, given that the virtue theory of Aquinas is a key suggestion of this book, it is relevant to discuss some criticisms of Aquinas.

DiLeo (2007) argues that there are contradictions in Aquinas; certainly there are difficulties with Aquinas but if the general approach of Aquinas of striking a balance plus the complexity of the issues that Aquinas deals with are considered, contradiction is perhaps too strong a term. Even if there are contradictions in Aquinas, these are less theoretically damaging than the largely complete inability of economic and legal approaches to guide policy when faced with an issue as unpredictable as abrupt climate change. This can be exemplified by the clearer contradictions, often within one paragraph, that there is in Earth System science and climate science as discussed in Chapter 2. This contradiction is between making clear that the earth cannot be predicted and then assuming prediction by assuming economics is the correct policy tool.

Attfield (1983, 1991) wrestles with the question of Aquinas being used to justify instrumental attitudes to nature and how valid these arguments are. If seen in the broader context of the rest of the writing of Aquinas, it appears that using Aquinas to justify such instrumental attitudes is a misuse of Aquinas, but this remains a complex question.

In addition to the above, I do have queries about the ease of application of a virtue theory as complex and subtle as that of Aquinas. Nonetheless, it can be understood at different levels of depth, with there being at least three levels: (1) a list of four or seven cardinal virtues; (2) the structure of sub-virtues; and (3) the full subtlety and complexity of the entire text. This is made more problematic as a full understanding of the most complex level would need to refer to expert knowledge, which is both scarce and will tend to be denominational. Fortunately, an understanding by more people of the four cardinal virtues that are shared across a range of philosophical and cultural traditions will be sufficient to move from intemperate (consumerist) societies to more temperate societies. History demonstrates that citizens using cardinal virtues as an aide memoir is successful in facilitating an applied understanding of virtue. Indeed, simply less promotion of greed as a virtue where it promotes economic growth and allowing moderation as a virtue should reduce stress to the Earth System. Global virtue tradition suggests that not promoting greed and allowing virtue will lead to happier individuals and societies as well.

It should not be assumed that virtue is an alternative that excludes other forms of ethic. Indeed, Aquinas is very explicit about the relationship between broadly deontological principles (i.e. precepts) and virtue in the second part of the second part of the *Summa Theologica* (cf. MacIntyre, 2009, 88–92).[43] Indeed, Lauren (2003, 13–14) argues that Aquinas was a not insignificant figure in the development of ideas that led to human rights as now understood. The relationship of virtue to consequential/utilitarian/economic ethics is less explicit in Aquinas's work, beyond discussion of property rights outlined earlier.

To summarise what a virtue ethic applied to environment and development questions in general and abrupt climate change specifically would look like, it would be prudent through temperance in that it would not take risks just to increase material wealth; it would be just through courage in that it would give preference to the needs of those who have not caused climate change in the past and to nature that has been dominated and abused rather than cared for.[44]

Ecological virtue applied to abrupt climate change

A broad picture of what ecological virtue might be like should be clear and something of how it could apply to unpredictable abrupt climate change, for example, should also be apparent; however, adding more specifics will be worthwhile. First, let us re-state why conventional economics cannot be the practical tool that we are looking for. Jamieson (1992, 139–46; cf. Berkhout *et al.*, 2003, 22–3) argues that because of limitations of human abilities to predict the climate, management approaches to climate change 'must fail', particularly management in the form of economics:

When our ignorance is so extreme, it is a leap of faith to say that some analysis is better than none. A bad analysis can be so wrong that it can lead us to do bad things, outrageous things – things that are much worse than what we would have done had we not tried to assess the costs and benefits at all.

(Jamieson, 1992, 146)

Jamieson (ibid., 146–51) goes on to suggest that virtue ethics responses are analytically more robust in situations where consequences cannot be assumed to be known. In the light of evidence for the possibility of abrupt climate change, the virtue of moderation could be extended to involve the reduction of GHG emissions immediately, without needing to wait for predictive evidence of when abrupt climate change will happen and what the effects will be. Thus, the key practical suggestion made is that policy decisions are no longer made principally by economics in the pursuit of efficiency but via political discourse and debate about what the right thing – most virtuous thing – to do is; for example, by choosing the best possible technique or technology with less concern for cost. This change of normative basis for policy should be made public, in order to send the correct signals to industry, civil servants, civil society and citizens.

Virtue can be a way to directly address concerns about paralysis caused by public discussion of unpredictable catastrophic change. To illustrate, Lowe (2006) (cf. Hulme, 2006, 2007) is a direct reflection on whether communication of catastrophic climate scenarios are effective in producing action by citizens to reduce the GHG emissions associated with their lifestyle. Lowe does not exclude the possibility of climate catastrophe, instead he emphasises that predictions of catastrophe are incomplete. It appears reasonable to characterise Lowe (2006) as arguing that scare stories on their own are not effective in producing the 'desired effect'. Lowe (ibid., 4–5) appears to want to feed citizens just sufficient fear to make them take the action that he feels is best. If this is so, it is questionable morally and strategically. Strategically, it is questionable as the 'scare stories' are already in the public domain, including documents such as the IPCC reports, as highlighted in Chapter 2. Morally, the position Lowe takes is questionable in a number of ways. First, it appears condescending and in some sense undemocratic. Second, it assumes that scary information can only be released as is, without taking measures to reduce the 'fatalism and apathy … rejection and anger' (ibid., 1) this might result in. Virtue schemes that include both hope and moderation are a basis of action to reduce the stress to the climate system from consumerism, without the need for prediction or management of the Earth System.

Sandler and Cafaro (2005) add significantly more examples than this chapter of how ecological virtue might be applied, even if the relationship between difficulties in prediction and tipping points is less clear. The emphasis is on the seven deadly sins (or vices), as being promoted by consumerism, with little reference to Aquinas and his account of how vices, including the deadly sins, can be countered by specific virtues. Van Wensveen (2000) and Hursthouse (in Walker and Ivanhoe, 2009) also add further philosophical texture and practical illustration of what environmental virtues might look like (cf. Barry, 1999; Dobson, 1998). It is worth noting that many of the theoretical questions some of these authors wrestle with would have been greatly aided by a reading of Aquinas. More significant though is the broad agreement about what ecological virtues and vices are. Indeed, to the extent that the literature talks about systematic coherent virtue systems, these tend to be quite Thomist though rarely explicitly stated. It is also striking that Brunner (1996), in his discussion of making climate policy in the context of difficulties of prediction, also makes suggestions that are quite Thomist without explicitly recognising this.

From a practical policy viewpoint more important still than the agreement in the academic literature, discussed in the previous paragraph, is indications of agreement in favour of similar environmental virtues across the globe. To illustrate, Palmer and Finlay (2003) articulate the views of eleven world religions on environment and development questions; according to the then President of the World Bank, these religions represent 'two thirds' (ibid., xi) of global citizens. In broad terms, the virtue ideas in Palmer and Finlay (2003) are not fundamentally in tension with the Thomistic system outlined above. Deeply significant is the agreement in Palmer and Finlay (ibid., xiii) of how virtues of care and justice could bring dignity even when faced with apocalypse. The use of a Thomist model does raise questions but it is beyond the scope of this book to propose a secularised version of Thomist virtue, let alone a systematic virtue model that can be universally agreed. However, as indicated in Palmer and Finlay (2003), Sandler and Cafaro (2005), Inglehart *et al.* (2004), BBC World Service polls (2007, 2009, 2010) and the World Economic Forum (2010), there is enough democratic weight that virtue approaches to ecological issues should be accorded consideration by policymakers. That is, the evidence suggests that most people in the globe would choose ecological virtue over maximum economic growth. Indeed, observation of even Anglo-Saxon countries suggests that a Thomistic model of virtue and vice coexists with the utilitarianism of economics and deontological ideas. Talk of greedy politicians and greedy financiers should provide sufficient illustration of this coexistence. Media discussion of virtue and more often self-righteous discussion of vice also illustrates how poorly understood models of virtue are in contemporary Anglo-Saxon societies.

What are the implications of virtue for policy at various levels? First, from global to local, virtue provides a stronger basis for precautionary approaches that override the current dominance of economic growth. Second, at all levels virtue can provide additional strength of argument for the application of common good over self or national interest. Conventional economics assumes and in effect promotes self-interest whereas the most influential approaches to virtue ethics tend to advocate a notion of common good. Indeed, socialist and social democracy ideas tend to use utilitarian ethics but also tend to advocate broadly common good approaches to the aim of policy.[45] However, the difficulties that typical socialist planning would have in the face of difficulties in prediction of abrupt climate change probably mean that historically dominant socialist approaches to policy details would not be effective at addressing unpredictable climate change.

More than this, it is likely that the US at least would be even more resistant to socialist ideas of common good than virtue-based notions. Indeed, classical notions of utilitarianism as summed up in the phrase 'the greatest good for the greatest number' also have a common good component. However, the current application of utilitarian ethics in economics tends to have faith that the greatest good will come from individuals pursuing their own self-interest, with common good coming through faith in 'an invisible hand'. Empirical evidence suggests the current neo-liberal economic policies are at least increasing inequity between the rich and the poor and probably increasing carbon dioxide emissions. The assumptions of conventional economics also tend to be scaled from individual citizens to nation states, whereby at climate negotiations nations tend to seek to maintain or promote national self-interest rather than a global common good approach.

To simplify, from international to local, typical economistic policy is currently made primarily by various economists rhetorically dressing up opaque assumptions with obscure complex calculations to arrive at seemingly simple answers to the question what produces the 'optimum' economic growth. Politicians then arbitrarily choose from these economic analyses on the basis of what suits their ideological position. Virtue policy would be made not by asking what maximises economic growth but by asking the broader question what is the right thing to do. This would be by political discourse about what is in the common good rather than self-interest or national interest. It would respect relevant rights and laws. It would consider questions of economic efficiency but not privilege them above all else. The aim of the discourse would be to gather an understanding of what citizens believe are the right (virtuous) things society should do. A secondary question may be helpful when considering policy options if it not clear what the right thing to do is; ask the question will this promote virtue in citizens or will it promote vice. Consumerism and conventional economics tends to promote vice. This has been painted in an oppositional way to aim at clarity; another way of looking at how virtue would work is that it would fill in the gaps where the world is too complex for laws, rights and economics to operate effectively. To put it another way, virtue would be the framework into which laws, rights and economics fits. Indeed, it might be argued from the descriptions of prudence by Aristotle and Aquinas, that political discourse in many nations (e.g. representative democracy), which currently establishes what laws and rights will be respected and what position economics holds, is unconsciously grounded in the virtue of prudence.

It is hoped that the following questions, which are intended to be asked when making policy, will be a helpful orientation:

1   Will the policy promote global common good? Or does it serve interests – national, vested or self?
2   In the broadest sense, is it the right thing to do? This would need to consider all relevant opinions, not just the rich and powerful.
3   Will it promote virtue or vice? This could be operationalised by articulating in a tabular manner explicitly which virtues and vices are being promoted and why?

From global to local, a virtue of justice can add to Rawlsian and other arguments for climate justice in the form of equity in per capita GHG emissions, consideration of current climate change harm and responsibility for past GHG emissions.

At all levels, questions of political economy will need to be considered. Ecological, green, pluralistic, heterodox and post-autistic economics provide, at least, effective criticism of conventional neo-classical economics. A more sustainable virtuous political economy could be built on the work of writers such as Schumacher (1974), Siddiqi (1981), Pesch (2002–3),[46] Braybrooke and Mofid (2005) and Bokare (1993). As already noted, the current emphasis by national governments on economic growth through consumerism tends to promote vice not virtue (Sandler and Cafaro, 2005); this is the opposite of the advice from Aristotle.

In some ways, application of virtue to personal action is easiest to imagine, articulate and put into practice. However, experience throughout human history also suggests that a perfect system to promote ecological virtue is unlikely ever to be found. This is why governments cannot be too small, though we can perhaps hope for a day when virtuous citizens and subsidiarity mean that governments are smaller than they have been in recent memory. This is likely to be a long time in the future. Within the boundaries that are set by geographical and ecological reality plus political, economic, administrative and technological structures, individuals and communities can apply ecological virtue immediately. To the extent that virtue is applied, it will help change structures and cultures to allow greater virtue than is now possible, though political activism will also be required.

Key ideas to inform a virtue of prudence for abrupt climate change and other environmental questions to minimise stress to the Earth System include 'The Natural Step' (Natural Step, 2011) particularly as a guide to policy and industry at the global level. At the local or micro level, permaculture (Mollison, 1988) is one good model for local practical action that should cause minimum stress to the Earth System. Both should be encouraged by policy.

Deliberation is at the heart of operational virtue epistemology so Dryzek's *Discursive Democracy* (1987, 1990, 2000) and Popper's *Open Society* (1966) provide key resources. This is the question to which the next chapter turns in detail.

7.6 Conclusions

Though not without difficulties, virtue approaches to policy have clear benefits in the current situation where abrupt climate change cannot be dismissed or predicted but paleoclimate evidence suggests is entirely possible, especially as we are already seeing more rapid climate change than had been predicted. With this discussion of how virtue approaches can be applied in practice to abrupt climate change, I hope that policymakers will begin to address seriously the possibility of abrupt climate change, whether using the approaches suggested here or alternatives.

Notes

1 In response to Crutzen (2006), both Bengtsson (2006) and Kiehl (2006) raise similar epistemological and/or ethical questions. Schneider (1996) and Bodansky (1996) also raise institutional difficulties with climate engineering.

2 Callicott (1990) claims Darwin was the first to see 'animals as members of a ... kinship group'. This appears to have poor historical foundations as, for example, St Francis of Assisi thought of animals and *other* parts of creation as being 'brothers'. This and an apparent unwillingness to engage with 'religious' ethical theories generally, rather than evaluate them (Callicott, 1994) is probably unfortunate, if as Callicott (1990) implies he intends his single moral theory to achieve universal acceptance by reason rather than by 'the "other" [being] bombed, terrorized, bought, pacified, or sweet-talked'.

3 Appleton (2013) provides a helpful, more academic update in a similar vein for those looking for that, with Taback and Ramanan (2013) providing some similar analysis that is helpfully applied but lacking the depth of analysis of epistemology related to ethics of this current volume.

4 For example, Naess (Engel and Engel, 1990, 93), reflecting on the thoughts of Mother Teresa, writes: 'We, the rich, are poor in deep satisfactions.'

5 Given his reasons for population reduction (i.e. not just to allow a few rich people to continue wanton consumption) and that he does not specify the means of population reduction, this position is broadly compatible with those of the world religions.

6 Cf. Westra (1998, 147–69, 249–56).

7 My biggest query with the analysis is that he appears to imply that frugality and temperance are seen as virtues in industrialised countries (Wenz, 2005, 197). This jars with his description of consumerism.

8 Which Wenz does not discuss, nor similar literature such as Engel and Engel (1990).

9 There are other more minor issues such as an implicit assumption that virtues necessarily come into conflict; these need not detain us here.

10 MacIntyre (1990 e.g. 186–93) provides a philosophically deeper treatment of the problems of selfishness.

11 Even more pointedly, from the tone of Smith (2003), it might be that the aim of Smith is to encourage citizens to be ecologically virtuous in a manner indicated by Barry (1999).

12 The discussion of teleology by Dubray (1912) does tend towards conclusions that some including this author may question. This is less important than the questions raised over the use of teleology by Solomon.

13 Aquinas may be a little more complicated; the virtue of love may be prior to judgements about specific actions.

14 Though the source for the cardinal virtues (van Wensveen, 2005, 173, endnote 2) might be questioned.

15 There is mention of achieving *predicted* goals in this discussion (van Wensveen, 2005, 184); however, this is at the individual level and does not clearly have a utilitarian flavour.

16 This perhaps contradicts his discussion of applied ethics if traditional moral communities use both virtue ethics and rules of intolerable behaviour.

17 There is discussion in Western tradition about what the capital vices are – some adding further vices; however, the broad thrust is similar enough for present purposes.

18 That is, notions of private property that assume that once something becomes private property, the owner is free to use, abuse and abandon the property as they see fit, without any consideration of the needs of others or the intrinsic worth of the property.

19 It is worth mentioning parallels of this description of how virtues, particularly prudence, are acquired with the description by Kuhn (1970, 270–75) of how scientists are trained.

20 That is, the virtuocracy or aristocracy that is suggested is certainly not a return to the rule by the landed gentry, as aristocracy is typically understood in the UK. It is worth noting that the worlds of Aristotle and Aquinas were probably no more materially unequal than today's 'liberal' societies.

21 Though Putnam's talk of social capital does suggest a more capitalist/utilitarian/instrumental take, that is human relationships being important primarily as an input to the machine of industrial societies, that some may find even more objectionable than David Hume seeing virtues including love/care as a way of producing more utility. This objection is stronger still when utility is approximated by money – this would see us all as enslaved prostitutes to industrialism and consumerism.

22 Further evidence of this can be seen in that Smith makes virtue gendered in a way that Aquinas does not.

23 That is, for Smith the 'utility' of virtue tends to be greater material utility to society rather than Smith seeing virtue as being good for individuals and society in other ways. Inconsistencies and lack of clarity in the reasons to be virtuous in Smith point to key limitations in using Smith as a basis for an environmental virtue ethic to address abrupt climate change. A similar argument can be developed for David Hume's work on virtue (cf. Crisp, 2005). It is worth noting that Crisp (ibid., 171–3) argues that Hume would not have sought to predict utility exactly; however, given the level of uncertainty discussed in earlier chapters, it is not clear how even an approximate answer to which policy option would maximise utility can be established – at best life cycle assessment may be able to suggest which technology or techniques minimise stress to the Earth System.

24 That is Mill was key in developing the 'harm principle' often articulated along the lines of an individual has the right to act as he wants, so long as these actions do not harm others; see Mill (1859, 21–2) for his more exact formulation. Given an issue such as climate change, a logical extension of this principle would be that all actions may harm others – even breathing produces carbon dioxide – thus this principle is of little help in making decisions.

25 The Oxford edition of the *Nicomachean Ethics* (Aristotle, 1980) adds very useful contents pages to the original text, which can aid understanding of the structure of these ethics. This provides evidence that the Nicomachean ethics were not designed to be systematic, but rather principally an account of discussions of individual virtues. www. newadvent.org/summa/3.htm provides a similar function for the virtues of Aquinas and comparing this with Aristotle (ibid.) illustrates the similarities and differences between the virtues of Aquinas and Aristotle. This comparison also illustrates the more detailed and systematic nature of the virtues of Aquinas. MacIntyre (1988, 164) concurs with the suggestion that Aquinas is more systematic than Aristotle (or Plato and Augustine). He also argues that virtue ethics is more coherent than rights-based and utilitarian ethics (MacIntyre, 1985). MacIntyre (1990) provides an account of why natural science has broadly been able to progress, whereas the case for moral and political philosophy is far less convincing. An interpretation of MacIntyre (ibid., e.g. 39–40) is that he argues that utilitarian/deontological ethics find it difficult to understand other forms of ethics; that the relativism around Nietzsche criticises this 'scientistic' ethics effectively but lacks the resources to question its own relativism and arrogance. In the same manner that Aquinas reconciled/synthesised Aristotle and Augustine, MacIntyre suggests that Thomistic method (e.g. ibid., 74–5, 79, 118–25) offers a potential way forward beyond fruitless misunderstood exchanges. Indeed, MacIntyre (ibid., e.g. 187) can be understood to suggest that Thomism is more rational than scientistic (Kantian and utilitarian) and relativistic ethics, as it understands the strengths and limitations of the alternatives but these do not understand Thomism and make little effort to do so. In other words, MacIntryre puts a philosophical case that by partial reading of Aristotle and Aquinas, philosophy and

society have been endarkened since Aquinas (including later scholasticism) by less coherent, more fragmented, more arrogant world views, rather than enlightened. MacIntyre implies that the move away from the rationality of Aquinas was associated with charismatic approaches such as Eckhart (ibid., 165–9). It is not irrelevant to discussions of Popper's 'open society' in this book, that a trajectory of approach can then be drawn to 'charismatic' fascist dictators.

26 For the sake of clarity and brevity, the *Summa Theologica* of Thomas Aquinas will be referred to as 'Aquinas (ST, II:II:n)' where II:II refers to the second part of the second part of the *Summa Theologica* and n is the number of the question in that part. No specific date is given in each specific reference to the *Summa* as the work was written from approximately 1265 and was incomplete at the time of Aquinas's death in 1274. The version used in this book is the second revised edition of the English translation from 1920 – specifically the 2008 online edition from www.newadvent.org/summa. For readers unfamiliar with the work, the objections listed immediately after each article of a question are objections that were or could be raised. The remainder of the text that follows each article is what Aquinas believes and states as a response to those objections. MacIntyre (1990, especially Chapter VI) includes more detailed exploration of how the *Summa* might be understood.

27 Even as economic and technical a paper as Jeroen van den Bergh 'Safe climate policy is affordable: 12 reasons', *Climatic Change* (2010, 349) suggests the precautionary principle is ultimately grounded in 'prudence'.

28 Cf. Paavola and Adger (2002); see also Schellnhuber *et al.* (2009, 2).

29 This second principle may be based on justice in exchange as well as justice in distribution.

30 That justice can be towards other than humans for Aquinas can readily be seen as Aquinas discusses justice of humans to God in as much detail as justice between humans.

31 Even as knowledgeable a virtue theorist as Dale Jamieson (2001) bases his defence of climate justice on moral intuition rather than a more analytical approach.

32 Though the fair trade movement is focused on making specific types of trade fairer rather than bringing about systematic change that will mean all trade is fairer.

33 The history of political revolutions is sufficiently mixed and their effectiveness and implementation promotion is sufficiently difficult that this author does not promote revolution in the way it is typically conceived. A move from consumerism to a sustainable post consumerist society would be revolutionary but would probably be better accomplished in years rather than weeks.

34 Aquinas's theory of 'Just War' is one area of his philosophy that is still widely discussed in contemporary philosophy; it should be noted that this discussion of a just war occurs as part of a discussion of war as a vice that opposes the virtue of peace.

35 E.g. Chico Mendes, Dorothy Stang and Ken Saro Wiwa.

36 Aquinas quotes Augustine approvingly: 'Pride ... wishes to usurp [God's] dominion over our fellow-creatures.' Cf. Aquinas on hope and trusting on worldly power.

37 An argument could be made that Dr Mengele's experiments had the potential to increase utility overall, which is another example of the problems of utilitarianism.

38 Indeed, even though Aquinas is a key foundation for Catholic theology, the Catholic Church would now only advocate the death penalty if this is the only way to 'protect people's safety from the aggressor', stating that 'today ... [these] cases ... are practically non-existent' (CCC, 2003, 2267). The practical consequences of this are that from the Pope down, Catholics are campaigning against the death penalty, e.g. the US Catholic Bishops (www.usccb.org/deathpenalty). Beyond this, some liberal theorists wrestle with the question of whether the use of force in defence of liberalism is justifiable, which might be considered to have parallels with heresy as Aquinas saw it. Further, Aquinas makes clear that his writing should not be seen as infallible (Aquinas, ST, II:II:10).

39 Indeed, one of the references in DiLeo argues: 'Thomistic theory of free will and the relationship of God to the free choices of man provides an even stronger basis for toleration than does Rawls' more pragmatic doctrine' (Magee, 1999). DiLeo (2007, 11) argues that there is a contradiction in Aquinas being 'supporter of both political pluralism and the execution of heretics'; given that virtue is about balancing goods, tension might be more accurate than contradiction as indicated in Magee (1999).

40 It should be noted that Jackson's discussion of theodicy is limited and that many of the authors he discusses would have had stronger resources to resolve 'theodicy' issues if they had greater awareness of Orthodox and Catholic approaches to questions around suffering and evil.

41 Aquinas states that the latter is a sin against the Holy Spirit that is typically seen as very serious. These types of argument appear to be key reasons behind some US politicians' use of uncertainty in science as a reason for inaction on climate change.

42 Even to the point 'we can love the nature of the demons even out of charity, in as much as we desire those spirits to endure, as to their natural gifts, unto God's glory'. With regard to love, Aquinas also discusses Bible passages such as 1 Corinthians 13 and sees the acceptance of suffering of Jesus during crucifixion for the benefit of all creation as the exemplar of love. See also Lewis (2002).

43 The teaching of the Catholic Church rooted in Thomistic theology makes clear statements about human rights that challenge the inequalities brought about by capitalism (CCC, 2003, 1928–1948) even if questions around human rights such as the ordination of women and practising homosexual men can be posed.

44 That is where human power has used and abused nature assuming that dominion is domination and a synonym of abuse when dominion is simply a synonym of power and a statement of fact of human power that can be applied to nature and not exhortation to abuse.

45 Roger Crisp and delegates at the 2006 ECPR environmental politics summer school should be thanked for discussions on the notion of the common good.

46 Pesch in particular (see Wishloff, 2006) could perhaps be used to reassure politically powerful US opponents of action to reduce climate change that virtue economics is not synonymous with socialism.

References

Anderson, K. (2009) *Climate change in a myopic world*, Tyndall Briefing Note No. 36 – May 2009, www.tyndall.ac.uk/sites/default/files/bn36.pdf. Accessed 22 May 2011

Appleton, J. (ed.) (2013) *Values in sustainable development*, Abingdon: Routledge

Aquinas, T. (1920 translation) (2nd rev. edn) *Summa Theologica*, www.newadvent.org/summa. Accessed 22 May 2011

Aristotle (1980) *The Nicomachean ethics*, translated with an introduction by D. Ross. Revised by J.L. Ackrill and J.O. Urmson, Oxford: Oxford University Press

Attfield, R. (1983) 'Western traditions and environmental ethics', in Elliot, R. and Gare, A. (eds) *Environmental philosophy: A collection of readings*, Pennsylvania: Pennsylvania State University Press

Attfield, R. (1991) *The ethics of environmental concern*, Athens: University of Georgia Press

Attfield, R. (1994) *Environmental philosophy: Principles and prospects*, Aldershot: Ashgate

Attfield, R. (2003) *Environmental ethics: An overview for the twenty-first century*, Cambridge: Polity

Barber, B. (2007) *Consumed: How markets corrupt children, infantilize adults and swallow citizens whole*, New York: W.W. Norton & Company

Baron, M., Pettit, P. and Slote, M. (1997) *Three methods of ethics*, Oxford: Blackwell

Barry, J. (1999) *Rethinking green politics: Nature, virtue and progress*, London: SAGE

Bass, S., Dalal-Clayton, B. and Pretty, J. (1995) *Participation in strategies for sustainable development*, London: International Institute for Environment and Development, http://pubs.iied.org/7754IIED.html. Accessed 29 March 2015

BBC World Service (2007) *Most would pay higher energy bills to address climate change, suggests global poll*, www.globescan.com/news_archives/bbc_climate2/bbcclimate2.pdf. Accessed 14 February 2015

BBC World Service (2009) *Climate concerns continue to increase according to global poll*, www.bbc.co.uk/pressoffice/pressreleases/stories/2009/12_december/07/poll.shtml. Accessed 22 May 2011

BBC World Service (2010) *Poverty most serious world problem, says global poll*, www.bbc.co.uk/pressoffice/pressreleases/stories/2010/01_january/17/poll.shtml. Accessed 22 May 2011

Bengtsson, L. (2006) 'Geo-engineering to confine climate change: Is it at all feasible?', *Climatic Change*, 77: 229–34

Bergmann, S. and Gerten, D. (2010) *Religion and dangerous environmental change: Transdisciplinary perspectives on the ethics of climate and sustainability*, Berlin: Lit Verlag

Berkhout, F., Leach, M. and Scoones, I. (2003) (eds) *Negotiating environmental change: New perspectives from social sciences*, Cheltenham: Edward Elgar

Bodansky, D. (1996) 'May we engineer the climate', *Climatic Change*, 33: 309–21

Bokare, M. (1993) *Hindu economics: Eternal economic order*, New Delhi: Janaki Prakashan

Blackburn, S. (2000) *Ruling passions: A theory of practical reason*, Oxford: Oxford University Press

Braybrooke, M. and Mofid, K. (2005) *Promoting the common good: Bringing economics and theology together again*, London: Shepheard-Walwyn

Broome, J. (2010) 'The most important thing about climate change', in Boston, J., Bradstock, A. and Eng, D. (eds) *Public policy: Why ethics matters*, Canberra: ANU E Press

Brosnan, S. and de Wall, F. (2003) 'Monkeys reject unequal pay', *Nature*, 425: 297–9

Brown, C. (2001) *Ethical theories compared*, www.trinity.edu/cbrown/intro/ethical_theories.html. Accessed 9 May 2011

Brunner, R.D. (1996) 'Policy and global change research', *Climatic Change*, 32: 121–47

Callicott, J. (1990) 'The case against moral pluralism', *Environmental Ethics*, 12: 99–124 (also in Light, A. and Rolston III, H. (2003) *Environmental Ethics: An Anthology*, Malden, MA: Blackwell)

Callicott, J. (1994) *Earth's insights: A survey of ecological ethics from the Mediterranean basin to the Australian outback*, Berkeley: University of California Press

CCC (2003) *Catechism of the Catholic Church*, Vatican: Vatican

Charlesworth, M. and Okereke, C. (2010) 'Policy responses to rapid climate change: An epistemological critique of dominant approaches', *Global Environmental Change*, 20: 121–9

Connelly, J. (2003) *Environmental politics as a vocation*, Southampton Institute: Inaugural Professorial Lecture

Connelly, J. (2006) 'The virtues of environmental citizenship', in Dobson, A. and Bell, D. (eds) *Environmental citizenship*, Cambridge, MA: MIT Press

Crisp, R. (2005) 'Hume on virtue, utility and morality', in Gardiner, S. (ed.) *Virtue ethics old and new*, Ithaca, NY: Cornell University Press

Crutzen, P.J. (2006) 'Albedo enhancement by stratospheric sulfur injections: A contribution to resolve a policy dilemma?', *Climatic Change*, 77: 211–20 de Castella, T. (2009) *Top climate scientists share their outlook, Financial Times* magazine, 20 November, www.ft.com/cms/s/2/f1d9f856-d4ad-11de-a935-00144feabdc0.html? nclick_check=1. Accessed 14 February 2015

DiLeo, D. (2007) 'Thomas Aquinas and the overlapping consensus', *Commonwealth: A Journal of Political Science*, 13(1): 1–21, http://sites.temple.edu/commonwealth/files/2013/11/2007-v13.pdf. Accessed 13 November 2014

Dobson, A. (1993) 'Ecologism', in Eatwell, R. and Wright, A. (eds) *Contemporary political ideology*, London: Pinter

Dobson, A. (1998) *Justice and the environment: Conceptions of environmental sustainability and theories of distributive justice*, Oxford: Oxford University Press

Dobson, A. (2003) *Citizenship and the environment*, Oxford: Oxford University Press

Dorscht, A. (2007) *Beyond managing from crisis to crisis dealing with the environment: Creating the necessary conditions for a sustainable, equitable, secure and peaceful future*, http://ihcmdonline.com/BeyondCrises-6.pdf. Accessed 14 February 2015

Dubray, C. (1912) 'Teleology', *The Catholic encyclopedia*, New York: Robert Appleton Company, www.newadvent.org/cathen/14474a.htm. Accessed 25 May 2011

Dryzek, J. (1987) *Rational ecology: Environment and political economy*, Oxford: Blackwell

Dryzek, J. (1990) *Discursive democracy: Politics, policy, and political science*, Cambridge: Cambridge University Press

Dryzek, J. (2000) *Deliberative democracy and beyond: Liberals, critics, contestations*, Oxford: Oxford University Press

Earth Charter (2000) *The Earth Charter*, www.earthcharterinaction.org/content/pages/Read-the-Charter.html. Accessed 19 May 2011

Eco, U. (1988) *The aesthetics of Thomas Aquinas*, Cambridge: Harvard University Press

Engel, J.R. and Engel, J.G. (eds) (1990) *Ethics of environment and development: Global challenge, international response*, London: Belhaven

Faber, M., Proops, J. and Manstetten, R. (1998) *Ecological economics: Concepts and methods*, Cheltenham: Edward Elgar

FAO (2006) *Livestock's long shadow: Environmental issues and options*, Rome: FAO, ftp://ftp.fao.org/docrep/fao/010/A0701E/A0701E00.pdf. Accessed 21 May 2011

Fleischacker, S. (2004) *On Adam Smith's wealth of nations: A philosophical companion*, Princeton, NJ: Princeton University Press

Foot, P. (2002) (2nd edn) *Virtues and vices and other essays in moral philosophy*, New York: Oxford University Press

Fox, M. (2003) *Sheer joy: Conversations with Thomas Aquinas on creation spirituality*, New York: Jeremy P Tarcher/Putnam

Frierson, P. (2006) 'Applying Adam Smith: From Adam Smith to environmental virtue ethics', in Schliesser, E. and Montes, L. (eds) *New voices on Adam Smith*, Abingdon: Routledge

Gallop, D. (2004) 'Aristotle: Aesthetics and philosophy of mind', in Furley, D. (ed.) *From Aristotle to Augustine*, London: Routledge

Hanley, R.P. (2009) *Adam Smith and the character of virtue*, New York: Cambridge University Press

Hay, P. (2002) *Main currents in Western environmental thought*, Bloomington: Indiana University Press

Hillerbrand, R. and Ghil, M. (2008) 'Anthropogenic climate change: Scientific uncertainties and moral dilemmas', *Physica D*, 237: 2132–8

Hinman, L. (1999) (2nd edn) *Contemporary moral issues*, Upper Saddle River, NJ: Prentice Hall

Hof, A.F., den Elzen, M.G.J. and van Vuuren, D.P. (2008). Analysing the costs and benefits of climate policy: Value judgements and scientific uncertainties, *Global Environmental Change*, 18: 412–24

Holden, B. (2002) *Democracy and global warming*, London: Continuum

Huckle, J. (2004) *Citizenship education for sustainable development in initial teacher training*, Canterbury: citizED, www.citized.info/pdf/induction/John_Huckle.pdf. Accessed 22 May 2011

Hulme, M. (2006) 'Chaotic world of climate truth', *BBC News*, 4 November, http://news.bbc.co.uk/1/hi/sci/tech/6115644.stm. Accessed 7 May 2011

Hulme, M. (2007) 'Newspaper scare headlines can be counter-productive', *Nature*, 445(7130): 818

Hursthouse, R. (2000) *Ethics, humans, and other animals: An introduction with readings*, London: Routledge

Inglehart, R., Basanez, M., Diez-Medrano, J., Halman, L. and Luijkx, R. (2004) (eds) *Human beliefs and values: A cross-cultural sourcebook based on the 1999–2002 values surveys*, Mexico City: Siglo XXI

IUCN/UNEP/WWF (1991) *Caring for the earth: A strategy for sustainable living*, Gland: The World Conservation Union, United Nations Environment Programme, World Wide Fund For Nature, https://portals.iucn.org/library/efiles/documents/CFE-003.pdf. Accessed 13 November 2014

Jackson, T. (2002) 'Consumer culture as a failure in theodicy', in *Consumption, Christianity and creation* – Proceedings from an academic seminar held on 5 July 2002, Sheffield: Centre for Sustainable Consumption

Jamieson, D. (1992) 'Ethics, public policy, and global warming', *Science, Technology and Human Values*, 17: 139–53 (also in Light, A. and Rolston III, H. (2003) *Environmental ethics: An anthology*, London: Blackwell)

Jamieson, D. (1996) 'Ethics and intentional climate change', *Climatic Change*, 33: 323–36

Jamieson, D. (2001) 'Climate change and global environmental justice', in Miller, C.A. and Edwards, P.N. (eds) *Changing the atmosphere: Expert knowledge and environmental governance*, Cambridge, MA: MIT Press

Jamieson, D. (2007) 'When utilitarians should be virtue theorists', *Utilitas*, 19: 160–83

Jantsch, E. (1980) *The self-organizing universe: Scientific and human implications of the emerging paradigm of evolution*, Oxford: Pergamon

Keynes, J-M. (1931) *Essays in persuasion*, London: Macmillan

Kiehl, J.T. (2006) 'Geoengineering climate change: Treating the symptom over the cause? An editorial comment', *Climatic Change*, 77: 227–8

King, R. and Vandiver-King, K. (2008) *It is*, http://globalpublic.org/ITIS.pdf. Accessed 22 May 2011

Korten, D. (1996) *When corporations rule the world*, West Hartford, CT: Kumarian Press

Kuhn, T.S. (1970) 'Reflections on my critics', in Lakatos, I. and Musgrave, A. (eds) *Criticism and the growth of knowledge*, London: Cambridge University Press

Lauren, P.G. (2003) (2nd edn) *The evolution of international human rights*, Philadelphia, PA: University of Pennsylvania Press

Lewis, C.S. (2001) *The abolition of man*, Grand Rapids, MI: Zondervan

Lewis, C.S. (2002) *The four loves*, London: HarperCollins

Light, A. (2003) 'Callicott and Naess on pluralism', in Light, A. and Rolston III, H. (eds) *Environmental ethics: An anthology*, Malden, MA: Blackwell

Louden, R. (1984) 'On some vices of virtue ethics', *American Philosophical Quarterly*, 21(3): 227–36

Lowe, T. (2006) *Tyndall briefing note no. 16*, Norwich: Tyndall, www.tyndall.ac.uk/sites/default/files/bn16.pdf. Accessed 7 May 2011

MacIntyre, A. (1985) (2nd edn) *After virtue: A study in moral theory*, London: Duckworth

MacIntyre, A. (1988) *Whose justice? Which rationality?* London: Duckworth

MacIntyre, A. (1990) *Three rival versions of moral enquiry*, London: Duckworth

MacIntyre, A. (2009) *God, philosophy, universities: A selective history of the Catholic philosophical tradition*, London: Continuum

Magee, M.F. (1999) *A Thomistic case for tolerance*, www.aquinasonline.com/Topics/tolernce.html. Accessed 25 May 2011

McInerney, D. and Keller, K. (2008) 'Economically optimal risk reduction strategies in the face of uncertain climate thresholds', *Climatic Change*, 91: 29–41

Merchant, C. (1983) *The death of nature: Women, ecology, and the scientific revolution*, San Francisco, CA: Harper & Row

Mill, J.S. (1859) *On liberty*, London: John W. Parker and Son

Mill, J.S. (1867) (3rd edn) *Utilitarianism*, London: Longman, Green, Reader and Dyer

Mollison, B. (1988) *Permaculture: A designers' manual*, Tyalgum, NSW: Tagari Publications

Natural Step (2011) *The four system conditions*, www.naturalstep.org/the-system-conditions. Accessed 11 May 2011

Newton, P. (1999) 'A manual for planetary management', *Nature*, 400: 399

Paavola, J. and Adger, W.N. (2002) *Justice and adaptation to climate change*, Tyndall Centre Working Paper 23, www.tyndall.ac.uk/sites/default/files/wp23.pdf. Accessed 22 May 2011

Palmer, M. and Finlay, V. (2003) *Faith in conservation: New approaches to religions and the environment*, Washington, DC: World Bank, http://go.worldbank.org/3L9IDQNFO0 or www.arcworld.org/books_resources.asp. Accessed 9 May 2011

Parliament of the World's Religions (1993) *Declaration toward a global ethic*, www.parliamentofreligions.org/_includes/FCKcontent/File/TowardsAGlobalEthic.pdf. Accessed 21 May 2011

Perrings, C. (2003) 'The economics of abrupt climate change', *Philosophical Transactions of the Royal Society of London A: Mathematical, Physical and Engineering Sciences*, 361(1810): 2043–59.

Pesch, H. (2002–3) *Teaching guide to economics*, Lewiston, NY; Lampeter: Edwin Mellen Press

Popper, K. (1966) (5th edn) *The open society and its enemies*, London: Routledge and Kegan Paul

Putnam, R.D. (2002) *Democracies in flux: The evolution of social capital in contemporary society*, New York: Oxford University Press

Salleh, A. (2009) *Eco-sufficiency and global justice: Women write political ecology*, London: Pluto

Sandler, R. (2004) 'Towards an adequate environmental virtue ethics', *Environmental Values*, 13(4): 477–95

Sandler, R. and Cafaro, P. (eds) (2005) *Environmental virtue ethics*, Lanham, MD: Rowman & Littlefield

Schellnhuber, H-J. (1998) 'Earth System analysis: The concept', in Schellnhuber, H-J. and Wenzel, V. (eds) *Earth System analysis: Integrating science for sustainability*, Berlin: Springer Verlag

Schellnhuber, H-J. (2001) 'Earth System analysis and management', in Ehlers, E. and Krafft, T. (eds) *Understanding the Earth System: Compartments, processes and interactions*, Berlin: Springer Verlag

Schellnhuber, H-J. and Held, H. (2002) 'How fragile is the Earth System', in Briden, J. and Downing, T. (eds) *Managing the Earth: The Linacre lectures 2001*, Oxford: Oxford University Press

Schellnhuber, H-J., Crutzen, P., Clark, W., Claussen, M. and Held, H. (eds) (2004) *Earth System analysis for sustainability*, Boston, MA: MIT Press

Schellnhuber, H-J., Messner, D., Leggewie, C., Leinfelder, R., Nakicenovic, N., Rahmstorf, S., Schlacke, S., Schmid, J. and Schubert, R. (2009) *Solving the climate dilemma: The budget approach*, Berlin: German Advisory Council on Global Change, www.wbgu.de/fileadmin/templates/dateien/veroeffentlichungen/sondergutachten/sn2009/wbgu_sn2009_en.pdf. Accessed 21 May 2011

Schneider, S. (1996) Geoengineering: Could – or should – we do it? *Climatic Change*, 33: 291–302

Schumacher, E.F. (1974) *Small is beautiful: A study of economics as if people mattered*, London: Abacus

Settle, C., Shogren, J.F. and Kane, S. (2007) 'Assessing mitigation–adaptation scenarios for reducing catastrophic climate risk, *Climatic Change*, 83: 443–56

Siddiqi, M. (1981) *Muslim economic thinking: A survey of contemporary literature*, Leicester: Islamic Foundation

Singer, P. (1972) 'Famine, affluence, and morality', *Philosophy and Public Affairs*, 1(1): 229–43

Smith, A. (1759/1790) (6th edn) *The theory of moral sentiments*, London: A. Millar

Smith, A. (1776/1904) (Edwin Cannan, ed., 5th edn) *An inquiry into the nature and causes of the wealth of nations*, London: Methuen & Co., Ltd

Smith, G. (2003) *Deliberative democracy and the environment*, London: Routledge

Smithson, I. (1983) 'The moral view of Aristotle's poetics', *Journal of the History of Ideas*, 44(1): 3–17

Spash, C. (2007) 'The economics of climate change impacts à la Stern: Novel and nuanced or rhetorically restricted?', *Ecological Economics*, 63: 706–13

Statman, D. (1997) (ed.) *Virtue ethics: A critical reader*, Edinburgh: Edinburgh University Press

Steffen, W. and Tyson, P. (eds) (2001) *Global change and the Earth System: A planet under pressure*, Stockholm: International Geosphere-Biosphere Programme, www.igbp.net/download/18.1b8ae20512db692f2a680007648/1376383135421/science-4.pdf. Accessed 7 November 2014

Steffen, W., Sanderson, A., Tyson, P., Jäger, J., Matson, P., Moore III, B., Oldfield, F., Richardson, K., Schellnhuber, H-J., Turner, B.L. and Wasson, R. (2004) Global change and the Earth System: A planet under pressure, Berlin: Springer Verlag, Executive Summary, www.igbp.net/download/18.56b5e28e13 7d8d8c09380001694/1376383141875/Springer+IGBP+Synthesis+Steffen+et +al+%282004%29_web.pdf. Accessed 9 May 2011

Stern Review (2006) *Stern Review on the economics of climate change*, http://webarchive. nationalarchives.gov.uk/20100407172811/www.hm-treasury.gov.uk/stern_review_ report.htm. Accessed 15 April 2012

Stone, C. (1988) 'Moral pluralism and the course of environmental ethics', *Environmental Ethics*, 10: 139–54

Taback, H. and Ramanan, R. (2013) *Environmental ethics and sustainability: A casebook for environmental professionals*, Boca Raton, FL: CRC Press

Tol, R.S.J. and Yohe, G.W. (2007), 'Infinite uncertainty, forgotten feedbacks, and cost–benefit analysis of climate change', *Climatic Change*, 83: 429–42

Torgerson, D. (1999) *The promise of green politics environmentalism and the public sphere*, Durham, NC: Duke University Press

van den Bergh, J. (2010) 'Safe climate policy is affordable: 12 reasons', *Climatic Change*, 101: 339–85

van Wensveen, L. (2000) *Dirty virtues: The emergence of ecological virtue ethics*, Amherst, MA: Prometheus Books

van Wensveen, L. (2005) 'Cardinal environmental virtues: A neurobiological perspective', in Sandler, R. and Cafaro, P. (eds) *Environmental virtue ethics*, Lanham, MD: Rowman & Littlefield

Velasquez, M., Moberg, D., Meyer, M.J., Shanks, T., McLean, M.R., DeCosse, D., André, C. and Hanson, K.O. (2009) *A framework for thinking ethically*, www.scu.edu/ethics/practicing/decision/framework.html. Accessed 29 March 2015

Walker, R.L. and Ivanhoe, P.J. (eds) (2009) *Working virtue: Virtue ethics and contemporary moral problems*, Oxford: Oxford University Press

Wattles, J. (1996) *The golden rule*, New York: Oxford University Press

Weitzman, M.L. (2009) 'On modeling and interpreting the economics of catastrophic climate change', *Review of Economics and Statistics*, 91(1): 1–19

Wenz, P. (1993) 'Minimal, moderate, and extreme moral pluralism', *Environmental Ethics*, 15: 61–74

Wenz, P. (2005) 'Synergistic environmental virtues: Consumerism and human flourishing', in Sandler, R. and Cafaro, P. (eds) *Environmental virtue ethics*, Lanham, MD: Rowman & Littlefield

Westra, L. (1998) *A global ethic to restore a fragmented earth*, Lanham, MD: Rowman & Littlefield

White, L. (1967) 'The historical roots of our ecological crisis', *Science*, 155: 1203–7

Wishloff, J. (2006) 'Solidarist economics: The legacy of Heinrich Pesch', *Review of business*, 27(2): 33–46

World Economic Forum (2010) *Faith and the global agenda: Values for the post-crisis economy*, Geneva: World Economic Forum, http://akgul.bilkent.edu.tr/WEF/2010/valuesreport. pdf. Accessed 14 February 2015

8 Democratising global stewardship

8.1 Introduction

The reader may not agree with the analysis in the previous chapter that virtue epistemology and ethics are good responses to an unpredictable Earth System which includes tipping points and inertia. However, they may find analysis of the limits to prediction of Earth System science and climate science in Chapter 2 sufficiently robust that they call into question the use of economic cost–benefit analysis as the policy tool of choice for these questions. More so given that twenty years of making climate policy through economics has failed to bring about reduction in GHGs. As indicated in the previous chapter, virtue politics would operate through public discourse and debate, in addition international agreements on sustainable development state that policy should be participatory. Even if these arguments and international law are not accepted, if we are looking for an alternative to economistic policy-making, the choice of alternatives will have to be made through political processes, as no authoritarian figure can claim epistemological authority to decide policy for an unpredictable Earth System.

Section 2.6 discussed the 'open society' (Popper, 1966), which indicated the basic logic of participatory decision-making when there are difficulties in prediction. That is, if experts or elites cannot robustly claim to know what is best for society, then the more people that are involved, the better solutions might be. In addition, participation should also maximise 'buy-in' to any solutions and involving citizens in policy might be regarded as intrinsically the right thing to do. Participation might also be used to resolve questions of when and how to use particular ethical assumptions. Specifically, if different ethical assumptions are articulated during participatory processes, then conscious decisions can be made about when and where to use them, rather than particular assumptions being imposed on policy and citizens by dominant groups.

This chapter will examine some of the large amount of literature that discusses participatory decision-making, much of which is concerned with decisions to be made about sustainable development questions. Again the focus is on the literature that applies particularly to 'developed' rather than 'developing' countries. Section 8.2 analyses the literature that looks at participation primarily from a theoretical point of view. Section 8.3 examines past experience of participation.

Section 8.4 makes suggestions for criteria for participatory processes for sustainable development, particularly in the light of difficulties in prediction of the Earth System and given ethical contestations.

8.2 Theoretical literature

Criticism of participation

A good introduction to participatory democracy in comparison with liberal democracy is provided by Holden (1993, 123–30) and he (ibid., 130–5) provides a good summary of arguments for participatory democracy. Of particular note is the discussion of how particular forms of liberal democracy might lead to relativism, perhaps particularly implying selfish individualistic moral relativism (ibid., 134–5; cf. Holden, 2002, 16–20) and the close association between particular forms of liberal democracy and particular forms of capitalism (Holden, 1993, 141–50, 173–7). Holden (ibid., 135–40) outlines arguments against participatory 'theory', broadly the difficulties in putting theory into practice and the dangers that participatory democracy would in effect turn into 'totalitarian rule by a minority of extremists' (ibid., 139) of those who decided to participate.

These are important questions and it is interesting that the intergovernmental literature and academic sustainable development literature tend not to raise such issues. However, there are responses, which together reduce the significance of these for the policy questions considered by this book. First is that this book is focused on particular issues where experts cannot tell us what to do. In this situation, it is reasonable to advocate participation in policy-making from a Popperian 'open society' perspective because it brings as much problem solving ability to the question as possible. For any policies that mean changes in citizen behaviour, maximising participation should also maximise cooperation with behaviour change. Indeed, Holden (2002, 30–52) himself advocates participation of citizens in decisions about 'global warming' for these reasons and more. Perhaps more importantly for the criticisms advanced by Holden is that participation can be within the limits set by 'representative liberal democracy', particularly as the issues discussed in this book are quite practical questions about the operation of society rather than the operations of political systems (cf. Dryzek, 2000, 170–1; Saward, 1993, 74). Thus, if an extremist 'green' minority made quite draconian policy that the moderate majority disagreed with, then such policy could be reversed or weakened. With regard to questions of how to put participation into practice, this chapter does offer some suggestions; however, I am under no illusions that one perfect or even a number of adequate systems will be available immediately or even in the short term. What is possible though is to experiment with different processes in different situations to see which are found to be more satisfactory, including the level of participation they encourage. This need not undermine any of liberal representative democracies' safeguards; it can simply reduce the power of elites, democratise policy decisions, engage citizens in questions that many already want to contribute to (cf. Holden, 1993, 195–6) and, through this, hopefully make societies more just and ecologically sustainable.

In a more practical vein, Lélé (1991, 616) cautions that 'participation or at least equity and social justice' can lead to less effective environmental steward-ship. However, he does not make clear for the examples he considers whether participation or equity were the key factors that led to poorer stewardship or whether other factors such as commercialisation, poorer terms of trade, the prom-ise of greater wealth by moving to a city, etc. were more important factors in creating increased environmental stress.

In reviewing 'scientisation', deliberation and precaution with regard to policy on transboundary air pollution and genetic modification, Bäckstrand (2004a) raises important epistemological questions. Specifically, 'even an educated cit-izenry would have problems in grasping the complexity of the knowledge of environmental risks' (ibid., 110). This is an important issue; however, scien-tific/academic communities appear to have problems grasping the complexity of key unsustainable development issues, let alone the interconnections of these issues, and this book suggests that this will remain the case for the foreseeable future. Holden (2002, 30–52) addresses these types of questions directly, argu-ing that limitations of science with regard to global warming mean that policy on this issue should be made democratically. That is, science cannot tell society exactly what to do, so citizens should be given the opportunity to employ their ingenuity and judgement for 'open society' (Popper, 1966) reasons. It should be noted that Bäckstrand does not tackle the deeper epistemological issues that this book highlights, even if she does allude to them. Indeed, it is possible that her conclusions would not apply to other issues, particularly where there are deeper epistemological issues. However, the work by Bäckstrand does raise an impor-tant note of caution about following participatory policy as an unquestioned dogma in every situation. Bass et al. (1995, particularly sections 5.2 to 5.4[1]) does offer some further insights about the costs, risks and weaknesses of participa-tion. However, these are largely of a pragmatic nature about the organisation of specific occurrences of participation, are addressed at least partially by Bass et al. (1995) and, despite being important, these need not detain us here. Bäckstrand (2004b) suggests that despite differences in approach and emphasis, nobody has yet suggested a better response to issues where prediction is not possible than some form of participation.

A useful discussion of how different levels and forms of participatory democ-racy might operate within representative democracy frameworks is presented by Weale (1999, 84–105). The definition of participation that he gives is 'taking part in the process of formulation, passage and implementation of public polices' (Parry et al., 1992, 16, quoted in ibid., 84–5). However, much of the discussion by Weale appears to be more about decision-making on policies largely developed by bureaucrats. In this, he does usefully point out that the elected representa-tives with specialist knowledge do provide an important balance to specialist bureaucrats and the benefits of representative democracy more generally. There is nothing in this book intended to suggest that representative democracy should be replaced entirely by participatory democracy. Nonetheless, if expertise is limited with regard to prediction and control of the Earth System, and if forms of open democratic participatory policy formulation and implementation are the best processes available to respond to this lack of predictive ability, then these can operate within a broader representative framework. Weale (ibid., 105) concludes:

> It is not possible to state a principle by which it would be wrong for the members of a political community to sacrifice a great deal of their other interests to achieve participation. ... I simply think that, considering the all-round nature of potential human achievements, it would be a pity to sacrifice too much to the mundane business of politics.

I wholeheartedly agree that there are things in life more important than political activity – let alone than increasing material wealth. Nonetheless, note the seriousness of the possible effects of current human stress to the Earth System indicated in Chapter 2. Thus, I am quite willing to sacrifice blind efforts towards economic growth, which appears to be the focus of much government activity and 'propaganda', in order to allow a greater focus of human will and ingenuity in participating in policies that might decide the continuance of industrial civilisation or not. A refocusing back towards economic growth at some point in the future, when 'development' is believed to be sustainable, is a question that can be left to future generations.

Further important technical issues around the forms of participatory democracy are raised by Elster (1998, 1–18) and Johnson (ibid., 161–84). These will need considering in the development of participatory processes. However, it is not clear that they suggest reasons to believe that purely representative processes will be better able to address issues where difficulties in prediction of the Earth System form a significant part of the epistemological context.

Arguments for participation

In responding to 'ambiguity and ignorance' that surround human abilities to predict the effects of human actions (in his case focusing primarily on broadly technology policy), Stirling (Berkhout *et al.*, 2003, 60–3) argues effectively for 'pluralism' and broad 'participatory' governance, despite concerns about specific applications of nominally participatory processes. This discussion by Stirling has quite a Popperian 'open society' flavour to it, e.g. 'the aim is to achieve as much transparency as possible in the elucidation of dissenting views' (ibid., 63).

The relationship between democracy and 'green' political thought is discussed in broad terms by Saward (1993). In this, he perhaps over-emphasises the tensions between democracy and other 'green' ideas, at least on the evidence presented. However, he is quite even handed in his critiques of 'ideologies' using democracy for 'legitimation of positions rather than illumination' (ibid.,

63–4). Importantly, Saward (ibid., 68; cf. Horton and Mendus, 1991, 7) specifically argues

> that liberal democracy is, historically and theoretically, much more liberal than democratic. Indeed, the 'founding father' of liberal democracy, Locke, put natural laws centring on property at the core of his political theory, which attenuated liberal variants of democracy from the start.

It is interesting that Saward mentions Locke, as his discussions of property are often used as justifications of private property, and perhaps unfairly, as a basis for the justification for consumerism (cf. Kramer, 1997; Oksanen, 1997). Indeed, it is perhaps intrinsic to representative forms of democracy to tend to promote utilitarian assumptions by trying to appeal to people's self-interest and in effect rhetorically try to 'buy votes', thus promoting the classical vices. Saward (1993, 76) reflects on the work of Barber suggesting:

> Rather than find foundations in nature, or in human nature, for democracy, he argues for a conception of 'politics as epistemology', where the 'quest for certainty' has been abandoned and participatory democracy becomes the basis for discovering practical and fulfilling actions in human communities.

The phrase 'politics as epistemology' is a helpful summary of the findings of this book. The 'quest for certainty' appears that it will not be resolved, with regard to unsustainable development, in the foreseeable future. This does not mean that the quest should be abandoned, particularly if some of the important epistemological issues discussed in this book appear resolved. However, at least until the limitations of prediction are resolved, it appears that the best process we have is that 'participatory democracy becomes the basis for discovering practical and fulfilling actions in human communities' (ibid.). Saward goes on to argue that discourse based on unpredictability is more rational than eco-authoritarianism, and that virtues including toleration are important for addressing unpredictable unsustainable development:

> It can only be the case that 'political change will only occur once people think differently or, more particularly, that sustainable living must be prefaced by sustainable thinking' ... This does not mean anyone has to stop believing in the need for a radically changed society. It does suggest that the grounds on which someone might seek to bring such a society about will not include the claim to have access to some immutable laws of nature, or of human nature. Therein lies respect for the nonbeliever, and a reconciliation between green principles and democracy.
>
> (Ibid.)

If we make an assumption, such as 'the dignity of the human person' which accords with standard types of justification of democracy, then it appears more moral to democratise policy as much as reasonable, rather than not.

A quotation that encapsulates a number of standard justifications of democracy is 'moral autonomy and sovereignty of the individual; the requirement for consent of the governed; the basic equality of individuals or at least citizens; and the educative capability of democratic citizenship' (Treanor, 2006). Saward (1996) discusses similar justifications of democracy before he goes on to suggest an additional reason, which he believes is philosophically more robust than those in the quotation by Treanor are. This additional justification for democracy is captured in the following quotation:

> Knowledge of political rightness may encompass technical expertise from case to case, but always goes beyond this to embrace knowledge of values, and ultimately of what makes a good life. That is knowledge that no person, or group, can rightly claim to possess perpetually and with a higher degree of certainty than all others. In this way, justifications for non-democratic rule fall, and can be resurrected only by unsavoury doses of wilfully tailored ideology.
>
> (Ibid., 78)

Although convincing, this argument raises questions about why a group would have the authority to impose democracy on an individual or other groups. In addition, this would derive from a belief or commitment to something such as 'the dignity of the human person'. Let us set aside these questions as it appears that no answer will be achieved that will satisfy all possible participants in democratic debate. Before leaving this question completely, let me suggest that in discussions about democracy, the widely recognised limitations of representative democracy need to be balanced by highlighting the potential of discursive democratic participation in policy development.

Questions of participative processes with particular regard to environmental questions are addressed by Munton (Berkhout *et al.*, 2003, 109–36). In this, he notes (ibid., 109–10) that there is some evidence that powerful (industrial?) interests resist participatory processes for ostensibly public-spirited reasons, even if these are perhaps based on economistic utilitarian ethical assumptions or even self-interest. Munton (ibid., 112–15) also provides an eloquent discussion of why participative processes should provide a more effective response to the epistemological difficulties, contested ethics and practical difficulties than representative–bureaucratic governance has had in addressing environmental issues. He also indicates useful questions and difficulties that need to be considered around local political cultures and processes; though Munton does note as much success as failure (ibid., 115–17). Usefully exploring theoretical questions around participative processes and to a lesser extent practical issues, Munton (ibid., 118–31) notes significant questions around the nature of deliberation, inclusion and representation in participation, as well as the evaluation of participation. The issues raised are significant; however, they are an indication that participation cannot expect to be perfect, rather than arguments that participative processes are necessarily worse than representative–bureaucratic governance. Indeed, the arguments perhaps indicate the relative strength of participative processes in comparison with representative–bureaucratic governance in a context of epistemological difficulties and contested ethics.[2]

Looking directly at the question of democracy and global warming, Holden (2002) advocates democracy for broadly Popperian reasons[3] and uses democratic and broader political theory to advocate democracy, as a response to the limitations of scientific expertise in responding to climate change. Indeed, his in-depth discussion of these questions concludes that democracy may make an 'invaluable contribution to dealing with the problem of global warming' (ibid., 177) even using the broadly utilitarian assumptions that he makes (e.g. ibid., 58–60). To expand a little, Holden broadly conceives of international environmental NGOs as providing a locus for a notion of global democracy, as a balance to state and transnational corporate (primarily economic) self-interests. He implies that if global democracy of citizens affected by global warming does not provide this balance, then short-term economic interests will prevent action to reduce GHG emission reduction. This can be questioned; however, this book would suggest the advocacy of NGOs, along with analysis by academics, the ethical position of the 'global virtue tradition' plus whatever other support can be gained from other organisations such as trade unions, may provide a counter-balance to economic interests, whether this is termed 'global democracy' or not.

Smith (2003, 53–130) eloquently argues for notions of deliberative democracy as a response to the reality of contested ethical positions about environmental questions. This is inspired by his criticisms of cost–benefit analysis as discussed in the previous chapter and particularly the privileging it receives, as well as 'liberal' assumptions that preferences should not be contested in general (cf. Jackson and Michaelis, 2003, 62). As an illustration of Smith's epistemological and moral criticism of liberal representative democratic political institutions, he writes: 'Given the lack of critical engagement on the part of citizens, the danger is that political elites are not effectively called upon to comply to demanding standards of political rationality and responsibility' (Smith, 2003, 55).

An effective summary of his reasons for favouring deliberative democracy is given by Smith (ibid., 72) specifically to improve the plurality of policy processes in general and with regard to environmental issues. In particular, he argues that in deliberative democracy, a 'plurality of environmental values will be voiced and considered in the political process' even if deliberative democracy does not guarantee ecological decisions:

> It is worth reflecting that, as currently practiced, there is a guarantee that in decision making procedures such as CBA environmental values *cannot* be adequately represented. Deliberative democracy at the very least opens up the political space for the plurality of values to be articulated and to be considered in the policy process.
>
> (Ibid., emphasis in original)

Smith wonders: 'Are we expecting too much from citizens in expecting them to display the moral courage necessary in cultivating an enlarged mentality and acknowledging conflicting values?' (ibid., 76). If the above is seen in the context of Palmer and Finlay (2003), this might mean that the 'fears of politics' (Smith, 2003, 76) might be easier to overcome than Smith assumes, at least with regard to sustainable development. Specifically, Palmer and Finlay (2003) suggest that, globally, value conflicts in this area are not as great as is typically assumed by academic 'green' literature and globally there are strong allies who should help promote 'moral courage' (Smith, 2003, 60, 76) and an 'enlarged mentality' (ibid., 26, 60, 64, 76).

Practical methods that might be used to make representative democracy more deliberative and pluralistic are reviewed by Smith (ibid., 77–128). He offers evidence that these can be effective, though each alternative does have (different) limitations and further alternatives, which allow even wider citizen participation, and would be welcome additions to the techniques that could be used for deliberative democracy. Smith tends to argue for deliberative democracy as a complement to representative democratic institutions; in this, he does make clear that deliberative improvements to existing democratic practices are possible.

Smith (ibid., 126–7) is also broadly sympathetic to the notion that 'green' democracy needs to have a critical attitude to aspects of (current) states (e.g. protection of capital accumulation), particularly as articulated by Dryzek (2000); even if Smith is concerned about a lack of an obvious 'method' for articulating these critical attitudes other than networks of organisations being publicly critical. This is a reasonable criticism; however, it is not clear that alternative institutionalised 'methods' for questions so critical of the state are theoretically possible and acceptable to nation states, at least as these tend to currently conceive their own sovereignty. It is not clear whether it may be possible in future for 'unwarranted assumption commissions' to operate, which may be given official standing but operate outside the state, to call into question implicit or explicit assumptions of governments. However, it is uncertain that constituted bodies would be able to do this more effectively than spontaneous networks, which can arise around specific questions.

There are numerous theoretical treatments of making policy more open and participatory. One that is very aware of the epistemological issues raised in this book (as demonstrated in Dryzek, 1987) is discursive democracy (Dryzek, 1990, 2000). This might form a robust basis for practical initiatives to develop processes for open participatory policy-making, to inform citizens of levels of difficulties of knowledge and prediction of the Earth System and to inform citizens of other ethical and epistemological assumptions. Saward (2001) suggests that discursive democracy (Dryzek, 1990, 2000) is the most advanced model of participation and nothing in his description of alternatives suggests that these are a better fit with unpredictable unsustainable development than discursive democracy. However, Dryzek (1990, 2000) does not detail practical methods of participation that can be readily applied, so it is to this question that we turn now.

8.3 Practical literature

There is a significant amount of literature that discusses applied techniques for citizen participation in policy processes and much of this is focused around sustainable development issues. It is beyond the scope of this book to review all this literature; however, brief mention of some literature in this field is worthwhile to gauge the state of the art, in order to assess whether there are dominant techniques that are clearly agreed to be applicable in all situations or whether the situation is more complex. The following literature has been chosen particularly because it gives an overview of the academic and policy literature in this area.

An important and useful article by Rowe and Frewer (2004)[4] reviews a large number of academic reports of numerous public participation exercises. This has quite a strong empirical flavour (e.g. ibid., 541–2), which the analysis by this book indicates might be based on questionable Baconian assumptions. However, the call for 'production of a definition of effectiveness' (ibid., 541) and development of such definitions is couched in sufficiently open terms that an empirical definition might only become dominant if this was justified. However, they acknowledge the difficulties of the research agenda they propose and if parliamentary democracy had to 'justify its existence' in a similar way when it was developing, feudalism might still be our form of government. Thus, if justification is required, it appears that the research agenda should also include comparison with other concepts such as technocratic and representative models. However, doing this in the quantitative way that Rowe and Frewer prefer might multiply the difficulties exponentially, potentially leading to precautionary maintenance of the status quo, until clear quantitative empirical evidence were available, whether this is possible or not.

The relationship between participation and the 'quality', legitimacy and implementation of environmental policy is reviewed by Fritsch and Newig (2007). They make clear that their conclusions are currently tentative, furthermore questions can be raised about how representative of the issues of concern to this book their research is. However, if we take their key conclusion at face value (ibid., 14), 'on the one hand, the "quality" of decisions with respect to more environmentally sound outputs was rather lessened than improved through participation. On the other hand, participation did indeed foster the effective implementation of these decisions.'

This might not be all that environmentalists would hope for. However, putting things very crudely, if technocratic policy processes agreed a target of 450ppm CO_2e (parts per million carbon dioxide equivalent in the atmosphere) but only achieved 650ppm and a participative process agreed a target of 550ppm and actually achieved it, then the latter should be better. Experience might subsequently suggest that environmentalists who advocated a target of 350ppm or 450ppm might have been wiser than a participative process. However, if 550ppm was the best possible, then this is the best possible. The research by Fritsch and Newig does not justify the conclusion painted in the scenario above. Nonetheless, given the complexity of the situation and the impossibility of running controlled experiments with a number of Earth Systems, we perhaps have to rely on whatever evidence and reasoning we can muster, both about processes of decision-making and the range of possible physical consequences for the Earth System. To clarify, virtue ethics as well as consequentialist (including utilitarian) ethics can both consider consequences. To illustrate crudely, let us assume the best Earth System science suggests the tipping point for dangerous climate change is 350ppm CO_2e to 750ppm. Then 'global virtue tradition' can easily and typically would say: if we are only going to lose some material wealth, let us moderate our consumption and aim for 395ppm in five years and 300ppm in 100 years – the current level is 395ppm (NOAA, 2014) and the residence period of carbon dioxide is 5–200 years (IPCCWG1, 2001, 38). For consequential ethics, the picture is more complicated and for economistic utilitarian or consumerist ethics, without other ethical factors added in, the logical conclusion might be: 'who cares about carbon dioxide, let us just have faith that we can sort out any problems with technology'.

An important and useful review of the effectiveness of 'participation in strategies for sustainable development' around the world was produced by Bass *et al* (1995). Their broad conclusions in this regard are that 'successful past strategies appear also to have been participatory. Conversely, "failed" strategies – those that appear to be going nowhere, even though the documentation may look good – frequently have been characterised by a lack of participation' (ibid., 13).

Rowe and Frewer (2004) raise questions about how Bass *et al*. (1995) assess success of participatory sustainable development strategies, as these assessments are quite qualitative and even anecdotal. However, the assessment does appear to be based on the opinions of a range of policy professionals and institutional stakeholders from the countries who produced the strategies. Overall, Bass *et al*. (ibid.) indicate that even with complex policy processes such as national sustainable development strategies, participatory processes can be successful. Their evidence suggests that with complex questions, which affect all aspects of society, participation is more effective than technocratic approaches. Their evidence does make clear that mistakes will be made with participatory processes, but also that they can succeed eventually even after set-backs, if sufficient political will is applied. Unfortunately, some of the successes they highlight have perhaps since been reversed by subsequent lack of political will. This has perhaps been particularly connected to the (temporary?) triumph globally of economistic utilitarian ethical assumptions over perhaps more virtuous assumptions. That is, the nations with ambitious sustainable development plans perhaps adopted these because of some notion of the global common good; however, other more powerful nations focused on maximising the consumption of their citizens. This increased difficulties of 'free riding' problems for nations prepared to commit to moderation of consumption. The guidance that Bass *et al*. (ibid.) offer, to help effective participation for the development of national sustainable development plans, from the national to the local level, appears to be a unique and useful source.[5] This includes details of both the difficulties and successes of participatory sustainable development. A quotation about representation in the participative process will illustrate the nature of the advice more generally:

> It is hard to achieve anything remotely resembling perfection … A reasonable aim is for as much representativeness, accountability and fairness as possible, within the constraints of budgets, timetables set by political deadlines, and capacity to manage a logistically complex process.
>
> (Ibid., 84)

Overall, Bass *et al.* (1995) suggest that participatory approaches can be made effective despite the difficulties. The next section will offer some suggestions that might complement their insights with regard to issues where science cannot predict the consequences of human disturbance to the Earth System. A few suggestions related to Bass *et al.* (ibid.) are worthwhile at this point. An updated review of lessons that can be learnt about participation from (national) sustainable development strategies is worthwhile. This review should look in particular for processes that might be effectively used to develop policy given difficulties in prediction of the Earth System. Also worthwhile will be some focus on gleaning how participative processes can be effectively applied, particularly to address contestation of economistic utilitarian ethics. Some useful insights in this regard can be found in Otsuki (2013) and more broadly in Stevenson and Dryzek (2014). In the light of Tickner (2003, 377–83) and the questions raised around Baconian assumptions by this book, it may be worth revisiting the risk assessment of key scientific experiments (cf. CERN, 2007; www.risk-evaluation-forum.org) and even opening these to greater public debate so that they have a broader democratic mandate.

8.4 Suggested criteria

In the literature discussed in the above section, similar literature and more technical literature (e.g. Stirling in Berkhout *et al.*, 2003, 55–60), and numerous practical approaches for participatory decision processes are described. A diversity of these will probably be helpful, particularly whilst participative approaches are being developed, but also to reflect people of different types of 'political' and epistemological aptitudes. Indeed, Stirling (ibid., 59–60) importantly implies that methods that adopt a 'quantitative idiom can convey the otherwise unpalatable implications of ambiguity and ignorance into the technocratic and power-laden institutional settings in which social appraisal typically takes place' (ibid., 59).

The following are suggested as criteria to judge the fit of approaches to established components of sustainable development (e.g. Jacobs, 1999, 26–7) and newly identified criticisms of 'modern' policy-making in this book (cf. Smith, 2003, 80–1), specifically for issues where current epistemology does not allow prediction, and where control of the Earth System and ethical assumptions are contested:[6]

- Can people readily choose to use or not use the process? Will the process skew results against the views or 'interests' of those who do not participate?

Can citizens readily enter into the process later if they disagree with current results (cf. Munton in Berkhout *et al.*, 2003, 123–5)?

- Does the approach promote or hide an understanding of the limitations of managerial approaches to society and the Earth System? Does it promote participation of citizens in policy decisions?
- Does the approach promote understanding of the global plurality of epistemological and ethical assumptions by participants? Does this understanding include reasons why these assumptions are held and the probable global democratic distribution of these assumptions?
- Does the approach allow the promotion of greater social cohesion and justice (equity)?
- Does the approach respect the dignity of each individual human and allow the promotion of respect (non-instrumental) for nature for its own sake?
- Does the approach promote an awareness of the possible effects of current actions on those around the world, now and in the future?
- Does the approach allow minimising managerial attitudes both with regard to how people and nature are treated?
- Does the approach allow the input of 'experts' but not privilege their opinions in the decision-making process, beyond the quality of their reasoning? Does the approach facilitate the communication of expert opinion in a way that is readily understood by non-specialists?
- Does the approach minimise the need for experts in the approach to operate the approach? Is the approach as transparent as possible?
- How neutral is the approach in respect of the strengths and weaknesses of particular technologies? Energy technologies and cultivation technologies could be useful test cases.
- How easy is the approach to understand and engage with, particularly to aid understanding of the whole Earth System and with different types of people, over time, with changing information and situations, with different types of question, etc.?

Obviously this list cannot be seen as definitive; it is based on the analysis of this author as indicated in this book. It is hoped that it is a useful starting point for further development by civil society, the academic and policy communities.[7]

8.5 Conclusions

The preceding analysis does not lead to a simple solution or simple solutions. This should not be surprising given the complex nature of unsustainable development and the Earth System. However, it is better to recognise this complexity and consider it directly than to hide policy problems behind economic calculus which looks scientific but is still normative political economy dressed up to look scientific. The status of economics as a science can be judged from the oft repeated phrase that you will not get two economists to agree on any policy issue.

However imperfect participatory policy-making is and will remain, it is nonetheless the best process that we have. This re-politicisation of policy and modern communication technologies mean that it is more important than ever for citizens to be engaged with policy questions. This can be more passive through citizens supporting organisations that they believe will represent their views but it is better still for citizens to take an active role. If we move towards a society less focused on maximising economic growth, this should be facilitated by people being less busy making money. To paraphrase even less accurately than the original, 'consumerism has become the opium of the masses'. As this chapter has hinted, there are myriad ways that citizens can become directly involved in making policy. To list a few:

1   Being involved in participatory policy initiatives that are organised by governments and civil servants.
2   Organising their own and presenting the results to government.
3   Organising their own and implementing the results. Transition towns being one example and local bans on the distribution of plastic carrier bags being another.
4   Starting and signing petitions.
5   Listening to the views of people who you disagree with – if dialogue is possible citizens from all sides may learn something.
6   Perhaps most importantly citizens who do not have a market fundamentalist faith in the invisible hand of the market, as the answer to all social problems, should resist the imposition or promotion of markets to allow space for alternatives.

In participatory processes, perhaps particularly those originating in government, citizens will need to be wary of these processes being hijacked by businesses and groups that want to promote economic growth above all things – they can use their money to cause good people to waste a lot of time and energy in consultations whose results will be ignored if the 'right' result does not occur. Nonetheless, the possibility of those for whom money is God being persuaded to weaken their position by discussion with people who do not share this faith cannot be discounted.

It will be appreciated that many of the ecological virtues suggested in the previous chapter will be needed in participative policy processes. Let me suggest the following will be particularly important: (1) learning well from others; (2) deliberating well; (3) caution; (4) seeking justice for humans and nature; (5) courage; (6) patience; (7) perseverance; (8) humility – to allow the possibility that one's position is wrong; (9) hope; (10) caring about someone enough to disagree with them; and (11) caring about those who are less powerful than you are.

Notes

1   Chapter 5 is available at www.environmental-mainstreaming.org/nssd/pdf/IIED08.pdf. The other version available directly from the IIED website is used as the basis for page numbering in other places in this book but is missing from Chapter 5.

2 Munton (Berkhout et al., 2003, 128–31) does imply a need to apply an empirical process to establish that participative processes are better than technocratic processes.
   However, given the complexity of the question, the 'research programme' suggested
   does not make clear how this can be done in an incontestable way in the foreseeable
   future.
3 Holden (2002, 13) explicitly mentions Popper's *Open Society*.
4 Thanks are owed to Oliver Fritsch for suggesting this article but also broader discussions particularly around the effectiveness of participatory approaches to sustainable
   development questions.
5 Chapter 8 is particularly useful but Chapters 6 and 7 do provide important insights.
6 The use of the term 'allow' is intended to be neutral, whereas the term 'promote' is typically intended to make up for deficiencies in current policy as identified in this book.
7 Chukwumerije Okereke and the current author are currently working on an article
   that is one attempt to go into greater practical detail of a possible process whereby the
   views of citizens globally may more effectively be brought as an input to climate change
   policy.

References

Bäckstrand, K. (2004a) 'Precaution, scientisation or deliberation? Prospects for greening
   and democratizing science', in Wissenburg, M. and Levy, Y. (eds) *Liberal democracy and
   environmentalism: The end of environmentalism?*, London: Routledge
Bäckstrand, K. (2004b) 'Science, uncertainty and participation in global environmental
   governance', *Environmental Politics*, 13(3): 650–6
Bass, S., Dalal-Clayton, B. and Pretty, J. (1995) *Participation in strategies for sustainable
   development*, London: International Institute for Environment and Development,
   http://pubs.iied.org/7754IIED.html. Accessed 29 March 2015
Berkhout, F., Leach, M. and Scoones, I. (2003) (eds) *Negotiating environmental change:
   New perspectives from social sciences*, Cheltenham: Edward Elgar
CERN (2007) The safety of the LHC, Geneva: CERN, http://public.web.cern.ch/public/
   en/LHC/Safety-en.html. Accessed 25 May 2011
Dryzek, J. (1987) *Rational ecology environment and political economy*, Oxford: Blackwell
Dryzek, J. (1990) *Discursive democracy: Politics, policy, and political science*, Cambridge:
   Cambridge University Press
Dryzek, J. (2000) *Deliberative democracy and beyond: Liberals, critics, contestations*, Oxford:
   Oxford University Press
Elster, J. (ed.) (1998) *Deliberative democracy*, Cambridge: Cambridge University Press
Fritsch, O. and Newig, J. (2007) *Public participation as a regulatory instrument in the EU and
   the US. Findings of a large-N meta-analysis of discursive governance in environmental politics*,
   1st Advanced Colloquium on Better Regulation Centre for Regulatory Governance,
   University of Exeter, 25–26 January 2007. Similar appears in Newig, J. and Fritsch, O.
   (2009) 'More input – Better output: Does citizen involvement improve the quality,
   legitimacy and implementability of environmental policy?', in Blühdorn, I. (ed.) *In
   search of legitimacy: Policy making in Europe and the challenge of complexity*, Opladen;
   Farmington Hills: Verlag Barbara Budrich
Holden, B. (1993) *Understanding liberal democracy*, Hemel Hempstead: Harvester
   Wheatsheaf
Holden, B. (2002) *Democracy and global warming*, London: Continuum
Horton, J. and Mendus, S. (1991) (eds) *John Locke – A letter concerning toleration: In Focus*,
   London: Routledge

IPCCWG1 (2001) *Climate change 2001: The scientific basis*, Cambridge: Cambridge University Press

Jackson, T. and Michaelis, L. (2003) *Policies for sustainable consumption*, London: Sustainable Development Commission

Jacobs, M. (1999) 'Sustainable development as a contested concept', in Dobson, A. (ed.) *Fairness and futurity: Essays on environmental sustainability and social justice*, Oxford: Oxford University Press

Kramer, M. (1997) *John Locke and the origins of private property: Philosophical explorations of individualism, community, and equality*, Cambridge: Cambridge University Press

Lélé, S. (1991) 'Sustainable development: A critical review', *World Development*, 19: 607–21

NOAA (2014) *Trends in atmospheric carbon dioxide*, www.esrl.noaa.gov/gmd/ccgg/trends/. Accessed 25 October 2014

Oksanen, M. (1997) 'The Lockean provisos and the privatisation of nature', in Hayward, T. and O'Neill, J. (eds) (1997) *Justice, property and the environment: Social and legal perspectives*, Aldershot: Ashgate

Otsuki, K. (2013) *Transformative sustainable development: Participation, reflection, and change*, Abingdon: Routledge

Palmer, M. and Finlay, V. (2003) *Faith in conservation: New approaches to religions and the environment*, Washington, DC: World Bank, http://go.worldbank.org/3L9IDQNFO0 or www.arcworld.org/books_resources.asp. Accessed 9 May 2011

Popper, K. (1966) (5th edn) *The open society and its enemies*, London: Routledge and Kegan Paul

Rowe, G. and Frewer, L. (2004) 'Evaluating public-participation exercises: A research agenda', *Science, Technology & Human Values*, 29(4): 512–56

Saward, M. (1993) 'Green democracy', in Dobson, A. and Lucardie, P. (eds) *The politics of nature: Explorations in green political theory*, London: Routledge

Saward, M. (1996) 'Must democrats be environmentalists', in Doherty, B. and de Geus, M. (eds) *Democracy and green political thought: Sustainability, rights, and citizenship*, London: Routledge

Saward, M. (2001) 'Reconstructing democracy: Current thinking and new directions', *Government and Opposition*, 36(4): 559–81

Smith, G. (2003) *Deliberative democracy and the environment*, London: Routledge

Stevenson, H. and Dryzek, J.S. (2014) *Democratizing global climate governance*, Cambridge: Cambridge University Press

Tickner, J. (ed.) (2003) *Precaution, environmental science, and preventative public policy*, Washington, DC: Island Press

Treanor, P. (2006) *Why democracy is wrong*, http://web.inter.nl.net/users/Paul.Treanor/democracy.html. Accessed 25 May 2011

Weale, A. (1999) *Democracy*, Basingstoke: Macmillan

9 Conclusion

Environmental policy in the light of at least one metre sea level rise

This book argues that managerial approaches typical of official sustainable development policy are questionable. It has identified and interrogated some of the assumptions that underpin managerial approaches. Alternative assumptions have been suggested as have alternative possible ways in which policy decisions might be made. Perhaps the first practical thing that could be done is to reduce making decisions based on economic cost–benefit analysis, as decisions made this way tend to increase stress to the Earth System, not diminish it. In addition, the infinite costs of eco-cataclysm, for which it currently appears no robust probability can be established, means that all options subject to cost–benefit analysis in theory should be rejected (assuming that possibilities of cataclysm are not ignored). That is, cost–benefit analysis cannot distinguish between different options in an unpredictable Earth System because each might conceivably lead to eco-cataclysm. Further, Berglund and Matti (2006) argue that economic approaches to environmental policy can reduce ecological virtue in citizens. That is, for those who feel the need for numbers, they present the results of a reasonably convincing survey that indicates that in Sweden, at least, virtue ethics is more important for ecological behaviour than economistic utilitarian motivations.

If it is still deemed essential[1] for decision-making to be informed by reductive analytical methods, life cycle analysis should be better than economic analysis, as it can give an indication of stress to the Earth System depending on which policy and/or technological options are followed. It can also highlight the moral and epistemological difficulties that remain to be resolved politically when technical analysis is complete. For policy-making, it would be important for life cycle analysis to record an indication of any social effects as well as environmental effects.

The analysis in this book suggests that humanity is under threat in at least three senses. First, both existing market fundamentalism and possible eco-dictatorships threaten the humaneness of societies. Second, market fundamentalism and the promotion of consumerism threaten what can be regarded as the best aspect of individual humans (their humanity) and the humaneness of societies, for example, consumerist societies' typically selfish responses to global injustices, which are important drivers of refugee crises, immigration pressures and international terrorism. Finally, unpredictable abrupt changes in the Earth System such as abrupt climate change – including possibly inevitable one metre or more sea level rise (cf. Joughin *et al.*, 2014; NASA, 2014; Rignot *et al.*, 2014) – brought about by industrial activity, threaten complex human societies and conceivably Homo sapiens. The ideas that have been offered in this book are intended to allow we wise apes to demonstrate our wisdom sufficiently, in saving ourselves and other complex life forms from irrational undemocratic blind industrialism, whether capitalist or communist.

Whether any combinations of the suggestions in this book will allow sustainable development is impossible to predict. What is clear is that there are options that have been indicated that can make policy-making less focused on predicting consequences and less vicious. It has been argued that these are worth further research and democratic debate on implementation. It is probable that there are further rational responses to an unpredictable Earth System that the author has not identified. It is likely that more important than this is that conventional economics is irrational, as the cost of policy options cannot be estimated in any valid sense, given the impossibility of predicting the Earth System. I currently believe that the two suggestions that will move us towards sustainable development most rapidly are the following.

The first suggestion is that natural scientists should have the courage to admit the limitations of natural science to tell policymakers what will bring about the best consequences, however consequences are defined. How long it will take sufficient influential scientists to summon this courage is not predictable. It should be noted that scientists clarifying the limitations of prediction would not mean less science, as societies may well call for more research to better describe the possible effects of human stress on the Earth System – particularly if economic costs are much less influential in decision-making. However, it might mean different science to that which currently receives the bulk of available funding.

The second suggestion is for influential critics of economistic utilitarianism to collectively and in an increasingly united way engage powerful advocates of economistic utilitarianism. This will be key if, as the analysis in this book suggests, it is the utilitarianism, or even hedonism of conventional economics and consumerism, that is the principal driver of our increasingly unsustainable societies. Policy decisions made by conventional economics take us in the wrong direction, both directly and in the attitudes and assumptions encouraged. Given the levels of prediction possible, estimating costs and benefits is impossible to do robustly. Thus, economics is an irrational (i.e. crazy) response to climate change. If ecological virtues are truly virtuous, then decisions made on the basis of these virtues allow progress in the right direction. Individuals and organisations are already criticising consumerism and related economic dogma.[2] However, more public and concerted collective effort, backed by strong analysis, should be more effective at causing advocates of economistic utilitarianism to, at least, question the faith in their creed. Importantly, this process could also catch the public imagination, though the economistic utilitarian context of much of the mass media will make this more difficult.

However, given the levels of prediction possible, these two actions might falter for reasons foreseen and unforeseen by this author and perhaps other drivers will lead to more rapid progress to less unsustainable development. What is clear from Earth System science is that all citizens have a duty to have an informed opinion about the possibility of human-caused eco-cataclysm, for humanity and many other species. This should include an opinion of whether the Earth System can be predicted adequately to be assessed by conventional economic practice. I believe those who live above subsistence should also divert some of their ingenuity and energy from pursuing consumerism to pursuing happier, more sustainable communities, whether that be via permaculture, political activity or both.

This book is offered as a trans-Atlantean, trans-modern start to earthsystemology, at least until a more elegant name can be found for research that integrates social science and humanities thought with Earth System science.

Notes

1 Because of Cartesian epistemological assumptions.
2 To give some examples beyond the literature already cited: www.ituc-csi.org/climate-change, www.creationcare.org, www.arcworld.org, www.interfaithdeclaration.org, www.creationjustice.org/members-etc.html

References

Berglund, C. and Matti, S. (2006) 'Citizen and consumer: The dual role of individuals in environmental policy', *Environmental Politics*, 15: 550–71

Joughin, I., Smith, B.E. and Medley, B. (2014) 'Marine ice sheet collapse potentially under way for the Thwaites Glacier Basin, West Antarctica', *Science*, 344(6185): 735–8

NASA (2014) *Decline of West Antarctic glaciers appears irreversible*, http://earthobservatory.nasa.gov/IOTD/view.php?id=83672. Accessed 6 November 2014

Rignot, E., Mouginot, J., Morlighem, M., Seroussi, H. and Scheuchl, B. (2014) 'Widespread, rapid grounding line retreat of Pine Island, Thwaites, Smith, and Kohler glaciers, West Antarctica, from 1992 to 2011', *Geophysical Research Letters*, 41(10): 3502–9

Index

For Product Safety Concerns and Information please contact our
EU representative GPSR@taylorandfrancis.com Taylor & Francis
Verlag GmbH, Kaufingerstraße 24, 80331 München, Germany